The Open
University

Understanding
OBJECT-ORIENTED
PROGRAMMING
with JAVA™

Second Updated Edition for the Open University

By Timothy Budd

ADDISON
WESLEY

An imprint of **Pearson Education**

Harlow, England · London · New York · Reading, Massachusetts · San Francisco · Toronto · Don Mills, Ontario · Sydney
Tokyo · Singapore · Hong Kong · Seoul · Taipei · Cape Town · Madrid · Mexico City · Amsterdam · Munich · Paris · Milan

Pearson Education Limited
Edinburgh Gate
Harlow
Essex CM20 2JE
England

and Associated Companies throughout the world

Visit us on the World Wide Web at:
www.pearsoned.co.uk

First published 2000 by Addison Wesley Longman, Inc.
Second updated edition published 2002

ISBN 0201 78704 0

British Library Cataloguing-in-Publication Data
A catalogue record for this book is available from the British Library

10 9 8 7 6 5 4 3
07 06 05 04 03

Typeset in 10/12 Sabon by Windfall Software
Printed in Great Britain by Henry Ling Limited, at the Dorset Press, Dorchester, DT1 1HD

Preface

There are many books on Java that teach you *how* to use the language, but few books that teach you *why* the language works in the way that it does.

Many books help you learn the mechanics of Java programming; few books teach you the deeper issues that lie behind the programming syntax. The goal of this book is to give you a fuller, more complete understanding of the philosophy behind Java, not just the mechanics of the language.

These principles and practices are illustrated throughout the book with extensive examples from the Java standard library. Here you can learn, for example, the many design patterns that are found in the AWT, the multitude of purposes for which inheritance is used in the standard classes, and why there are 22 different types of input/output file streams. Here you can discover why the lack of an ordered container class in the standard library is not a simple omission but is instead a reflection of a fundamental and deep property of the Java language.

In short, this book should not be considered a reference manual for the Java language, but rather a tool for understanding the Java philosophy.

STRUCTURE OF THE BOOK

The book is structured in five major sections:

Part 1 is a general, language-independent introduction to the ideas that lie at the heart of the Java world. The first major object-oriented concepts–those of classes, encapsulation, behavior, and responsibilities–will be introduced in this part and reinforced in Part 2. Chapter 1 presents the idea that the solution to a problem can be structured as interactions among a community of agents. Chapter 2 presents a brief history of the development of Java, and can be omitted at the instructor's discretion. However, Chapter 3, on design, should in no way be avoided. In fact, I strongly encourage students to conduct at least one, if not several, design exercises using CRC cards, similar to the one presented here, even before they start to learn aspects of the Java programming language.

Part 2 introduces Java through several graduated example programs (paradigms, in the original sense of the word). These examples lead students through successive steps in learning the Java language, introducing new features as they are required for specific applications. This is not a systematic introduction to all of the Java language, but rather provides examples designed to motivate the need for mechanisms discussed in other parts of the text.

Part 3 discusses inheritance, the next major object-oriented concept that the student must master after learning about classes and objects. Inheritance is a technique that is superficially obvious, but that possesses many subtle aspects that can trap the unwary programmer. The introduction of inheritance into a programming language has an impact on almost every other aspect of the language. For this reason, students familiar with conventional non-object-oriented languages should pay careful attention to this part of the book.

Part 4 discusses polymorphism, which is often an even subtler concept for the student to understand than inheritance. As the mechanism through which much of the power and applicability of object-oriented techniques is manifest, polymorphism is found in Java in many ways, as shown by the extensive examples studied in this part of the book.

Part 5 discusses features of the Java world that are important for the student to understand but not particularly notable for their object-oriented features. These items are separated from the remainder of the text so that they do not interrupt the flow of the narrative developed earlier in the book. However, the features discussed are not as difficult as their late placement in the book might indicate. At the instructor's discretion, these features can be omitted altogether, or introduced in parallel with earlier material.

OBTAINING THE SOURCE

Source code for the case studies presented in the book can be accessed via the mechanism of anonymous ftp from the machine `ftp.cs.orst.edu`, in the directory `/pub/budd/java`. This directory is also used to maintain a number of other items, such as an errata list. This information can also be accessed via the World Wide Web, from my personal home pages at `http://www.cs.orst.edu/~budd/`. Requests for further information can be forwarded to the electronic mail address `budd@cs.orst.edu`, or to Professor Timothy A. Budd, Department of Computer Science, Oregon State University, Corvallis, Oregon, 97331.

ACKNOWLEDGMENTS

Invaluable advice was provided by the reviewers who examined an early draft of the book. These included Richard Anderson, University of Washington; Richard Carver, George Mason University; Deborah Frincke, University of Idaho; Matt Greenwood, Bell Laboratories; David Riley, University of Wisconsin–La Crosse; and J. Richard Rinewalt, Texas Christian University.

I would like to thank my editors at Addison-Wesley, Susan Hartman and Deborah Lafferty, who patiently and quietly suffered through countless delays and postponements. It is my sincere hope that they, as well as the reader, will find the result to have been worth the wait.

ACKNOWLEDGMENTS FOR THE REVISION

A number of people have been very helpful in bringing about this update of the original manuscript. The impetus for the revision came from Ray Weedon and Pete Thomas of the Open University in the United Kingdom, who wanted to adopt the book for a course they were developing but first wanted to see "just a few changes." Ray and Pete have worked closely with me during the revision process, but the blame for any remaining errors should rest on my shoulders, not theirs.

The process of revision also gave me the opportunity to correct a number of small errors or omissions that had been reported in the first printing. Many of these were first noticed and brought to my attention by alert readers. In particular, I would like to thank Walter Beck, University of Nothern Iowa; Andrew Black, Oregon Graduate Institute; Thomas Gross, Carnegie-Mellon University; Jon Heggland, Forsvarets Forskningsinstitutt, Norway; Mattias Karlström, student at the Royal Institute of Technology, Stockholm; Thomas Larsson, Mälardalen University, Sweden; Mark Morrissey, Oregon Graduate Institute; Eyal Shifroni, Center for Educational Technology, Israel; Neal Smith, Oregon State University; and John Trono, St. Michael's College, Vermont.

Susan Hartman has once again been my able and talented editor at Addison-Wesley, assisted this time by Lisa Kalner. Paul Anagnostopoulos of Windfall Software was in charge of converting my original manuscript into a more pleasing format. He has been most patient in helping me understand the process of that conversion and how I could most easily make the new material blend in with the old. As always, I have found it a pleasure to work with the entire editorial and production staff at Addison-Wesley.

Contents

I

Understanding the
Object-Oriented Worldview

1 Object-Oriented Thinking

This is a book about object-oriented programming. In particular, this is a book that explores the principal ideas of object-oriented programming in the context of the Java programming language. Object-oriented programming has been a hot topic for over a decade, and more recently Java has become the commonly perceived embodiment of object-oriented ideas. This book will help you *understand* Java. It makes no pretensions to being a language reference manual; there are many other books that fall into that category. But knowing the syntax for a language should not be confused with understanding why the language has been developed in the way it has, why certain things are done the way they are, or why Java programs look the way they do. This book explores the *why*'s.

Object-oriented programming is frequently referred to as a new programming *paradigm*. The word "paradigm" originally meant example, or model. For example, a paradigm sentence would help you remember how to conjugate a verb in a foreign language. More generally, a model is an example that helps you understand how the world works. For example, the Newtonian model of physics explains why apples fall to the ground. In computer science, a paradigm explains how the elements that go into making a computer program are organized and how they interact with one another. For this reason the first step in understanding Java is appreciating the object-oriented worldview.

1.1 A Way of Viewing the World

To illustrate the major ideas in object-oriented programming, let us consider how we might go about handling a real-world situation and then ask how we could make the computer more closely model the techniques employed. Suppose I wish to send flowers to a friend who lives in a city many miles away. Let me call my friend Sally. Because of the distance, there is no possibility of my picking the

3

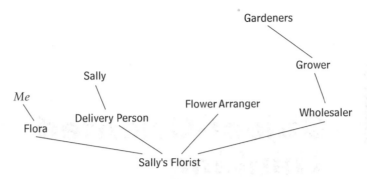

Figure 1.1   The community of agents helping me.

flowers and carrying them to Sally's door myself. Nevertheless, sending her the flowers is an easy enough task; I merely go down to Flora, my local florist, tell her the variety and quantity of flowers I wish to send and Sally's address, and I can be assured the flowers will be delivered expediently and automatically.

1.1.1   *Agents and Communities*

At the risk of belaboring a point, let me emphasize that the mechanism I used to solve my problem was to find an appropriate *agent* (namely, Flora) and to pass to her a *message* containing my request. It is the *responsibility* of Flora to satisfy my request. There is some *method*—some algorithm or set of operations— used by Flora to do this. I do not need to know the particular method she will use to satisfy my request; indeed, often I do not want to know the details. This information is usually *hidden* from my inspection.

If I investigated, however, I might discover that Flora delivers a slightly different message to another florist in my friend's city. That florist, in turn, perhaps has a subordinate who makes the floral arrangement. The florist then passes the flowers, along with yet another message, to a delivery person, and so on. Earlier, the florist in Sally's city had obtained her flowers from a flower wholesaler who, in turn, had interactions with the flower growers, each of whom had to manage a team of gardeners.

So, our first observation of object-oriented problem solving is that the solution to my problem required the help of many other individuals (Figure 1.1). Without their help, my problem could not be easily solved. We phrase this in a general fashion as the following:

> An object-oriented program is structured as a *community* of interacting agents, called *objects*. Each object has a role to play. Each object provides a service, or performs an action, that is used by other members of the community.

1.1.2 *Messages and Methods*

The chain reaction that ultimately resulted in the solution to my program began with my request to Flora. This request led to other requests, which led to still more requests, until my flowers ultimately reached my friend. We see, therefore, that members of this community interact with one another by making requests. So, our next principle of object-oriented problem solving is the vehicle by which activities are initiated:

> Action is initiated in object-oriented programming by the transmission of a *message* to an agent (an *object*) responsible for the action. The message encodes the request for an action and is accompanied by any additional information (arguments) needed to carry out the request. The *receiver* is the object to whom the message is sent. If the receiver accepts the message, it accepts the responsibility to carry out the indicated action. In response to a message, the receiver will perform some *method* to satisfy the request.

We have noted the important principle of *information hiding* in regard to message passing—that is, the client sending the request need not know the actual means by which the request will be honored. Another all too human principle is implicit in message passing. If there is a task to perform, the first thought of the client is to find somebody else he or she can ask to do the work. This second reaction often becomes atrophied in many programmers with extensive experience in conventional techniques. Frequently, a difficult hurdle to overcome is the programmer's belief that he or she must write everything and not use the services of others. An important part of object-oriented programming is the development of reusable components, and an important first step in the use of reusable components is a willingness to trust software written by others.

Information hiding is also an important aspect of programming in conventional languages. In what sense is a message different from, say, a procedure call? In both cases, there is a set of well-defined steps that will be initiated following the request. But, there are two important distinctions.

The first is that a message has a designated *receiver*; the receiver is some object to which the message is sent. In a procedure call, there is no designated receiver.

The second is that the *interpretation* of the message (that is, the method used to respond to the message) is dependent on the receiver and can vary with different receivers. I can give a message to my wife Elizabeth, for example, and she will understand it and a satisfactory outcome will be produced (that is, flowers will be delivered to my friend). However, the method Elizabeth uses to satisfy the request (in all likelihood, simply passing the request on to Flora) will be different from that used by Flora in response to the same request. If I ask Kenneth, my dentist, to send flowers to my friend, he may not have a method for solving that problem. If he understands the request at all, he will probably issue an appropriate error diagnostic.

Let us move our discussion back to the level of computers and programs. There, the distinction between message passing and procedure calling is that message passing has a designated receiver, and the interpretation—the selection of a method to execute in response to the message—may vary with different receivers. Usually, the specific receiver for any given message will not be known until run time, so the determination of which method to invoke cannot be made until then. Thus, we say there is late *binding* between the message (function or procedure name) and the code fragment (method) used to respond to the message. This situation is in contrast to the very early (compile-time or link-time) binding of name to code fragment in conventional procedure calls.

1.1.3 *Responsibilities*

A fundamental concept in object-oriented programming is to describe behavior in terms of *responsibilities*. My request for action indicates only the desired outcome (flowers for my friend). Flora is free to pursue any technique that achieves the desired objective and is not hampered by interference on my part.

By discussing a problem in terms of responsibilities, we increase the level of abstraction. This permits greater *independence* between objects, a critical factor in solving complex problems. The entire collection of responsibilities associated with an object is often termed the *protocol*.

A traditional program often operates by acting *on* data structures, for example changing fields in an array or record. In contrast, an object-oriented program *requests* data structures (that is, objects) to perform a service. This difference between viewing software in traditional, structured terms and viewing it from an object-oriented perspective can be summarized by a twist on a well-known quote:

> Ask not what you can do *to* your data structures, but what your data structures can do *for* you.

1.1.4 *Classes and Instances*

Although I have only dealt with Flora a few times, I have a rough idea of the behavior I can expect when I walk into her shop and present my request. I am able to make certain assumptions because I have information about florists in general, and I expect that Flora, being an instance of this category, will fit the general pattern. We can use the term Florist to represent the category (or *class*) of all florists. Let us incorporate these notions into our next principle of object-oriented programming:

> All objects are *instances* of a *class*. The method invoked by an object in response to a message is determined by the class of the receiver. All objects of a given class use the same method in response to similar messages.

1.1.5 *Class Hierarchies—Inheritance*

I have more information about Flora—not necessarily because she is a florist but because she is a shopkeeper. I know, for example, that I probably will be asked for money as part of the transaction, and that in return for payment I will be given a receipt. These actions are true of grocers, stationers, and other shopkeepers. Since the category Florist is a more specialized form of the category Shopkeeper, any knowledge I have of Shopkeepers is also true of Florists and hence of Flora.

One way to think about how I have organized my knowledge of Flora is in terms of a hierarchy of categories (see Figure 1.2). Flora is a Florist, but Florist is a specialized form of Shopkeeper. Furthermore, a Shopkeeper is also a Human; so I know, for example, that Flora is probably bipedal. A Human is a Mammal (therefore they nurse their young and have hair), and a Mammal is an Animal (therefore it breathes oxygen), and an Animal is a Material Object (therefore it has mass and weight). Thus, quite a lot of knowledge that I have that is applicable to Flora is not directly associated with her, or even with her category Florist.

The principle that knowledge of a more general category is also applicable to a more specific category is called *inheritance*. We say that the class Florist will inherit attributes of the class (or category) Shopkeeper.

Another graphical technique is often used to illustrate this relationship, particularly when there are many individuals with differing lineages. This technique

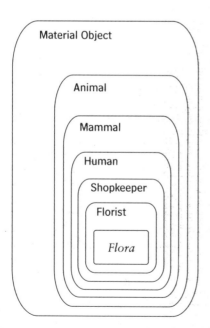

Figure 1.2 The categories surrounding Flora.

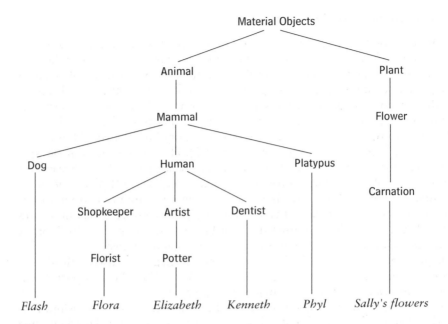

Figure 1.3 A class hierarchy for various material objects.

shows classes listed in a hierarchical treelike structure, with more abstract classes (such as Material Object or Animal) listed near the top of the tree, and more specific classes, and finally individuals, listed near the bottom. Figure 1.3 shows this class hierarchy for Flora. This same hierarchy also includes Elizabeth, my dog Flash, Phyl the platypus who lives at the zoo, and the flowers I am sending to my friend.

Information that I possess about Flora because she is an instance of class Human is also applicable to my wife Elizabeth. Information that I have about her because she is a Mammal is applicable to Flash as well. Information about all members of Material Object is equally applicable to Flora and to her flowers. We capture this in the idea of inheritance:

> Classes can be organized into a hierarchical *inheritance* structure. A *child class* (or *subclass*) will inherit attributes from a *parent class* higher in the tree. An *abstract parent class* is a class (such as Mammal) for which there are no direct instances; it is used only to create subclasses.

1.1.6 *Method Binding, Overriding, and Exceptions*

Phyl the platypus presents a problem for our simple organizing structure. I know that mammals give birth to live offspring, and Phyl is certainly a Mammal, yet

Phyl (or rather his mate Phyllis) lays eggs. To accommodate this variation, we need to find a technique to encode *exceptions* to a general rule.

We do this by decreeing that information contained in a subclass can *override* information inherited from a parent class. Most often, implementations of this approach take the form of a method in a subclass having the same name as a method in the parent class, combined with a rule stating how to conduct the search for a method to match a specific message:

> The search for a method to invoke in response to a given message begins with the *class* of the receiver. If no appropriate method is found, the search is conducted in the *parent class* of this class. The search continues up the parent class chain until either a method is found or the parent class chain is exhausted. In the former case, the method is executed; in the latter case, an error message is issued. If methods with the same name can be found higher in the class hierarchy, the method executed is said to *override* the inherited behavior.

Even if the compiler cannot determine which method will be invoked at run time, in many object-oriented languages, such as Java, it can determine whether there will be an appropriate method and issue an error message as a compile-time error diagnostic rather than as a run-time message.

That my wife Elizabeth and my florist Flora will respond to my message by different methods is an example of one form of *polymorphism*, an important aspect of object-oriented programming discussed in Chapter 12. As explained, that I do not, and need not, know exactly what method Flora will use to honor my message is an example of *information hiding*.

1.1.7   *Summary of Object-Oriented Concepts*

Alan Kay, considered by some to be the father of object-oriented programming (OOP), identified the following characteristics as fundamental to OOP [Kay 1993]:

1. Everything is an *object*.

2. Computation is performed by objects communicating with each other, requesting that other objects perform actions. Objects communicate by sending and receiving *messages*. A message is a request for action bundled with whatever arguments may be necessary to complete the task.

3. Each object has its own *memory*, which consists of other objects.

4. Every object is an *instance* of a *class*. A class simply represents a grouping of similar objects, such as integers or lists.

5. The class is the repository for *behavior* associated with an object. That is, all objects that are instances of the same class can perform the same actions.

6. Classes are organized into a singly rooted tree structure, called the *inheritance hierarchy*. Memory and behavior associated with instances of a class are automatically available to any class associated with a descendant in this tree structure.

1.2 COMPUTATION AS SIMULATION

The view of programming represented by the example of sending flowers to my friend is very different from the conventional conception of a computer. The traditional model describing the behavior of a computer executing a program is a *process-state* or *pigeonhole* model. In this view, the computer is a data manager, following some pattern of instructions, wandering through memory, pulling values out of various slots (memory addresses), transforming them in some manner, and pushing the results back into other slots (see Figure 1.4). By examining the values in the slots, we can determine the state of the machine or the results produced by a computation. Although this model may be a more or less accurate picture of what takes place inside a computer, it does little to help us understand how to solve problems using the computer, and it is certainly not the way most people (pigeon handlers and postal workers excepted) go about solving problems.

In contrast, in the object-oriented framework we never mention memory addresses, variables, assignments, or any of the conventional programming terms. Instead, we speak of objects, messages, and responsibility for some action. In Dan Ingalls's memorable phrase:

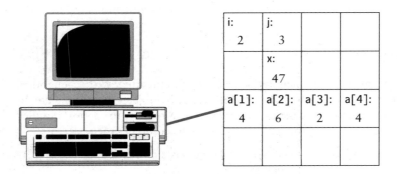

Figure 1.4 Visualization of imperative programming.

> Instead of a bit-grinding processor . . . plundering data structures, we have a universe of well-behaved objects that courteously ask each other to carry out their various desires. [Ingalls 1981]

Another author has described object-oriented programming as "animistic": a process of creating a host of helpers that form a community and assist the programmer in the solution of a problem (see the *Actor Language Manual*) [Actor 1987].

This view of programming as creating a "universe" is in many ways similar to a style of computer simulation called "discrete event-driven simulation." In brief, in a discrete event-driven simulation the user creates computer models of the various elements of the simulation, describes how they will interact with one another, and sets them moving. This is almost identical to the average object-oriented program, in which the user describes what the various entities in the universe for the program are, and how they will interact, and finally sets them in motion. Thus, in object-oriented programming, we have the view that *computation is simulation* [Kay 1977].

1.2.1 The Power of Metaphor

An easily overlooked benefit to the use of object-oriented techniques is the power of *metaphor*. When programmers think about problems in terms of behaviors and responsibilities of objects, they bring with them a wealth of intuition, ideas, and understanding from their everyday experience. When solutions to problems are envisioned as pigeonholes, mailboxes, or slots containing values, there is little in the programmer's background to provide insight into how problems should be structured.

Although anthropomorphic descriptions such as the quote by Ingalls may strike some people as odd, in fact they reflect the great expositive power of metaphor. Journalists make use of metaphor every day, as in the following description of object-oriented programming from *Newsweek*:

> Unlike the usual programming method—writing software one line at a time—NeXT's "object-oriented" system offers larger building blocks that developers can quickly assemble the way a kid builds faces on Mr. Potato Head.

Possibly it is this power of metaphor, more than any other feature, that is responsible for the frequent observation that it is often easier to teach object-oriented programming concepts to computer novices than to computer professionals. Novice users quickly adapt the metaphors with which they are already comfortable from their everyday life, whereas seasoned computer professionals are blinded by an adherence to more traditional ways of viewing computation.

As you start to examine the Java programs presented in the book, as well as create your own Java programs, you may find it useful to envision the process of programming as like the task of "training" a universe of agents to interact smoothly with each other, each providing a certain small and well-defined service to the others, each contributing to the effective execution of the whole. Think about how you have organized communities of individuals, such as a club or committee. Each member of the group is given certain responsibilities, and the achievement of the goals for the organization depends upon each member fulfilling his or her role.

1.3   CHAPTER SUMMARY

- Object-oriented programming is not simply a few new features added to programming languages. Rather, it is a new way of *thinking* about the process of decomposing problems and developing programming solutions.

- Object-oriented programming views a program as a collection of loosely connected agents, termed *objects*. Each object is responsible for specific tasks. It is by the interaction of objects that computation proceeds. In a certain sense, therefore, programming is nothing more or less than the simulation of a model universe.

- An object is an encapsulation of *state* (data values) and *behavior* (operations). Thus, an object is in many ways similar to a module or an abstract data type.

- The behavior of objects is dictated by the object *class*. Every object is an instance of some class. All instances of the same class will behave in a similar fashion (that is, invoke the same method) in response to a similar request.

- An object will exhibit its behavior by invoking a method (similar to executing a procedure) in response to a message. The interpretation of the message (that is, the specific method used) is decided by the object and may differ from one class of objects to another.

- Objects and classes extend the concept of abstract data types by adding the notion of *inheritance*. Classes can be organized into a hierarchical inheritance tree. Data and behavior associated with classes higher in the tree can also be accessed and used by classes lower in the tree. Such classes are said to inherit their behavior from the parent classes.

- Designing an object-oriented program is like organizing a community of individuals. Each member of the community is given certain responsibilities. The achievement of the goals for the community as a whole comes about through the work of each member, and the interactions of members with each other.

- By reducing the interdependency among software components, object-oriented programming permits the development of reusable software systems. Such components can be created and tested as independent units, in isolation from other portions of a software application.

- Reusable software components permit the programmer to deal with problems on a higher level of abstraction. We can define and manipulate objects simply in terms of the messages they understand and a description of the tasks they perform, ignoring implementation details.

FURTHER READING

I said at the beginning of the chapter that this is not a reference manual. The reference manual written by the developers of the language, James Gosling, Billy Joy, and Guy Steele is [Gosling, Joy, and Steele 1996]. But perhaps even more useful for most programmers is the annotated description of the Java class library presented by Patrick Chan and Rosanna Lee [Chan 1996]. Information on the internal workings of the Java system is presented by Tim Lindholm and Frank Yellin [Lindholm and Yellin 1997].

I noted earlier that many consider Alan Kay to be the father of object-oriented programming. Like most simple assertions, this one is only somewhat supportable. Kay himself [Kay 1993] traces much of the influence on his development of Smalltalk to the earlier computer programming language Simula, developed in Scandinavia in the early 1960s by Ole-Johan Dahl and Kristen Nygaard [Dahl and Nygaard 1966]. A more accurate history would be that most of the principles of object-oriented programming were fully worked out by the developers of Simula, but that these would have been largely ignored by the profession had they not been rediscovered by Kay in the creation of the Smalltalk programming language. I will discuss the history of OOP in more detail in the next chapter.

Like most terms that have found their way into the popular jargon, *object-oriented* is used more often than it is defined. Thus, the question "What is object-oriented programming?" is surprisingly difficult to answer. Bjarne Stroustrup has quipped that many arguments appear to boil down to the following syllogism:

- X is good.
- Object-oriented is good.
- *Ergo*, X is object-oriented [Stroustrup 1988].

Roger King argued [Kim and Lochovsky 1989], that his cat is object-oriented. After all, a cat exhibits characteristic behavior, responds to messages, is heir to a long tradition of inherited responses, and manages its own quite independent internal state.

Many authors have tried to provide a precise description of the properties a programming language must possess to be called *object-oriented*. I myself have written an earlier book [Budd 1997] that tries to explain object-oriented concepts in a language-independent fashion. See also, for example, the analysis by Josephine Micallef [1998], or Peter Wegner [1986]. Wegner distinguishes *object-based* languages, which support only abstraction (such as Ada), from *object-oriented* languages, which must also support inheritance.

Other authors—notably Brad Cox [1990]—define the term much more broadly. To Cox, object-oriented programming represents the *objective* of programming by assembling solutions from collections of off-the-shelf subcomponents, rather than any particular *technology* we may use to achieve this objective. Rather than drawing lines that are divisive, we should embrace any and all means that show promise in leading to a new software industrial revolution. Cox's book on OOP [Cox 1986], although written early in the development of object-oriented programming and now somewhat dated in details, is nevertheless one of the most readable manifestos of the object-oriented movement.

STUDY QUESTIONS

1. What is the original meaning of the word *paradigm*?

2. How do objects interact with one another?

3. How are messages different from procedure calls?

4. What is the name applied to an algorithm an object uses to respond to a request?

5. Why does the object-oriented approach naturally imply a high degree of information hiding?

6. What is a class? How are classes linked to behavior?

7. What is a class inheritance hierarchy? How is it linked to classes and behavior?

8. What does it mean for one method to override another method from a parent class?

9. What are the basic elements of the process-state model of computation?

10. How does the object-oriented model of computation differ from the process-state model?

11. In what way is an object-oriented program like a simulation?

EXERCISES

1. In an object-oriented inheritance hierarchy, each level is a more specialized form of the preceding level. Give an example of a hierarchy found in everyday life that has this property. Some types of hierarchy found in

everyday life are not inheritance hierarchies. Give an example of a hierarchy that is not an inheritance hierarchy.

2. Look up the definition of *paradigm* in at least three dictionaries. Relate these definitions to computer programming languages.

3. Take a real-world problem, like the task of sending flowers described earlier, and describe its solution in terms of agents (objects) and responsibilities.

4. Consider an object in the real world, such as a pet. Describe some of the classes, or categories, to which the object belongs. Can you organize these categories into an inheritance hierarchy? What knowledge concerning the object is represented in each category?

5. If you are familiar with two or more distinct computer programming languages, give an example of a problem showing how one language would direct the programmer to one type of solution, and a different language would encourage an alternative solution.

6. Argue either for or against the position that computing is basically simulation. (You may want to read the article by Alan Kay in *Scientific American* [Kay 1977].)

2 A Brief History of Object-Oriented Programming

It is commonly thought that object-oriented programming (OOP) is a relatively recent phenomenon in computer science. To the contrary in fact, almost all the major concepts we now associate with object-oriented programs, such as objects, classes, and inheritance hierarchies, were developed in the 1960s as part of a language called Simula, designed by researchers at the Norwegian Computing Center. Simula, as the name suggests, was a language inspired by problems involving the simulation of real-life systems. However the importance of these constructs, even to the developers of Simula, was only slowly recognized [Nygaard and Dahl 1981].

In the 1970s, Alan Kay organized a research group at Xerox PARC (the Palo Alto Research Center). With great prescience, Kay predicted the coming revolution in personal computing that was to develop nearly a decade later (see, for example, his 1977 article in *Scientific American* [Kay 1977]). Kay was concerned with discovering a programming language that would be understandable to people who were not computer professionals, to ordinary people with no prior training in computer use.[1] He found in the notion of classes and computing as simulation a metaphor that could easily be understood by novice users, as he then demonstrated by a series of experiments conducted at PARC using children as programmers. The programming language developed by his group was named Smalltalk. This language evolved through several revisions during the decade. A

---

[1] I have always found it ironic that Kay missed an important point. He thought that to *use* a computer one would be required to *program* a computer. Although he correctly predicted in 1977 the coming trend in hardware, few could have predicted at that time the rapid development of general purpose computer applications that was to accompany, perhaps even drive, the introduction of personal computers. Nowadays the vast majority of people who use personal computers have no idea how to program.

widely read 1981 issue of *Byte* magazine, in which the remark by Ingalls quoted in the first chapter appears, did much to popularize the concepts developed by Kay and his team at Xerox.

Roughly contemporaneous with Kay's work was another project being conducted on the other side of the country. Bjarne Stroustrup, a researcher at Bell Laboratories who had learned Simula while completing his doctorate at Cambridge University in England, was developing an extension to the C language that would facilitate the creation of objects and classes [Stroustrup 1982]. This was eventually to evolve into the language C++ [Stroustrup 1994].

With the dissemination of information on these and similar projects, an explosion of research in object-oriented programming techniques began. By the time of the first major conference on object-oriented programming, in 1986, there were literally dozens of new programming languages vying for acceptance. These included Eiffel [Meyer 1988], Objective-C [Cox 1986], Actor, Object Pascal, and various Lisp dialects.

In the decade since the 1986 OOPSLA conference, object-oriented programming has moved from being revolutionary to being mainstream, and in the process has transformed a major portion of the field of computer science as a whole.

2.1 THE HISTORY OF JAVA

The language we now call Java was originally named Oak, and was developed in 1991 by a computer scientist at Sun Microsystems named James Gosling. Oak's intended purpose was as a language for use in embedded consumer electronic applications, such as VCRs. Although this intended use might at first seem to be only a bit of historical computer trivia, in fact it was important in determining the characteristics of the language we see today.

In designing Oak, Gosling envisioned a world where many electronic devices, such as your telephone, your VCR, your television, and your computer, would all be connected together over a vast computer network. Such applications would generally possess embedded computer processors, which would control the essential running of the component. (Although we have not yet reached the point where telephones are routinely connected to the Internet, the part about electronic devices having embedded processors is now almost universally true.)

Several characteristics of embedded systems make them different from the average general purpose computer. Two of the most important features are size and reliability. Generally, the processors that run in embedded systems are very small, possessing only meager amounts of memory. Thus, a programming language designed for an embedded system must be able to be translated into a very concise encoding. An even more important aspect is reliability. When a program fails on a typical general purpose computer, the user is annoyed, but even in the worst case the user can generally recover and continue the program by rebooting the computer. The annoyance is greater if, for example, the software controlling a telephone fails. For this reason embedded systems should almost never fail, and should respond as gracefully as possible to exceptional and erroneous conditions.

Many features of Java reflect this original mindset. The language itself is small and simple, and can be translated into a very compact internal representation. Programming constructs, such as pointers or the goto statement, which experience had shown to be a source of many programming errors, were simply eliminated from the language. A powerful concept called exception handling was borrowed from earlier languages but greatly extended and intimately tied into the other aspects of the language. This *exception-handling* facility meant that any programmer writing in Java would be forced to deal with the possibilities of how programs could fail in unpredictable ways, and create code to handle the unexpected in a (hopefully) graceful fashion.

For a number of reasons, Java (or Oak) as a language for embedded consumer electronics did not materialize. But as interest in embedded systems at Sun was starting to wane, the phenomenon known as the World Wide Web was just beginning. The Web was originally developed in the early 1990s by a small group of scientists at a research lab in Switzerland as a means of quickly communicating research results to a physically far-flung set of colleagues. It was quickly realized, however, that the framework provided by the Web was applicable to a wide range of information. First, scientists in all disciplines started using the Web, and eventually the ideas found their way into the mainstream. Now, almost every organization, large or small, must have a Web page. Similarly, almost every advertisement in print or television contains an obligatory Web address (the universal resource locator, or URL).

To understand how Java fits into the World Wide Web, and to grasp the importance of Internet computing, one must first understand a little about the concept of clients and servers, and the difference between server-side computing and client-side computing.

2.2   CLIENT-SIDE COMPUTING

Although Java is a general purpose programming language that can be used to create almost any type of computer program, much of the excitement surrounding Java has been generated by its employment as a language for creating programs intended for execution across the Internet. To understand the process of programming for the Web, one must first understand a few basic characteristics of the Internet in general. The Internet is a classic example of a *client/server* system. A person using the Internet works at his or her own computer, which runs an Internet-aware application, such as a Web browser (Figure 2.1). This is

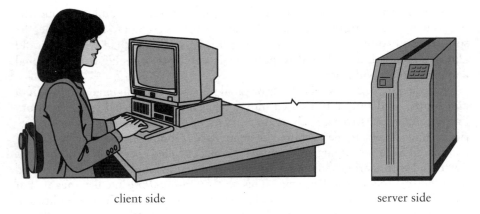

client side   server side

Figure 2.1   Client and server-side computing.

called the *client* system. The client application communicates over the Internet with another computer, perhaps one physically very far away. For example, a Web browser might request the information on a Web page stored on a distant computer. The second computer, the *server* computer, transmits the contents of the Web page to the client application. The client computer then determines how to display this information to the user.

From the beginning of the Web, it has been possible to add dynamic behavior to Web pages by executing programs. However, in the past these programs executed on the server computer. The client transmitted a request, and the server responded by executing a program, and transmitting the result. Many Web-based forms are still implemented in this fashion. Such an arrangement is sometimes termed *CGI–bin* processing, after the directory where executable programs are conventionally located on the server computer.

Several problems occur with this arrangement. For one, transmission times are often slow, causing a noticeable delay between the moment when the client asks that a program be executed and the time the results are returned. In addition, server programs often deal with many clients at once (perhaps hundreds or thousands), further reducing performance. In contrast, the client machines are often lightly loaded personal machines. Frequently the client machine is executing little more than the single Internet application.

The key idea of *client-side* computing is that rather than executing the program on the server side and transmitting the result, the server will transmit the *program* to the client. The client will then execute the program locally. Not only is the program then run on a less heavily loaded system, but the only delay is the time to transmit the program. Once the program starts executing, any interactions between the user and the program take place locally, and do not need to cross the Internet.

2.2.1 *Bytecode Interpreters and Just-In-Time Compilers*

Of course, many difficulties must be overcome for this process to succeed. The first is that the client computer must be able to execute the program. Often the server and client machines will be different types of computers. Indeed, the client may not even know what type of machine the server is using. Thus, the traditional concept of computer programs being translated into machine code for a specific machine will not work in this environment; machine code that executes well on the server computer may not work at all for the client computer.

Instead, Java is translated into a device-independent *bytecode*. This bytecode (so-called because most instructions are one or two bytes long), is like a machine language for an imaginary machine, a Java-specific machine, or *virtual machine*. Each computer that runs Java programs then processes these bytecodes into a form that works correctly on the current system.

There are several ways this can be done. The easiest scheme is to have an *interpreter* that reads and executes bytecodes one by one as they are needed. Better performance can be obtained by using a *just-in-time (JIT) compiler*. This system takes the Java bytecodes and translates them into the machine code native to the client system. These programs then run as fast as any compiled program created specifically for the client computer.

2.2.2 *Security Issues*

Another problem that must be overcome for client-side computing to be widely accepted is the issue of security. A program running on a server machine can do very little damage to a client machine; the server simply does not have access to memory or to files to which damage could be done. But a program running on the client side could, in theory, have full access to the client computer resources. There is great potential for such a program to do significant damage, such as erasing files from a hard drive.

Java programs get around this problem by using a *security manager*. The security manager is provided by the client, and limits the actions that can be performed by the Java program provided by the server. For example, most security managers will not allow a Java program to access the file system or to transmit information across the Internet to machines other than the client or server processors. Thus, the potential damage that a Java program can cause is very limited.

Despite the use of a security manager, the issue of security remains one of the more controversial aspects of Java programming. In fact, the security manager is only part of a multilayer approach to providing security for client machines that run Java programs. Despite these, the short history of experiences with computer viruses and other attacks should caution us that a truly malicious programmer can probably still find weaknesses to exploit. However, the use of techniques such as the security manager has made the task of the malicious programmer greatly more difficult.

2.2.3 *Specialization of Interfaces*

Yet another issue arises due to the fact that the client and server systems can be entirely different types of computers. As anybody who has tried to write a graphical program in another language for multiple platforms has discovered, the sequences of commands needed to perform graphical operations, such as placing a window on the display, varies greatly from one machine to another. As will be explained in Section 15.11, the solution to this problem requires a careful coordination between the client and server computers, with portions of a Java program originating on one machine, and other parts coming from the second.

The server program is structured in terms of generic classes, such as Window and Button. These classes are the same regardless of the type of system on which the Java program is run. But when executed, the first task these components perform is to create a *peer* component. The peer component originates on the client system and is not part of the server program. Thus, a button running on a PC will create a PC-Button peer, while the same program running on a Macintosh will create a Mac-Button peer. All the device-specific aspects of drawing the image on the local computer system are held in the peer class, and not in the generic button class.

2.3   THE WHITE PAPER DESCRIPTION

In one of the first papers published by Sun Microsystems that dealt with Java, the language was described in the following fashion:

> Java: A simple, object-oriented, network-savvy, interpreted, robust, secure, architecture neutral, portable, high-performance, multithreaded, dynamic language.

The tongue-in-cheek description is intentionally reminiscent of the hyperbole-laden and buzzword-heavy descriptions characteristic of advertising copy. Nevertheless, each phrase had been carefully selected, and in total, they accurately sum up the language.

2.3.1 *Java Is Simple*

Although much of the syntax of Java is based on the earlier object-oriented language C++, the Java language is considerably simpler than C++. Many keywords have been eliminated, there is no preprocessor, there are far fewer special cases, and the language is augmented with a much larger library of high-level development tools. Confusing features such as operator overloading have been eliminated, as have independent functions, global variables, the `goto` statement, structures, and pointers.

One of the more notable omissions from Java is the latter, the concept of the pointer. In many other languages there is a distinction between a *value* and a *pointer to a value*. Values are static, fixed-size entities. Pointers are dynamic quantities that are filled at run time. As explained in Chapter 11, there are important reasons why an object-oriented language should make heavy use of pointers. Java does so, but hides this fact from the programmer. As far as the programmer is concerned, there are no pointers, although in truth this illusion is only possible because almost everything is internally a pointer. However, the elimination of this construct removes an entire class of common programming errors, making it greatly easier to construct reliable and correct programs.

2.3.2   *Java Is Object-Oriented*

The language Java is founded upon the object-oriented principles described in Chapter 1. The only unit of programming is the class description. Unlike other languages, Java has no functions and no variables that can exist outside of class boundaries. Thus, all Java programs must be built out of objects. Other languages, notably C++ and Object Pascal, have tried to combine object-oriented features on top of an existing, non–object-oriented language. The unfortunate consequence of such a design is that programmers can continue working in their old, non–object-oriented fashion. By forcing all programs into an object-oriented structure, the many benefits of object-oriented design (an emphasis on encapsulation, an orientation toward reusability) are much more easily realized.

2.3.3   *Java Is Network Savvy*

From the start, Java was designed with the Internet in mind. Although it is possible to construct Java programs that do not deal with the Internet (indeed, most of the programs in this book will not), the language provides a rich set of tools for programming across a network. The Java standard library provides a plethora of classes for describing universal resource locators (URLs), for making connections between client and server computers (see Chapter 21), and for execution in controlled environments such as a World Wide Web browser.

2.3.4   *Java Is Interpreted*

Java was designed for a multicomputer execution environment. From the first, it was intended that the computer a program was developed on might not be the same as the computer on which it is stored, which might again be different from the computer on which it is finally executed. Thus, the traditional model where a program is translated by a *compiler* into the machine language for a particular machine will not work for Java; the machine language for the system on which the program is developed will probably not work for the machine on which the program is eventually executed.

Java systems initially got around this problem by using an *interpreter*. Java programs were compiled into an assembly language for an imaginary machine, called the *virtual machine*. These assembly language instructions, called *byte-codes*, could be stored on any type of machine. Any machine that supported Java programs would provide a simulator, an *interpreter*, that would read the bytecode values and execute them. In this fashion, any type of computer could be used as a Java virtual machine.

However, interpreters have one serious disadvantage over conventional systems. They are generally much slower in execution. Recent innovations in the Java world have advanced upon this idea of interpreters, and largely eliminated this performance penalty. A *just-in-time (JIT) compiler* is a system that reads the machine-independent bytecode representation of a Java program, and immediately prior to execution translates the bytecode representation into actual machine instructions for the system on which the Java program is being run. Because Java programs then execute as machine instructions, they can be almost as fast as programs compiled in more conventional languages for the specific hardware platform, and still retain the portability of the virtual machine.

2.3.5 *Java Is Robust*

The Java language and associated libraries are designed to be graceful in the presence of hardware and software errors. An example of this is the extensive use of *exception handling*. Statements that can potentially receive an error, such as a file operation that could attempt to read from a nonexistent source, will generate an exception instead of performing an erroneous operation. The semantics of the language insist that the programmer *must* deal with this possibility any time a file operation is intended. Thus, programmers are forced into thinking about potential sources of error, and their programs are therefore much more robust in the presence of error-producing conditions.

Another feature that makes Java programs more robust is automatic memory management, or garbage collection. Programmers writing in languages that use manual memory management, for example C++, frequently forget to release memory resources once they are finished with them. Long-running programs therefore slowly increase their memory requirements, until they catastrophically fail. The Java run-time system instead automatically detects and recovers memory that is no longer being used by the currently running program. This both simplifies the programmer's task and makes programs more reliable.

2.3.6 *Java Is Secure*

By eliminating pointers, the Java language removes what is perhaps the most common source of programming errors, inadvertently overwriting memory locations that are being addressed by pointers with improperly set values. The Java language also insists that array index values are checked for validity before they are referenced and that all variables must be assigned a value before being used.

But the Java language is just the first layer in a multilevel security system. Bytecodes themselves (which may or may not have been produced by a Java compiler) are examined before they are executed by the Java interpreter. This check determines that bytecodes are free of a number of common errors, for example that they do not access classes incorrectly, overflow or underflow the operand stack, or use illegal data conversions.

Finally, as we will discuss in Chapter 21, many of the applications envisioned for Java involve programs that are stored on one computer but executed on another. Typically, the computer on which the Java program will execute is a user's personal computer. Few users would trust Java if it were possible that programs brought over a network could possibly cause damage, such as erasing a hard drive or removing a file. For this reason, the designers of Java purposely created a programming environment where programs are severely restricted in the type of operations they can perform. Because of these restrictions, users can be largely assured that when they execute a program brought over the network, their local computer is safe from tampering.

2.3.7 *Java Is Architecture Neutral*

Because Java bytecodes do not correspond to any particular machine, they work with all machines. A Java program is the same whether it runs on a PC, a Macintosh, or a Unix system. This is very different from conventional languages. Although C++ is a standard language, and therefore should be the same on all machines, the libraries needed to perform activities such as placing a window on a display, or responding to a button press, differ considerably from one platform to another. This is why it is very difficult to, for example, move programs designed for the PC onto a Macintosh, or vice versa. But Java hides these application-specific details under a layer of abstraction in the standard Java library. Thus, from the programmer's point of view, all machines look the same.

2.3.8 *Java Is Portable*

Because the Java library hides architecture-specific concepts, and because byte-codes are the same regardless of the machine on which they are generated, Java programs possess an unparalleled degree of portability. Indeed, the exact same program can be compiled on one system, then executed on many different types of systems.

2.3.9   *Java Is High-Performance*

Although the initial implementations of Java bytecode interpreters exacted a heavy performance penalty, the technology of Java execution has rapidly evolved since the language was introduced. Systems such as just-in-time compilers now allow platform-independent Java programs to be executed with nearly the same run-time performance as conventional compiled languages.

2.3.10   *Java Is Multithreaded*

Java is one of the first languages to be designed explicitly for the possibility of multiple threads of execution running in one program. As shown in Chapter 20, not only is it easy to set up such multitasking, but the coordination of these parallel processes is also relatively simple.

2.3.11   *Java Is Dynamic*

Finally, because Java programs move across the Internet and execute on the user's local computer, they permit a degree of dynamic behavior impossible in older style systems.

2.4   CHAPTER SUMMARY

Although much of the excitement of Java stems from its use in developing Web-based application programs, or *applets*, the Java language itself is a general purpose programming language suitable for any task that can be solved using a computer. For most of this book we will deal with more general application programs. We will return to a discussion of Web-based programming and applets in Chapter 21.

   The intent of this book is to discuss the principles of object-oriented programming, and in particular, the way that object-oriented concepts are manifest in the Java programming language. Nevertheless, an understanding of Java is not possible without an appreciation of the history and intent of the language. In this chapter we have examined how the Java language was developed and the original purpose for the language. The characteristics required for this original purpose, namely a small language with a high degree of reliability, turn out also to be desirable characteristics for any programming language. Thus, the Java language has potential uses that far exceed the original designers' intent.

STUDY QUESTIONS

   1. What was the name of the first object-oriented language? In what country was it developed?

2. What problem was the research group founded by Alan Kay concerned with when they developed the language Smalltalk?

3. What was the original name given to the Java language?

4. What was the original intended use of Java programs?

5. What are some characteristics of embedded systems?

6. What is the difference between server-side computing (also known as CGI-bin processing) and client-side computing?

7. What is a bytecode interpreter?

8. What is a just-in-time compiler?

EXERCISES

1. Read Alan Kay's 1977 paper in *Scientific American*. List the issues that Kay thought would be important when truly personal computers attained widespread use. In hindsight, in what ways were his predictions correct, and in what ways did his predictions miss the mark?

2. Try to identify all the embedded computer processors found in a typical home.

3 Object-Oriented Design

A superficial description of the distinction between an object-oriented language, such as Java, and a conventional programming language, such as Pascal, might concentrate on syntactic differences. In this area, discussion would center on topics such as classes, inheritance, message passing, and methods. But such an analysis would miss the most important point of object-oriented programming, which has nothing to do with syntax.

Working in an object-oriented language (that is, one that supports inheritance, message passing, and classes) is neither a necessary nor sufficient condition for doing object-oriented programming. As emphasized in Chapter 1, an object-oriented program is like a community of interacting individuals, each having assigned responsibilities, working together toward the attainment of a common goal. As in real life, a major aspect in the design of such a community is determining the specific responsibilities for each member. To this end, practitioners of object-oriented design have developed a design technique driven by the specification and delegation of responsibilities. Rebecca Wirfs-Brock and Brian Wilkerson have called this technique *responsibility-driven design* [Wirfs-Brock 1989, 1990].

3.1 RESPONSIBILITY IMPLIES NONINTERFERENCE

As anyone can attest who can remember being a child, or who has raised children, responsibility is a sword that cuts both ways. When you make an object (be it a child or a software system) responsible for specific actions, you expect a certain behavior, at least when the rules are observed. But just as important, responsibility implies a degree of independence or noninterference. If you tell a child that she is responsible for cleaning her room, you do not normally stand over her and watch while that task is being performed—that is not the nature of responsibility. Instead, you expect that, having issued a directive in the correct fashion, the desired outcome will be produced.

Similarly, in the floral delivery example from Chapter 1, I give the request to deliver flowers to my florist without stopping to think about how my request will be serviced. Flora, having taken on the responsibility for this service, is free to operate without interference on my part.

The difference between conventional programming and object-oriented programming is in many ways the difference between actively supervising a child while she performs a task, and delegating to the child responsibility for that performance. Conventional programming proceeds largely by doing something *to* something else—modifying a record or updating an array, for example. Thus, one portion of code in a software system is often intimately tied, by control and data connections, to many other sections of the system. Such dependencies can come about through the use of global variables, through use of pointer values, or simply through inappropriate use of and dependence on implementation details of other portions of code. A responsibility-driven design attempts to cut these links, or at least make them as unobtrusive as possible.

This notion might at first seem no more subtle than the notions of information hiding and modularity, which are important to programming even in conventional languages. But responsibility-driven design elevates information hiding from a technique to an art. The principle of information hiding becomes vitally important when one moves from programming in the small to programming in the large.

One of the major benefits of object-oriented programming is reaped when software subsystems are reused from one project to the next. For example, a simulation system might work for both a simulation of balls on a billiards table and a simulation of fish in a fish tank. This ability to reuse code implies that the software can have almost no domain-specific components; it must totally delegate responsibility for domain-specific behavior to application-specific portions of the system. The ability to create such reusable code is not one that is easily learned— it requires experience, careful examination of case studies (paradigms, in the original sense of the word), and use of a programming language in which such delegation is natural and easy to express. In subsequent chapters, we will look at several such examples.

3.2   Programming in the Small and in the Large

The difference between the development of individual projects and of more sizable software systems is often described as programming in the small versus programming in the large. *Programming in the small* characterizes projects with the following attributes:

- Code is developed by a single programmer, or perhaps by a very small collection of programmers. A single individual can understand all aspects of a project, from top to bottom, beginning to end.

- The major problem in the software development process is the design and development of algorithms for dealing with the problem at hand.

Programming in the large, on the other hand, characterizes software projects with features such as the following:

- The software system is developed by a large team of programmers. Individuals involved in the specification or design of the system may differ from those involved in the coding of individual components, who may differ as well from those involved in the integration of various components in the final product. No single individual can be considered responsible for the entire project or even necessarily understand all aspects of the project.

- The major problem in the software development process is the management of details and the communication of information between diverse portions of the project.

While the beginning student will usually be acquainted with programming in the small, aspects of many object-oriented languages are best understood as responses to the problems encountered while programming in the large. Thus, some appreciation of the difficulties involved in developing large systems is a helpful prerequisite to understanding OOP.

3.3 WHY BEGIN WITH BEHAVIOR?

Why begin the design process with an analysis of behavior? The simple answer is that the behavior of a system is usually understood long before any other aspect.

Earlier software development techniques concentrated on ideas such as characterizing the basic data structures or the overall sequence of function calls, often within the creation of a formal specification of the desired application. But structural elements of the application can be identified only after a considerable amount of problem analysis. Similarly, a formal specification often ended up as a document understood by neither programmer nor client. But *behavior* is something that can be described almost from the moment an idea is conceived, and (often unlike a formal specification) can be described in terms meaningful to both the programmers and the client.

The following case study illustrates the application of responsibility-driven design (RDD).

3.4 A CASE STUDY IN RDD

Imagine you are the chief software architect in a major computer firm. One day your boss walks into your office with an idea that, it is hoped, will be the next major success in your product line. Your assignment is to develop the Interactive Intelligent Kitchen Helper (IIKH) (Figure 3.1). The task given to your software team is stated in very few words, written on what appears to be the back of a slightly used paper napkin, in handwriting that appears to be your boss's.

3.4.1 *The Interactive Intelligent Kitchen Helper*

Briefly, the Interactive Intelligent Kitchen Helper is a PC-based application that will replace the index-card system of recipes found in the average kitchen. But more than simply maintaining a database of recipes, the kitchen helper assists in the planning of meals for an extended period, say a week. The user of the IIKH can sit down at a terminal, browse the database of recipes, and interactively create a series of menus. The IIKH will automatically scale the recipes to any number of servings and will print out menus for the entire week, for a particular day, or for a particular meal. And it will print an integrated grocery list of all the items needed for the recipes for the entire period.

As is usually true with the initial descriptions of most software systems, the specification for the IIKH is highly ambiguous on a number of important

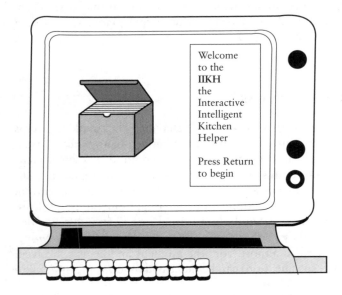

Figure 3.1 View of the Interactive Intelligent Kitchen Helper.

points. It is also true that, in all likelihood, the eventual design and development of the software system to support the IIKH will require the efforts of several programmers working together. Thus, the initial goal of the software team must be to clarify the ambiguities in the description and to outline how the project can be divided into components to be assigned for development to individual team members.

The cornerstone of object-oriented programming is to characterize software in terms of *behavior*, that is, actions to be performed. We will see this repeated on many levels in the development of the IIKH. Initially, the team will try to characterize, at a very high level of abstraction, the behavior of the entire application. This then leads to a description of the behavior of various software subsystems. Only when all behavior has been identified and described will the software design team proceed to the coding step. In the next several sections, we will trace the tasks the software design team will perform in producing this application.

3.4.2 *Working With Components*

The first task is to refine the specification. As already noted, initial specifications are almost always ambiguous and unclear on anything except the most general points. There are several goals for this step. One objective is to get a better handle on the "look and feel" of the eventual product. This information can then be carried back to the client (in this case, your boss) to see if it is in agreement with the original conception. It is likely, perhaps inevitable, that the specifications for the final application will change during the creation of the software system, and it is important that the design be developed to easily accommodate change and that potential changes be noted as early as possible. (See Section 3.6.2, "Preparing for Change.") Equally important, at this point very high-level decisions can be made concerning the structure of the eventual software system. In particular, the activities to be performed can be mapped onto components.

3.4.3 *Identification of Components*

The engineering of a complex physical system, such as a building or an automobile engine, is simplified by dividing the design into smaller units. So, too, the engineering of software is simplified by the identification and development of software components. A *component* is simply an abstract entity that can perform tasks—that is, fulfill some responsibilities. At this point, it is not necessary to know exactly the eventual representation for a component or how a component will perform a task. A component may ultimately be turned into a function, a structure or class, or a collection of other components (a *pattern*). At this level of development, just two characteristics are important:

- A component must have a small, well-defined set of responsibilities.

- A component should interact with other components as little as possible.

We will shortly discuss the reasoning behind the second characteristic. For the moment, we are simply concerned with the identification of component responsibilities.

3.5 CRC CARDS — RECORDING RESPONSIBILITY

In order to discover components and their responsibilities, the programming team walks through scenarios. That is, the team acts out the running of the application just as if it already possessed a working system. Every activity that must take place is identified and assigned to some component as a responsibility. (See Figure 3.2.)

As part of this process, it is often useful to represent components using small index cards. On the face of the card the programming team writes the name of the software component, the responsibilities of the component, and the names of other components with which the component must interact. Such cards are sometimes known as CRC (component, responsibility, collaborator) cards [Beck and Cunningham 1989], [Bellin and Simone 1997], and are associated with each software component. As responsibilities for the component are discovered, they are recorded on the face of the CRC card.

3.5.1 Giving Components a Physical Representation

While working through scenarios, it is useful to assign CRC cards to different members of the design team. The member holding the card representing a component records the responsibilities of the associated software component, and acts as the "surrogate" for the software during the scenario simulation. He or

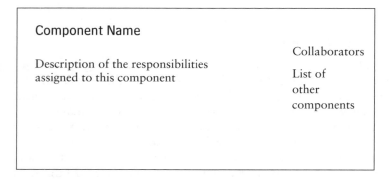

Figure 3.2 A component, responsibility, collaborator (CRC) card.

she describes the activities of the software system, passing "control" to another member when the software system requires the services of another component.

An advantage of CRC cards is that index cards are widely available, inexpensive, and erasable. This encourages experimentation, since alternative designs can be tried, explored, or abandoned with little investment. The physical separation of the cards encourages an intuitive understanding of the importance of the logical separation of the various components, helping to emphasize the cohesion and coupling (described shortly). The constraints of an index card are also a good measure of approximate complexity—a component that is expected to perform more tasks than can fit easily in the space of a card is probably too complex, and the team should find a simpler solution, perhaps by moving some responsibilities elsewhere to divide a task between two or more new components.

3.5.2 The What/Who Cycle

As noted at the beginning of this discussion, the identification of components takes place during the process of imagining the execution of a working system. Often this proceeds as a cycle of what/who questions. First, the programming team identifies *what* activity needs to be performed next. This is immediately followed by answering the question of *who* performs the action. In this manner, designing a software system is much like organizing a collection of people, such as a club. Any activity that is to be performed must be assigned as a responsibility to some component.

We know, from real life, that if any action is to take place, there must be an agent assigned to perform it. Just as in the running of a club, any action to be performed must be assigned to some individual; in organizing an object-oriented program, all actions must be the responsibility of some component. The secret to good object-oriented design is to first establish an agent for each action.

3.5.3 Documentation

At this point the development of documentation should begin. Two documents should be essential parts of any software system: the user manual and the system design documentation. Work on both of these can commence even before the first line of code has been written.

The user manual describes the interaction with the system from the user's point of view; it is an excellent means of verifying that the development team's conception of the application matches the client's. Since the decisions made in creating the scenarios will closely match the decisions the user will be required to make in the eventual application, the development of the user manual naturally dovetails with the process of walking through scenarios.

Before any actual code has been written, the mindset of the software team is most similar to that of the eventual users. Thus, it is at this point that the developers can most easily anticipate the sort of questions to which a novice user will need answers.

The second essential document is the design documentation. Because the design documentation records the major decisions made during software design, it should thus be produced when these decisions are fresh in the minds of the creators, and not after the fact when many of the relevant details will have been forgotten. It is often far easier to write a general global description of the software system early in the development. Too soon, the focus will move to the level of individual components or modules. And although it is also important to document the module level, too much concern with the details of each module will make it difficult for subsequent software maintainers to form an initial picture of the larger structure.

CRC cards are one aspect of the design documentation, but they do not reflect *all* important decisions. Arguments for and against any major design alternatives should be recorded, as well as factors that influenced the final decisions. A log or diary of the project schedule should be maintained. Both the user manual and the design documents are refined and evolve over time in exactly the same way the software is refined and evolves.

3.6   COMPONENTS AND BEHAVIOR

To return to the Interactive Kitchen Helper application, the IIKH, the team decides that when the system begins, the user will be presented with an attractive informative window (shown in Figure 3.1). The responsibility for displaying this window is assigned to a component called the Greeter. In some as yet unspecified manner (perhaps by pull-down menus, button or key presses, or use of a pressure-sensitive screen), the user can select one of several actions. Initially, the team identifies just five actions:

1. Casually browse the database of existing recipes, but without reference to any particular meal plan.

2. Add a new recipe to the database.

3. Edit or annotate an existing recipe.

4. Review an existing plan for several meals.

5. Create a new plan of meals.

These activities seem to divide themselves naturally into two groups. The first three are associated with the recipe database; the latter two are associated with menu plans. As a result, the team next decides to create components corresponding to these two responsibilities. Continuing with the scenario, the team elects to ignore the meal plan management for the moment and move on to

```
┌─────────────────────────────────────────────────────────────────────┐
│                                                                       │
│   Greeter                                                             │
│                                             Collaborators             │
│   Display informative initial message                                 │
│                                             Database Manager          │
│   Offer user choice of options              Plan Manager             │
│   Pass control to either                                              │
│       Recipe Database Manager                                         │
│       Plan Manager for processing                                     │
│                                                                       │
└─────────────────────────────────────────────────────────────────────┘
```

Figure 3.3 CRC card for the Greeter.

refine the activities of the Recipe Database component. Figure 3.3 shows the initial CRC card representation of the Greeter.

Broadly speaking, the responsibility of the recipe database component is simply to maintain a collection of recipes. We have already identified three elements of this task: The recipe component database must facilitate browsing the library of existing recipes, editing the recipes, and including new recipes in the database.

3.6.1 *Postponing Decisions*

A number of decisions must eventually be made concerning how best to let the user browse the database. For example, should the user first be presented with a list of categories, such as "Soups," "Salads," "Main Courses," and "Desserts"? Alternatively, should the user be able to describe keywords to narrow a search, perhaps by providing a list of ingredients, and then see all the recipes that contain those items ("Almonds, Strawberries, Cheese"), or a list of previously inserted keywords ("Bob's favorite cake")? Should scroll bars be used or simulated thumbholes in a virtual book? These choices are fun to think about, but the important point is that such decisions do not need to be made at this point (see next section). Since they affect only a single component and do not affect the functioning of any other system, all that is necessary to continue the scenario is to assert that by some means the user can select a specific recipe.

3.6.2 *Preparing for Change*

It has been said that all that is constant in life is the inevitability of change. The same is true of software. No matter how carefully one tries to develop the initial specification and design of a software system, it is almost certain that changes in the user's needs or requirements will, sometime during the life of the system, force changes to be made in the software. Programmers and software designers need to anticipate this and plan accordingly.

- The primary objective is that changes should affect as few components as possible. Even major changes in the appearance or functioning of an application should be possible with alterations to only one or two sections of code.

- Try to predict the most likely sources of change and isolate the effects of such changes to as few software components as possible. The most likely sources of change are interfaces, communication formats, and output formats.

- Try to isolate and reduce the dependency of software on hardware. For example, the interface for recipe browsing in our application may depend in part on the hardware on which the system is running. Future releases may be ported to different platforms. A good design will anticipate this change.

- Reducing coupling between software components will reduce the dependence of one upon another and increase the likelihood that one can be changed with minimal effect on the other.

- In the design documentation, maintain careful records of the design process and the discussions surrounding all major decisions. It is almost certain that the team responsible for maintaining the software and designing future releases will be at least partially different from the team producing the initial release. The design documentation will allow future teams to know the important factors behind a decision and help them avoid spending time discussing issues that have already been resolved.

3.6.3 *Continuing the Scenario*

Each recipe will be identified with a specific recipe component. Once a recipe is selected, control is passed to the associated recipe object. A recipe must contain certain information. Basically, it consists of a list of ingredients and the steps needed to transform the ingredients into the final product. In our scenario, the recipe component must also perform other activities. For example, it will display the recipe interactively on the terminal screen. The user may be given the ability to annotate or change either the list of ingredients or the instruction portion. Alternatively, the user may request a printed copy of the recipe. All of these actions are the responsibility of the Recipe component. (For the moment, we will continue to describe the Recipe in singular form. During design we can think of this as a prototypical recipe that stands in place of a multitude of actual recipes. We will later return to a discussion of singular versus multiple components.)

Having outlined the actions that must take place to permit the user to browse the database, we return to the recipe database manager and pretend the user has indicated a desire to add a new recipe. The Database Manager somehow decides in which category to place the new recipe (again, the details of how this is done are unimportant for our development at this point), requests the name of the new recipe, and then creates a new recipe component, permitting the user to edit this new blank entry. Thus, the responsibilities of performing this new task are a subset of those we already identified in permitting users to edit existing recipes.

Having explored the browsing and creation of new recipes, we return to the Greeter and investigate the development of daily menu plans, which is the Plan Manager's task. In some way (again, the details are unimportant here) the user can save existing plans. Thus, the Plan Manager can either be started by retrieving an already developed plan or by creating a new plan. In the latter case, the user is prompted for a list of dates for the plan. Each date is associated with a separate Date component. The user can select a specific date for further investigation, in which case control is passed to the corresponding Date component. Another activity of the Plan Manager is printing out the recipes for the planning period. Finally, the user can instruct the Plan Manager to produce a grocery list for the period.

The Date component maintains a collection of meals as well as any other annotations provided by the user (birthdays, anniversaries, and other reminders). It prints information on the display concerning the specified date. By some means (again unspecified), the user can indicate a desire to print all the information concerning a specific date or choose to explore in more detail a specific meal. In the latter case, control is passed to a Meal component.

The Meal component maintains a collection of augmented recipes, where the augmentation refers to the user's desire to double, triple, or otherwise increase a recipe. The Meal component displays information about the meal. The user can add or remove recipes from the meal, or can instruct that information about the meal be printed. In order to discover new recipes, the user must be permitted at this point to browse the recipe database. Thus, the Meal component must interact with the recipe database component. The design team will continue in this fashion, investigating every possible scenario.

The major category of scenarios we have not developed here is exceptional cases. For example, what happens if a user selects a number of keywords for a recipe and no matching recipe is found? How can the user cancel an activity, such as entering a new recipe, if he or she decides not to continue? Each possibility must be explored, and the responsibilities for handling the situation assigned to one or more components.

Having walked through the various scenarios, the software design team eventually decides that all activities can be adequately handled by six components (Figure 3.4). The Greeter needs to communicate only with the Plan Manager and the Recipe Database components. The Plan Manager needs to communicate only

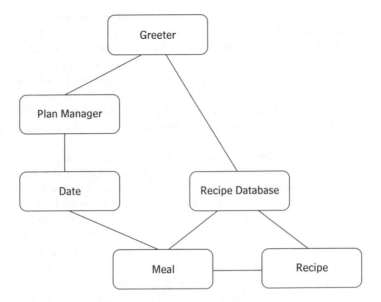

Figure 3.4   Communication among the six components in the IIKH.

with the Date component; and the Date agent, only with the Meal component. The Meal component communicates with the Recipe Database and, through this agent, with individual recipes.

3.6.4   *Interaction Diagrams*

While a description such as that shown in Figure 3.4 may describe the static relationships between components, it is not very good for describing their dynamic interactions during the execution of a scenario. A better tool for this purpose is an *interaction diagram*. Figure 3.5 shows the beginning of an interaction diagram for the Interactive Kitchen Helper. In the diagram, time moves forward from the top to the bottom. Each component is represented by a labeled vertical line. A component sending a message to another component is represented by a horizontal arrow from one line to another. Similarly, a component returning control and perhaps a result value back to the caller is represented by an arrow. (Some authors use two different arrow forms, such as a solid line to represent message passing and a dashed line to represent returning control.) The commentary on the right-hand side of the figure explains more fully the interaction taking place.

With a time axis, the interaction diagram is able to describe better the sequencing of events during a scenario. For this reason, interaction diagrams can be a useful documentation tool for complex software systems.

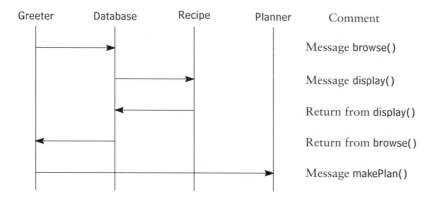

Figure 3.5 An example interaction diagram.

3.7 SOFTWARE COMPONENTS

In this section we will explore a software component in more detail. As is true of all but the most trivial ideas, there are many aspects to this seemingly simple concept.

3.7.1 *Behavior and State*

We have already seen how components are characterized by their behavior, that is, by what they can do. But components may also hold certain information. Let us take as our prototypical component a Recipe structure from the IIKH. One way to view such a component is as a pair consisting of *behavior* and *state*.

- The *behavior* of a component is the set of actions it can perform. The complete description of all the behavior for a component is sometimes called the *protocol*. For the Recipe component this includes activities such as editing the preparation instructions, displaying the recipe on a terminal screen, or printing a copy of the recipe.

- The *state* of a component represents all the information held within it. For our Recipe component the state includes the ingredients and preparation instructions. Notice that the state is not static and can change over time. For example, by editing a recipe (a behavior) the user can make changes to the preparation instructions (part of the state).

It is not necessary that all components maintain state information. For example, it is possible that the Greeter component will not have any state since it does not need to remember any information during the course of execution. However, most components will consist of a combination of behavior and state.

3.7.2   Instances and Classes

The separation of state and behavior permits us to clarify a point we avoided in our earlier discussion. Note that in the real application there will probably be many different recipes. However, all of these recipes will *perform* in the same manner. That is, the behavior of each recipe is the same; it is only the state—the individual lists of ingredients and instructions for preparation—that differs between individual recipes. In the early stages of development our interest is in characterizing the behavior common to all recipes; the details particular to any one recipe are unimportant.

The term *class* is used to describe a set of objects with similar behavior. We will see in later chapters that a class is also used as a syntactic mechanism in Java. An individual representative of a class is known as an *instance*. Note that behavior is associated with a class, not with an individual. That is, all instances of a class will respond to the same instructions and perform in a similar manner. On the other hand, state is a property of an individual. We see this in the various instances of the class Recipe. They can all perform the same actions (editing, displaying, printing) but use different data values.

3.7.3   Coupling and Cohesion

Two important concepts in the design of software components are coupling and cohesion. *Cohesion* is the degree to which the responsibilities of a single component form a meaningful unit. High cohesion is achieved by associating in a single component tasks that are related in some manner. Probably the most frequent way in which tasks are related is through the necessity to access a common data area. This is the overriding theme that joins, for example, the various responsibilities of the Recipe component.

Coupling, on the other hand, describes the relationship between software components. In general, it is desirable to reduce the amount of coupling as much as possible, since connections between software components inhibit ease of development, modification, or reuse.

In particular, coupling is increased when one software component must access data values—the state—held by another component. Such situations should almost always be avoided in favor of moving a task into the list of responsibilities of the component that holds the necessary data. For example, one might conceivably first assign responsibility for editing a recipe to the Recipe Database component, since it is while performing tasks associated with this component that the need to edit a recipe first occurs. But if we did so, the Recipe Database agent would need the ability to directly manipulate the state (the internal data values representing the list of ingredients and the preparation instructions) of an individual recipe. It is better to avoid this tight connection by moving the responsibility for editing to the recipe itself.

3.7.4 *Interface and Implementation: Parnas's Principles*

The emphasis on characterizing a software component by its behavior has one extremely important consequence. It is possible for one programmer to know how to *use* a component developed by another programmer, without needing to know how the component is *implemented*. For example, suppose each of the six components in the IIKH is assigned to a different programmer. The programmer developing the Meal component needs to allow the IIKH user to browse the database of recipes and select a single recipe for inclusion in the meal. To do this, the Meal component can simply invoke the browse behavior associated with the Recipe Database component, which is defined to return an individual Recipe. This description is valid regardless of the particular implementation used by the Recipe Database component to perform the actual browsing action.

The purposeful omission of implementation details behind a simple interface is known as *information hiding*. We say the component *encapsulates* the behavior, showing only how the component can be used, not the detailed actions it performs. This naturally leads to two different views of a software system. The interface view is the face seen by other programmers. It describes *what* a software component can perform. The implementation view is the face seen by the programmer working on a particular component. It describes *how* a component goes about completing a task.

The separation of interface and implementation is perhaps *the* most important concept in software engineering. Yet it is difficult for students to understand, or to motivate. Information hiding is largely meaningful only in the context of multiperson programming projects. In such efforts, the limiting factor is often not the amount of coding involved, but the amount of communication required among the various programmers and among their respective software systems. As will be described shortly, software components are often developed in parallel by different programmers, and in isolation from one another.

There is also an increasing emphasis on the reuse of general purpose software components in multiple projects. For this to be successful, there must be minimal and well-understood interconnections between the various portions of the system. These ideas were captured by computer scientist David Parnas in a pair of rules, known as *Parnas's principles*:

- The developer of a software component must provide the intended user with all the information needed to make effective use of the services provided by the component, and should provide *no* other information.

- The developer of a software component must be provided with all the information necessary to carry out the given responsibilities assigned to the component, and should be provided with *no* other information.

A consequence of the separation of interface from implementation is that a programmer can experiment with several different implementations of the same structure without affecting other software components.

3.8   FORMALIZING THE INTERFACE

We continue with the description of the IIKH development. In the next several steps the descriptions of the components will be refined. The first step in this process is to formalize the patterns and channels of communication.

A decision should be made as to the general structure that will be used to implement each component. A component with only one behavior and no internal state may be made into a function—for example, a component that simply takes a string of text and translates all capital letters to lowercase. Components with many tasks are probably more easily implemented as classes. Names are given to each of the responsibilities identified on the CRC card for each component, and these will eventually be mapped onto procedure names. Along with the names, the types of any arguments to be passed to the procedure are identified. Next, the information maintained within the component itself should be described. All information must be accounted for. If a component requires some data to perform a specific task, the source of the data, either through argument or global value, or maintained internally by the component, must be clearly identified.

3.8.1   *Coming Up with Names*

Careful thought should be given to the names associated with various activities. Shakespeare has Juliet claiming that a name change does not alter the object being described, but certainly not all names will conjure up the same mental images in the listener.[1] As government bureaucrats have long known, obscure and idiomatic names can make even the simplest operation sound intimidating. The selection of useful names is extremely important, as names create the vocabulary with which the eventual design will be formulated. Names should be internally consistent, meaningful, preferably short, and evocative in the context of the problem. Often a considerable amount of time is spent finding just the right set of terms to describe the tasks performed and the objects manipulated. Far from being a barren and useless exercise, proper naming early in the design process greatly simplifies and facilitates later steps.

The following general guidelines have been suggested [Keller 1990]:

---

[1] "What's in a name? That which we call a rose, by any other name would smell as sweet; So Romeo would, were he not Romeo call'd, retain that dear perfection which he owes without that title." *Romeo and Juliet*, Act II, Scene 2.

- Use pronounceable names. As a rule of thumb, if you cannot read a name out loud, it is not a good one.

- Use capitalization (or underscores) to mark the beginning of a new word within a name, such as "CardReader" or "Card_reader," rather than the less readable "cardreader."

- Examine abbreviations carefully. An abbreviation that is clear to one person may be confusing to the next. Is a "TermProcess" a terminal process, something that terminates processes, or a process associated with a terminal?

- Avoid names with several interpretations. Does the empty function tell whether something is empty, or empty the values from the object?

- Avoid digits within a name. They are easy to misread as letters (0 as O, 1 as l, 2 as Z, 5 as S).

- Name functions and variables that yield Boolean values so they describe clearly the interpretation of a true or false value. For example, "Printer-IsReady" clearly indicates that a true value means the printer is working, whereas "PrinterStatus" is much less precise.

- Take extra care in the selection of names for operations that are costly and infrequently used. Doing so can avoid errors caused by using the wrong function.

Once names have been developed for each activity, the CRC cards for each component are redrawn, with the name and formal arguments of the function used to elicit each behavior identified. An example of a CRC card for the Date is shown in Figure 3.6. What is not yet specified is how each component will perform the associated tasks.

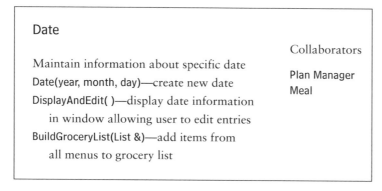

Figure 3.6 Revised CRC card for the Date component.

Once more, scenarios or role playing should be carried out at a more detailed level to ensure that all activities are accounted for and that all necessary information is maintained and made available to the responsible components.

3.9 DESIGNING THE REPRESENTATION

At this point, if not before, the design team can be divided into groups, each responsible for one or more software components. The task now is to transform the description of a component into a software system implementation. The major portion of this process is designing the data structures that will be used by each subsystem to maintain the state information required to fulfill the assigned responsibilities.

It is here that the classic data structures of computer science come into play. The selection of data structures is an important task, central to the software design process. Once they have been chosen, the code used by a component in the fulfillment of a responsibility is often almost self-evident. But data structures must be carefully matched to the task at hand. A wrong choice can result in complex and inefficient programs, while an intelligent choice can result in just the opposite.

It is also at this point that descriptions of behavior must be transformed into algorithms. These descriptions should then be matched against the expectations of each component listed as a collaborator, to ensure that expectations are fulfilled and necessary data items are available to carry out each process.

3.10 IMPLEMENTING COMPONENTS

Once the design of each software subsystem is laid out, the next step is to implement each component's desired behavior. If the previous steps were correctly addressed, each responsibility or behavior will be characterized by a short description. The task at this step is to implement the desired activities in a computer language. In a later section we will describe some of the more common heuristics used in this process.

If they were not determined earlier (say, as part of the specification of the system), then decisions can now be made on issues that are entirely self-contained within a single component. A decision we saw in our example problem was how best to let the user browse the database of recipes.

As multiperson programming projects become the norm, it becomes increasingly rare that any one programmer will work on all aspects of a system. More often, the skills a programmer will need to master are understanding how one section of code fits into a larger framework and working well with other members of a team. Often, in the implementation of one component it will become clear that certain information or actions might be assigned to yet another component that will act "behind the scene," with little or no visibility to users of the software abstraction. Such components are sometimes known as *facilitators*. We will see examples of facilitators in some of the later case studies.

An important part of analysis and coding at this point is characterizing and documenting the necessary preconditions a software component requires to complete a task, and verifying that the software component will perform correctly when presented with legal input values. This is establishing the correctness aspect of the algorithms used in the implementation of a component.

3.11 INTEGRATION OF COMPONENTS

Once software subsystems have been individually designed and tested, they can be integrated into the final product. This is often not a single step, but part of a larger process. Starting from a simple base, elements are slowly added to the system and tested, using *stubs*—simple dummy routines with no behavior or with very limited behavior—for the as yet unimplemented parts.

For example, in the development of the IIKH, it would be reasonable to start integration with the Greeter component. To test the Greeter in isolation, stubs are written for the Recipe Database manager and the daily Plan manager. These stubs need not do any more than print an informative message and return. With these, the component development team can test various aspects of the Greeter system (for example, that button presses elicit the correct response). Testing of an individual component is often referred to as *unit testing*.

Next, one or the other of the stubs can be replaced by more complete code. For example, the team might decide to replace the stub for the Recipe Database component with the actual system, maintaining the stub for the other portion. Further testing can be performed until it appears that the system is working as desired. (This is sometimes referred to as *integration testing*.)

The application is finally complete when all stubs have been replaced with working components. The ability to test components in isolation is greatly facilitated by the conscious design goal of reducing connections between components, since this reduces the need for extensive stubbing.

During integration it is not uncommon for an error to be manifested in one software system, and yet to be caused by a coding mistake in another system. Thus, testing during integration can involve the discovery of errors, which then results in changes to some of the components. Following these changes, the components should once again be tested in isolation before an attempt to reintegrate the software, once more, into the larger system. Reexecuting previously developed test cases following a change to a software component is sometimes referred to as *regression testing*.

3.12   MAINTENANCE AND EVOLUTION

It is tempting to think that once a working version of an application has been delivered, the task of the software development team is finished. Unfortunately, that is almost never true. The term *software maintenance* describes activities subsequent to the delivery of the initial working version of a software system. A wide variety of activities fall into this category.

- Errors, or *bugs*, can be discovered in the delivered product. These must be corrected, either in *patches* to existing releases or in subsequent releases.

- Requirements may change, perhaps as a result of government regulations or standardization among similar products.

- Hardware may change. For example, the system may be moved to different platforms, or input devices, such as a pen-based system or a pressure-sensitive touch screen, may become available. Output technology may change—for example, from a text-based system to a graphical window-based arrangement.

- User expectations may change. Users may expect greater functionality, lower cost, and easier use. This can occur as a result of competition with similar products.

- Better documentation may be requested by users.

A good design recognizes the inevitability of changes and plans an accommodation for them from the very beginning.

3.13   CHAPTER SUMMARY

Object-oriented programming begins with object-oriented analysis and design. Object-oriented design is characterized by an emphasis on responsibility, rather than on structure. Responsibility and behavior are attributes that can be discovered for a software system well before any other features can be identified. By systematically tracing the behavior of a system, the design of the software elements flows naturally from the general specification.

A key tool in the characterization of behavior is the idea of scenarios. Developers trace through the execution of an imaginary system, identifying actions that need to be performed, and more importantly assigning the responsibilities for these actions to individual software components. A useful tool in this activity is the CRC card, which is an index card that records the responsibilities of a software system. As design evolves, the descriptions of the actions of each component can be rewritten in more precise formats.

Developing a working software system involves many steps, frequently termed the software life cycle. Design and implementation are the first major steps. Implementation can be broken into the identification of components, development and testing of components in isolation, integration of components into larger units, and finally testing of the completed application. The life of a software system does not, however, halt with the first completed applications. Errors are uncovered, requirements change, and hardware modifications can all cause changes in the software system. The management of these changes that come after the first release is known as software maintenance.

STUDY QUESTIONS

1. What is the key idea driving object-oriented design?

2. How is the idea of responsibility tied to information hiding?

3. What are some of the characteristics of programming in the small?

4. How does programming in the large differ from programming in the small?

5. Why is information hiding an important aspect of programming in the large?

6. Why should the design of a software system begin with the characterization of behavior?

7. What is a scenario? How does a scenario help the identification of behaviors?

8. What do the three fields of a CRC card represent?

9. What are some of the advantages of using a physical index card to represent a CRC card?

10. What is the what/who cycle?

11. Why should the user manual be written before actual coding of an application is begun?

12. What are the most common sources of change in the requirements for an application over time? How can some of the difficulties inherent in change be mitigated?

13. What information is being conveyed by an interaction diagram?

14. Describe in your own words the following aspects of software components:

    (a) Behavior and state

    (b) Instances and classes

    (c) Coupling and cohesion

    (d) Interface and implementation

15. What are Parnas's principles of information hiding?

16. What are some guidelines to follow in the selection of names for components, arguments, behaviors, and so on?

17. After design, what are the later stages of the software life cycle?

18. What is software maintenance?

EXERCISES

1. Finish the development of CRC cards for the IIKH.

2. Having done Exercise 1, give a complete interaction diagram for one scenario use of the IIKH.

3. Describe the responsibilities of an organization that includes at least six types of members. Examples of such organizations are a school (students, teachers, principal, janitor), a business (secretary, president, worker), and a club (president, vice-president, member). For each member type, describe the responsibilities and the collaborators.

4. Create a scenario for the organization you described in Exercise 3 using an interaction diagram.

5. For a common game such as solitaire or twenty-one, describe a software system that will interact with the user as an opposing player. Example components include the deck and the discard pile.

6. Describe the software system to control an automated teller machine (ATM). Give interaction diagrams for various scenarios that describe the most common uses of the machine.

7. Consider a large program with which you are familiar (not necessarily object-oriented), and examine the names of variables and functions. Which names do you think are particularly apt? Why? Which names do you think might have been badly selected?

II

Understanding Paradigms

4 A Paradigm

As we noted in Chapter 1, to a medieval scholar a *paradigm* was an example sentence, one that could be used as a model or as an aid in learning a language. You are learning a new language, the programming language Java. This book will introduce Java by means of many small paradigms, or example code fragments. You as the reader should examine these programs carefully, paying close attention to those features that are new or different in comparison to earlier programs. Learning to view programs as a form of literature, that is, learning how to read programs as well as to write them, is a skill well worth an investment in time.

Our first paradigm is shown in Figure 4.1. Line numbers have been provided in comments along the right side. Like all comments, these are mainly intended to help the human reader, and are not actually part of the program. While exceedingly short and largely lacking in interesting functionality (the program prints one line of output and exits), this program nevertheless exhibits characteristics found in all Java programs, and is therefore a good place to begin our explorations. In the remainder of this chapter we will analyze the features of this program from several different perspectives.

```
import java.lang.*;                                        // 1

public class FirstProgram {                                // 2

   public static void main ( String [ ] args ) {           // 3
      System.out.println( "My first Java program!" );      // 4
   }                                                        // 5
}                                                           // 6
```

Figure 4.1 A simple Java program.

4.1 PROGRAM STRUCTURE

The first step is to understand the structure of a Java program. As noted in Chapter 1, the Java universe is a community populated by *objects*, and by little else (for more on the types of values found in the Java world, see the next section). Objects are all instances of *classes*, and thus the overall structure of a Java program is simply a series of class descriptions. In our example program there is a single class, named FirstProgram. The name of the class (given on line number 2) is important in several respects. First, it will be the handle we use to create instances of the class. Of more pragmatic concern in running your first program, it is also the name used to create the file in which the executable version of the class will be stored. On most systems this file will be named FirstProgram.class. To execute the program, this would be the file you hand to the Java interpreter.

Figure 4.2 shows the commands used to compile and execute this first program on a computer running the Unix operating system. The text of the program is stored in a file named FirstProgram.java. The command javac, the Java compiler, analyzes this program, creating the file FirstProgram.class to hold the executable version of the program. The command ls lists the contents of the directory, showing these two files. The command java, the Java bytecode interpeter, is used to execute the program. The output of the program is shown immediately after this command.

The names of the applications used to compile and execute a Java program, the steps needed to invoke these applications, and the location of the output are all features that differ greatly between platforms. We will not discuss these further here, concentrating instead on the features of the Java programming language, which will be the same on all platforms.

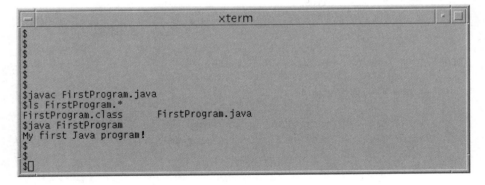

Figure 4.2 Compiling and executing a Java program.

A class consists of a class *header* and a class *body*. The header is found on line 2, and provides the name of the class. The keyword class indicates (both to the compiler, and to you as a program reader) that this is a new class description, and that the text following the class keyword should be taken to be the class name.

```
public class FirstProgram {                                        // 2
     .
     .
     .
}                                                                  // 6
```

The class body begins with the curly brace at the end of line 2 and terminates with the matching curly brace on line 6. The Java language places few restrictions on the use of spaces in programs, and the placement of elements such as curly braces relative to the rest of the line is largely a matter of personal taste—and consequently the subject of a great deal of heated debate. I personally like to place the starting brace on the same line as the unit it is grouping, with the closing brace on a line all by itself. I deviate from this only when an entire statement group can be placed on a line by itself. Others prefer to place both braces on separate lines, as in the following:

```
public class FirstProgram
{
    public static void main ( String [ ] args )
    {
        System.out.println( "My first Java program!");
    }
}
```

Find a style that seems comfortable to you personally, and use it consistently.

Within the body of a class are found a series of *members*. A member can be either a *data field*, or a *method*. The former characterize the internal data being held by an object, while the latter define the behaviors an instance of the class can perform.

In our initial program there are no data fields, and only one method. This method is named main, which *must* be the name used in describing the first method that will be invoked when execution commences.

Like a class, a method consists of two parts; a method *header* and a method *body*. All method headers have the same form, which can be described as a sequence of zero or more modifiers, a return type, a name, and a list of arguments. Thus, a prototypical method has the following form:

```
modifiers return-type method-name ( arguments ) {
    sequence-of-statements
}
```

The method header for main is given on line number 3 of the example program. It includes two modifiers, public and static. The first, as indicated earlier, will be subsequently discussed in Section 4.4, while the latter is described in Section 4.5. The return type for this method is void, which will be introduced in Section 4.3. The remaining parts are the name of the method (main) and the list of arguments to the method. The initial method for execution always takes a single argument, which is an array of string values. More will be said about Java types, such as the types shown in the argument declaration, in Section 4.3.

```
public static void main ( String [ ] args ) {                    // 3
    .
    .
    .
}                                                                // 5
```

The method body begins with the curly brace on line 3, and ends with the corresponding curly brace on line 5. Method bodies must always be properly nested within a class description.

Within a method body are a series of statements that indicate the actions to be executed when an instance of the given class is asked to perform the indicated method. In our sample program, there is one action, which is to print a single line of output. We will discuss this statement in more detail in the next section.

4.2   THE CONNECTION TO THE JAVA WORLD

A Java program is never entirely self-contained but must instead execute in the "universe" provided by the Java run-time system. We see this characteristic exhibited in two ways in our sample program. The first connection to the Java world is created by the import statement in line 1.

```
import java.lang.*;                                              // 1
```

This statement makes a portion (or *package*) of the Java library (usually referred to as the Java Application Programming Interface, or API) visible to the class description that follows it. The Java API is both powerful and exceedingly large. Because of its size, the API is arranged in packages of related classes that are only made available when the user explicitly requests them. The import statement in line 1 above requests that a package of the Java API (in this case java.lang) should be treated as part of this program.

The package java.lang has been selected because it is where the class System is defined.[1] Among the data members held by System is one named out that holds various features associated with output. Among the behaviors provided by out is

---

[1] Technically, importing java.lang is not required since it is automatically available to all Java programs. It has been included in this first program to illustrate the process of importing a package.

the method println, which takes as argument a text string, and uses the argument to print a single line of output on a standard output area (often called the *output console*).

```
System.out.println( "My first Java program!" );          // 4
```

The data member out is declared as a static variable of the class System. You have already met a static method in line 3 of FirstProgram. An important property of static variables (or class variables as they are sometimes called) is that they can be accessed from anywhere in a program by prefixing them with the name of their class, provided of course that they are public and that their class is part of the program. Line 4 shows how FirstProgram accesses the variable out by prefixing it with its class name System. Another useful class is Math. The Math class has public static methods for performing a variety of useful mathematical operations. We will encounter several other static values in later case studies.

4.3 TYPES

In addition to a variety of useful objects, the initial Java world contains the descriptions for a large collection of useful *types*, called *primitive data types*, that programmers can employ in their own code. The most basic types are integers and real (or floating-point) values. Integer variables are declared using the keyword int, as in the following assignment, which both declares a new integer variable and initializes it with a value.

```
int newVar = 42;
```

Such variables could be declared either as data members within a class or as local variables within a method. Floating-point values are declared using either the primitive data type float or the type double. Another basic type is boolean. A Boolean value is either true or false. Boolean values are produced by the relational operators (less-than, written <; less-than-or-equal, written <=; and so on) as well as the logical operators (and, written &&; or, written ||; and the like)[2]. The most common use for Boolean values is in the test portion of an if or a while statement.

The keyword void is used as a type mainly to describe methods that do not, in fact, return any value. We see this in our example program, as the return type for the method main:

---

[2] Two other operators, & and |, can be used in place of && and ||. For boolean values, they produce exactly the same result as && and || but evaluate their result in a slightly different manner. Both will evaluate their left argument before the right. If the value of the result can be determined by the left argument alone, the doubled operators will ignore, and not evaluate, their right argument. This is sometimes called *short circuit evaluation*. The single character operators also have a different meaning altogether when used with integers.

```
public static void main ( String [ ] args ) {                    // 3
```

The argument list for this method also illustrates another useful type provided by the Java language, the type String. A literal value, for example like "Fred Smith" below, has the type String.

```
String name = "Fred Smith";
```

Notice that the types int, float, double, and boolean all begin with lowercase letters, while the type String, as well as the majority of other types provided by the Java library, begin with an uppercase letter. The reason for this is that the primitive data types (int and the like) are technically not objects, while all other values are objects. That is, there is no class definition that corresponds to int, while there *is* a class description that defines the characteristics of the String data type. This is a minor distinction that in rare situations is important, and one we will return to in a later chapter.

An *array* in Java is rather different from arrays in many other languages. One difference is that the array type declaration does not specify the number of elements, or extent, of the array. We see this in our sample program in line 3:

```
public static void main ( String [ ] args ) {                    // 3
```

The parameter value for this method is named args, and is an array of string values. The square brackets in the declaration give us the clue that the value is an array; however, they do not specify the size of the array. The size will have been set when the array was created (we will see examples in later chapters). Methods provided by the class Array can be used to access information about the array. For example, consider the following program, which is only slightly more complicated than the first example:

```
import java.lang.*;

public class SecondProgram {

    public static void main ( String [ ] args ) {
        if (args.length > 0)
            System.out.println("Hello " + args[0]);
        else
            System.out.println( "Hello  everybody!");
    }
}
```

Here, the data member length is being used to determine the number of values held by the array named args. If the user entered a command line argument, such as the string "Fred", the output would be "hello Fred".[3]

If the size of the array args is larger than zero (that is, if there are array elements) then the subscript operator is used to access the first element. The set of legal index values for an array in Java begins with zero, and extends to the value one smaller than the number of elements in the array.

Finally, this example shows the use of the + operator with a string value. When at least one argument to the "addition" operator is a String, the other argument is automatically converted into a string, and the operation of string catenation is performed. The result will be a new string value in which the left argument is immediately followed by the right argument. This feature is often used to format output. For example, suppose x is an integer variable; we could display the value of x by means of the following statement:

```
System.out.println("The value of x is " + x);
```

There are other interesting features of both strings and the array data type in Java that we will discuss in subsequent chapters.

4.4 Access Modifiers

The modifier public appears twice in our example program, first in line 2 and then again in line 3.

```
public class FirstProgram {                          // 2
    public static void main ( String [ ] args ) {    // 3
```

This modifier is one of a trio that are used to control the *accessibility* of names. The other possibilities are protected and private. By controlling access we mean that these modifiers control which objects in a program can make use of a name, and in which portions of a program that name can appear.

Recall once again our intuitive description of an object-oriented program as a community populated by many agents, or objects, that interact with one another in order to achieve some desired objective. Each object has a role to play, and that role is defined by the data values it holds and the services it can provide to the other objects in the universe.

Those features that are public are the aspects of an object that another object can see; the outward appearance of the object. Any feature that another object might want to use should be declared as public.

---

[3] Exactly how command-line arguments are entered differs depending upon which platform you are executing your Java programs. Consult a reference manual for further information.

```
class BankAccount {

  private int accountBalance = 0;

  public void deposit (int amount) {
      accountBalance = accountBalance + amount;
  }

  public void withdrawal (int amount) {
      accountBalance = accountBalance - amount;
  }
}
```

Figure 4.3   A data member being hidden using the keyword private.

The use of the public modifier in front of the class keyword in our first program indicates that the entire class description is public; it is visible to the program loader that gets an application ready for execution.

```
public class FirstProgram {                                              // 2
```

Similarly, the keyword used in front of the method named main indicates that the method is visible outside of the class. This means that the program loader not only can see the class FirstProgram, but also can see the method inside of the class. This is important; otherwise the program loader would not be able to execute the method.

```
public static void main ( String [ ] args ) {                           // 3
```

Frequently a programmer desires that features of a class, or entire classes themselves, be "hidden" from other classes. This means that other objects in the program universe cannot "see" these features, and since they cannot be seen, they cannot be manipulated.

Data members are most commonly hidden. An object might want to hold a data value and not let the value be seen by other objects. It can do this by using the keyword private. For example, the class description shown in Figure 4.3 is a simple model of a bank account. The bank account object holds an "internal" piece of information, which represents the account balance. Because the variable holding this value is declared private, other objects in the program universe are not allowed to directly examine or modify the account balance. There are, however, two methods that are declared public. These allow deposits or withdrawals to be made from the bank account object. Thus, other objects in the simulation can indirectly modify the value of the balance (by performing a deposit or a withdrawal) even though they cannot directly set the account balance.

Private features (both data members and methods) can only be accessed within the bounds of a class description. A third possibility, termed protected, comes into play when inheritance is used as a technique to create new types of objects out of an existing, older class description. A protected member is one that is still inaccessible to other objects but that *is* accessible within the bounds of any subclass (or derived class). We will see examples of this in subsequent chapters.

4.5   LIFETIME MODIFIERS

Another important keyword in our first program is the term static, which appears preceding the method main. Like the accessibility keywords, the keyword static can be applied both to data fields and to methods.

```
public static void main ( String [ ] args ) {                    // 3
```

There are two ways to envision the effect that static has on the member it modifies. One way is to imagine that static members are shared by all instances of a class. That is, no matter how many similar objects are created, only one manifestation of a static member will be created. This one member will be shared by all the instances of the class.

Because a static member is shared by all instances, it is not *part* of any one instance. In this sense, it can be imagined to be outside of all instances. (Although accessibility modifiers can still be applied, a private but static data member is outside of all objects but can only be accessed from inside the class definition.) Since a static data member is outside of the object definitions, it also exists no matter how many instances of a class have been created. In particular, a static member exists even if *no instances of a class have yet been created*!

It is for this reason that the main method in any program must be declared to be static. The main method must exist, even before any instances of the class have been created. The program loader selects this static method (which must also be public) and runs it. If it were not declared static, it would be necessary to first create an instance of the class before executing the method.

Also, as described in Section 4.2, static (or class) members that are public have another very useful purpose; they can be accessed from anywhere within the program by prefixing them with their class name, as for example System.out.

4.6   CHAPTER SUMMARY

The first *paradigm*, or example program, we have examined will print a single line of output and halt. Although trivial in purpose, the structure of this program is similar to every Java program we will subsequently encounter. Thus, a good appreciation of this simple example is a necessary prerequisite to understanding the remainder of this book:

```
import java.lang.*;

public class FirstProgram {

    public static void main (String [ ] args ) {
        System.out.println ( "My first Java program!" );
    }
}
```

- The import statement connects *this* Java program to the initial Java universe; it indicates which portions of the Java run-time system will be used by this program.

- A Java program is a sequence of class descriptions.

- Each class description consists of a class heading and a class body.

- The class heading consists of modifiers, the keyword class, and a class name.

- A class body is a sequence of members.

- A member is either a data member or a method.

- A method consists of a method heading and a method body.

- A method heading consists of modifiers, the method name, and the argument list.

- A method body is a sequence of statements.

- The modifier public indicates attributes (entire classes, or members within a class) that can be accessed and used by other objects.

- The modifier static indicates attributes (data members of methods) that are shared by all instances of a class. Such members exist even when no instances of the class have yet been created.

- The method main must be declared as both public and static, since it must be visible to the program loader and must exist even before instances of the class have been created.

CROSS REFERENCES

Other, more extensive paradigms will be introduced in the remaining chapters in this part of the book. The keyword protected, discussed briefly in Section 4.4, becomes important when *inheritance* is used to create new classes. Inheritance will be investigated more fully beginning in Chapter 8. The class String and related facilities will be explored in Chapter 17.

STUDY QUESTIONS

1. What is the original meaning of the word *paradigm*?

2. What is the overall structure of a Java program?

3. What are the two major parts of a class description?

4. How is the body of a class delineated?

5. What are the two types of members that can be found within a class body?

6. What is the connection between a class name and the file it is stored in?

7. What is a method?

8. What are the parts of a method header?

9. What operation is performed by System.out.println?

10. What is the purpose of an import statement?

11. What is the type void mainly used for?

12. What does the difference in case in the initial letter of the types int and String indicate?

13. How in Java does one determine the number of elements held by an array?

14. What is the meaning of the + operator when one of the arguments is a String?

15. What are the three access modifier keywords? What does each of them signify?

16. When applied to a data member, what does the modifier static signify?

EXERCISES

1. Add a member method named display to the class description shown in Figure 4.3. When invoked, this method should print the current account balance.

2. The looping statement in Java uses the for keyword, and consists of three parts. The first part is an initialization statement, which can also be used to declare the loop variable. The second part is a test for termination; the loop will execute as long as the expression returns true. The final part is

the increment, which is a statement that is evaluated to update the loop variable.

Consider the following main program. Describe the effect produced by the program when it is executed with three command-line arguments.

```
public static void main ( String [ ] args ) {
   for (int i = 0; i < args.length; i = i + 1)
      System.out.println(args[i]);
}
```

3. Now consider the following, slightly more complex program:

```
public static void main ( String [ ] args ) {
   for (int i = 0; i < args.length; i = i + 1)
      for (int j = 0; j <= i; j = j + 1)
         System.out.println(args[i]);
}
```

Describe the pattern of the output when the program is executed with three command-line arguments.

4. Consider the following main program:

```
public static void main ( String [ ] args ) {
   String result = "";
   for (int i = args.length - 1; i >= 0; i = i - 1)
      result = result + " " + args[i];
   System.out.println(result);
}
```

What does this method do? What will be the result printed given the arguments Sam saw Sarah said Sally ?

5. Another useful method provided by the class String is the substring operation. This takes an integer argument, and returns the portion of the string that remains following the given index position. For example, if word is a variable containing the string "unhappy", then word.substring(2) is the string "happy".

This operation is used in the following program. What will the output be given the command-line argument Sally?

```
static public void main ( String [ ] args ) {
   String name = args[0];
   String shortName = name.substring(1);
   System.out.println(name + "," + name + ", bo-B" + shortName);
   System.out.println("Banana-fana Fo-F" + shortName);
```

```
    System.out.println("Fee, Fie, mo-M" + shortName);
    System.out.println(name + "!");
}
```

6. By placing the code shown in the previous question inside a loop, write a program that will take any number of command-line arguments, and write one verse of the name game for each.

5 ■ Ball Worlds

In the intuitive description of object-oriented programming presented in Chapter 1, an object-oriented program was described as a universe of interacting agents. However, in our first example Java program, in Chapter 4, we did not actually create any new objects, but only used the static method named main in the program class.

Our second program is slightly more complex in structure, although hardly more complicated in functionality. It places a graphical window on the user's screen, draws a ball that bounces around the window for a few moments, and then halts. A screen shot of this application in execution is shown as Figure 5.1.

Our second example program, or paradigm, is constructed out of two classes. The first of these appears in Figure 5.2. Again, we have added line numbers for the purposes of reference; however, these are not part of the actual program.[1] The reader should compare this program to the example program described in the previous chapter, noting both the similarities and differences. Like the previous program, this program imports (on lines 1 and 2) information from the Java library. Like the earlier program, execution will begin in the method named main (lines 4–10), which is declared as static, void, and public. Like all main programs, this method must take as argument an array of string values, which are, in this case, being ignored. The main procedure creates the window for the application, instructs this window to display itself (the method show), then moves the ball 1000 times (the loop surrounding the invocation of the method run) before halting the application.

---

[1] In order to draw more attention to the Java code itself, the programs presented in this text have purposely been written using very few comments. In practice, comments would usually be used to describe each method in a class.

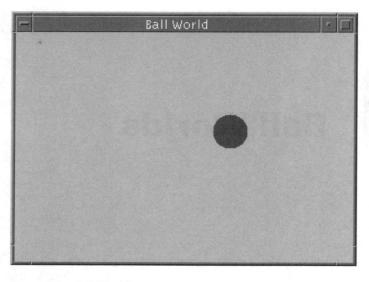

Figure 5.1   Ball World screen.

This program also incorporates a number of new features. These are summarized by the following list, and will be the subject of more detailed discussion in subsequent sections.

- The class defines a number of private internal variable data fields, some of which are constant, some of which are initialized but not constant. These data fields will be described in detail in Section 5.1.

- The main( ) method creates an instance of the class BallWorld. This object is initialized by means of a constructor. A *constructor* automatically ties together the actions of object *creation* and object *initialization*. Constructors will be introduced in Section 5.2.

- The class is declared as an *extension* of an existing Java class named JFrame. This technique is called *inheritance*, and is the principal means in object-oriented languages for constructing new software abstractions that are variations on existing data types. Inheritance will be introduced in Section 5.3 and will be more extensively studied beginning in Chapter 8.

- The output displayed in a window by this program is created using some of the graphics primitives provided by the Java run-time library. These graphics operators are explained in Section 5.4.

```
import java.awt.*;                                                  // 1
import javax.swing.JFrame;                                          // 2

public class BallWorld extends JFrame {                             // 3
    public static void main (String [ ] args) {                     // 4
        BallWorld world = new BallWorld (Color.red);                // 5
        world.show();        inherited from JFrame.                 // 6
        for (int i = 0; i < 1000; i++)                              // 7
            world.run();                                            // 8
        System.exit(0); // halt program                            // 9
    }                                                               // 10

    public static final int FrameWidth = 600;                       // 11
    public static final int FrameHeight = 400;                      // 12
    private Ball aBall = new Ball (new Point(50, 50), 20);           // 13

    private BallWorld (Color ballColor) {                           // 14
            // general application initialization                   // 15
        setSize (FrameWidth, FrameHeight);                          // 16
        setTitle("Ball World");                                     // 17
            // application specific initialization                  // 18
        aBall.setColor (ballColor);                                 // 19
        aBall.setMotion (3.0, 6.0);                                 // 20
    }                                                               // 21

    public void paint (Graphics g)                                  // 22
        { super.paint(g); aBall.paint(g); }                         // 23

    public void run () {                                            // 24
        aBall.move();                                               // 25
        Point pos = aBall.location();                               // 26
        if ((pos.x < aBall.radius()) ||                             // 27
            (pos.x > FrameWidth - aBall.radius()))                  // 28
                aBall.reflectHorz();                                // 29
        if ((pos.y < aBall.radius()) ||                             // 30
            (pos.y > FrameHeight - aBall.radius()))                 // 31
                aBall.reflectVert();                                // 32
        repaint();                                                  // 33
        try {                                                       // 34
            Thread.sleep(50);                                       // 35
        } catch (InterruptedException e) { System.exit(0); }        // 36
    }                                                               // 37
}                                                                   // 38
```

Figure 5.2   Class description for Ball World.

5.1 DATA FIELDS

We have seen in the previous chapter (Section 4.4) how data fields can be declared within a class and how they can be initialized. The example program here includes features we have not seen in our previous programs in the three data fields declared on lines 11–13:

```
public static final int FrameWidth = 600;                    // 11
public static final int FrameHeight = 400;                   // 12
private Ball aBall = new Ball (new Point(50, 50), 20);        // 13
```

Recall that the keyword public means that the variables being declared can be accessed (that is, used directly) anywhere in a Java program, while those that are declared as private can be used only within the bounds of the class description in which the declaration appears. Recall also that the keyword static means that there is one instance of the data field, shared by all instances of the class. The modifier keyword final means that this is the last time when an object is changed. It is here applied to a variable declaration; we will in later chapters, see how the modifier can also be applied to a method definition.

Data fields that are declared static and final behave as constants, because they exist in only one place and cannot change value. The identifier of such a data field is sometimes called a symbolic name. Because they cannot be modified, there is less reason to encapsulate a static final variable by declaring it private. Such values are often made public, as shown here. The particular symbolic values being defined in this program represent the height and width of the window in which the application will eventually produce its output. Symbolic constants are useful in programs for a number of different reasons:

- By being defined in only one place, they make it easy to change subsequently, should circumstances require. For example, changing the height and or width of the window merely requires editing the file to change the values being used to initialize these symbolic constants, rather than hunting down all locations in the code where the quantities are used.

- When subsequently used elsewhere in the program, the symbolic name helps document the purpose of the constant values.

The third data field is declared as an instance of class Ball, which is the second class used in the creation of our example program. A Ball is an abstraction that represents a bouncing ball. It is represented by a colored circular disk that can move around the display surface. The class Ball will be described in Section 5.5.

5.2 CONSTRUCTORS

As noted at the beginning of the chapter, one of the major topics of this chapter is the creation of new objects. This occurs in two places in the program shown in Figure 5.2. The first is in the main program, which creates an instance of the class BallWorld.

```
BallWorld world = new BallWorld (Color.red);                    // 5
```

The new operator is always used to create a new object. In this case, it is being used to create an instance of BallWorld, which (the next section shows) is the name given to the window in which the program will display its output. The new operator is followed by a class name, indicating the type of object being created. A parenthesized list then gives any arguments needed in the *initialization* of the object.

Object *creation* and object *initialization* are intimately tied in concept, and it is important that a programming language also bring these concepts together. Without support from the programming language, two types of errors can easily occur:

- An object is created, but it is used before it is initialized.

- An object is created and is initialized several times before it is used.

The language Java uses a concept called a *constructor* to guarantee that objects are placed into a proper initial state the moment they are created. A constructor bears a strong resemblance to a method; however, the name of the constructor matches the name of the class in which it appears, the constructor does not specify a return type, and the user will never (indeed, can never) execute the constructor except as part of creating a new object. Like a method a constructor can have arguments, and the body of the constructor consists of a sequence of statements. In our example program the body of the constructor is found on lines 14–21:

```
private BallWorld (Color ballColor) {                           // 14
    // general application initialization                        // 15
    setSize (FrameWidth, FrameHeight);                           // 16
    setTitle("Ball World");                                      // 17
    // application specific initialization                       // 18
    aBall.setColor (ballColor);                                  // 19
    aBall.setMotion (3.0, 6.0);                                  // 20
}                                                                // 21
```

When an object is created (via the new operator), the first method invoked using the newly created object is the constructor method. The arguments passed to the constructor are the arguments supplied in the new expression.

In this particular case, the argument represents a color. The class Color is part of the Java run-time library. The value red is simply a constant (a value declared both as static and final) in the class description of Color.

```
BallWorld world = new BallWorld (Color.red);                    // 5
```

The corresponding parameter value in the constructor method is named ball-Color (see line 14). The constructor method must ensure that the instance of the class BallWorld is properly initialized. As noted earlier, the BallWorld represents the window in which the output will be displayed. The first two statements in the constructor set some of the attributes for this window; namely, the size and the title.

The declaration of aBall also uses two occurrences of the new operator to create and initialize a new ball. One is creating an instance of the class Point, which is a Java library abstraction for representing a two-dimensional coordinate. The arguments to the constructor will set the x and y values of the point. The second new operation will create an instance of the class Ball. Not only will memory for this object be created by the new statement, but also the arguments will be matched by a corresponding constructor in the class Ball, which will then be invoked to initialize the newly created ball:

```
public class Ball { // a generic round colored object that moves

    public Ball (Point loc, int r) { // ball center and radius
        :
        :
    }
}
```

The complete class description for Ball is shown in Figure 5.3. Not all aspects of a Ball are set by the constructor. The final two statements in the constructor for BallWorld set the color of the ball, and set the direction of motion for the ball. These attributes will be discussed in more detail in Section 5.5.

5.2.1 Constructing the Application

It is perhaps helpful at this point to say a word about the role and positioning of the main method. As you learned in Chapter 4, this method is invoked when execution of the program begins. This is possible because it is declared as static and therefore exists before any objects of its class exist. Consequently, an object of class BallWorld need not already exist in order to invoke the main() method.

Because it exists, in a sense, outside of all objects of the class, the main procedure can be used to create an instance of the class. This accounts for what might seem the strange phenomenon of main being a method in the BallWorld class, but at the same time being used to create a BallWorld object.

```
import java.awt.*;

public class Ball {

    public Ball (Point lc, int r) { loc = lc; rad = r; }

    protected Point loc; // position in window
    protected int rad; // radius
    protected double changeInX = 0.0; // motion in the X direction
    protected double changeInY = 0.0; // motion in the Y direction
    protected Color color = Color.blue; // color of ball

    public void setColor (Color newColor) { color = newColor; }

    public void setMotion (double dx, double dy)
        { changeInX = dx; changeInY = dy; }

    public int radius () { return rad; }

    public Point location () { return loc; }
        // reverse the motion in the vertical direction
    public void reflectVert () { changeInX = - changeInX; } // should be
                                                            // changeInY
        // reverse the motion in the horizontal direction
    public void reflectHorz () { changeInY = - changeInY; } // should be changeInX

    public void moveTo (int x, int y) { loc.move(x, y); }

    public void move ()
        { loc.translate((int) changeInX, (int) changeInY); }

    public void paint (Graphics g) {
        g.setColor (color);
        g.fillOval (loc.x-rad, loc.y-rad, 2*rad, 2*rad);
    }
}
```

Figure 5.3 Implementation of the class Ball.

Some developers believe that it is less confusing to place the main method for a program into a class of its own, and to use this additional class merely to create an instance of the application class (in this case BallWorld), and then send it an appropriate message to begin the application. The code for such a class might look as follows:

```
public class BallWorldProgram {

    public static void main(String [ ] args) {
        BallWorld world = new BallWorld(Color.red);
        world.show( );
        for (int i = 0; i < 1000; i++)
            world.run( );
        System.exit(0);
    }
}
```

A disadvantage of this approach is that it creates two classes which, on many platforms, must reside in two separate files. Since this is in many ways just as cumbersome as the approach we have taken, and in most cases results in a longer program, we have adopted the style of incorporating the main method into the application class itself.

5.3   INHERITANCE

The most important feature of this program is the use of *inheritance* (sometimes also called *extension*). As noted earlier, the ball world is a rectangular window in which the action of the program (the bouncing ball) is displayed. The code needed to display and manipulate a window in a modern graphical user interface is exceedingly complex, in part because of the fact that the user can indicate actions such as moving, resizing, or iconifying the window. As a consequence, recent languages attempt to provide a means of reusing existing code so that the programmer need only be concerned with those features of the application that distinguish the program from other window applications.

The programming language Java uses the class JFrame to represent a generic window.[2] By saying that the class BallWorld extends the class JFrame, we indicate that our new class, BallWorld, is a type of frame, but a more specialized type with a single purpose. The class JFrame defines code to perform actions such as resizing the window, arranging for the window to be displayed on the workstation screen, and so on. By extending the class JFrame, our new class *inherits* this functionality, which means the abilities are made available to the new class, and do not need to be rewritten anew.

```
public class BallWorld extends JFrame {                            // 3
```

By executing the example program, the reader can verify that the window exhibits the functionality we expect of graphical windows—the ability to move,

---

[2] Users without access to the newer swing library will use the base class Frame instead of JFrame. Other minor differences between the program that uses the original AWT library and the swing version will be described in Appendix C.

resize, and iconify, even though the program does not explicitly define any code to support these behaviors. (The reader might also note some expected behaviors that are not provided. For example, the handling of menu items and the close or quit box. In subsequent chapters we will describe how these features can be provided.)

We can observe the use of inheritance in the variety of methods that are invoked in our example program, but are not defined by the class BallWorld. These methods are instead inherited from the *parent class* JFrame, or from the classes that JFrame in turn inherits from. Two examples are the methods setSize and setTitle invoked in the BallWorld constructor. These methods set the dimensions (in pixels) and title value for the window, respectively.

```
private BallWorld (Color ballColor) {              // 14
        // general application initialization        // 15
    setSize (FrameWidth, FrameHeight);              // 16
    setTitle("Ball World");                         // 17
        .
        .
        .
}                                                   // 21
```

Another example is the method show, which is invoked in the static method main after the instance of BallWorld has been created. The show method arranges for the window to appear on the display, and then for the surface of the window to be drawn.

```
public static void main (String [ ] args) {        // 4
    BallWorld world = new BallWorld (Color.red);    // 5
    world.show( );                                  // 6
    for (int i = 0; i < 1000; i++)                  // 7
        world.run( );                               // 8
    System.exit(0); // halt program                 // 9
}                                                   // 10
```

After displaying the window, the program will execute the method run one thousand times before halting execution. A graphical application will not halt simply because the end of the main method is encounterd, but must explicitly call the system method System.exit to terminate execution. The ++ operator is used to increment an integer variable. The statement

```
i++
```

is equivalent to

```
i = i + 1
```

We will describe the effect of the run method in the next section.

5.4   THE JAVA GRAPHICS MODEL

Graphics in Java is provided as part of the Abstract Windowing Toolkit (AWT). The Java AWT is an example of a software *framework*. The idea of a framework is to provide the structure of a program but no application-specific details. The overall control, the flow of execution, is provided by the framework and therefore does not need to be rewritten for each new program. Thus, the programmer does not "see" the majority of the program code.

This is illustrated by the actions that occur subsequent to the program issuing the show method that is inherited from the class JFrame. The window in which the action will take place is created, and the image of the window must be rendered (drawn on the screen). To do so, the show method invokes a method named paint, passing as argument a *graphics object*.

The programmer defines the appearance of the window by providing an implementation of the method paint. The graphics object passed as argument provides the ability to draw a host of items, such as lines and polygons as well as text. In our example program the paint method simply instructs the ball to paint itself. Before doing this, the method invokes the paint method in the parent class JFrame. The method in the parent class erases any previous contents of the window, so that we only concern ourselves with drawing the new image. The variable super is used to distinguish the parent method from the child method, as both have the same name, paint. (As an experiment, you can try removing the call to super, and notice that our ball movement then becomes a continuous blur).

```
public void paint (Graphics g)                              // 22
   { super.paint(g); aBall.paint(g); }                      // 23
```

In later examples we will investigate more of the abilities of the graphics objects provided by the Java library. (Including how to avoid the annoying flicker that may on some platforms be observed as the animation progresses.)

The loop in the run method instructs the ball to move slightly, checks to see if the ball has struck the edge of the playing surface, reflects the ball if necessary, and finally requests that the window be repainted. Note that the method to do this is called repaint; an application does not call the paint method directly, but only indirectly by requesting a repainting.

```
public void run () {                                        // 24
   aBall.move();                                            // 25
   Point pos = aBall.location();                            // 26
   if ((pos.x < aBall.radius()) ||                          // 27
       (pos.x > FrameWidth - aBall.radius()))               // 28
         aBall.reflectHorz();                               // 29
   if ((pos.y < aBall.radius()) ||                          // 30
       (pos.y > FrameHeight - aBall.radius()))              // 31
         aBall.reflectVert();                               // 32
```

```
        repaint();                                                // 33
        try {                                                     // 34
            Thread.sleep(50);                                     // 35
        } catch (InterruptedException e) { System.exit(0); }      // 36
    }                                                             // 37
```

Graphical operations, such as repainting the window, are relatively slow in comparison to Java execution. Therefore it is necessary to halt the program for a short period of time so that the graphics system can catch up. This is accomplished by using the command Thread.sleep(). The command sleep will suspend the program for a small period of time, measured in milliseconds. While suspended, the window will be repainted. Because this method can raise an exception, it must be surrounded by a try block that will catch the exception and deal with it. In this case, an exception might indicate the program was interrupted while sleeping. To handle this we will terminate the program.

5.5   THE CLASS Ball

We will use a ball, that is, a round colored object that moves, in a number of our subsequent example programs. It is therefore useful to define the behavior of a Ball in a general fashion so that it can be used in a variety of ways. The description of class Ball is placed in its own file (Ball.java) and is linked together with the BallWorld class to create the executable program.

A Ball (Figure 5.3) maintains five data fields. The location of the ball is represented by a Point, a general purpose class provided in the Java run-time library. The radius of the ball is an integer amount. Two floating point values are used to represent the horizontal and vertical components of the motion for the ball. Finally, the color of the ball is represented by an instance of class Color, a Java library class we have previously encountered.

These five data fields are declared as protected. This allows classes within the same package, as well as any subsequent child classes we might create to have access to the data fields, without exposing the data to modification by other objects. It is good practice to declare data fields protected, rather than private, even if you do not anticipate extending the class to make new classes.

The constructor for the class Ball records the location by creating a new instance of class Point. The constructor also provides default values for color (blue) and motion. As we have seen in our example program, these can be redefined by invoking the method setColor and setMotion.

A number of methods are used to access some of the attributes of a ball. Attributes that can be obtained in this fashion include the radius, and the position of the ball. Methods that allow access to a data field in a class are termed *accessor methods*. The use of accessor methods is strongly encouraged in preference to making the data fields themselves public, as an accessor method permits the value to be *read* but not modified. This ensures that any modification to a data field will be mediated by the proper method, such as through the methods setMotion or moveTo.

The methods reflectVert and reflectHorz reflect the motion of a ball in a vertical or a horizontal direction, respectively. We have seen already how these are used to alter the direction of the ball.

The method move makes use of an operation provided by the class Point. A point can have its position changed (translated) by giving an amount the point should move in the two-dimensional surface.

Finally, the method paint uses two operations that are provided by the class Graphics in the Java library. These are the methods to set the current color for rendering graphics (setColor) and to display a painted oval at a given location on the window (fillOval).

5.6   MULTIPLE OBJECTS OF THE SAME CLASS

Every instance of a class maintains its own internal data fields. We can illustrate this by making variations on our sample program. The simplest change is to modify the main routine to create two independent windows. Each window will have a different ball, each window can be independently moved or resized.

```
public static void main (String [ ] args) {
       // create first window with red ball
    BallWorld world = new BallWorld (Color.red);
    world.show( );
       // now create a second window with yellow ball
    BallWorld world2 = new BallWorld (Color.yellow);
    world2.show( );
       // now put them both in motion
    for (int i = 0; i < 1000; i++) {
       world.run();
       world2.run();
    }
    System.exit(0);
}
```

The reader should try making this change, and observe the result. (On some platforms the two windows will be placed one on top of the other, and so it will be necessary to move the topmost window in order to see the second window underneath). Note how one window is bouncing a red ball and the second is bouncing a yellow ball. This indicates that each instance of class BallWorld must be maintaining its own Ball value, given that a ball cannot be both red and yellow at the same time.

```
public class MultiBallWorld extends JFrame {
   .
   .
   .
   private static final int BallCollectionSize = 10;
   private Ball [ ] balls = new Ball [ BallCollectionSize ];

   private MultiBallWorld (Color ballColor) {
         // general application initialization
      setSize (FrameWidth, FrameHeight);
      setTitle("Ball World");
         // application specific initialization
      for (int i = 0; i < BallCollectionSize; i++) {
         balls[i] = new Ball(new Point(10, 15), 5);
         balls[i].setColor(ballColor);
         balls[i].setMotion(3.0+i, 6.0-i);
      }
   }

   public void paint (Graphics g) {
      super.paint(g);
      for (int i = 0; i < BallCollectionSize; i++)
         balls[i].paint(g);
   }

   public void run () {
      for (int i = 0; i < BallCollectionSize; i++) {
         balls[i].move();
         Point pos = balls[i].location();
         if ((pos.x < balls[i].radius()) ||
            (pos.x > FrameWidth - balls[i].radius()))
               balls[i].reflectHorz();
         if ((pos.y < balls[i].radius()) ||
            (pos.y > FrameHeight - balls[i].radius()))
               balls[i].reflectVert();
      }
      repaint();
      try {
         Thread.sleep(5);
      } catch (InterruptedException e) { System.exit(0); }
   }
}
```

Figure 5.4   Class description for Multiple Ball World.

A second variation illustrates even more dramatically the independence of different objects, even when they derive from the same class. The class MultiBallWorld (Figure 5.4) is similar to our initial program except that it creates a collection of balls rather than just a single ball. Only the lines that have changed are included, and those that are elided are the same as the earlier program. The new program declares an array of Balls, rather than just a single ball. Note the syntax used to declare an array. As noted in the previous chapter, arrays in Java are different from arrays in most other languages. Even though the array is declared, space is still not set aside for the array elements. Instead, the array itself must be created (again with a new command):

```
private Ball [] balls = new Ball [ BallCollectionSize ];
```

Note how the size of the array is specified by a symbolic constant, defined earlier in the program. Even then, however, the array elements cannot be accessed. Instead, each array element must be individually created, once more using a new operation:

```
for (int i = 0; i < BallCollectionSize; i++) {
   balls[i] = new Ball(new Point(10, 15), 5);
   balls[i].setColor(ballColor);
   balls[i].setMotion(3.0+i, 6.0-i);
}
```

Each ball is created, then initialized with the given color, and set in motion. We have used the loop index variable i to change the direction of motion slightly, so that each ball will initially move in a different direction.

When the program is executed, ten different balls will be created. Each ball will maintain its own location and direction. Each ball will move, independently of all other balls. To paint the window each of the ten balls is asked to paint itself.

5.7   CHAPTER SUMMARY

The two major themes introduced in this chapter have been the creation and initialization of new objects using a combination of the operator new and a constructor, and the definition of new classes using *inheritance* to extend an existing class. Topics discussed in this chapter include the following:

- Data fields that are declared final cannot be subsequently redefined. A static and final value is the technique normally used to create a symbolic constant.

- New objects are always created using the operator new.

- When a new object is created, the *constructor* for the class of the object is automatically invoked as part of the creation process. The constructor should guarantee the object is properly initialized.

- A constructor is a method that has the same name as the class in which it is defined.

- Any arguments used by the constructor must appear in the new statement that creates the corresponding object.

- Classes can be defined using *inheritance*. Such classes extend the functionality of an existing class. Any public or protected data fields or methods defined in the parent class become part of the new class.

- The class JFrame can be used to create simple Java windows. This class can be extended to define application-specific windows.

- The *framework* provided by the Java AWT displays a frame (a window) when the frame object is given the message show.

- To create the image shown in the window the programmer executes the inherited message repaint. The framework eventually responds by issuing the message paint. The programmer can redefine the paint method to produce application-specific pictures.

- The paint method is given as argument an instance of the library class Graphics. This object can be used to create a variety of graphical images.

- The class Point (used in our class Ball) is a library class that represents a two-dimensional point on the window surface. The class provides a large amount of useful functionality.

- Multiple instances of the same class each maintain their own separate data fields. This was illustrated by creating multiple independent Ball objects, which move independently of each other.

CROSS REFERENCES

We will use the Ball class in case studies in Chapters 6–8 and 20. The topic of inheritance is simple to explain but has many subtle points that can easily trap the unwary. We will examine inheritance in detail in Chapters 8 through 11. The AWT and Swing will be examined in more detail in Chapter 13.

STUDY QUESTIONS

1. How would you change the color of the ball in our example application to yellow?

2. How would you change the size of the application window to 500 by 300 pixels?

3. What does the modifier keyword final mean when applied in a data field declaration?

4. Why do symbolic constants make it easier to read and maintain programs?

5. What two actions are tied together by the concept of a constructor?

6. What types of error does the use of constructors prevent?

7. What does it mean to say that a new class inherits from an existing class?

8. What methods inherited from class JFrame are used in our example application?

9. What methods provided by our example program are invoked by the code inherited from class JFrame?

10. What abstraction does the Java library class Point represent?

11. What are some reasons that data fields should be declared as private or protected, and access provided only through public methods?

EXERCISES

1. The method Math.random returns a random floating-point value between 0 and 1.0. This value can be multiplied by a constant to yield a value from a larger range. If needed, assigning the result to an integer yields a random integer value. For example, the following will generate a random integer between 0 and 10:

```
int i = (int) (10 * Math.random());
```

Using this method, modify the example program shown in Figure 5.2 so that the ball will initially move in a random direction.

2. Modify the MultiBallWorld class so that the colors of the various balls created are selected randomly from the values red, blue and yellow. (*Hint*: Call Math.random() and test the resulting value for various ranges, selecting red if the value is in one range, blue if it is in another, and so on.)

3. Modify the MultiBallWorld so that it will produce balls of different radiuses, as well as different colors.

4. Rather than testing whether or not a ball has hit the wall in our main program, we could have used inheritance to provide a specialized form of Ball. Create a class BoundedBall that inherits from class Ball. The constructor for this class should provide the height and width of the window, which

should subsequently be maintained as data fields in the class. Rewrite the move method so that if the ball moves outside the bounds, it automatically reflects its direction. Finally, rewrite the BallWorld class to use an instance of BoundedBall, rather than an ordinary Ball, and eliminate the bounds test in the main program.

5. Our Ball abstraction is not as simple as it could have been. Separate the Ball class into two separate classes. The first, the new class Ball, knows only a location, its size, and how to paint itself. The second class, MovableBall, extends the class Ball and adds all behavior related to motion, such as the data fields changeInX and changeInY, the methods setMotion, reflectVert, reflectHorz and move, and so on. Rewrite the MultiBallWorld to use instances of class MovableBall.

6. Modify the run method in the multi-ball world so that after it has advanced a ball a small distance it will check to see if it has run into any other balls. (You can do this by seeing if its center is less than 2 radius distance from the center of any other ball). If so, alter (reflect) the directions of both balls.

6 A Cannon Game

In this chapter we will examine an implementation of a classic "shooting cannon" game. In this simple game there is a cannon on the left portion of the user's window, and a target on the right portion, as shown in Figure 6.1. The user can control the angle of elevation for the cannon and fire a cannonball. The objective of the game is, of course, to hit the target.

As with all the case studies, our objective is not so much the cannon application itself, which is only moderately interesting, but the use of a simple program to illustrate a number of different features of the Java language. In particular, in this chapter we will examine the features of the Java library that simplify the creation of a graphical user interface (GUI). We will develop two variations on this game:

- The first version is the simplest. The user enters the angle of the cannon from the command argument line, the cannon fires once, and the program halts.

Figure 6.1 A window of the Cannon Game.

- In the second version, we improve user interaction, by providing both a scroll bar with which the angle of the cannon can be changed, and a button to fire the cannon. By manipulating these, multiple attempts to hit the target can be made during one execution of the program.

6.1 THE SIMPLE CANNON GAME

The principal class for our cannon application is shown in Figure 6.2. The main method is similar to those described in the previous chapters. The universe for our application is termed CannonGame. An instance of this class is created, then passed the message show. The message show causes the window in which the application is played to be displayed. The method run then repeatedly moves the ball and redraws the window.

In our first version of the Cannon Game, the angle for the cannon is read from the command-line argument. The first string in the command-line argument list is assumed to be an integer value, representing the angle (in degrees) for the cannon to be set prior to launch of the cannonball. This value is converted by a method from the Java library class Integer, and passed as argument to the constructor for the cannon game. There, the method intValue() is used to convert an Integer into an int. We will return to a discussion of the relationship between these two data types in Section 6.1.4.

The cannon game is declared to be a type of JFrame, which you will recall from the preceding chapter is how Java declares a new type of window. The class description defines two public constant values (declared as static final, see Section 5.1) that describe the height and width of the window that represents the cannon application. In addition, several new data fields are declared. These are the cannon ball (an instance of the class Ball we described in the previous chapter), a message that will be displayed in the middle of the playing window, the target, and the cannon. The latter is an instance of class Cannon, which will be described shortly.

The constructor for the class CannonGame resizes the window frame to the declared bounds, and sets the window title. The argument value is converted from the type Integer to the built-in type int using the method intValue. The string representing the message is set to a value that will, when printed, indicate the current angle of the cannon. Finally, the cannonball is created using the angle to determine the initial direction of movement. There are two other methods defined in this class. The method moveCannonBall will move the cannon ball slightly and see if the target has been hit, updating the message string appropriately if so. The method run cycles over a loop that moves the cannon ball, redraws the window, then sleeps while the slower graphics operations are being performed.

The paint method for the cannon game simply paints the window, the cannon, the cannon ball (if there is one), the target, and the message in the middle of the screen:

```
import java.awt.*;
import javax.swing.JFrame;

public class CannonGame extends JFrame {
   public static void main (String [ ] args) {
      CannonGame world = new CannonGame (Integer.valueOf(args[0]));
      world.show(); while (true) world.run();  }

   public CannonGame (Integer theta) {
      setSize (FrameWidth, FrameHeight); setTitle ("Cannon Game");
      cannon.setAngle(theta.intValue());
      message = "Angle = " + theta;
      aBall = cannon.fire();
   }

   public static final int FrameWidth = 600;
   public static final int FrameHeight = 400;
   private Cannon cannon = new Cannon(new Point(20, FrameHeight-10));
   private CannonTarget target =
      new CannonTarget(new Point(FrameWidth-100, FrameHeight-12));
   private Ball aBall = null;
   private String message;

   public void paint (Graphics g) { ... }

   private void moveCannonBall () {
      aBall.move();
      if (aBall.location().y > FrameHeight) {
         if (target.hitTarget(aBall.location().x))
            message = "You Hit It!";
         else message = "Missed!";
         aBall = null;
      }
   }

   private void run () {
      if (aBall != null) moveCannonBall();
      repaint();
      try { Thread.sleep(50); } catch (Exception e) { System.exit(0); }
   }
}
```

[handwritten annotation: converts String to Integer]

[handwritten annotation: converts Integer to int]

Figure 6.2 Description of the principal class for the Cannon Game.

```
public void paint (Graphics g) {
   super.paint(g);
   cannon.paint(g);
   target.paint(g);
   if (aBall != null)
      aBall.paint(g);
   g.drawString(message, FrameWidth/2, FrameHeight/2);
}
```

The call on super.paint(g) is necessary to first erase the screen. Without it each image is drawn on top of the previous, leaving the cannon ball looking like a large ink stain running across the page.

6.1.1   *The Target*

The target is a simple object that has only two responsibilities. It must draw itself (as a rounded rectangle) and it must determine if a horizontal value is within the bounds of the target:

```
public class CannonTarget {
   public CannonTarget (Point loc) { location = loc; }

   private Point location;
   private static final int width = 50;

   public boolean hitTarget (int x) {
         // see if target has been hit
      return (x > location.x) && (x < location.x + width);
   }

   public void paint (Graphics g) {
      g.setColor (Color.red);
      g.fillRoundRect(location.x, location.y, width, 10, 6, 6);
   }
}
```

6.1.2   *The Cannon*

The most complicated graphics occurs in the class Cannon, which manipulates the angle of the cannon and the firing of cannon balls. This class is shown in Figure 6.3.

Rendering pictures is complicated by the fact that Java, like almost all windowing systems, uses a coordinate system that is "upside down." As shown in Figure 6.4, the upper left corner of a window is the 0,0 coordinate, with x values

```java
import java.awt.*;

class Cannon {
   public Cannon (Point location) { loc = location; setAngle(45); }

   private final Point loc;
   private int angle;
   private double radianAngle;

   public void setAngle (int a) {
      angle = a;
      radianAngle = angle * Math.PI / 180.0;
   }

   public Ball fire () {
      Ball cannonBall = new CannonBall(new Point(loc), 10,
         15 * Math.cos(radianAngle),
         - 12 * Math.sin(radianAngle));
      return cannonBall;
   }

   public void paint (Graphics g) {
      int barrelLength = 40;
      int barrelWidth = 8;
      int wheelRadius = 12;
         // draw wheel
      g.drawOval (loc.x - wheelRadius, loc.y - wheelRadius,
         2 * wheelRadius, 2 * wheelRadius);
         // draw barrel
      int lv = (int) (barrelLength * Math.sin(radianAngle));
      int lh = (int) (barrelLength * Math.cos(radianAngle));
      int sh = (int) (barrelWidth * Math.sin(radianAngle));
      int sv = (int) (barrelWidth * Math.cos(radianAngle));
      g.drawLine(loc.x-sh, loc.y-sv, loc.x+sh, loc.y+sv);
      g.drawLine(loc.x-sh, loc.y-sv, loc.x+lh-sh, loc.y-lv-sv);
      g.drawLine(loc.x+sh, loc.y+sv, loc.x+lh+sh, loc.y-lv+sv);
      g.drawLine(loc.x+lh-sh, loc.y-lv-sv, loc.x+lh+sh, loc.y-lv+sv);
   }
}
```

Figure 6.3   The cannon used in the Cannon Game application.

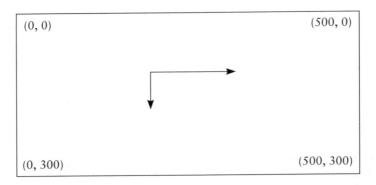

Figure 6.4 The "upside down" coordinate system of Java and other windowing software.

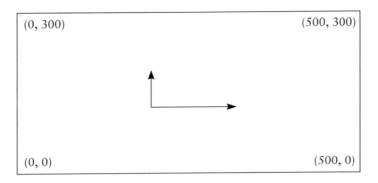

Figure 6.5 Coordinate system as most people think of it.

increasing as they move right, and *y* values increasing as they move *down*. However, most people prefer to think in a coordinate system where the 0,0 location is the bottom left corner, and *y* values increase as they move *up* as depicted in Figure 6.5.

This upside down geometry should be kept in mind when reading the graphics code in Figure 6.3. To draw the cannon we first draw the circle that represents the wheel. A small amount of trigonometry is used to determine the lines that will be used to draw the barrel of the cannon. To move upwards a value is subtracted from the current y location, while to move to the right a value is added to the x location.

The data fields in the cannon game have all been declared private. The location (here representing the center of the wheel) is set by the constructor. The angle is set by the method setAngle. Since the methods Math.sin and Math.cos use radians instead of degrees, a conversion is performed. The method fire creates a new cannonball that is headed in the appropriate direction.

6.1.3 Balls That Respond to Gravity

The class Ball was introduced in Chapter 5. A Ball, you will recall, possessed a radius, a location, a color, and a direction. The latter was represented by a pair of values, representing the extent of motion in the x coordinate and the extent of motion in the y coordinate.

A CannonBall is built using inheritance as an extension of class Ball. This means that a CannonBall has all the properties of a Ball and also includes new properties or alters existing properties. In this case, a CannonBall changes the move method, simulating the effect of gravity by reducing the change in the vertical direction by a small amount (stored in constant GravityEffect) each update cycle.

```java
import java.awt.Point;

public class  CannonBall extends Ball {
    public CannonBall (Point loc, int r, double dx, double dy) {
        super(loc, r);
        setMotion (dx, dy);
    }

    public static final double GravityEffect = 0.3;

    public void move () {
        changeInY += GravityEffect;
        super.move(); // update the ball position
    }
}
```

We have already encountered the pseudovariable super, shown here in both methods, but have not yet provided an explanation of this construct. When a method *overrides* (that is, replaces) a similarly named method in the parent class, a technique must be provided to indicate that the method should invoke the method inherited from the parent class. The method cannot simply be named, as the name in the child class and the parent class are the same. Thus, for example, if one was to try to invoke the move method in class Ball by simply executing the method move, the result would be an infinite series of recursive method calls; which is not the outcome we wish.

The pseudovariable super is used to represent the receiver but is viewed as an instance of the parent class, not the current class. Thus, by invoking super.move( ), the method move is asking that the move method from the parent class be executed, and not the version overridden by the class CannonBall. Similarly, the call on super.paint( ) in the paint method is instructing that the paint method inherited from JFrame be executed.

In a similar fashion, the use of the name super as a method in a constructor is used to indicate that the constructor for the parent class should be invoked, using the arguments shown. Note how the class CannonBall is invoked with a slightly different set of arguments than were used for the class Ball.

6.1.4   *Integers and* ints

As noted in Section 4.3 of Chapter 4, integer values are not actually *objects*, in the technical sense of the world. Thus, integers do not have classes, there are no methods associated with integers, and so on. For each of the nonclass primitive types, the Java library defines a "wrapper" class that can be used as an object. For integers this wrapper class is named Integer. The class Integer provides a number of useful operations. The one we utilize in our example program is the ability to take a String (the command-line argument), and convert it into a numeric value. To do this, a string is passed as argument in the call to the method valueOf:

```
CannonGame world = new CannonGame (Integer.valueOf(args[0]));
```

The result produced by the message valueOf is a new instance of class Integer, initialized to the indicated value. The conversion from Integer to int is performed using the message intValue:

```
cannon.setAngle(theta.intValue());
```

6.2   ADDING USER INTERACTION

The user interaction in our first application was very primitive. The user could select one angle, run the program, and see the result. In our second variation, we improve user interaction by providing the ability to dynamically set the angle of the cannon, and fire several times during one execution.

In the language of graphical user interfaces, buttons are used to signal actions, scroll bars are used to set a variable quantity, checkboxes or radio buttons are used to select alternatives, and text boxes are used to enter textual information. In our revised game we will incorporate two of these features, placing a button on the top of the screen, and a scroll bar to the right of the playing area, as shown in Figure 6.6.

The program for the revised game, now named CannonWorld, is shown in Figure 6.7. One feature to note is that we must now import the Java libraries java.awt.event.* and javax.swing.event.*, in order to include the definitions of the event-handling routines for the Java system. This is in addition to the java.awt.*

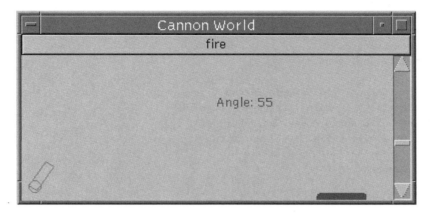

Figure 6.6 A screen of the revised game, renamed CannonWorld.

and javax.swing.* libraries we have been including from the start.[1] Although in code length the amount of change from the first version of our program is relatively small, a number of important features distinguish this program. We will explore these in the following sections.

6.2.1 Listeners

User interaction in Java is based on a model termed *event-driven* execution. An event-driven program will wait for an event, and then respond to it. In Java, the technique used to wait for events is termed a *listener*. A listener is simply an object whose sole responsibility is to wait for a specific event. When the event occurs, the listener wakes up, and performs whatever action is necessary.

Our first listener is a useful tool we will employ in many subsequent programs. You may have noticed that it was difficult to halt our first version of the program. Halting a running program in inherently platform-specific. On Unix systems you can type Control-C to force a halt. On other platforms you may or may not have this ability. We can get around this problem and provide a platform independent way to halt our program by defining a listener and attaching it to the close-box that is part of any window.

Clicking the mouse in the close box for a window will generate a window event. To trap this condition, we need a listener specialized for window events. The Java method windowClosing defined as part of the standard library class WindowAdapter defines the behavior we want. By using inheritance to subclass from WindowAdapter we can attach whatever actions we want to this method. In

---

[1] It is possible to rewrite this program to use the older AWT library, and avoid the newer swing components. See appendix C.

```
import java.awt.*;
import java.awt.event.*;
import javax.swing.*;
import javax.swing.event.*;

public class CannonWorld extends JFrame {
   public static void main (String [ ] args) {
      CannonWorld world = new CannonWorld ();
      world.show(); while (true) world.run(); }

   public CannonWorld () {
      ...
      addWindowListener(new CloseQuit());
         // add graphical objects
      JButton fire = new JButton("fire");
      fire.addActionListener(new FireButtonListener());
      getContentPane().add("North", fire);
      scrollbar.addAdjustmentListener(new ScrollBarListener());
      getContentPane().add("East", scrollbar);
   }

   private JScrollBar scrollbar =
      new JScrollBar(JScrollBar.VERTICAL, 45, 5, 0, 90);

   public void paint (Graphics g) { ... }
   private void moveCannonBall () { ... }
   private void run () { ... }

   private class FireButtonListener implements ActionListener {
      public void actionPerformed (ActionEvent evt) {
         aBall = cannon.fire();
      }
   }

   private class ScrollBarListener implements AdjustmentListener {
      public void adjustmentValueChanged (AdjustmentEvent e) {
         int angle = scrollbar.getValue();
         cannon.setAngle(angle);
         message = "Angle: " + angle;
         repaint();
      }
   }
}
```

Figure 6.7 Revised program renamed CannonWorld with button and scroll bar.

the present program, we simply want to halt the application. Thus, we create the following simple class:

```
import java.awt.event.*;

public class CloseQuit extends WindowAdapter {
   public void windowClosing (WindowEvent e) {
      System.exit(0);
   }
}
```

The argument to the method windowClosing contains information about the mouse-click event, for example the location of the mouse-click action. In the class CloseQuit we simply ignore this additional information.

Having defined the class CloseQuit, we next must register the listener with the window. This is accomplished by the method addWindowListener:

```
addWindowListener(new CloseQuit());
```

Now to stop the program the user can simply click the close box, and the application will immediately halt.

6.2.2 *Inner Classes*

One of the more notable features of the program in Figure 6.7 is the declaration of two new classes *within* the application class itself. A class declared in such a fashion is known as an *inner class*. Modifiers used in declaring an inner class match the meanings we have previously described for data fields and methods; thus, an inner class that is declared as private (such as shown here) can only be used within the outer class in which it is defined.

Inner classes are allowed to access their surrounding environment. That is, methods in an inner class can use data fields declared in the surrounding outer class, as well as invoke methods from the surrounding context. We see this in the method defined in class ScrollBarListener, which is allowed access to both the data fields cannon and message.

6.2.3 *Interfaces*

Both the inner classes created in this example use the keyword implements in their header. The *implementation* of an *interface* is yet another program-structuring mechanism, one that can be understood by comparison to the technique of *inheritance* we have been using previously.

An interface in Java is a description of *behavior*. It is written in a fashion that appears similar to a class definition; however, there are no implementations (method bodies) associated with methods, and the only data fields permitted must be declared static. An interface for ActionListener, used in our sample program, might be written as follows:

```
interface ActionListener {
    public void actionPerformed (ActionEvent);
}
```

The Java library, particularly in those sections that relate to the handling of events (such as pressing buttons or moving scroll bars), makes extensive use of interfaces. When a class is declared as implementing an interface, it is a guarantee (one that is checked by the compiler) that the class must provide a certain behavior. In this case, an assertion that a class is an ActionListener means that the class must provide a method named actionPerformed.

The reader should consider carefully the difference between the implementation of an interface and the extension of a class by means of inheritance. Using inheritance, methods and data fields that are declared in the parent class may be used in the child class. Thus, the child class inherits the *structure* of the parent, as well as being able to mimic the parent behavior. Using an interface, on the other hand, there is no implementation of the methods in the "parent interface" at all. Instead, the parent simply defines the names of the methods, which *must* then be implemented in the child class. In this manner a child class inherits a *specification* of methods from an interface, but no structure, no data fields, and no member functions.

Despite the fact that methods of an interface have no implementation, an interface can be used as a type name in an argument declared in a method header. The matching parameter value must then be an instance of a class that implements the interface. In our example program, the addActionListener method in class JButton expects an argument that implements the ActionListener interface, and the addAdjustmentListener method in class JScrollBar expects an argument that implements the AdjustmentListener interface.

6.2.4   *The Java Event Model*

As we noted earlier, modern graphical user interfaces are structured around the concept of events. An *event* is an action, such as the user clicking the mouse on a button, selecting a menu item, pressing a key, or inserting a disk into a drive. The program responds to an event by performing certain actions. Thus, such interfaces are said to be *event-driven*. For each type of event, there is an associated listener. When the event occurs, the listener goes into action and performs its assigned behavior.

Our sample program uses several listeners. One listener, an instance of Close-Quit, waits for the user to click in the close box. Another is waiting for the fire button to be pressed. The class JButton is one of many graphical elements provided by the Java Swing library. The string argument passed to the constructor for the class is the text that will appear on the face of the button. A listener for a button must implement the interface ActionListener. The listener in our sample program is declared as an instance of the inner class FireButtonListener, and is attached to a newly created button by the following code:

```
JButton fire = new JButton("Fire");
fire.addActionListener(new FireButtonListener( ));
```

When the button is pressed, the message actionPerformed will be passed to the listener. In this case, this message will be handled by the one method in the class body:

```
private class FireButtonListener implements ActionListener {
    public void actionPerformed (ActionEvent e) {
        aBall = cannon.fire();
    }
}
```

The argument of type ActionEvent which is passed to the method actionPerformed describes details of the event with more precision. However, the value is ignored, since in this case there is only one event a button can perform that is of any interest, namely the event that occurs when it is pressed. In this case we simply fire the cannon, which will return a new Ball that is then put into motion.

The scroll bar that is used to control the elevation of the cannon is created in a similar fashion. The constructor for class ScrollBar takes as argument an indication whether the scroll bar is horizontal or vertical, an initial value, and the range of accepted values. The scroll bar itself is created as part of the declaration of the variable named scrollbar, while the listener is added as part of the constructor for the game:

```
scrollbar.addAdjustmentListener(new ScrollBarListener());
```

The listener must implement the AdjustmentListener interface. When the scroll bar is moved, the listener is given the message adjustmentValueChanged. Note that, unlike the situation involving the button, the slide bar must be made available to the listener, so that the current value of the slide bar can be determined (using the message getValue). It is for this reason that the slide bar is saved in a data field, but the button need not be. Once the value of the slide bar has been determined, the angle and message can be changed, and the window scheduled for repainting.

```
private class ScrollBarListener implements AdjustmentListener {
    public void adjustmentValueChanged (AdjustmentEvent e) {
        int angle = scrollbar.getValue();
        cannon.setAngle(angle);
        message = "Angle: " + angle;
        repaint();
    }
}
```

6.2.5 *Window Layout*

Part of every Java program is a *layout manager*. The layout manager controls the placement of graphical items in a Java program. By using sophisticated layout managers the programmer can have a great deal of control over the appearance of a Java window. For simple programs, however, we can use the default layout manager, BorderLayout, which permits values to be placed on the four sides of the screen. These four portions of the screen are identified as North (the top), East (the right), West (the left), and South (the bottom).

The current layout manager is accessed indirectly by first getting hold of the window pane, and then using add to insert an object into the pane.[2] The constructor for our application places the button on the top of the window, and the scroll bar on the right hand side.

```
public CannonWorld ( ) {
    .
    .
    .

        // add graphical objects
    JButton fire = new JButton("fire");
    fire.addActionListener(new FireButtonListener());
    getContentPane().add("North", fire);
    scrollbar.addAdjustmentListener(new ScrollBarListener());
    getContentPane().add("East", scrollbar);
}
```

In later chapters we will explore a variety of other layout managers.

6.3 CHAPTER SUMMARY

This chapter has once again made use of a relatively simple application as a vehicle to introduce a number of new concepts. The following list summarizes some of the ideas introduced in this chapter:

- The class Integer, which is a wrapper class that can hold an integer value. Instances of this class are objects, unlike normal integer values, which are not objects. The class Integer provides some useful functionality, such as the ability to parse a string value that holds the textual representation of an integer quantity.

- The use of inheritance in the construction of the class CannonBall, so that the majority of the behavior for the ball is inherited from the parent class Ball.

---

[2] The method getContentPane is specific to the swing graphics library. Users of the older AWT library should see Appendix C.

- The pseudovariable super, which when used as a value inside a method refers to the parent class from which the current class inherits.

- The idea of an *inner class*, which is a class definition nested within another class definition. Inner classes are allowed full access to the data values and methods provided by surrounding classes.

- The idea of an *interface*, which is a means to ensure that classes satisfy certain behavior. An interface defines the names and arguments for member functions but does not provide an implementation. A class that declares itself as implementing an interface must then provide an implementation for these operations. A method can insist that an argument implement certain functionality, by declaring the argument using the interface as a type.

- The Java event model, in which *listener* objects are attached to event producing objects, such as buttons. When an event occurs, the listener is notified and then performs whatever action is appropriate.

- The graphical component classes JButton and JScrollBar, which simplify the creation of graphical features in a user interface.

- The idea of a window layout manager. In our application program we used the default layout manager, which is an instance of the class BorderLayout.

Note that as our application has become more complex, we have moved closer to the idea that an object-oriented program is a "community" of agents that interact to produce the desired behavior. Instances of the following categories of objects are all used in this example program:

- The class CannonWorld, which inherits from the class JFrame provided by the Java library.

- The class CannonBall, built as an extension of the earlier class Ball developed in Chapter 5. Note that each instance of Ball also includes a Point object.

- A Cannon object.

- The instance of CannonTarget, which also maintains an instance of Point.

- The class Integer, used here for its ability to translate a number in text into a numeric quantity.

- The instance of class CloseQuit that waits for the user to click in the close box.

- The graphical component classes JButton and JScrollBar, and their listener classes FireButtonListener and ScrollBarListener, the latter two constructed as inner classes within our application class.

- Instances of the class ActionEvent and AdjustmentEvent, which are created when an event occurs and carry information to the event listener.

- The layout manager, an instance of class BorderLayout.

CROSS REFERENCES

Wrapper classes, such as Integer and Double, will be explained in more detail in Chapter 19. The distinction between inheritance and implementation, and the uses of each, will be a topic addressed in Chapter 10. Window layouts, layout managers, graphical components, and other features of the AWT will be examined in more detail in Chapter 13.

STUDY QUESTIONS

1. What is the parent class for class CannonGame?

2. In the first cannon game, how is the angle of the cannon determined?

3. What is the difference in behavior between a Ball and a CannonBall?

4. How is the pseudovariable super used in a method? What effect does it have in a message expression?

5. What is the difference between the types Integer and int?

6. What is an inner class?

7. What is an interface?

8. What would an interface for the class CannonBall look like?

9. What does it mean to say that a class implements an interface?

10. What does it mean to say that a program is event-driven?

11. What is an event listener?

12. What is a window layout manager?

13. In Figure 6.7, although both the fire button and the scroll bar are graphical components, one is declared as a member data field and the other a local variable. Explain why. Could they both have been declared as member data fields? As local variables?

EXERCISES

1. Change the CannonGame so that the message being displayed provides not only the angle of the cannon, but also the current position of the cannonball. This value should change as the cannonball moves through the air.

2. Modify the class CannonBall so that the ball is colored blue when the ball is moving upward, and colored red when the ball is descending. Will this change have any impact on the rest of the program?

3. Modify the CannonWorld program so that it maintains both a count of the number of balls fired and the number of times the target was hit. Display both of these values in the message area, as well as the angle of the cannon.

4. Add a button labeled "Quit" to the bottom (south) part of the application window. When pressed, this button should execute the method System.exit(0).

5. Create a simple program that draws a window with a colored ball in the center. Place a button at the top of the window. When the user presses the button, the color of the ball will change from red to yellow, or from yellow to green, or from green to red.

6. Create a simple program that draws a window with a colored ball in the center. Place a scroll bar on the right side of the window. As the user moves the scroll bar, move the ball up and down the window.

7. The constructor for class Color can also take three integer arguments, which represent the saturation values for red, blue, and green. The arguments must be integers between 0 and 255. Create a simple program that draws a window with a colored ball in the center. Place scroll bars on three sides. As the user moves the scroll bars, the saturation values change for one of these arguments, and the ball changes color.

7 Pinball Game Construction Kit

In this chapter we will expand on the techniques introduced in the Cannon Game of Chapter 6, creating an entirely different type of interactive application. Along the way, we will use the development of this program to discuss standard data structures, event handling, inheritance, exceptions, and interfaces.

The application we will develop, the Pinball Construction Kit, simulates a pinball game. Users can fire a ball from the small square in the right corner of the bottom of the screen. (See Figure 7.1.) Balls rise, then encounter a variety of different types of targets as they fall back to the ground. The user scores points that depend upon the type and number of targets encountered as the ball descends. The objective of the game is to score as many points as possible.

As we did with the Cannon World application in Chapter 6, we will develop this program in a sequence of stages, each stage emphasizing a small number of new programming concepts. The intent is simply to introduce these concepts in the context of a relatively simple and easy to understand program. Many of the major ideas introduced here will be discussed in more detail in later chapters.

7.1 FIRST VERSION OF GAME

Our first version (Figure 7.2) is in many ways the same as the Cannon World application from Chapter 6, but with a number of new features. Because we will later be creating objects that will need to communicate with the window object, the variable world is declared as a public static value, rather than as a local variable to the main method. Balls are "fired" from a square box labelled with a red disk that appears at the bottom right corner of the window. A notable difference between this version and the Cannon Game application of Chapter 6 is the mechanism for placing a new ball into motion. Whereas in the earlier program firing was tied to a button, in this version we will trap mouse activities

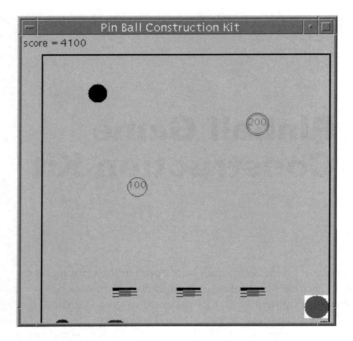

Figure 7.1   The Pinball Application

in a more general routine. One more notable change is that the pinball game allows several balls to be in the air at once (the Cannon Game fired only a single ball).

The class PinBallFire, shown in Figure 7.3, is the fire button for the application. It knows how to draw itself. It also can test a point to see if it is in the region of the fire button, and return a new ball.

The class PinBall (Figure 7.4) extends the class CannonBall described in Chapter 6 (Section 6.1.3). Differences are that here the initial direction is slightly to the left of vertical, and includes a small random number perturbation so as to be less predicatable. Also, a PinBall can return an instance of the standard class Rectangle that represents the bounding rectangle for the ball. We will use the latter feature to help detect when a ball has hit a target.

7.1.1   *Collection Classes*

Unlike the Cannon Game described in the previous chapter, the pinball game allows several balls to be moving at one time. Every time the user clicks on the "fire" button, a new ball is placed in motion, even if earlier balls have not yet ceased moving.

```java
import java.awt.*;
import java.awt.event.*;
import java.util.Vector;
import javax.swing.JFrame;

public class PinBallGame extends JFrame {

   public static void main (String [ ] args) {
      world = new PinBallGame( );
      world.show( );
      world.run( );
   }

   public PinBallGame ( ) {
      setTitle("Pin Ball Construction Kit");
      setSize(FrameWidth, FrameHeight);
      addWindowListener(new CloseQuit( ));
      balls = new Vector( );
      addMouseListener(new MouseKeeper( ));
   }

   public static final int FrameWidth = 400;
   public static final int FrameHeight = 400;
   private Vector balls;
   private PinBallFire fireButton =
      new PinBallFire(new Point(FrameWidth-40, FrameHeight-40));

   public static PinBallGame world;

   private void run ( ) { ... }

   private class MouseKeeper extends MouseAdapter { ... }

   public void paint (Graphics g) {
      super.paint(g); // clear window
      fireButton.paint(g); // draw target
      for (int i = 0; i < balls.size( ); i++) { // draw balls
         PinBall aBall = (PinBall) balls.elementAt(i);
         aBall.paint(g);
      }
   }
}
```

Figure 7.2 First version of PinBallGame class.

```
class PinBallFire {
   public PinBallFire (Point where) { location = where; }

   private Point location;

   public void paint(Graphics g) {
      g.setColor(Color.white);
      g.fillRect(location.x, location.y, 30, 30);
      g.setColor(Color.red);
      g.fillOval(location.x, location.y, 30, 30);
   }

   public boolean includes (int x, int y)
      { return (x > location.x) && (y > location.y); }

   public PinBall fire (int x, int y)
      { return new PinBall(new Point(x, y)); }
}
```

Figure 7.3   The class PinBallFire.

```
class PinBall extends CannonBall {
   public PinBall (Point loc)
      { super(loc, 8, -5 + Math.random( ), -15); }

   public Rectangle box( ) {
      int r = radius( );
      return new Rectangle(location( ).x-r, location( ).y-r, 2*r, 2*r);
   }
}
```

Figure 7.4   The class PinBall.

To manage this, we need a data structure that can hold a collection of values.
The one collection data structure we have seen up to now is the array (see Chapter
5). However, the array is limited by the fact that when we allocate a new array
object we must state the number of elements the array will hold. In the present
case, we cannot make any such estimate since we do not know how many times
the user will hit the "fire" button.

Fortunately, the Java library provides a number of other data structures we
can employ. One of the simplest is a Vector. A vector is, like an array, an indexed
data structure; meaning that each element has a position in the collection, and
elements are accessed by requesting the value at a given position. However, unlike

an array, a vector can dynamically grow as new values are inserted into the collection.

To use a vector, the programmer must first import the vector class definition from the standard library:

```
import java.util.Vector;
```

The vector is declared by simply providing a name:

```
private Vector balls;
```

Note, in particular, that unlike an array, it is not necessary to state the type of values that a Vector will hold. For technical reasons having to do with their internal structure, a vector is restricted to holding only objects. Thus, for example, one cannot create a vector of integer values (ints) but one *can* create a vector of instances of class Integer. This is one reason for the existence of "wrapper" classes, such as Integer and Float.

Just as an array in Java separates the declaration of the array name and the allocation of space for the array, the space for a Vector must be similarly created and assigned. In our example program this occurs in the constructor for the class PinBallGame. Note that no fixed limit is set for the space:

```
balls = new Vector( );
```

Although we have not seen it yet, a new element will be inserted into the vector by the method addElement:

```
balls.addElement (newBall);
```

The number of values stored in a Vector can be determined by invoking the method size.

```
for (int i = 0; i < balls.size( ); i++)
```

Finally, values are accessed in a vector using the method elementAt. Like an array, the set of legal index values ranges from zero to one less than the number of elements in the collection. The compiler only knows that the accessed element is a value of type object; it must be *cast* to the appropriate type before it can be used. Here we cast the value into the type PinBall. A run-time check is performed to ensure that the conversion is actually valid:

```
PinBall aBall = (PinBall) balls.elementAt (i);
```

The reader should note how the paint method in Figure 7.2 cycles over the collection of balls, asking each to paint itself.

7.1.2 *Mouse Listeners*

As noted in Chapter 6, the Java event model is based around the concept of *listeners*; objects that wait and "listen" for an event to take place, and then respond appropriately. The earlier examples showed how to create a listener by defining a class that implements the corresponding *interface* for the event in question.

Mouse events are treated in a similar fashion; however, there are five different mouse-related events that could potentially be of interest. Thus, the interface for a MouseListener has the following structure:

```
public interface MouseListener {
    public void mouseClicked (MouseEvent e);
    public void mouseEntered (MouseEvent e);
    public void mouseExited (MouseEvent e);
    public void mousePressed (MouseEvent e);
    public void mouseReleased (MouseEvent e);
}
```

Often a programmer is interested in only one or two of these five events. However, to implement an interface the Java language insists that the programmer provide a definition for all operations. To simplify such cases, the Java library provides a simple class named MouseAdapter. The class MouseAdapter implements the MouseListener interface but uses an empty method for each method. That is, a MouseAdapter does nothing in response to any mouse event. However, the programmer can write a new class that *inherits* from MouseAdapter, and overrides (or redefines) the methods of interest.

That is what we do in the example program. An inner class defines a MouseListener by extending MouseAdapter. An instance of this class is created, and passed as an argument to the method addMouseListener, which is inherited from class JFrame.

```
addMouseListener (new MouseKeeper( ));
```

The class MouseKeeper inherits all five methods defined by MouseAdapter and redefines only one. The other four messages will be handled by the methods inherited from the parent class, which will do nothing.

```
private class MouseKeeper extends MouseAdapter {

    public void mousePressed (MouseEvent e) {
        int x = e.getX( ); // get coordinates where
        int y = e.getY( ); // mouse was pressed
            // only handle mouse event in the fire region
        if (fireButton.includes(x, y))
            balls.addElement(fireButton.fire(x, y));
```

```
        }
    }
```

The argument passed to each method in the MouseListener interface is a value
of type MouseEvent. The mouse event encodes certain information relating to the
type of event that occurred. In our case, the most important information is the
position (or coordinate) of the mouse at the moment the button was pressed.
This information can be derived from the mouse event object using the methods
getX and getY. With these values, a new ball is created, added to the list of balls,
and placed into motion.

7.1.3 *Running the Application*

Once the initial window has been displayed, the heart of the application is
found in the method run and the other methods it calls. The run method repeatedly
calls moveBalls to move the balls, then repaints the window, sleeping for a short
period in order to permit the window to be redrawn.

```
private void run ( ) {
    while (true) {
        moveBalls( );
        repaint( );
        try {
            Thread.sleep(10);
        } catch (InterruptedException e) { System.exit(0); }
    }
}
```

The moveBalls routine cycles over the list of balls, moving each one:

```
private void moveBalls ( ) {
    for (int i = 0; i < balls.size( ); i++) {
        PinBall theBall = (PinBall) balls.elementAt(i);
        if (theBall.location( ).y < FrameHeight)
            theBall.move( );
    }
}
```

7.2 ADDING TARGETS: INHERITANCE AND INTERFACES

To provide realism and interest to our pinball game, we need to add targets for the
ball to encounter on its way down the playing surface. As in real pinball games,
we will want to include a variety of different types of targets. Some targets simply
add values to the score, some move the ball in a new direction, and some swallow

the ball, removing it from play. In order to simplify the program, we will want to maintain all the different types of targets in a single data structure, a vector.

7.2.1   *The* Pinball Target *Interface*

Because we want to process targets uniformly, for example in a loop that asks whether a ball has hit any target, we need all the targets to have a uniform interface. However, the various different types of targets will be represented internally by different data structures. Thus, we do not want to use *inheritance*, such as we have been doing with the different forms of Ball up to this point. Inheritance is a mechanism for sharing *structure*; a PinBall, for example, is simply a type of Ball that has the same structure and behavior as a Ball, adding a few new features, but maintaining all the characteristics of the original. There is little in the way of common structure between a Peg (a target that when hit by a ball scores a number of points and moves the ball in a new direction) and a Wall (a target that when struck simply reflects the motion of the ball).

What is needed in this case is the ability to state that the two concepts (Peg and Wall, in this case), share the same *behavior*, although they have nothing in common in *structure*. As we saw in our earlier case study, in Java this is accomplished by describing the common behavior as an interface, and declaring that both objects implement the same interface. An interface for our pinball targets can be described as follows:

```
interface PinBallTarget {
    public boolean intersects (PinBall aBall);
    public void moveTo (int x, int y);
    public void paint (Graphics g);
    public void hitBy (PinBall aBall);
}
```

The interface in this case is declaring that there are four characteristics of interest in a pinball target. Each target can tell if it has been hit by a ball; that is, if it intersects the region occupied by a ball. Each target can be moved to a specific point on the playing surface, each can paint itself, and each provides some response when it has been hit by a given ball. However, the means by which each of these behaviors will be achieved is left unspecified, and different targets are free to *implement* the interface in different fashions.

An examination of a few different targets will help illustrate the point. Our first type of target will be a Spring. When hit by a falling ball, a Spring rebounds the ball back into the playing area, moving it upward where we hope it will encounter further targets. A spring is represented graphically by a small horizontal box, and a series of zigzag lines, as in Figure 7.5.

The class description for Spring is shown in Figure 7.6. Note how the class Spring must explicitly state that it implements the PinBallTarget interface, and must provide a specific meaning for each of the four elements of that interface. In this

Figure 7.5   Graphical representation of a spring.

case, we will state that a spring intersects a ball if the rectangle surrounding the ball intersects with the rectangle representing the spring platform. When the spring is hit by the ball, it reverses the vertical direction of movement for the ball.

One slight element of interest has been added to the drawing of the Spring object. We have provided two different graphical representations for the Spring object, selected by an integer variable named state. Normally, a spring will be held in state 1. When struck, the value of state is changed to 2, and the *next* time the spring is redrawn it will present an alternative image, one in which the spring has been elongated. Drawing this second image changes the state back to state 1, and a subsequent redraw will display the original. The effect is a simple form of animation, where a moving spring will appear to stretch momentarily, then return to a ready state.

A second type of target is a Wall. A Wall (Figure 7.7) is a narrow rectangular region. A ball intersects a wall if their regions overlap, and if so the ball is simply reflected back, in effect bouncing off the wall. The bounce is obtained by reversing either the horizontal or vertical component of the direction of motion, depending upon which wall has been hit.

The advantage of declaring these two different structures as both implementing an interface is that an interface name can be used as a *type*. That is, we can declare a variable as holding a value of type PinBallTarget. In much the same way that a variable declared as maintaining a value of type Ball could, in fact, be holding a cannonball, a pinball, or any other value derived from a class that extends the original class Ball, a variable declared as maintaining a PinBallTarget could, in fact, be holding either a Spring, a Wall, or any of the other varieties of target to be described subsequently. (This is one aspect of *polymorphism*, a topic we will return to in more detail in Chapter 12.) We will shortly make use of this property, by storing all the targets in our game in a single data structure, and testing the motion of the ball against the location of each target in turn.

Consider now a third type of target, a Hole. A Hole (Figure 7.8) consumes any ball it comes in contact with, removing the ball from the playing surface. A Hole is represented by a circular colored image, just like a ball. A Hole has a location on the playing surface, just like a Ball. In fact, because a hole is *structurally*

```java
class Spring implements PinBallTarget {
  public Spring (int x, int y)
      { pad = new Rectangle(x, y, 30, 3); }

  private Rectangle pad;
  private int state = 1;

  public void moveTo (int x, int y)
      { pad.setLocation(x, y); }

  public void paint (Graphics g) {
    int x = pad.x; int y = pad.y;
    g.setColor(Color.black);
    if (state == 1) { // draw compressed spring
       g.fillRect(x, y, pad.width, pad.height);
       g.drawLine(x, y+3, x+30, y+5);
       g.drawLine(x+30, y+5, x, y+7);
       g.drawLine(x, y+7, x+30, y+9);
       g.drawLine(x+30, y+9, x, y+11);
       }
    else {  // draw extended spring
       g.fillRect(x, y-8, pad.width, pad.height);
       g.drawLine(x, y+5, x+30, y-1);
       g.drawLine(x+30, y-1, x, y+3);
       g.drawLine(x, y+3, x+30, y+7);
       g.drawLine(x+30, y+7, x, y+11);
       state = 1;
    }
  }

  public boolean intersects (PinBall aBall)
      { return pad.intersects(aBall.box( )); }

  public void hitBy (PinBall aBall) {
    aBall.reflectHorz( );
    state = 2;
  }
}
```

Figure 7.6   Definition for class Spring.

```
class Wall implements PinBallTarget {
   public Wall (int x, int y, int width, int height)
      { location = new Rectangle(x, y, width, height); }

   public Rectangle location;

   public void moveTo (int x, int y)
      { location.setLocation(x, y); }

   public void paint (Graphics g) {
      g.setColor(Color.black);
      g.fillRect(location.x, location.y,
         location.width, location.height);
   }

   public boolean intersects (PinBall aBall)
      { return location.intersects(aBall.box()); }

   public void hitBy(PinBall aBall) {
      Point ballPos = aBall.location();
      if ((ballPos.y < location.y) ||
         (ballPos.y > (location.y + location.height)))
            aBall.reflectVert();
      else
         aBall.reflectHorz();
   }
}
```

Figure 7.7 Definition of class Wall.

similar to a Ball, we can use inheritance to simplify the implementation of the Hole abstraction.[1]

This illustrates the important difference between the use of inheritance and the use of interfaces. The mechanism of inheritance should be used when two (or more) concepts have a *structural* relationship. Note that with objects, a structural relationship almost always implies at least some behavioral relationship. In contrast, the interface mechanism should be used with two (or more) concepts having a *behavioral* relationship but no structural relationship. We will explore these ideas in more detail in Chapter 8.

---

[1] Whether the structural similarity of Ball and Hole is sufficient grounds for the use of inheritance is a debatable point we will return to in Chapter 8.

```
class Hole extends Ball implements PinBallTarget {

    public Hole (int x, int y) {
        super(new Point(x, y), 12);
        setColor(Color.black);
    }

    public boolean intersects (PinBall aBall) {
        int dx = aBall.location( ).x - location( ).x;
        int dy = aBall.location( ).y - location( ).y;
        int r = 2 * radius( );
        return (-r < dx) && (dx < r) && (-r < dy) && (dy < r);
    }

    public void hitBy (PinBall aBall) {
        // move ball totally off frame
        aBall.moveTo(0, PinBallGame.FrameHeight + 30);
        // stop motion of ball
        aBall.setMotion(0, 0);
    }
}
```

Figure 7.8   Definition of class Hole.

Note how a Hole uses both inheritance and an interface. The hole *inherits* much of its behavior from the class Ball, including the methods paint and moveTo. The Hole declares that it implements the PinBallTarget interface, and to do so must provide a method to see if the hole has intersected with a ball, and the actions to be performed when such an event occurs. In the case of a hole, the ball is moved clear off the playing surface, and motion of the ball is halted.

A class that inherits from an existing class that implements an interface must of necessity also implement the interface. We will use this property in defining the next two types of targets in our pinball game. A ScorePad is, like a hole, represented by a circular region. When struck by a ball, the score pad has no effect on the ball (the ball simply moves over it); however, the score pad adds a certain amount to the player's score. The particular amount to add is defined as part of the state for the score object.

Note how the ScorePad class (Figure 7.9) inherits the intersects behavior from class Hole and the moveTo behavior from class Ball, but overrides the paint and hitBy methods that would otherwise be inherited from class Hole. The first now draws a colored circle with the scoring amount in the middle, while the latter adds the given value to the player score.

```
class ScorePad extends Hole {
   public ScorePad (int x, int y, int v) {
      super(x, y);
      value = v;
      setColor(Color.red);
   }

   protected int value;

   public void hitBy (PinBall aBall)
      { PinBallGame.world.addScore(value); }

   public void paint (Graphics g) {
      g.setColor(color);
      int r = radius( );
      g.drawOval(location( ).x-r, location( ).y-r, 2*r, 2*r);
      String s = "" + value;
      g.drawString(s, location( ).x-7, location( ).y+1);
   }
}
```

Figure 7.9 Definition of the class ScorePad.

```
public class PinBallGame extends JFrame {

   public PinBallGame ( ) {
          .
          .
          .
      getContentPane( ).add("North", scoreLabel);
   }

   private int score = 0;
   private Label scoreLabel = new Label("Score = 0");

   public void addScore (int v) {
      score = score + v;
      scoreLabel.setText("Score = " + score);
      }
    .
    .
    .
}
```

Figure 7.10 Adding labels to our pinball game.

Because a ScorePad inherits from class Hole, which implements the PinBallTarget interface, the class ScorePad is also said to implement the interface. This means, for example, that a ScorePad could be assigned to a variable that was declared to be a PinBallTarget.

7.2.2 *Adding a Label to Our Pinball Game*

In the revised version of our program we will add a new graphical element, a textual label in a banner across the top of the window. This is accomplished by declaring a new Label, and adding it in the "North" part of the window (Figure 7.10). As the user scores new points, the text of the label is updated. Note that a ScorePad refers back to the application object through the variable world.

A Peg is similar to a ScorePad, but it sticks up above the playing surface. Thus, when a Peg is struck, it deflects the ball off in a new direction, depending upon the angle of the ball and the point at which it encounters the peg. (The algorithm used in Figure 7.11 is not exactly correct as far as actual physics is concerned, but it does have the advantage of being easy to compute.) The ball is then updated until it no longer intersects with the peg, thereby avoiding having the method executed multiple times for a single encounter. We have once again added a simple animation to the class Peg, so that the first time a peg is redrawn after it has been struck, the circle surrounding the peg will appear to enlarge and then return to a normal size.

To create the second version of our game (Figure 7.12), we simply create a Vector of targets, along with the vector of balls. We initialize the targets in the constructor for the game, including placing walls on the sides and top of the playing area, to reflect wayward balls. The user fires balls as before, which then proceed to interact with the various targets as the balls move down the playing surface. Each time a ball moves, a loop is executed to determine if the new location of the ball has struck a target. If so, the target is informed, and the location of the ball potentially updated. Finally, the entire screen is repainted, which involves repainting both the targets and the collection of balls.

7.3 PINBALL GAME CONSTRUCTION KIT: MOUSE EVENTS RECONSIDERED

Although the second version of the pinball game is certainly more interesting than the first, it is still limited by the fact that the layout of the various targets is determined by the original programmer. To create a different layout, the program must be changed and then recompiled and executed. In our final version, we will show how this limitation can be overcome, by providing a *pallet* of target elements from which the *user* can select, dynamically constructing the pinball game while the program is executing.

In appearance, our revised game will move the playing area slightly to the right, placing a sequence of potential target components along a strip in the far left. (See Figure 7.13.) The user can click the mouse down in one of these alternatives, then slide the mouse (still down) over into the playing area. When the user releases the mouse, the selected target element will be installed into the new location.

The effect is produced by overriding both the mousePressed and the mouseReleased methods inherited from the mouse adapter (Figure 7.14). The two methods communicate with each other by means of a variable named element. The mousePressed method creates a potential target, determined by the coordinates of the point at which the mouse goes down. Note that we have not eliminated the

```java
class Peg extends ScorePad {

    public Peg (int x, int y, int v)
      { super(x, y, v); }

    private int state = 1;

    public void paint (Graphics g) {
      super.paint(g);
      int r = radius();
      if (state == 2) { // draw expanded circle
          g.drawOval(location().x-(r+3), location().y-(r+3),
            2*(r+3), 2*(r+3));
          state = 1;
          }
      else
          g.drawOval(location().x-(r+2), location().y-(r+2),
            2*(r+2), 2*(r+2));
    }

    public void hitBy (PinBall aBall) {
      super.hitBy(aBall); // update the score
      aBall.reflectVert();
      aBall.reflectHorz();
      while (intersects(aBall)) // move out of range
          aBall.move();
      state = 2; // next draw will expand circle
    }
}
```

Figure 7.11 Definition of the class Peg.

```java
public class PinBallGame extends JFrame {

    private Vector targets;

    public PinBallGame ( ) {
        .
        .
            // create the targets
            targets = new Vector( );
            targets.addElement(new Wall(30, 50, 2, 350));
            targets.addElement(new Wall(30, 50, 360, 2));
            targets.addElement(new Wall(390, 50, 2, 380));
            targets.addElement(new Hole(100, 100));
            targets.addElement(new ScorePad(150, 220, 100));
            targets.addElement(new Peg(300, 140, 200));
            targets.addElement(new Spring(120, 350));
    }

    public void moveBalls ( ) {
        for (int i = 0; i < balls.size( ); i++) {
            PinBall theBall = (PinBall) balls.elementAt(i);
            if (theBall.location( ).y < FrameHeight) {
                theBall.move( );
                    // see if we ran into anything
                for (int j = 0; j < targets.size( ); j++) {
                    PinBallTarget target =
                        (PinBallTarget) targets.elementAt(j);
                    if (target.intersects(theBall)) target.hitBy(theBall);
                }
            }
        }
    }

    public void paint (Graphics g) {
        .
        .
        for (int j = 0; j < targets.size( ); j++) { // draw targets
            PinBallTarget target = (PinBallTarget) targets.elementAt(j);
            target.paint(g);
        }
    }
}
```

Figure 7.12   Addition of targets to the class PinBallGame.

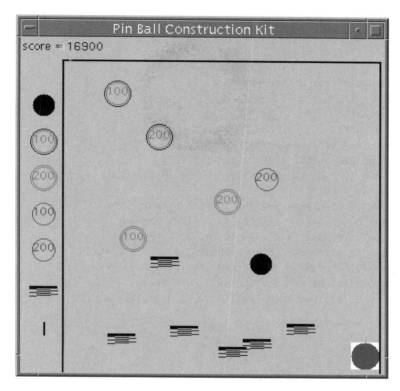

Figure 7.13 The revised Pinball Game Construction Kit.

original use of the mousePressed method, simply added a new condition. The MouseReleased method checks the location of the release, and if it is in the playing area and if a target item was previously selected (*both* conditions must be true), then it adds a new target to the game.

Other changes needed to provide our final version of the Pinball Construction Kit simply involve repositioning the left wall, and drawing the images of the selection pallet.

7.4 CHAPTER SUMMARY

In this chapter the development of an example program has once again served as a vehicle to introduce a number of features of the Java programming language. Introduced in this chapter were the following features:

- The use of collection classes, in particular the collection class Vector. We will discuss collection classes in more detail in Chapter 19.

```
private class MouseKeeper extends MouseAdapter {

    private PinBallTarget element;

    public void mousePressed (MouseEvent e) {
        element = null;
        int x = e.getX( );
        int y = e.getY( );
        if (firebutton.includes(x, y))
            balls.addElement(fireButton.fire(x, y));
        if (x < 40) { // each target occupies a 40 by 40 pixel box
            switch (y / 40) {
                case 2: element = new Hole(0, 0); break;
                case 3: element = new Peg(0, 0, 100); break;
                case 4: element = new Peg(0, 0, 200); break;
                case 5: element = new ScorePad(0, 0, 100); break;
                case 6: element = new ScorePad(0, 0, 200); break;
                case 7: element = new Spring(0, 0); break;
                case 8: element = new Wall(0, 0, 2, 15); break;
            }
        }
    }

    public void mouseReleased (MouseEvent e) {
        int x = e.getX( ); // only perform release action if mouse is
        int y = e.getY( ); // released on playing surface
        if ((element != null) && (x > 50)){
            element.moveTo(x, y);
            targets.addElement(element);
            repaint( );
        }
    }
}
```

Figure 7.14 Capturing both mouse presses and releases.

- An expanded discussion of the Java listener event model (started in Chapter 6), focusing on how to create objects that will listen for mouse events.

- Our first example of a statement that could potentially produce an *exception*, and the way the Java language permits the programmer to specify what actions to take when an exception occurs.

- More on interfaces, contrasting the use of the interface mechanism with the use of inheritance.

- One aspect of the important concept of *polymorphism*. A variable declared as an instance of a parent class (such as Ball) can, in fact, be holding a value derived from a child class (such as PinBall). Similarly, a variable declared as an interface value (such as PinBallTarget) can, in fact, hold any object that implements that interface (such as Peg). This property allows us to create arrays of different objects, such as an array of pinball targets, and process them in a uniform fashion.

CROSS REFERENCES

The distinction between interfaces and inheritances is explored in more detail in Chapter 8. Collection classes will be investigated in detail in Chapter 19. Chapter 13 presents a more systematic investigation of the services provided by the AWT.

STUDY QUESTIONS

1. Why must the variable world be declared static?

2. In what ways is a Vector object similar to an array? In what ways is it different?

3. What method is used to determine the number of elements held in a Vector? What method is used to access the values? What method is used to insert a new value into the collection?

4. What is the relationship between MouseAdapter and MouseListener? In what ways are they different?

5. What is an exception?

6. What action is performed by the method System.exit? Under what circumstances in our program will this method be called?

7. When should two software components be tied together through the use of inheritance rather than a common interface?

8. What type of objects can be held by a variable declared using the interface PinBallTarget?

9. In what ways does the class Hole modify the behavior inherited from class Ball?

10. What is a Label? How is a label attached to a window? What methods are used to change the text of a label?

EXERCISES

1. The class Peg inherits from ScorePad, which in turn inherits from Hole, which in turn inherits from Ball. For each of these classes, describe all the methods defined in the class or inherited from parent classes, and for each of the latter indicate in which parent class the method definition occurs.

2. The pinball game as presented allows the user an unlimited number of balls. Change the program to fire only a fixed number of balls, disallowing firing once the supply is exhausted. Change the display at the top of the screen so that it will indicate the number of remaining balls, as well as the score.

3. Add a "reset" button to the bottom of the screen. When pressed, the reset button sets the score back to zero and, if you implemented the suggestion in the previous question, resets the number of balls in play.

4. On some platforms it may be difficult to halt the PinBall application once it has finished. Add a button labeled "Quit" to the bottom (south) part of the application window. When pressed, this button should execute the method System.exit(0).

5. In the final program, the items on the pallet are still stored in the targets vector, so that they will be checked for a hit, even though they can never be hit by a ball. A better solution would have been to create a new vector pallet that will hold these items, redrawing both the pallet and the targets on a repaint, but only if a target in the targets vector is hit by a ball. Modify the program in this fashion.

6. Currently balls do not test to see if they intersect with other balls. We could support this modification by making PinBall implement the PinBallTarget interface, and adding balls to the list of targets as well as the list of balls. Describe what changes would need to be added to modify the program in this fashion.

7. Another change could allow the programmer to reposition items even after they have been placed in the playing area. If a mouse click occurs on the playing surface over a target, select the target and move it to the location given by the associated mouse up. Be careful that you don't end up placing the element in the target vector twice.

8. Create a program that opens a window, listens for mouse clicks, and when a mouse is released will display the distance (in pixel units) between the location the mouse was pressed and the location it was released.

9. Write a program that places a red circle in the middle of the window. The circle should change color to blue when the mouse enters the window, then return to red when the mouse leaves the window. When the mouse is clicked inside the window, the circle should change color to green and remain green

for 1000 milliseconds, before returning to blue. Finally, if the mouse is clicked within the bounds of the circle and released outside the circle, the circle should be moved so as to be centered on the location of the mouse release.

10. Develop a "paddle" target object. When the user clicks the mouse over the paddle, the paddle should move back and forth (perhaps only once). If a paddle encounters a ball, the ball is reflected off the paddle.

III

Understanding Inheritance

8 Understanding Inheritance

The first step in learning object-oriented programming is understanding the basic philosophy of organizing a computer program as the interaction of loosely coupled software components. This idea was the central lesson in the case studies presented in the first part of the book. The next step in learning object-oriented programming is organizing classes into a hierarchical structure based on the concept of inheritance. By *inheritance*, we mean the property that instances of a child class (or subclass) can access both data and behavior (methods) associated with a parent class (or superclass).

Although in Java the term *inheritance* is correctly applied only to the creation of new classes using subclassing (the extends keyword), there are numerous correspondences between subclassification and the designation that classes satisfy an interface (the implements keyword). The latter is sometimes termed "inheritance of specification," contrasted with the "inheritance of code" provided by subclassification. In this chapter we will use the word in a general fashion, meaning both mechanisms.

Although the intuitive meaning of inheritance is clear, and we have used inheritance in many of our earlier case studies, and the mechanics of using inheritance are relatively simple, there are nevertheless subtle features involved in the use of inheritance in Java. In this and subsequent chapters we will explore some of these issues.

8.1 AN INTUITIVE DESCRIPTION OF INHERITANCE

Let us return to Flora the florist from the first chapter. There is a certain behavior we expect florists to perform, not because they are florists but simply because they are shopkeepers. For example, we expect Flora to request money for the transaction and in turn give us a receipt. These activities are not unique to florists, but are common to bakers, grocers, stationers, car dealers, and other merchants. It is as though we have associated certain behavior with the general category Shopkeeper, and as Florists are a specialized form of shopkeepers, the behavior is automatically identified with the subclass.

In programming languages, inheritance means that the behavior and data associated with child classes are always an *extension* (that is, a larger set) of the properties associated with parent classes. A child class will be given all the properties of the parent class, and may in addition define new properties. On the other hand, since a child class is a more specialized (or restricted) form of the parent class, it is also, in a certain sense, a *contraction* of the parent type. For example, the Java library JFrame represents any type of window, but a PinBallGame frame is restricted to a single type of game. This tension between inheritance as expansion and inheritance as contraction is a source for much of the power inherent in the technique, but at the same time it causes much confusion as to its proper employment. We will see this when we examine a few of the uses of inheritance in a subsequent section.

Inheritance is always transitive, so that a class can inherit features from superclasses many levels away. That is, if class Dog is a subclass of class Mammal, and class Mammal is a subclass of class Animal, then Dog will inherit attributes both from Mammal and from Animal.

A complicating factor in our intuitive description of inheritance is the fact that subclasses can *override* behavior inherited from parent classes. For example, the class Platypus overrides the reproduction behavior inherited from class Mammal, since platypuses lay eggs. The mechanics of overriding is treated briefly in this chapter and in more detail in Chapter 11.

8.2   THE BASE CLASS OBJECT

In Java all classes use inheritance. Unless specified otherwise, all classes are derived from a single root class, named Object. If no parent class is explicitly provided, the class Object is implicitly assumed. Thus, the class declaration for FirstProgram (Chapter 4, Figure 4.1) is the same as the following:

```
class FirstProgram extends Object {
    // ...
    };
```

The class Object provides minimal functionality guaranteed to be common to all objects. These include the following methods:

equals (Object obj)   Determine whether the argument object is the same as the receiver. This method is often overridden to change the equality test for different classes.

getClass ()   Returns the class of the receiver, an object of type Class (see Section 15.5).

hashCode () Returns a hash value for this object (see Section 19.7). This method should also be overridden when the equals method is changed.

toString () Converts object into a string value. This method is also often overridden.

8.3 Subclass, Subtype, and Substitutability

The concept of *substitutability* is fundamental to many of the most powerful software development techniques in object-oriented programming. The idea of substitutability is that the type given in a declaration of a variable does not have to match the type associated with a value the variable is holding. Note that this is never true in conventional programming languages but is a common occurrence in object-oriented programs.

We have seen several examples of substitutability in our earlier case studies. In the Pin Ball Game program described in Chapter 7, the variable target was declared as a PinBallTarget, but in fact held a variety of different types of values that were created using implementations of PinBallTarget. (These target values were held in the vector named targets.)

```
PinBallTarget target = (PinBallTarget) targets.elementAt(j);
```

Substitutability can also occur through the use of interfaces. An example is the instance of the class FireButtonListener created in the Cannon Game (Chapter 6). The class from which this value was defined was declared as implementing the interface ActionListener. Because it implements the ActionListener interface, we can use this value as a parameter to a method (in this case, addActionListener) that expects an ActionListener value.

```
public class CannonWorld extends JFrame {
    .
    .

    private class FireButtonListener implements ActionListener {
        public void actionPerformed (ActionEvent e) {
            .
            .
        }
    }

    public CannonWorld () {
        .
        .

        fire.addActionListener(new FireButtonListener());
    }
}
```

Because Object is a parent class to all objects, a variable declared using this type can hold any nonprimitive value. The collection class Vector makes use of this property, holding its values in an array of Object values. Because the array is declared as Object, any object value can be stored in a Vector.

When new classes are constructed using inheritance from existing classes, the argument used to justify the validity of substitutability is as follows:

- Instances of the subclass must possess all data fields associated with the parent class.

- Instances of the subclass must implement, through inheritance at least (if not explicitly overridden) all functionality defined for the parent class. (They can also define new functionality, but that is unimportant for the argument.)

- Thus, an instance of a child class can mimic the behavior of the parent class and should be *indistinguishable* from an instance of the parent class if substituted in a similar situation.

We will see later in this chapter, when we examine the various ways in which inheritance can be used, that this is not always a valid argument. Thus, not all subclasses formed using inheritance are candidates for substitution.

The term *subtype* is used to describe the relationship between types that explicitly recognizes the principle of substitution. That is, a type B is considered to be a subtype of A if two conditions hold. The first is that an instance of B can legally be assigned to a variable declared as type A. And the second is that this value can then be used by the variable with no observable change in behavior.

The term *subclass* refers merely to the mechanics of constructing a new class using inheritance, and is easy to recognize from the source description of a program by the presence of the keyword extends. The *subtype* relationship is more abstract, and is only loosely documented directly by the program source. In the majority of situations a subclass is also a subtype. However, later in this chapter we will discover ways in which subclasses can be formed that are not subtypes. In addition, subtypes can be formed using interfaces, linking types that have no inheritance relationship whatsoever. So it is important to understand both the similarities and the differences between these two concepts.

8.4   FORMS OF INHERITANCE

Inheritance is employed in a surprising variety of ways. Presented in this section are a few of its more common uses. Note that the following list represents general abstract categories and is not intended to be exhaustive. Furthermore, it sometimes happens that two or more descriptions are applicable to a single situation, because some methods in a single class use inheritance in one way while others use it in another. In the following list, pay attention to which uses of inheritance support the subtyping relationship and which do not.

8.4.1 *Inheritance for Specialization*

Probably the most common use of inheritance and subclassification is for specialization. In this form, the new class is a specialized variety of the parent class but it satisfies the specifications of the parent in all relevant respects. Thus, this form always creates a subtype, and the principle of substitutability is explicitly upheld. Along with the following category (subclassification for specification) this is the most ideal form of inheritance, and something that a good design should strive for.

The creation of application window classes using inheritance from the Java library class JFrame is an example of subclassification for specialization. The following is from the PinBallGame program in Chapter 7.

```
public class PinBallGame extends JFrame {
    :
    :
}
```

To run such an application, an instance of PinBallGame is first created. Various methods inherited from class JFrame, such as setSize, setTitle, and show, are then invoked. These methods do not realize they are manipulating an instance of PinBallGame, but instead act as if they were operating on an instance of JFrame. The actions they perform would be the same for any instance of class JFrame.

Where application-specific behavior is necessary, for example, in repainting the window, a method is invoked that is overridden by the application class. For example, the method in the parent class will invoke the method paint. Although the parent class JFrame possesses a method of this name, the parent method is not the one executed. Instead, the method defined in the child class is executed.

We say that subclassification for specialization occurs in this example because the child class (in this example, PinBallGame) satisfies all the properties that we expect of the parent class (JFrame). In addition, the new class overrides one or more methods, specializing them with application-specific behavior.

8.4.2 *Inheritance for Specification*

Another frequent use for inheritance is to guarantee that classes maintain a certain common interface—that is, they implement methods having the same headings. The parent class can be a combination of implemented operations and operations that are deferred to the child classes. Often, there is no interface change of any sort between the parent class and the child class—the child merely implements the methods described, but not implemented, in the parent.

This is actually a special case of subclassification for specialization, except that the subclasses are not refinements of an existing type but rather realizations of an incomplete abstract specification. That is, the parent class defines the operation but has no implementation. It is only the child class that provides an implementation. In such cases the parent class is sometimes known as an *abstract specification class*.

There are two different mechanisms provided by the Java language to support the idea of inheritance of specification. The most obvious technique is the use of interfaces. We have seen examples of this in the way that events are handled by the Java library. For instance, the characteristics needed for an ActionListener (the object type that responds to button presses) can be described by a single method, and the implementation of that method cannot be predicted, since it differs from one application to another. Thus, an interface is used to describe only the necessary requirements, and no actual behavior is inherited by a subclass that implements the behavior.

```
interface ActionListener {
    public void actionPerformed (ActionEvent e);
    }
```

When a button is created, an associated listener class is defined. The listener class provides the specific behavior for the method in the context of the current application.

```
public class CannonWorld extends JFrame {
    :
    :

        // a fire button listener implements the action listener interface
    private class FireButtonListener implements ActionListener {
        public void actionPerformed (ActionEvent e) {
        ... // action to perform in response to button press
        }
    }
}
```

Subclassification for specification can also take place with inheritance of classes formed using extension. One way to guarantee that a subclass must be constructed is to use the keyword abstract. A class declared as abstract must be subclassed; it is not possible to create an instance of such a class using the operator new. In addition, individual methods can also be declared as abstract, and they, too, must be overridden before instances can be constructed.

An example abstract class in the Java library is Number, a parent class for the numeric wrapper classes Integer, Long, Double, and so on. The class description is as follows:

```
public abstract class Number {

    public abstract int intValue( );

    public abstract long longValue( );

    public abstract float floatValue( );

    public abstract double doubleValue( );

    public byte byteValue( )
        { return (byte) intValue( ); }

    public short shortValue( )
        { return (short) intValue( ); }
}
```

Subclasses of Number must override the methods intValue, longValue, floatValue, and doubleValue. Notice that not all methods in an abstract class must themselves be declared abstract. Subclasses of Number need not override byteValue or shortValue, as these methods are provided with an implementation that can be inherited without change.

In general, subclassification for specification can be recognized when the parent class does not implement actual behavior but merely provides the headings for methods that must be implemented in child classes.

8.4.3 *Inheritance for Construction*

A class can often inherit almost all of its desired functionality from a parent class, perhaps changing only the names of the methods used to interface to the class, or modifying the arguments. This may be true even if the new class and the parent class fail to share any relationship as abstract concepts.

An example of subclassification for construction occurred in the pinball game application described in Chapter 7. In that program, the class Hole was declared as a subclass of Ball. There is no logical relationship between the concepts of a Ball and a Hole, but from a practical point of view much of the behavior needed for the Hole abstraction matches the behavior of the class Ball. Thus, using inheritance in this situation reduces the amount of work necessary to develop the class Hole.

```
class Hole extends Ball implements PinBallTarget {

    public Hole (int x, int y) {
        super (x, y, 12);
        setColor (Color.black);
    }
```

```
    public boolean intersects (Ball aBall)
        { return location.intersects(aBall.location); }

    public void hitBy (Ball aBall) {
            // move ball totally off frame
        aBall.moveTo (0, PinBallGame.FrameHeight + 30);
            // stop motion of ball
        aBall.setMotion(0, 0);
    }
}
```

Another example of inheritance for construction occurs in the Java library. There, the class Stack is constructed using inheritance from the class Vector:

```
class Stack extends Vector {

    public Object push(Object item)
        { addElement(item); return item; }

    public boolean empty ()
        { return isEmpty( ); }

    public synchronized Object pop() {
        Object obj = peek( );
        removeElementAt(size( ) - 1);
        return obj;
    }

    public synchronized Object peek()
        { return elementAt(size( ) - 1); }
}
```

As abstractions, the concept of the stack and the concept of a vector have little in common; however, from a pragmatic point of view using the Vector class as a parent greatly simplifies the implementation of the stack.

Inheritance for **construction** is sometimes frowned upon, since it often directly breaks the principle of substitutability (forming subclasses that are not subtypes). On the other hand, because it is often a fast and easy route to developing new data abstractions, it is nevertheless widely used. See Chapter 10 for a more detailed discussion of the construction of the Stack abstraction.

8.4.4 *Inheritance for Extension*

Subclassification for extension occurs when a child class only adds new behavior to the parent class and does not modify or alter any of the inherited attributes. An example of inheritance for extension in the Java library is the class Properties, which inherits from class HashTable. A hash table is a dictionary structure (see Section 19.7). A dictionary stores a collection of key/value pairs and allows the user to retrieve the value associated with a given key. Properties represent information concerning the current execution environment. Examples of properties are the name of the user running the Java program, the version of the Java interpreter being used, the name of the operating system under which the Java program is running, and so on. The class Properties uses the parent class, HashTable, to store and retrieve the actual property name/value pairs. In addition, the class defines a few methods specific to the task of managing properties, such as reading or writing properties to or from a file.

```
class Properties extends Hashtable {
   .
   .
   .

   public synchronized void load(InputStream in) throws
      IOException { ... }

   public synchronized void save(OutputStream out, String header)
      { ... }

   public String getProperty(String key) { ... }

   public Enumeration propertyNames() { ... }

   public void list(PrintStream out) { ... }
}
```

As the functionality of the parent remains available and untouched, subclassification for extension does not contravene the principle of substitutability, and so such subclasses are always subtypes.

8.4.5 *Inheritance for Limitation*

Subclassification for limitation occurs when the behavior of the subclass is smaller or more restrictive than the behavior of the parent class. Like subclassification for extension, subclassification for limitation occurs most frequently when a programmer is building on a base of existing classes that should not, or cannot, be modified.

Although there are no examples of subclassification for limitation in the Java library, we could imagine the following. Suppose you wanted to create the class Set, in a fashion similar to the way the class Stack is subclassed from Vector. Say you also wanted to *ensure* that only Set operations were used on the set, and not vector operations. One way to accomplish this would be to override the undesired methods, so that if they were executed they would produce obviously incorrect results, or print a message indicating they should not be used.[1]

```
class Set extends Vector {
    // methods addElement, removeElement, contains
    // isEmpty and size
    // are all inherited from vector

    public int indexOf (Object obj)
        { System.out.println("Do not use Set.indexOf"); return 0; }

    public Object elementAt (int index)
        { return null; }
}
```

In theory an alternative would be to have the undesired methods throw an exception. However, the Java compiler does not permit subclasses to override a method and introduce new exceptions that are not already declared in the parent class.

Subclassification for limitation is characterized by the presence of techniques that take a previously permitted method and make it illegal. Because subclassification for limitation is an explicit contravention of the principle of substitutability, and because it builds subclasses that are not subtypes, it should be avoided whenever possible.

8.4.6 *Inheritance for Combination*

When discussing abstract concepts, it is common to form a new abstraction by combining features of two or more abstractions. A teaching assistant, for example, may have characteristics of both a teacher and a student, and can therefore logically behave as both. The ability of a class to inherit from two or more parent classes is known as *multiple inheritance*.

Although the Java language does not permit a subclass to be formed by inheritance from more than one parent class, several approximations to the concept are possible. For example, it is common for a new class to both extend an

---

[1] In actuality, the methods indexOf and elementAt are declared as final in class Vector, so this example will not compile. But it does illustrate the concept.

existing class and implement an interface. We saw this in the example of the class Hole that both extended class Ball and implemented the interface for PinBallTarget.

```
class Hole extends Ball implements PinBallTarget {
   :
   :
}
```

It is also possible for classes to implement more than one interface, and thus be viewed as a combination of the two categories. Many examples occur in the input/output sections of the Java library. A RandomAccessFile, for example, implements both the DataInput and DataOutput protocols.

8.4.7 *Summary of the Forms of Inheritance*

We can summarize the various forms of inheritance by the following list:

Specialization The child class is a special case of the parent class; in other words, the child class is a subtype of the parent class.

Specification The parent class defines behavior that is implemented in the child class but not in the parent class.

Construction The child class makes use of the behavior provided by the parent class but is not a subtype of the parent class.

Extension The child class adds new functionality to the parent class, but does not change any inherited behavior.

Limitation The child class restricts the use of some of the behavior inherited from the parent class.

Combination The child class inherits features from more than one parent class. Although multiple inheritance is not supported directly by Java, it can be simulated in part by classes that use both inheritance and implementation of an interface, or implement two or more interfaces.

The Java language implicitly assumes that subclasses are also subtypes. This means that an instance of a subclass can be assigned to a variable declared as the parent class type. Methods in the child class that have the same name as those in the parent class override the inherited behavior. We have seen that this assumption that subclasses are subtypes is not always valid, and creating subclasses that are not subtypes is a possible source of program error.

8.5 MODIFIERS AND INHERITANCE

The language Java provides several modifiers that can be used to alter aspects of the inheritance process. For example, in the case studies in earlier chapters, we made extensive use of the visibility (or access control) modifiers public, protected, and private.

- A public feature (data field or method) can be accessed outside the class definition. A public class can be accessed outside the package in which it is declared.

- A protected feature can be accessed only within the class definition in which it appears, within other classes in the same package, or within the definition of subclasses.

- A private feature can be accessed only within the class definition in which it appears.

The earlier case studies illustrated how both methods and data fields can be declared as static. A static field is shared by all instances of a class. A static method can be invoked even when no instance of the class has been created. Static data fields and methods are inherited in the same manner as nonstatic items, except that static methods cannot be overridden.

Both methods and classes can be declared to be abstract. An abstract class cannot be instanciated. That is, it is not legal to create an instance of an abstraction class using the operator new. Such a class can only be used as a parent class, to create a new type of object. Similarly, an abstract method must be overridden by a subclass.

An alternative modifier, final, is the opposite of abstract. When applied to a class, the keyword indicates that the class *cannot* be subclassified. Similarly, when applied to a method, the keyword indicates that the method cannot be overridden. Thus, the user is guaranteed that the behavior of the class will be as defined and not modified by a later subclass.

```
final class newClass extends oldClass {
   .
   .
   .
}
```

We have seen that program constants are generally defined by variables that are both static and final:

```
public class CannonGame extends JFrame {
   .
   .
   .
   public static final int FrameWidth = 600;
```

```
    public static final int FrameHeight = 400;
       .
       .
       .
}
```

Optimizing compilers can sometimes make use of the fact that a data field, class, or method is declared as final and can thus generate better code than would otherwise be possible.

8.6 PROGRAMMING AS A MULTIPERSON ACTIVITY

When programs are constructed out of reusable, off-the-shelf components, programming moves from an individual activity (one programmer and the computer) to a community effort. A programmer may operate both as the *developer* of new abstractions and as the *user* of a software system created by an earlier programmer. The reader should not confuse the term *user* when applied to a programmer with the same term denoting the application end-user. Similarly, we will often speak of the organization of several objects by describing a *client* object that is requesting the services of a *provider*. Again, the client in this case is likely a programmer (or the code being developed by a programmer) making use of the services developed by an earlier programmer. This should not be confused with the idea of *client/server* computing, as described in Chapter 2.

8.7 THE BENEFITS OF INHERITANCE

In this section we will describe some of the many important benefits of the proper use of inheritance.

8.7.1 Software Reusability

When behavior is inherited from another class, the code that provides that behavior does not have to be rewritten. This may seem obvious, but the implications are important. Many programmers spend much of their time rewriting code they have written many times before—for example, to search for a pattern in a string or to insert a new element into a table. With object-oriented techniques, these functions can be written once and reused.

8.7.2 Increased Reliability

Code that is executed frequently tends to have fewer bugs than code that is executed infrequently. When the same components are used in two or more applications, the code will be exercised more than code that is developed for a single application. Thus, bugs in such code tend to be discovered more quickly, and latter applications gain the benefit of using components that are more error free. Similarly, the costs of maintenance of shared components can be split among many projects.

8.7.3 Code Sharing

Code sharing can occur on several levels with object-oriented techniques. On one level, many users or projects can use the same classes. (Brad Cox [1986] calls these software-ICs, in analogy to the integrated circuits used in hardware design.) Another form of sharing occurs when two or more classes developed by a single programmer as part of a project inherit from a single parent class. For example, a Set and an Array may both be considered a form of Collection. When this happens, two or more types of objects will share the code that they inherit. This code needs to be written only once and will contribute only once to the size of the resulting program.

8.7.4 Consistency of Interface

When two or more classes inherit from the same superclass, we are assured that the behavior they inherit will be the same in all cases. Thus, it is easier to guarantee that interfaces to similar objects are in fact similar and that the user is not presented with a confusing collection of objects that are almost the same but behave, and are interacted with, very differently.

8.7.5 Software Components

Inheritance enables programmers to construct reusable software components. The goal is to permit the development of new and novel applications that nevertheless require little or no actual coding. The Java library offers a rich collection of software components for use in the development of applications.

8.7.6 Rapid Prototyping

When a software system is constructed largely out of reusable components, developers can concentrate their time on understanding the new and unusual portion of the system. Thus, software systems can be generated more quickly and easily, leading to a style of programming known as *rapid prototyping* or *exploratory programming*. A prototype system is developed, users experiment with it, a second system is produced that is based on experience with the first, further experimentation takes place, and so on for several iterations. Such programming is particularly useful in situations where the goals and requirements of the system are only vaguely understood when the project begins.

8.7.7 *Polymorphism and Frameworks*

Software produced conventionally is generally written from the bottom up, although it may be *designed* from the top down. That is, the lower-level routines are written, and on top of these, slightly higher abstractions are produced, and on top of these even more abstract elements are generated. This process is like building a wall, where every brick must be laid on top of an already laid brick.

Normally, code portability decreases as one moves up the levels of abstraction. That is, the lowest-level routines may be used in several different projects, and perhaps even the next level of abstraction may be reused, but the higher-level routines are intimately tied to a particular application. The lower-level pieces can be carried to a new system and generally make sense standing on their own; the higher-level components generally make sense (because of declarations or data dependencies) only when they are built on top of specific lower-level units.

Polymorphism in programming languages permits the programmer to generate high-level reusable components that can be tailored to fit different applications by changes in their low-level parts. The Java AWT is an example of a large software framework that relies on inheritance and substitutability for its operation.

8.7.8 *Information Hiding*

A programmer who reuses a software component needs only to understand the nature of the component and its interface. It is not necessary for the programmer to have detailed information concerning matters such as the techniques used to implement the component. Thus, the interconnectedness between software systems is reduced. As mentioned earlier in this book, the interconnected nature of conventional software is one of the principal causes of software complexity.

8.8 THE COSTS OF INHERITANCE

Although the benefits of inheritance in object-oriented programming are great, almost nothing is without cost of one sort or another. For this reason, we must consider the cost of object-oriented programming techniques, and in particular the cost of inheritance.

8.8.1 *Execution Speed*

It is seldom possible for general purpose software tools to be as fast as carefully handcrafted systems. Thus, inherited methods, which must deal with arbitrary subclasses, are often slower than specialized code.

Yet, concern about efficiency is often misplaced.[2] First, the difference in speed or complexity is often small. Second, the reduction in execution speed may be balanced by an increase in the speed of software development. Finally, most programmers actually have little idea of how execution time is being used in their programs. It is far better to develop a working system, monitor it to discover where execution time is being used, and improve those sections, than to spend an inordinate amount of time worrying about efficiency early in a project.

8.8.2   *Program Size*

The use of any software library frequently imposes a size penalty not imposed by systems constructed for a specific project. Although this expense may be substantial, as memory costs decrease, the size of programs becomes less important. Containing development costs and producing high-quality and error-free code rapidly are now more important than limiting the size of programs.

8.8.3   *Message-Passing Overhead*

Much has been made of the fact that passing messages is by nature a more costly operation than simply invoking procedures. As with overall execution speed, however, overconcern about the cost of message passing is frequently penny wise and pound foolish. For one thing, the increased cost is often marginal—perhaps two or three additional assembly-language instructions and a total time penalty of 10 percent. This increased cost, like others, must be weighed against the many benefits of the object-oriented technique.

8.8.4   *Program Complexity*

Although object-oriented programming is often touted as a solution to software complexity, in fact, overuse of inheritance can often simply replace one form of complexity with another. Understanding the control flow of a program that uses inheritance may require several multiple scans up and down the inheritance graph. This is what is known as the *yo-yo* problem, which we will discuss in more detail in a later chapter.

8.9   CHAPTER SUMMARY

Inheritance is a mechanism for relating a new software abstraction being developed to an older, existing abstraction. By stating that the new component inherits

---

[2] The following quote from an article by Bill Wulf is an apt remark on the importance of efficiency: "More computing sins are committed in the name of efficiency (without necessarily achieving it) than for any other single reason—including blind stupidity" [Wulf 1972/1979].

(or *extends*) the older abstraction, the programmer means that all the public and protected properties of the original class are also now part of the new abstraction. In addition, the new class can add new data fields and behavior, and can override methods that are inherited from the original class. Interfaces are a closely related mechanism, which tie the concrete realization of behavior to an abstract description.

All classes in Java use inheritance. If their inheritance is not explicitly stated, classes are assumed to inherit from the fundamental root class Object.

Inheritance is tied to the principle of substitutability. A variable that is declared as one class can be assigned a value that is created from a child class. A similar mechanism also works with interfaces. A class that can be used in lieu of another class is said to be a *subtype*. Java implicitly assumes that all subclasses are subtypes. However, this need not be true (a subclass can override a method in an incompatible fashion, for example). Subtypes can also be constructed from interfaces, avoiding subclasses altogether.

There are many different types of inheritance, used for different purposes. Variations include specialization, specification, construction, extension, limitation, and combination.

A variety of modifiers alter the meaning of inheritance. A private feature is not inherited by subclasses. A static feature (data field or method) is shared by all instances. An abstract method must be overridden. A final feature (data field or method) cannot be overridden.

STUDY QUESTIONS

1. Give an intuitive description of inheritance.

2. What does it mean for a method to override an inherited method?

3. What is the name of the root class for all objects in Java?

4. What behavior is provided by the root class in Java?

5. What does it mean to say that child classes are substitutable for parent classes in Java?

6. What is the difference between a subclass and a subtype?

7. What are the characteristics of inheritance for specialization?

8. What are the characteristics of inheritance for specification? How does this differ from inheritance for specialization?

9. What is the difference between an abstract class and an interface?

10. What are the characteristics of inheritance for construction? Why is construction not generally considered to be a good use of inheritance?

11. What are the characteristics of inheritance for extension?

12. What are the characteristics of inheritance for limitation? Why is limitation not generally considered to be a good use of inheritance?

13. Why would it not make sense for a method in Java to be declared both abstract and final?

14. What are some of the benefits of developing classes using inheritance, rather than developing each new class from scratch?

15. What are some of the costs of using inheritance for software development?

EXERCISES

1. Suppose you were required to program a project in a non-object-oriented language, such as Pascal or C. How would you simulate the notion of classes and methods? How would you simulate inheritance? Could you support multiple inheritance? Explain your answer.

2. We noted that the execution overhead associated with message passing is typically greater than the overhead associated with a conventional procedure call. How might you measure these overheads? For a language that supports both classes and procedures (such as C++ or Object Pascal), devise an experiment to determine the actual performance penalty of message passing.

3. Consider the three geometric concepts of a line (infinite in both directions), a ray (fixed at a point, infinite in one direction), and a segment (a portion of a line with fixed end points). How might you structure classes representing these three concepts in an inheritance hierarchy? Would your answer differ if you concentrated more on the data representation or more on the behavior? Characterize the type of inheritance you would use. Explain the reasoning behind your design.

4. Why is the example used in the following explanation not a valid illustration of inheritance?

> Perhaps the most powerful concept in object-oriented programming systems is inheritance. Objects can be created by inheriting the properties of other objects, thus removing the need to write any code whatsoever! Suppose, for example, a program is to process complex numbers consisting of real and imaginary parts. In a complex number, the real and imaginary parts behave like real numbers, so all of the operations (+, −, /, *, sqrt, sin, cos, etc.) can be inherited from the class of objects called REAL, instead of having to be written in code. This has a major impact on programmer productivity.

9 A Case Study: Solitaire

A program for playing the card game *Solitaire* will illustrate the utility and power of inheritance and overriding. A major part of the game of Solitaire is moving cards from one pile of cards to another. There are a number of different types of card piles, each having some features in common with the others, while other features are unique. A parent class can therefore be used to capture the common elements, while inheritance and overriding can be used to produce specialized types of piles. The development of this program will illustrate how inheritance can be used to simplify the creation of these components and ensure that they can all be manipulated in a similar fashion.

9.1 THE CLASS Card

To create a card game, we first need to define a class to represent a playing card. Each instance of class Card (Figure 9.1) maintains a suit value and a rank. To prevent modification of these values, the instance variables maintaining them are declared private and access is mediated through *accessor methods*. The value of the suit and rank fields are set by the constructor for the class. Integer constant values (in Java defined by the use of final static constants) are defined for the height and width of the card as well as for the suits. Another method permits the user to determine the color of the card. The Java library class Color is used to represent the color abstraction. The Color class defines constants for various colors. The values Color.red, Color.black, Color.yellow, and Color.blue are used in the Solitaire program.

There are important reasons that data values representing suit and rank should be returned through an accessor method, as opposed to defining the data fields s and r as public and allowing direct access to the data values. One of the most important is that access through a method ensures that the rank and suit characteristics of a card can be read but not altered once the card has been created.

145

```
import java.awt.*;

public class Card {
      // public constants for card width and suits
   public final static int width = 50;
   public final static int height = 70;
   public final static int heart = 0;
   public final static int spade = 1;
   public final static int diamond = 2;
   public final static int club = 3;
      // internal data fields for rank and suit
   private boolean faceup;
   private int r;
   private int s;

      // constructor
   Card (int sv, int rv) { s = sv; r = rv; faceup = false; }

      // access attributes of card
   public final int rank () { return r; }

   public final int suit() { return s; }

   public final boolean faceUp() { return faceup; }

   public final void flip() { faceup = ! faceup; }

   public final Color color() {
      if (faceUp())
         if (suit() == heart || suit() == diamond)
            return Color.red;
         else
            return Color.black;
      return Color.yellow;  → card is face down.
      }

   public void draw (Graphics g, int x, int y) { ... }
}
```

Figure 9.1 Description of the class Card.

Note that many of the methods in the Card abstraction have been declared as final. This modifier serves two important purposes. First, it is a documentation aid, signaling to the reader of the listing that the methods cannot be overridden by subclasses. Second, in some situations the Java compiler can optimize the invocation of final methods, creating faster code than could be generated for the execution of non-final methods.

The only other actions a card can perform, besides setting and returning the state of the card, are to flip over and to display itself. The method flip() is a one-line function that simply reverses the value held by an instance variable. The drawing method is more complex, making use of the drawing facilities provided by the Java standard application library. As seen in the earlier case studies, the application library provides a data type called Graphics that provides a variety of methods for drawing lines and common shapes, as well as for coloring. An argument of this type is passed to the draw method, as are the integer coordinates representing the upper left corner of the card.

The card images are simple line drawings, as shown in Figure 9.3. Diamonds and hearts are drawn in red, spades and clubs in black. The hash marks on the back are drawn in yellow. A portion of the method for drawing a playing card is shown in Figure 9.2.

The most important feature of the playing-card abstraction is the manner in which each card is responsible for maintaining within itself all card-related information and behaviors. The card knows both its value and how to draw itself. In this manner the information is encapsulated and isolated from the application using the playing card. If, for example, one were to move the program to a new platform using different graphics facilities, only the draw method within the class itself would need to be altered.

9.2   THE GAME

The version of Solitaire we will describe is known as Klondike. The countless variations on this game make it probably the most common version of Solitaire; so much so that when you say "Solitaire," most people think of Klondike. The version we will use is that described in [Morehead and Mott-Smith 1949]; in the exercises we will explore some of the common variations.

The layout of the game is shown in Figure 9.4. A single standard pack of 52 cards is used. The *tableau*, or playing table, consists of 28 cards in 7 piles. the first pile has 1 card, the second 2, and so on up to 7. The top card of each pile is initially face up; all other cards are face down.

The suit piles (sometimes called *foundations*) are built up from aces to kings in suits. They are constructed above the tableau as the cards become available. The object of the game is to build all 52 cards into the suit piles.

The cards that are not part of the tableau are initially all in the *deck*. Cards in the deck are face down, and are drawn one by one from the deck and placed,

```
public class Card {
    .
    .
    .
    public void    draw (Graphics g, int x, int y) {
        String names[] = {"A", "2", "3", "4", "5", "6",
                "7", "8", "9", "10", "J", "Q", "K"};
            // clear rectangle, draw border
        g.clearRect(x, y, width, height);
        g.setColor(Color.blue);
        g.drawRect(x, y, width, height);
            // draw body of card
        g.setColor(color());
        if (faceUp()) {
            g.drawString(names[rank()], x+3, y+15);
            if (suit() == heart) {
                g.drawLine(x+25, y+30, x+35, y+20);
                g.drawLine(x+35, y+20, x+45, y+30);
                g.drawLine(x+45, y+30, x+25, y+60);
                g.drawLine(x+25, y+60, x+5, y+30);
                g.drawLine(x+5, y+30, x+15, y+20);
                g.drawLine(x+15, y+20, x+25, y+30);
                }
            else if (suit() == spade) { ... }
            else if (suit() == diamond) { ... }
            else if (suit() == club) {
                g.drawOval(x+20, y+25, 10, 10);
                g.drawOval(x+25, y+35, 10, 10);
                g.drawOval(x+15, y+35, 10, 10);
                g.drawLine(x+23, y+45, x+20, y+55);
                g.drawLine(x+20, y+55, x+30, y+55);
                g.drawLine(x+30, y+55, x+27, y+45);
                }
            }
        else { // face down
            g.drawLine(x+15, y+5, x+15, y+65);
            g.drawLine(x+35, y+5, x+35, y+65);
            g.drawLine(x+5, y+20, x+45, y+20);
            g.drawLine(x+5, y+35, x+45, y+35);
            g.drawLine(x+5, y+50, x+45, y+50);
            }
        }
}
```

Figure 9.2   Method to draw a playing card.

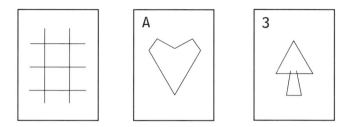

Figure 9.3   Card images for Solitaire.

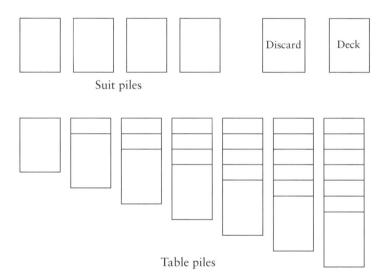

Figure 9.4   Layout for the Solitaire game.

face up, on the *discard pile*. From there, they can be moved onto either a tableau pile or a foundation. Cards are drawn from the deck until the pile is empty; at this point, the game is over if no further moves can be made.

Cards can be placed on a tableau pile only on a card of next-higher rank and opposite color. They can be placed on a foundation only if they are the same suit and next higher card or if the foundation is empty and the card is an ace. Spaces in the tableau that arise during play can be filled only by kings.

The topmost card of each tableau pile and the topmost card of the discard pile are always available for play. The only time more than one card is moved is when an entire collection of face-up cards from a tableau (called a *build*) is moved to another tableau pile. This can be done if the bottommost card of the build can be legally played on the topmost card of the destination. Our initial game will not support the transfer of a build, but we will discuss this as a possible extension. The topmost card of a tableau is always face up. If a card is moved from a tableau, leaving a face-down card on the top, the latter card can be turned face up.

From this short description, it is clear that the game of Solitaire mostly involves manipulating piles of cards. Each type of pile has many features in common with the others and a few aspects unique to the particular type. In the next section, we will investigate in detail how inheritance can be used in such circumstances to simplify the implementation of the various card piles by providing a common base for the generic actions and permitting this base to be redefined when necessary.

9.3   CARD PILES—INHERITANCE IN ACTION

Much of the behavior we associate with a card pile is common to each variety of pile in the game. For example, each pile maintains a collection of the cards in the pile (held in a Stack), and the operations of inserting and deleting elements from this collection are common. Other operations are given default behavior in the class CardPile, but they are sometimes overridden in the various subclasses. The class CardPile is shown in Figure 9.5.

Each card pile maintains the coordinate location for the upper left corner of the pile, as well as a Stack. The stack is used to hold the cards in the pile. All three of these values are set by the constructor for the class. The data fields are declared as protected and thus accessible to member functions associated with this class, with other classes in the same package, and to member functions associated with subclasses.

The three methods top(), pop(), and isEmpty() manipulate the list of cards, using methods provided by the Stack utility class. Note that these three methods have been declared final, and can not therefore be overridden in subclasses.

The topmost card in a pile is returned by the method top(). This card will be the last card in the underlying container. Note that the method peek() provided by the Stack class returns a value declared as Object. This result must be cast to a Card value before it can be returned as the result.

The method pop() uses the similarly named operation provided by the underlying stack. The stack method generates an exception if an attempt is made to remove an element from an empty stack. The pop() method in the class CardPile catches the exception and returns a null value in this situation.

The five operations that are not declared final are common to the abstract notion of our card piles, but they differ in details in each case. For example, the method canTake(Card) asks whether it is legal to place a card on the given pile. A card can be added to a foundation pile, for instance, only if it is an ace and the foundation is empty, or if the card is of the same suit as the current topmost card

```java
import java.util.Stack;
import java.util.EmptyStackException;

public class CardPile {
    protected int x; // coordinates of the card pile
    protected int y;
    protected Stack thePile; // the collection of cards

    CardPile (int xl, int yl) { x = xl; y = yl; thePile = new Stack( ); }

    public final Card top( ) { return (Card) thePile.peek( ); }

    public final boolean isEmpty( ) { return thePile.empty( ); }

    public final Card pop( ) {
        try {
            return (Card) thePile.pop( );
        } catch (EmptyStackException e) { return null; }
    }

    // the following are sometimes overridden
    public boolean includes (int tx, int ty) {
        return x <= tx && tx <= x + Card.width &&
            y <= ty && ty <= y + Card.height;
    }

    public void select (int tx, int ty) { }

    public void addCard (Card aCard)  { thePile.push(aCard); }

    public void display (Graphics g) {
        g.setColor(Color.blue);
        if (isEmpty( )) g.drawRect(x, y, Card.width, Card.height);
        else top( ).draw(g, x, y);
    }

    public boolean canTake (Card aCard) { return false; }
}
```

Figure 9.5 Description of the class CardPile.

in the pile and has the next-higher value. A card can be added to a tableau pile, on the other hand, only if the pile is empty and the card is a king, or if it is of the opposite color as the current topmost card in the pile and has the next lower value.

The actions of the five non-final methods defined in CardPile can be characterized as follows:

includes   Determines if the coordinates given as arguments are contained within the boundaries of the pile. The default action simply tests the topmost card; this is overridden in the tableau piles to test all card values.

canTake   Tells whether a pile can take a specific card. Only the tableau and suit piles can take cards, so the default action is simply to return no; this is overridden in the two classes mentioned.

addCard   Adds a card to the card list. It is redefined in the discard pile class to ensure that the card is face up.

display   Displays the card deck. The default method merely displays the topmost card of the pile, but it is overridden in the tableau class to display a column of cards. The top half of each hidden card is displayed. So that the playing surface area is conserved, only the topmost and bottommost face-up cards are displayed (this permits us to give definite bounds to the playing surface).

select   Performs an action in response to a mouse click. It is invoked when the user selects a pile by clicking the mouse in the portion of the playing field covered by the pile. The default action does nothing, but it is overridden by the table, deck, and discard piles to play the topmost card, if possible.

Table 9.1 illustrates the important benefits of inheritance. Given five operations and five classes, there are 25 potential methods we might have had to define. By making use of inheritance we need to implement only 13. Furthermore, we are guaranteed that each pile will respond in the same way to similar requests.

Table 9.1   The benefits of inheritance.

	CardPile	SuitPile	DeckPile	DiscardPile	TableauPile
includes	×				×
canTake	×	×			×
addCard	×			×	
display	×				×
select	×		×	×	×

```
class SuitPile extends CardPile {

    SuitPile (int x, int y) { super(x, y); }

    public boolean canTake (Card aCard) {
        if (isEmpty())
            return aCard.rank() == 0;
        Card topCard = top();
        return (aCard.suit() == topCard.suit()) &&
            (aCard.rank() == 1 + topCard.rank());
    }
}
```

Figure 9.6 The class SuitPile.

9.3.1 *The Suit Piles*

We will examine each of the subclasses of CardPile in detail, pointing out various uses of object-oriented features as they are encountered. The simplest subclass is the class SuitPile, shown in Figure 9.6, which represents the pile of cards at the top of the playing surface, the pile being built up in suit from ace to king.

The class SuitPile defines only two methods. The constructor for the class takes two integer arguments and does nothing more than invoke the constructor for the parent class CardPile. Note the use of the keyword super to indicate the parent class. The method canTake determines whether or not a card can be placed on the pile. A card is legal if the pile is empty and the card is an ace (that is, has rank zero) or if the card is the same suit as the topmost card in the pile and of the next higher rank (for example, a three of spades can only be played on a two of spades).

All other behavior of the suit pile is the same as that of our generic card pile. When selected, a suit pile does nothing. When a card is added, it is simply inserted into the collection of cards. To display the pile only the topmost card is drawn.

9.3.2 *The Deck Pile*

The DeckPile (Figure 9.7) maintains the original deck of cards. It differs from the generic card pile in two ways. When constructed, rather than creating an empty pile of cards, it creates the complete deck of 52 cards, inserting them in order into the collection. Once all the cards have been created, the collection is then shuffled. To do this, a *random number generator* is first created. This generator is provided by the Java utility class Random. A loop then examines each card in turn, exchanging the card with another randomly selected card. To produce the index of the latter card, the random number generator first produces a randomly selected integer value (using by the method nextInt). Since this value could potentially be negative, the math library function abs is called to make it

```
class DeckPile extends CardPile {

    DeckPile (int x, int y) {
            // first initialize parent
        super(x, y);
            // then create the new deck
            // first put them into a local pile
        for (int i = 0; i < 4; i++)
            for (int j = 0; j <= 12; j++)
                addCard(new Card(i, j));

            // then shuffle the cards
        Random generator = new Random();
        for (int i = 0; i < 52; i++) {
            int j = Math.abs(generator.nextInt()) % 52;
            // swap the two card values
            Object temp = thePile.elementAt(i);
            thePile.setElementAt(thePile.elementAt(j), i);
            thePile.setElementAt(temp, j);
            }
        }

    public void select(int tx, int ty) {
        if (isEmpty())
            return;
        Solitare.discardPile.addCard(pop());
        }
}
```

Figure 9.7   The class DeckPile.

positive. The modular division operation is finally used to produce a randomly selected integer value between 0 and 51.

A subtle feature to note is that we are here performing a random access to the elements of a Stack. The conventional view of a stack does not allow access to any but the topmost element. However, in the Java library the Stack container is constructed using inheritance from the Vector class. Thus, any legal operation on a Vector, such as the method elementAt(), can also be applied to a Stack.

The method select is invoked when the mouse button is used to select the card deck. If the deck is empty, it does nothing. Otherwise, the topmost card is removed from the deck and added to the discard pile.

Java does not have global variables. Where a value is shared between multiple instances of similar classes, such as the various piles used in our Solitaire game, an instance variable can be declared static. As noted in Chapter 4, one copy of a static variable is created and shared among all instances. In the present program, static variables will be used to maintain all the various card piles. These will be held in an instance of class Solitaire, described subsequently. To access these values we use a complete qualified name, which includes the name of the class as well as the name of the variable. This is shown in the select method in Figure 9.7, which refers to the variable Solitare.discardPile to access the discard pile.

9.3.3 *The Discard Pile*

The class DiscardPile (Figure 9.8) is interesting in that it exhibits two very different forms of inheritance. The select method *overrides* or *replaces* the default behavior provided by class CardPile, replacing it with code that when invoked (when the mouse is pressed over the card pile), checks to see if the topmost card can be played on any suit pile or, alternatively, on any tableau pile. If the card cannot be played, it is kept in the discard pile.

The method addCard is a different sort of overriding. Here the behavior is a *refinement* of the default behavior in the parent class. That is, the behavior of the parent class is completely executed, and, in addition, new behavior is added. In this case, the new behavior ensures that when a card is placed on the discard pile it is always face up. After satisfying this condition, the code in the parent class is invoked to add the card to the pile by passing the message to the pseudovariable named super.

Another form of refinement occurs in the constructors for the various subclasses. Each must invoke the constructor for the parent class to guarantee that the parent is properly initialized before the constructor performs its own actions. The parent constructor is invoked by the pseudovariable super being used as a method inside the constructor for the child class. Chapter 12 has much more about the distinction between replacement and refinement in overriding.

9.3.4 *The Tableau Piles*

The most complex of the subclasses of CardPile is that used to hold a tableau, or table pile. It is shown in Figures 9.9 and 9.10. Table piles differ from the generic card pile in the following ways:

- When initialized (by the constructor), the table pile removes a certain number of cards from the deck, placing them in its pile. The number of cards so removed is determined by an additional argument to the constructor. The topmost card of this pile is then displayed face up.

- A card can be added to the pile (method canTake) only if the pile is empty and the card is a king, or if the card is the opposite color from that of the current topmost card and one smaller in rank.

```
class DiscardPile extends CardPile {

    DiscardPile (int x, int y) { super (x, y); }

    public void addCard (Card aCard) {
        if (! aCard.faceUp( ))
            aCard.flip( );
        super.addCard(aCard);
        }

    public void select (int tx, int ty) {
        if (isEmpty( ))
            return;
        Card topCard = pop( );
        for (int i = 0; i < 4; i++)
            if (Solitare.suitPile[i].canTake(topCard)) {
                Solitare.suitPile[i].addCard(topCard);
                return;
                }
        for (int i = 0; i < 7; i++)
            if (Solitare.tableau[i].canTake(topCard)) {
                Solitare.tableau[i].addCard(topCard);
                return;
                }
        // nobody can use it, put it back on our list
        addCard(topCard);
        }
}
```

Figure 9.8   The class DiscardPile.

- When a mouse press is tested to determine if it covers this pile (method includes) only the left, right, and top bounds are checked; the bottom bound is not tested since the pile may be of variable length.

- When the pile is selected, the topmost card is flipped if it is face down. If it is face up, an attempt is made to move the card first to any available suit pile, and then to any available table pile. Only if no pile can take the card is it left in place.

- To display the pile, each card in the pile is drawn in turn, each moving down slightly. To access the individual elements of the stack, an Enumeration is created. Enumeration objects are provided by all the containers in the Java library; they allow the programmer to easily loop over the elements in the container.

```
class TablePile extends CardPile {

    TablePile (int x, int y, int c) {
            // initialize the parent class
        super(x, y);
            // then initialize our pile of cards
        for (int i = 0; i < c; i++) {
            addCard(Solitare.deckPile.pop( ));
            }
            // flip topmost card face up
        top( ).flip( );
        }

    public boolean canTake (Card aCard) {
        if (isEmpty( ))
            return aCard.rank( ) == 12;
        Card topCard = top( );
        return (aCard.color( ) != topCard.color( )) &&
            (aCard.rank( ) == topCard.rank( ) - 1);
        }

    public boolean includes (int tx, int ty) {
            // don't test bottom of card
        return x <= tx && tx <= x + Card.width &&
            y <= ty;
        }

    public void display (Graphics g) {
        int localy = y;
        for (Enumeration e = thePile.elements( ); e.hasMoreElements( ); ) {
            Card aCard = (Card) e.nextElement( );
            aCard.draw (g, x, localy);
            localy += 35;
            }
        }
        .
        .
        .
}
```

Figure 9.9   The class TablePile, part 1.

```
class TablePile extends CardPile {
   .
   .
   .

  public void select (int tx, int ty) {
     if (isEmpty( ))
        return;

        // if face down, then flip
     Card topCard = top( );
     if (! topCard.faceUp( )) {
        topCard.flip( );
        return;
        }

        // else see if any suit pile can take card
     topCard = pop( );
     for (int i = 0; i < 4; i++)
        if (Solitare.suitPile[i].canTake(topCard)) {
           Solitare.suitPile[i].addCard(topCard);
           return;
           }
        // else see if any other table pile can take card
     for (int i = 0; i < 7; i++)
        if (Solitare.tableau[i].canTake(topCard)) {
           Solitare.tableau[i].addCard(topCard);
           return;
           }
        // else put it back on our pile
     addCard(topCard);
     }
}
```

Figure 9.10   The class TablePile, part 2.

9.4 THE APPLICATION CLASS

Figure 9.11 shows the central class for the Solitaire application. As in our earlier
case studies, the control is initially given to the static method named main, which
creates an instance of the application class. The constructor for the application
creates a window for the application, by constructing an instance of a nested
class SolitareFrame that inherits from the library class JFrame. After invoking the

init method, which performs the application initialization, the window is given the message show, which will cause it to display itself.

```
public class Solitare {
   static public DeckPile deckPile;
   static public DiscardPile discardPile;
   static public TablePile tableau [ ];
   static public SuitPile suitPile [ ];
   static public CardPile allPiles [ ];
   private JFrame window;

   static public void main (String [ ] args) {
      Solitare world = new Solitare( );
      }

   public Solitare ( ) {
      window = new SolitareFrame( );
      init( );
      window.show( );
      }

   public void init ( ) {
         // first allocate the arrays
      allPiles = new CardPile[13];
      suitPile = new SuitPile[4];
      tableau = new TablePile[7];
         // then fill them in
      allPiles[0] = deckPile = new DeckPile(335, 30);
      allPiles[1] = discardPile = new DiscardPile(268, 30);
      for (int i = 0; i < 4; i++)
         allPiles[2+i] = suitPile[i] =
            new SuitPile(15 + (Card.width+10) * i, 30);
      for (int i = 0; i < 7; i++)
         allPiles[6+i] = tableau[i] =
            new TablePile(15+(Card.width+5)*i, Card.height+35, i+1);
      }

   private class SolitareFrame extends JFrame { ... }
}
```

Figure 9.11 The class Solitaire.

As noted earlier, the variables maintaining the different piles, which are shared in common between all classes, are declared as static data fields in this class. These data fields are initialized in the method name init.

Arrays in Java are somewhat different from arrays in most computer languages. Java distinguishes the three activities of array declaration, array allocation, and assignment to an array location. Note that the declaration statements indicate only that the named objects are an array and not that they have any specific bound. One of the first steps in the initialization routine is to allocate space for the three arrays (the suit piles, the tableau, and the array allPiles we will discuss shortly). The new command allocates space for the arrays, but does not assign any values to the array elements.

The next step is to create the deck pile. Recall that the constructor for this class creates and shuffles the entire deck of 52 cards. The discard pile is similarly constructed. A loop then creates and initializes the four suit piles, and a second loop creates and initializes the tableau piles. Recall that as part of the initialization of the tableau, cards are removed from the deck and inserted in the tableau pile.

The inner class SolitareFrame, used to manage the application window, is shown in Figure 9.12. In addition to the cards, a button will be placed at the bottom of the window. Listeners are created both for mouse events (see Chapter 7) and for the button. When pressed, the button will invoke the button listener method. This method will reinitialize the game, then repaint the window. Similarly, when the mouse listener is invoked (in response to a mouse press) the collection of card piles will be examined, and the appropriate pile will be displayed.

9.5   PLAYING THE POLYMORPHIC GAME

Both the mouse listener and the repaint method for the application window make use of the array allPiles. This array is used to represent all 13 card piles. Note that as each pile is created it is also assigned a location in this array, as well as in the appropriate static variable. We will use this array to illustrate yet another aspect of inheritance. The principle of substitutability is used here: The array allPiles is declared as an array of CardPile, but in fact is maintaining a variety of card piles.

This array of all piles is used in situations where it is not important to distinguish between various types of card piles; for example, in the repaint method. To repaint the display, each different card pile is simply asked to display itself. Similarly, when the mouse is pressed, each pile is queried to see if it contains the given position. If the pile does contain the given position, the pile is selected. Remember, of the piles being queried here, seven are tableau piles, four are foundations, and the remaining are the discard pile and the deck. Furthermore, the actual code executed in response to the invocation of the includes and select routines may be different in each call, depending upon the type of pile being manipulated. In other object-oriented languages, such methods are often described as *virtual*.

```
private class SolitareFrame extends JFrame {

    private class RestartButtonListener implements ActionListener {
        public void actionPerformed (ActionEvent e) {
            init( );
            repaint( );
        }
    }

    private class MouseKeeper extends MouseAdapter {
        public void mousePressed (MouseEvent e) {
            int x = e.getX( );
            int y = e.getY( );
            for (int i = 0; i < 13; i++)
                if (allPiles[i].includes(x, y)) {
                    allPiles[i].select(x, y);
                    repaint( );
                }
        }
    }

    public SolitareFrame( ) { // constructor for window
        setSize(600, 500);
        setTitle("Solitaire Game");
        addMouseListener (new MouseKeeper( ));
        Button restartButton = new Button("New Game");
        restartButton.addActionListener(new RestartButtonListener( ));
        add("South", restartButton);
    }

    public void paint(Graphics g) {
        for (int i = 0; i < 13; i++)
            allPiles[i].display(g);
    }
}
```

Figure 9.12   The inner class SolitareFrame.

The use of a variable declared as an instance of the parent class holding a value from a subclass is one aspect of *polymorphism*, a topic we will return to in more detail in a subsequent chapter.

9.6   BUILDING A MORE COMPLETE GAME

The Solitaire game described here is minimal and exceedingly hard to win. A more realistic game would include at least a few of the following variations:

- The method select in class TablePile would be extended to recognize builds. That is, if the topmost card could not be played, the bottommost face-up card in the pile should be tested against each tableau pile; if it could be played, the entire collection of face-up cards should be moved.

- Our game halts after one series of moves through the deck. An alternative would be that when the user selected the empty deck pile (by clicking the mouse in the area covered by the deck pile) the discard pile would be reshuffled and copied back into the deck, allowing execution to continue.

Various other alternatives are described in the exercises.

9.7   CHAPTER SUMMARY

The Solitaire program in this chapter is used as a case study to present many of the features and benefits of inheritance. The various different types of card piles found in the game can all be specialized from one common parent class. This parent class provides default behavior, which can be overridden when a pile requires more specialized code. In the program presented here, the default behavior is overridden less than half the time.

The following are some of the aspects of inheritance discussed in this chapter:

- By creating a common parent class, default behavior can be shared among several different software components.

- Methods can be declared as final, in which case they cannot be overridden in subclasses. (As noted in the previous chapter, methods can also be declared as abstract, in which case they *must* be overridden in subclasses.)

- Overriding methods can be divided into those that *replace* the code inherited from the parent, and those that *refine* the parent code. In the former case only the child code is executed, while in the latter both the child and the parent code is executed. In Java refinement is specified by explicitly executing the parent method, using the pseudovariable super.

- Inheritance is tied to polymorphism through the concept of substitutability. An instance of a child class can be assigned to a variable that is declared as a parent class type. Using this idea, we can create a variable (or, in this case, an array of values) that maintains any type of card pile.

- When an overridden method is applied to a polymorphic variable, the code executed is determined by the value the variable currently holds, not the

declared type of the variable. Such methods are sometimes described as *virtual*.

STUDY QUESTIONS

1. What data values are maintained by class Card? What behaviors can a card perform? (That is, what methods are implemented by the class Card?)

2. Explain why the suit and rank data fields are declared private.

3. What is a default constructor? What is a copy constructor?

4. What is an accessor method? What is the advantage of using an accessor methods as opposed to direct access to a data member?

5. What are the 13 different card piles that are used in the Solitaire game?

6. What does it mean when a method is declared final?

7. Describe the five non-final methods implemented in class CardPile and overridden in at least one child class.

8. How does the use of inheritance reduce the amount of code that would otherwise be necessary to implement the various types of card piles?

9. Explain the difference between overriding used for replacement and overriding used for refinement. Find another example of each in the methods associated with class CardPile and its various subclasses.

10. Explain how polymorphism is exhibited in the Solitaire game application.

EXERCISES

1. The Solitaire game has been designed to be as simple as possible. A few features are somewhat annoying, but they can be easily remedied with more coding. These include the following:

   (a) The topmost card of a tableau pile should not be moved to another tableau pile if there is another face-up card below it.

   (b) An entire build should not be moved if the bottommost card is a king and there are no remaining face-down cards.

   For each, describe what methods need to be changed, and give the code for the updated routine.

2. The following are common variations of Klondike. For each, describe which portions of the Solitaire program need to be altered to incorporate the change.

(a) If the user clicks on an empty deck pile, the discard pile is moved (perhaps with shuffling) back to the deck pile. Thus, the user can traverse the deck pile repeatedly.

(b) Cards can be moved from the suit pile back into the tableau pile.

(c) Cards are drawn from the deck three at a time and placed on the discard pile in reverse order. As before, only the topmost card of the discard pile is available for playing. If fewer than three cards remain in the deck pile, all the remaining cards (as many as that may be) are moved to the discard pile. (In practice, this variation is often accompanied by variation 1, permitting multiple passes through the deck.)

(d) The same as variation 3, but any of the three selected cards can be played. (This requires a slight change to the layout as well as an extensive change to the discard pile class.)

(e) Any royalty card, not simply a king, can be moved onto an empty tableau pile.

3. The game Thumb and Pouch is similar to Klondike except that a card may be built on any card of next-higher rank, of any suit but its own. Thus, a nine of spades can be played on a ten of clubs, but not on a ten of spades. This variation greatly improves the chances of winning. (According to Morehead and Mott-Smith [1949], the chances of winning Klondike are 1 in 30, whereas the chances of winning Thumb and Pouch are 1 in 4.) What portions of the program need to be changed to accommodate this variation?

4. The game Whitehead is superficially similar to Klondike, in the sense that it uses the same layout. However, it uses different rules for when a card can be played in the tableau:

(a) A card can be moved onto another face-up card in the tableau only if it has the *same* color and is one smaller in rank. For example, a five of spades can be played on either a six of clubs or a six of spades, but not on a six of diamonds or a six of hearts.

(b) A build can only be moved if all cards in the build are of the same suit.

What portions of the program need to be changed to accommodate this variation?

10 Mechanisms for Software Reuse

Object-oriented programming has been billed as the technology that will finally permit software to be constructed from general purpose reusable components. Writers such as Brad Cox have even gone so far as to describe object orientation as heralding the "industrial revolution" in software development [Cox 1986]. While reality may not quite match the expectations of OOP pioneers, it *is* true that object-oriented programming makes possible a level of software reuse that is orders of magnitude more powerful than that permitted by previous software construction techniques. In this chapter, we will investigate the two most common mechanisms for software reuse, which are known as *inheritance* and *composition*.

Inheritance in Java is made more flexible by the presence of two different mechanisms, interfaces and subclassification. In addition to contrasting inheritance and composition, we will contrast inheritance performed using subclassification and inheritance performed using interfaces, and relate all to the concept of substitutability.

10.1 SUBSTITUTABILITY

The concept of substitutability is fundamental to many of the most powerful software development techniques in object-oriented programming. You will recall that substitutability referred to the situation that occurs when a *variable* declared as one type is used to hold a *value* derived from another type.

In Java, substitutability can occur either through the use of classes and inheritance, or through the use of interfaces. Examples of both occurred in the case studies in earlier chapters. In the PinBall Game program described in Chapter 7, the variable targets was declared a PinBallTarget, but in fact it held a variety of

165

different types of values that were created using implementations of PinBallTarget. In the Solitaire program from Chapter 9, the variable allPiles was declared as holding a CardPile, but in fact it held values that were subclasses of CardPile, such as DeckPile and DiscardPile as follows:

```
public class Solitare {
    static public CardPile allPiles [ ];

    public void init () {
        .
        .

        allPiles = new CardPile[13];
        // then fill them in
        allPiles[0] = new DeckPile(335, 30);
        allPiles[1] = new DiscardPile(268, 30);
    }
    .
    .
    .

}
```

We have also seen examples of substitutability arising through interfaces. An example is the instance of the class FireButtonListener created in the Cannon Game (Chapter 6). The class from which this value was defined was declared as implementing the interface ActionListener. Because it implements the ActionListener interface, we can use this value as a parameter to a method (in this case, addActionListener) that expects an ActionListener value.

```
public class CannonWorld extends JFrame {
    .
    .
    .

    private class FireButtonListener implements ActionListener {
        public void actionPerformed (ActionEvent e) {
            .
            .
            .
        }
    }

    public CannonWorld () {
        .
        .

        fire.addActionListener(new FireButtonListener());
    }
}
```

We will return to the distinction between inheritance of classes and inheritance of interfaces in Section 10.1.2.

10.1.1 *The* Is-a *Rule and the* Has-a *Rule*

A commonly employed rule of thumb that can be used to understand when inheritance is an appropriate software technique is known colloquially as *is-a* and *has-a* (or *part-of*) relationship.

The *is-a* relationship holds between two concepts when the first is a specialized instance of the second. That is, for all practical purposes the behavior and data associated with the more specific idea form a subset of the behavior and data associated with the more abstract idea. For example, all the examples of inheritance described in the early chapters satisfy the *is-a* relationship (a Florist *is-a* Shopkeeper, a Dog *is-a* Mammal, a PinBall *is-a* Ball, and so on). The relationship derives its name from a simple rule of thumb that tests the relationship. To determine if concept X is a specialized instance of concept Y, simply form the English sentence *"An X is a Y"*. If the assertion "sounds correct," that is, if it seems to match your everyday experience, you may judge that X and Y have the *is-a* relationship.

The *has-a* relationship, on the other hand, holds when the second concept is a component of the first but the two are not in any sense the same thing, no matter how abstract the generality. For example, a Car *has-a* Engine, although clearly it is not the case that a Car *is-a* Engine or that an Engine *is-a* Car. A Car, however, *is-a* Vehicle, which in turn *is-a* MeansOfTransportation. Once again, the test for the *has-a* relationship is to simply form the English sentence *"An X has a Y"*, and let common sense tell you whether the result sounds reasonable.

Most of the time, the distinction is clear-cut. But, sometimes it may be subtle or may depend on circumstances. In Section 10.2 we will use one such indefinite case to illustrate the two software development techniques that are naturally tied to these two relationships.

10.1.2 *Inheritance of Code and Inheritance of Behavior*

There are at least two different ways in which a concept can satisfy the *is-a* relationship with another concept, and these are reflected in two different mechanisms in the Java language. Inheritance is the mechanism of choice when two concepts share a *structure* or *code* relationship with each other, while an interface is the more appropriate technique when two concepts share the *specification of behavior*, but no actual code.

This can be illustrated with examples from the Java run-time library. The class JFrame, from which most Java windows inherit, provides a great deal of code, in the form of methods that are inherited and used without being overridden.

Thus, inheritance using the extends modifier in the class heading is the appropriate mechanism to use in this situation.

```
// a cannon game is a type of Frame
public class CannonGame extends JFrame {
   .
   .
   .
}
```

On the other hand, the characteristics needed for an ActionListener (the object type that responds to button presses) can be described by a single method, and the implementation of that method cannot be predicted, since it differs from one application to another. Thus, an interface is used to describe only the necessary requirements, and no actual behavior is inherited by a subclass that implements the behavior.

```
public class CannonWorld extends JFrame {
   .
   .
   .

      // a fire button listener implements the action listener interface
   private class FireButtonListener implements ActionListener {
      public void actionPerformed (ActionEvent e) {
         .
         .
         .
      }
   }
}
```

In general, the class-subclass relationship should be used whenever a subclass can usefully inherit code, data values, or behavior from the parent class. The interface mechanism should be used when the child class inherits only the specification of the expected behavior, but no actual code.

10.2   COMPOSITION AND INHERITANCE DESCRIBED

Two different techniques for software reuse are *composition* and *inheritance*. Although uses of inheritance were explicitly noted in earlier chapters, and composition was used in several places as well, this was not pointed out. One way to view these two different mechanisms is as manifestations of the *has-a* rule and the *is-a* rule, respectively.

Although in most situations the distinction between *is-a* and *has-a* is clear-cut, it does happen occasionally that it can be difficult to determine which mechanism is most appropriate to use in a particular situation. By examining one such indefinite case, we can more easily point out the differences between the use of inheritance and the use of composition. The example we will use is taken from the Java library and concerns the development of a Stack abstraction from an existing Vector data type.

The Vector data type is described in detail in Chapter 19. While abstractly a vector is most commonly thought of as an indexed collection, the Java implementation also permits values to be added or removed from the end of the collection, growing and shrinking the container as necessary. The methods of interest for this discussion can be described as follows:

```java
public class Vector {
    // see if collection is empty
    public boolean isEmpty () { ... }

    // return size of collection
    public int size () { ... }

    // add element to end of collection
    public void addElement (Object value) { ... }

    // return last element in collection
    public Object lastElement () { ... }

    // remove element at given index
    public Object removeElementAt (int index) { ... }  // Object ⇒ void
    :
    :
}
```

A *stack* is an abstract data type that allows elements to be added or removed from one end only. If you think about a stack of dishes sitting on a counter, you can get a good intuitive image. It is easy to access the topmost dish, or to place a new dish on the top. It is much more difficult to access any dish other than the topmost dish. In fact, it might be that the only way to do this is to remove dishes one by one until you reach the dish you want.

The Stack abstractions defined here will be slightly simpler than the version provided by the Java library. In particular, the library abstraction will generate an exception if an attempt is made to access or remove an element from an empty stack, a condition we will ignore. The Java library stack routine names the empty test method *empty*, instead of the method isEmpty from class Vector, and finally the Stack abstraction provides a method to search the stack to determine if it includes a given element. We will not describe this method here.

10.2.1 *Using Composition*

We will first investigate how the stack abstraction can be formed with composition. Recall from our earlier discussion that an object is simply an encapsulation of data values and behavior. When composition is employed to reuse an existing data abstraction in the development of a new data type, a portion of the state of the new data structure is simply an instance of the existing structure. This is illustrated in Figure 10.1, where the data type Stack contains a private instance field named theData, which is declared to be of type Vector.

Because the Vector abstraction is stored as part of the data area for our stack, it must be initialized in the constructor. The constructor for class Stack allocates space for the vector, giving a value to the variable theData.

Operations that manipulate the new structure are implemented by making use of the existing operations provided for the earlier data type. For example, the implementation of the empty operation for our stack data structure simply invokes the method already defined for vectors. The peek operation is known by a different name, but the task is already provided by the lastElement operation in the Vector class. Similarly, the push operation is simply performed by executing an addElement on the vector.

```
public class Stack {
    private Vector theData;

    public Stack ()
       { theData = new Vector(); }

    public boolean empty ()
       { return theData.isEmpty(); }

    public Object push (Object item)
       { theData.addElement (item); return item; }

    public Object peek ()
       { return theData.lastElement(); }

    public Object pop () {
       Object result = theData.lastElement();
       theData.removeElementAt(theData.size()-1);
       return result;
       }
}
```

Figure 10.1 A stack created using composition.

The only operation that is slightly more complex is popping an element from the stack. This involves using two methods provided by the Vector class, namely obtaining the topmost element and removing it from the collection. Notice that to remove the element we must first determine its index position, then remove the element by naming its position.

The important point to emphasize is the fact that composition provides a way to leverage off an existing software component in the creation of a new application. By use of the existing Vector class, we have already addressed the majority of the difficult work in managing the data values for our new component.

But composition makes no explicit or implicit claims about substitutability. When formed in this fashion, the data types Stack and Vector are entirely distinct and neither can be substituted in situations where the other is required.

10.2.2 *Using Inheritance*

An entirely different mechanism for software reuse in object-oriented programming is the concept of inheritance, with which a new class can be declared a *subclass*, or *child class*, of an existing class. In this way, all data areas and methods associated with the original class are automatically associated with the new data abstraction. The new class can, in addition, define new data values or new methods; it can also *override* methods in the original class, simply by defining new methods with the same names as those of methods that appear in the parent class.

These possibilities are illustrated in the class description shown in Figure 10.2, which implements a different version of the Stack abstraction. By naming the class Vector in the class heading, we indicate that our Stack abstraction is an extension, or a refinement, of the existing class Vector. Thus, all data fields and operations associated with vectors are immediately applicable to stacks as well.

The most obvious features of this class in comparison to the earlier are the items that are missing. There are no local data fields. There is no constructor, since no local data values need be initialized. The method isEmpty need not be provided, since the method is inherited already from the parent class Vector.

Compare this method with the earlier version, shown in Figure 10.1. Both techniques are powerful mechanisms for code reuse, but unlike composition, inheritance carries an implicit assumption that subclasses are, in fact, subtypes. This means that instances of the new abstraction should react similarly to instances of the parent class.

In fact, the version using inheritance provides more useful functionality than the version using composition. For example, the method size in the Vector class yields the number of elements stored in a vector. With the version of the Stack formed using inheritance we get this method automatically for free, while the composition version needs to explicitly add a new operation if we want to include this new ability. Similarly, the ability to access intermediate values directly

```
public class Stack extends Vector {

   public Object push (Object item)
      { addElement (item); return item; }

   public Object peek ( )
      { return elementAt(size( ) - 1); }

   public Object pop ( ) {
      Object obj = peek( );
      removeElementAt(size( )-1);
      return obj;
   }
}
```

Figure 10.2   A stack created using inheritance.

using an index is in this version possible with a stack, but not permitted in the abstraction created using composition.

10.3   COMPOSITION AND INHERITANCE CONTRASTED

Having illustrated two mechanisms for software reuse, and having seen that they are both applicable to the implementation of stacks, we can comment on some of the advantages and disadvantages of the two approaches.

- Inheritance carries with it an implicit, if not explicit, assumption of substitutability. That is, classes formed by inheritance are assumed to be subtypes of the parent class, and therefore candidates for values to be used when an instance of the parent class is expected. No such assumption of substitutability is associated with the use of composition.

- Composition is the simpler of the two techniques. Its advantage is that it more clearly indicates exactly what operations can be performed on a particular data structure. Looking at the declaration for the Stack data abstraction, it is clear that the only operations provided for the data type are the test for emptiness, push, peek, and pop. This is true regardless of what operations are defined for vectors.

- In inheritance the operations of the new data abstraction are a superset of the operations of the original data structure on which the new object is built. Thus, to know exactly what operations are legal for the new structure, the programmer must examine the declaration for the original. An examination of the Stack declaration, for example, does not immediately indicate that the size method can be legally applied to stacks. It is only by examination of the declaration for the earlier Vector data abstraction that the entire set of legal operations can be ascertained.

The difficulty that occurs when, to understand a class constructed using inheritance, the programmer must frequently flip back and forth between two (or more) class declarations has been labeled the "yo-yo" problem by Taenzer, Ganti, and Podar [Taenzer 1989].

- The brevity of data abstractions constructed with inheritance is, in another light, an advantage. Using inheritance it is not necessary to write any code to access the functionality provided by the class on which the new structure is built. For this reason, implementations using inheritance are almost always, as in the present case, considerably shorter in code than are implementations constructed with composition, and they often provide greater functionality. For example, the inheritance implementation makes available not only the size test for stacks but also the index-related operations (inserting, modifying, or removing elements by giving their index locations).

- Inheritance does not prevent users from manipulating the new structure using methods from the parent class, even if these are not appropriate. For example, when we use inheritance to derive the class Stack from the class Vector, nothing prevents users from adding new elements to the stack using the inherited method insertElementAt, and thereby placing elements in locations other than the top of the stack.

- In composition the fact that the class Vector is used as the storage mechanism for our stack is merely an implementation detail. With this technique it would be easy to reimplement the class to make use of a different technique (such as a linked list), with minimal impact on the users of the Stack abstraction. If users counted on the fact that a Stack is merely a specialized form of Vector, such changes would be more difficult to implement.

- A component constructed using inheritance has access to fields and methods in the parent class that have been declared as protected. A component constructed using composition can only access the public portions of the included component.

- Inheritance may allow us to use the new abstraction as an argument in an existing *polymorphic* method. We will investigate this possibility in more detail in Chapter 12. Because composition does not imply substitutability, it usually precludes polymorphism.

- Understandability and maintainability are difficult to judge. Inheritance has the advantage of brevity of code but not of protocol. Composition code, although longer, is the only code that another programmer must understand to use the abstraction. A programmer faced with understanding the inheritance version needs to ask whether any behavior inherited from the parent class was necessary for proper utilization of the new class, and would thus have to understand both classes.

- Data structures implemented through inheritance tend to have a very small advantage in execution time over those constructed with composition, since one additional method call is avoided (although optimization techniques, such as inline functions, can in theory be used to eliminate much of this overhead).

Of the two possible implementation techniques, can we say which is better in this case? One answer involves the substitution principle. Ask yourself whether, in an application that expected to use a Vector data abstraction, it is correct to substitute instead an instance of class Stack.

The bottom line is that the two techniques are very useful, and an object-oriented programmer should be familiar with both of them.

10.4 COMBINING INHERITANCE AND COMPOSITION

The Java input/output system, which we will investigate in more detail in Chapter 14, provides an interesting illustration of the way in which inheritance and composition can interact with each other, and the particular problems each mechanism is designed to solve.

To begin with, there is an abstract concept, and several concrete realizations of the concept. For the file input system the abstract concept is the idea of reading a stream of bytes in sequence, one after the other. This idea is embodied in the class InputStream, which defines a number of methods for reading byte values. The concrete realizations differ in the source of the data values. Values can come from an array of bytes being held in memory, from an external file, or from another process that is generating values as needed. There is a different subclass of InputStream for each of these, as shown in Figure 10.3.

Because each of these is declared as a subclass of InputStream, they can be substituted for a value of type InputStream. In this fashion methods can be written to process a stream of byte values, without regard to where the values originate (whether in memory, or from an external file, or from another process).

However, there is an additional source of variation among input streams. Or rather, there is additional functionality that is sometimes required when using an input stream. Furthermore, this functionality is independent of the source for the byte values. One example is the ability to keep track of line numbers, so that the programmer can determine on which line of the input the current byte originates. Another useful function is the ability to buffer input so as to have the possibility of rereading recently referenced bytes once again.

These features are provided by defining a subclass of InputStream, named FilterInputStream. Thus, using the principle of substitutability, a FilterInputStream can be used in places where an InputStream is expected. On the other hand, a

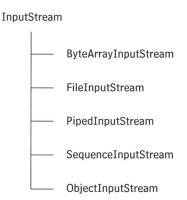

InputStream

- ByteArrayInputStream
- FileInputStream
- PipedInputStream
- SequenceInputStream
- ObjectInputStream

Figure 10.3 Subclasses of InputStream.

FilterInputStream holds as a component another instance of InputStream, which is used as the source for data values. Thus, the class InputStream is both parent and component to FilterInputStream. As requests for values are received, the FilterInputStream will access the InputStream it holds to get the values it needs, performing whatever additional actions are required (for example, counting newline characters in order to keep track of the current line number).

```
public class FilterInputStream extends InputStream {

    protected InputStream in;
    .
    .
    .
}
```

Because the component held by the FilterInputStream can be any type of InputStream, this additional functionality can be used to augment any type of InputStream, regardless of where the byte values originate. This idea of *filters* (sometimes called *wrappers* in other object-oriented literature) can be quite powerful when there are orthogonal sources of variation. Here the two reasons of variation are (1) the source of the input values and (2) the additional functionality that may or may not be needed in any particular application.

10.5 NOVEL FORMS OF SOFTWARE REUSE

There are several novel ways in which composition, or inheritance, or both, are used to achieve different effects.

```
public class Frog {
   private FrogBehavior behavior;

   public Frog ( ) {
      behavior = new TadpoleBehavior( );
      }

   public grow ( ) { // see if behavior should change
      if (behavior.growUp( ))
         behavior = new AdultFrogBehavior( );
      behavior.grow( ); // behavior does actual work
      behavior.swim( );
      }
}
```

Figure 10.4   Class Frog holds dynamically changing behavior component.

10.5.1   *Dynamic Composition*

One advantage of composition over inheritance concerns the delay in binding time. With inheritance, the link between child class and parent class is established at compile time and cannot later be modified. With composition, the link between the new abstraction and the older abstraction is created at run time, and is therefore much weaker, since it can also be changed at run time. This is sometimes called *dynamic composition*.

To illustrate, imagine a class that is simulating the behavior of a Frog. Although the frog interface can be fixed throughout its life, the actual actions it performs might be very different when the frog is a tadpole or when it is an adult. One way to model this is to create a class Frog (Figure 10.4) that uses composition to hold a value of type FrogBehavior. The Frog class is largely a facade, invoking the FrogBehavior object to do the majority of the real work.

The novel idea is that the variable holding the instance of FrogBehavior can actually be polymorphic. There might be more than one class that implements the FrogBehavior specification, such as TadpoleBehavior and AdultFrogBehavior. Figure 10.5 illustrates these classes. The parent class FrogBehavior is here declared *abstract*, which means that it *must* be overridden before any instances can be created. As the frog "grows," it can dynamically change behavior by reassigning the value behavior to a different value (for example, moving from a TadpoleBehavior to an AdultFrogBehavior). The user of the Frog abstraction need not know about this change, or even be aware when it occurs.

Dynamic composition is a useful technique if the behavior of an object varies dramatically according to some internal concept of "state," and the change in state occurs infrequently.

```
abstract class FrogBehavior {
   public boolean growUp () { return false; }

   public void grow ();

   public void swim ();
}

class TadpoleBehavior extends FrogBehavior {
   private int age = 0;

   public boolean growUp () { if (++age > 24) return true; }

   public void grow () { ... }

   public void swim () { ... }
}

class AdultFrogBehavior extends FrogBehavior {

   public void grow () { ... }

   public void swim () { ... }
}
```

Figure 10.5   Class FrogBehavior can dynamically change

10.5.2   *Inheritance of Inner Classes*

We have seen another combination of inheritance and composition in some of
the case studies presented in earlier chapters. For example, the "listener" classes
that responded to events were constructed using inheritance, but were themselves
components in the application class. The following is a skeleton of the class
PinBallGame from Chapter 7.

```
public class PinBallGame extends JFrame {
   .
   .
   private class MouseKeeper extends MouseAdapter { ... }

   private class PinBallThread extends Thread { ... }
}
```

The classes MouseKeeper and PinBallThread are each constructed using inheritance. Each is then used to create a new component, which will be held as part of the state of the pinball game. When used in this fashion, inner classes combine aspects of both inheritance and composition.

10.5.3   *Unnamed Classes*

In several of the earlier case studies we have seen situations where inheritance is used to override an existing class, yet only one instance of the new class is created. An alternative to naming the new class and then creating an instance of the named class is to use a class definition expression. Such an expression places the entire class definition inside the instance creation expression.

An example where this could be used is in the definition of an event listener. For example, the Cannon Game described in Chapter 6 contained the following code:

```
public class CannonWorld extends JFrame {
   .
   .
   .

   private class FireButtonListener implements ActionListener {
      public void actionPerformed (ActionEvent e) {
         .
         .
      }
   }

   public CannonWorld ( ) {
      fire.addActionListener(new FireButtonListener( ));
      .
      .
      .
   }
}
```

Note how the constructor for the class CannonWorld creates an instance of the inner class FireButtonListener. This is the only instance of this class created. An alternative way to achieve the same effect would be as follows:

```
public class CannonWorld extends JFrame {
   .
   .
   .

   public CannonWorld ( ) {
      fire.addActionListener(new ActionListener( ) {
```

```
public void actionPerformed (ActionEvent e) {
   .
   .
   .
   }
});
.
.
.
   }
}
```

Notice that in this example the object being created is declared only as being an instance of ActionListener. However, a class definition follows immediately the ending parenthesis, indicating that a new and *unnamed* class is being defined. This class definition would have exactly the same form as before, ending with a closing curly brace. The parenthesis that follows this curly brace ends the argument list for the addActionListener call. (The reader should carefully match curly braces and parenthesis to see how this takes place.) An unnamed class is also sometimes known as an *anonymous class*.

An advantage to the use of the class definition expression in this situation is that it avoids the need to introduce a new class name (in this case, the inner class name FireButtonListener). A disadvantage is that such expressions tend to be difficult to read, since the entire class definition must be wrapped up as an expression, and the close of the expressions occurs after the end of the class definition.

10.6 CHAPTER SUMMARY

The two most common techniques for reusing software abstractions are inheritance and composition. Both are valuable techniques, and a good object-oriented system will usually have many examples of each.

A good rule of thumb for deciding when to use inheritance is the *is-a* rule. Form the sentence "An X is a Y", and if it sounds right to your ear, then the two concepts X and Y can probably be related using inheritance. The corresponding rule for composition is the *has-a* rule.

The decision whether to use inheritance or not is not always clear. By examining one borderline case, one can more easily see some of the advantages and disadvantages of the two software structuring techniques.

The idea of *filters*, found in the portion of the Java library used for input and output, is an interesting technique that combines features of both inheritance and composition.

STUDY QUESTIONS

1. Explain in your own words the principle of substitutability.

2. What is the *is-a* rule? What is the *has-a* rule? How are these two rules related to inheritance and composition?

3. How are interfaces and inheritance related?

4. What are some of the advantages of composition over inheritance?

5. What are some of the advantages of using inheritance that are not available when composition is used?

6. How does a FilterStream combine inheritance and composition?

EXERCISES

1. A set is simply an unorganized collection of values. Describe how one could use a Vector to implement a set. Would inheritance or composition be the more appropriate mechanism in this case?

2. Modify the Stack data abstractions given in this chapter so that they will throw a EmptyStackException if an attempt is made to read or remove a value from an empty stack.

3. Modify each of the Stack data abstractions given in this chapter so that when given the message size they will return the number of elements they hold.

4. Give some rules for deciding when it is appropriate to use inheritance and when it is appropriate to use composition.

11 Implications of Inheritance

The decision to support inheritance and the principle of substitutability in a language sets off a series of chain reactions that end up impacting almost every aspect of a programming language. In this chapter, we will illustrate this point by considering some of the implications of the decision to support in a natural fashion the idea of the polymorphic variable.

The links between inheritance and other language features can be summarized as follows:

- In order to make the most effective use of object-oriented techniques, the language must support the polymorphic variable. A polymorphic variable is a variable that is declared as one type but actually maintains either a value of that type or a value derived from a subtype of the declared type.

- Because at compile time we cannot determine the amount of memory that will be required to hold the value assigned to a polymorphic variable, all objects must reside on the heap, rather than on the stack.

- Because values reside in heaps, the most natural interpretation of assignment and parameter passing uses reference semantics, rather than copy semantics.

- Similarly, the most natural interpretation of equality testing is to test object identity. However, since often the programmer requires a different meaning for equality, two different operators are necessary.

- Because values reside on the heap, there must be some memory management mechanism. Because assignment is by reference semantics, it is difficult for the programmer to determine when a value is no longer being used. Therefore a garbage collection system is necessary to recover unused memory.

Each of these points will be more fully developed in the following sections.

11.1 THE POLYMORPHIC VARIABLE

As we will see in Chapter 12, a great deal of the power of the object-oriented features of Java comes through the use of a *polymorphic variable*. A polymorphic variable is declared as maintaining a value of one type but in fact holds a value from another type. We have seen many such examples in the sample programs presented in Part 1. For instance, much of the standard user interface code thinks only that an application is an instance of class Frame, when in fact each program we created used inheritance to create a new type of application. Similarly, in the Pin Ball Game Construction Kit program (Chapter 7) a variable was declared

```
class Shape {
   protected int x;
   protected int y;

   public Shape (int ix, int iy)
      { x = ix; y = iy; }

   public String describe ()
      { return "unknown shape"; }
}

class Square extends Shape {
   protected int side;

   public Square (int ix, int iy, int is)
      { super(ix, iy); side = is; }

   public String describe ()
      { return "square with side " + side; }
}

class Circle extends Shape {
   protected int radius;

   public Circle (int ix, int iy, int ir)
      { super(ix, iy); radius = ir; }

   public String describe ()
      { return "circle with radius " + radius; }
}
```

Figure 11.1 Shape classes and a polymorphic variable.

as holding a value of type PinBallTarget, when in fact it would hold a Hole or a ScorePad.

Figure 11.1 provides a class hierarchy consisting of three classes, Shape and two subclasses Circle and Square. In the small test program shown below the variable named form is declared as type Shape, then assigned a value of type Circle. As expected, when the method describe() is invoked, the method that is executed is the method in class Circle, not the method inherited from class Shape. We will use this example class in the subsequent discussion in this chapter.

```
class ShapeTest {
   static public void main (String [ ] args) {
      Shape form = new Circle (10, 10, 5);
      System.out.println("form is " + form.describe( ));
      form = new Square (15, 20, 10);
      System.out.println("form is " + form.describe( ));
   }
}
```

11.2 MEMORY LAYOUT

Before we can observe the impact of the polymorphic variable on memory management, it is first necessary to review how variables are normally represented in memory in most programming languages. From the point of view of the memory manager, there are two major categories of memory values. These are *stack-based* memory locations, and *heap-based* memory values.

Stack-based memory locations are tied to method entry and exit. When a method is started, space is allocated on a run-time stack for local variables. These values exist as long as the method is executing, and are erased, and the memory recovered, when the method exits. Figure 11.2 shows, for example, a snapshot of the run-time stack for the following simple recursive algorithm:

```
class FacTest {
   static public void main (String [ ] args) {
      int f = factorial(3);
      System.out.println("Factorial of 3 is " + f);
   }

   static public int factorial (int n) {
      int c = n - 1;
      int r;
```

0	n: 1	third
4	r: 1	activation record
8	c: 0	
0	n: 2	second
4	r: ?	activation record
8	c: 1	
0	n: 3	first
4	r: ?	activation record
8	c: 2	

Figure 11.2   A snapshot of the activation frame stack.

```
if (c > 0)
    r = n * factorial(c);
else
    r = 1;
return r;
}
}
```

The snapshot is taken after the method has recursed three times, just as the innermost method is starting to return. The data values for three methods are shown. In the innermost method the variable r has been assigned the value 1, while for the two pending methods the value of r has yet to be determined.

There are a number of advantages of stack-based memory allocation. All local variables can be allocated or deallocated as a block, for example, instead of one by one. This block is commonly called an *activation record*. Internally, variables can be described by their numeric offset within the activation record, rather than by their symbolic address. These numeric offsets have been noted in Figure 11.2. Most machines are much more efficient at dealing with numeric offsets than with symbolic names. Notice that each new activation record creates a new set of offsets, so that the offset is always relative to the activation frame in which a variable appears.

Stack-based allocation has one serious disadvantage: These numeric offsets associated with variables must be determined at compile time, not at run time. In order to do this, the compiler must know the amount of memory to assign to each variable. In Figure 11.2, the compiler only knows that variable c can be found at address 8 because it knows that variable r, which starts at location 4, requires only four bytes.

But, this is exactly the information we do not know for a polymorphic variable. The storage requirements for a polymorphic variable value are determined when the value is created at run time, and can even change during the course of execution. Recall the classes shown in Figure 11.1, and the memory requirements for the method main in the sample program described earlier. Here the variable form, which is declared as holding a Shape, can at one moment be holding a circle, at another a square, and so on. Both the subclasses add more data fields that are not found as part of the parent class. Thus the translator cannot know at compile time exactly how much memory will be required to hold the variable form.

In Java the solution to this problem is that objects are not stored on the activation record stack but are instead stored on the *heap*. A heap is an alternative memory-management system, one that is not tied to method entry and exit. Instead, memory is allocated on the heap when explicitly requested (to create a new object, using the new operator) and is freed, and recycled, when no longer needed. At run time, when the memory is requested, the Java system knows precisely how much memory is required to hold a value. In this fashion the Java language avoids the need to predict, at compile time, the amount of memory that will be needed at run time.

The code generated by the compiler, however, must still be able to access variables through numeric offsets, even though the actual heap addresses will not be known until run time. The solution to this dilemma is to use one level of indirection. Local variables are represented on the stack as pointer values. The size of a pointer is known at compile time and is independent of the size of the object it points to. This pointer field is filled when an object is created.

It is said that the programming language Java has no pointers. This is true as far as the language the programmer sees is concerned. But ironically, this is only possible because *all* object values are, in fact, represented internally by pointers.

11.2.1 *An Alternative Technique*

It should be noted that the solution to this problem selected by the designers of Java is not the only possibility. This can be illustrated by considering the language C++, which uses an entirely different approach. C++ treats assignment of *variables* and assignment of *pointers* very differently.

The designers of C++ elected to store variable values on the stack. Thus, the memory allocated to a variable of type Shape is only large enough to hold a value of type Shape, not the additional fields added by the subclass Circle. During the process of assignment these extra fields are simply sliced off and discarded. Of course, the resulting value is then no longer a Circle. For this reason, when we try to execute a member function, such as the describe method, the code executed will be that associated with class Shape, not the value associated with class Circle, as in Java. The programmer who uses both C++ and Java should be aware of this subtle, but nevertheless important difference.

11.3 ASSIGNMENT

In Section 11.2 we saw why values in Java are most naturally maintained on the heap, rather than being held in the activation record stack. Because to the compiler the underlying "value" of a variable is simply a pointer into the heap, the most natural semantics for assignment simply copy this pointer value. In this manner, the right and left sides of an assignment statement end up referring to the same object. This is often termed *reference* semantics (sometimes also called *pointer* semantics). The consequences of this interpretation of assignment are subtle but are, again, a key point for Java programmers to remember. Suppose we create a simple class Box as follows:

```
public class Box {
   private int value;

   public Box () { value = 0; }
   public void setValue (int v) { value = v; }
   public int getValue () { return value; }
}
```

Now imagine that we create a new box, assign it to a variable x, and set the internal value to 7. We then assign the box held by x to another variable, named y. Since both x and y now hold non-null values of type Box, the programmer might assume that they are distinct. But, in fact, they are exactly the same box, as can be verified by changing the value held in the y box and printing the value held by the x box:

```
public class BoxTest {
   static public void main (String [ ] args) {

      Box x = new Box( );
      x.setValue (7);      // set value of x

      Box y = x;      // assign y the same value as x
      y.setValue (11);      // change value of y

      System.out.println("contents of x " + x.getValue( ));
      System.out.println("contents of y " + y.getValue( ));
   }
}
```

The key observation is that the two variables, although assigned separate locations on the activation record stack, nevertheless point to the same location on the heap, as shown in Figure 11.3.

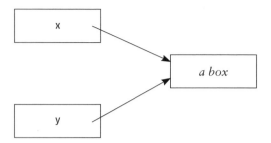

Figure 11.3 Two variables pointing to the same location.

11.3.1 *Clones*

If the desired effect of an assignment is indeed a copy, then the programmer must indicate this. One way would be to explicitly create a new value, copying the internal contents from the existing value:

```
//  create new box with same value as x
Box y = new Box ( );
y.setValue(x.getValue( ));
```

If making copies is a common operation, it might be better to provide a method in the original class:

```
public class Box {
   .
   .
   public Box copy( ) { // make copy of box
      Box b = new Box( );
      b.setValue (getValue( ));
      return b;
   }
   .
   .
}
```

A copy of a box is then created by invoking the copy( ) method:

```
//  create new box with same value as x
Box y = x.copy( );
```

There is no general mechanism in Java to copy an arbitrary object; however, the base class Object does provide a protected method named clone( ) that creates a bitwise copy of the receiver, as well as an interface Cloneable that represents objects that can be cloned. Several methods in the Java library require that arguments be values that are cloneable.

To create a class that is cloneable, the programmer must not only override the clone method to make it public but also explicitly indicate that the result satisfies the Cloneable interface. The following, for example, shows how to create a cloneable box.

```
public class Box implements Cloneable {
    private int value;

    public Box () { value = 0; }
    public void setValue (int v) { value = v; }
    public int getValue () { return value; }

    public Object clone () {
        Box b = new Box();
        b.setValue (getValue());
        return b;
    }
}
```

The clone method is declared as yielding a result of type Object. This property cannot be modified when the method is overridden. As a consequence, the result of cloning a value must be cast to the actual type before it can be assigned to a variable.

```
public class BoxTest {
    static public void main (String [ ] args) {

        Box x = new Box();
        x.setValue (7);

        Box y = (Box) x.clone(); // assign copy of x to y

        y.setValue (11); // change value of x

        System.out.println("contents of x " + x.getValue());
        System.out.println("contents of y " + y.getValue());
    }
}
```

As always, subtleties can trap the unwary programmer. Consider the object that is being held by our box. Imagine, instead of simply an integer, that it is something more complex, such as a Shape. Should a clone also clone this value, or just copy it? A copy results in two distinct boxes, but ones that share a common value. This is called a *shallow copy* (Figure 11.4).

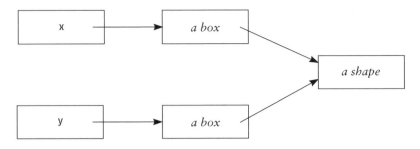

Figure 11.4 A shallow copy.

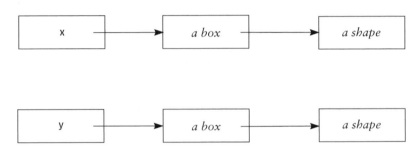

Figure 11.5 A deep copy.

Cloning the contents of the box (which must therefore be itself a type that is cloneable) results in two box values that are not only themselves distinct, but that point to values that are also distinct. This is termed a *deep copy* (Figure 11.5).

Whether a copy should be shallow or deep is something that must be determined by the programmer when overriding the clone interface.

11.3.2 *Parameters as a Form of Assignment*

Note that passing a variable as an argument to a member function can be considered to be a form of assignment, in that parameter passing, like assignment, results in the same value being accessible through two different names. Thus, the issues raised in Section 11.3 regarding assignment apply equally to parameter values. Consider the method sneaky in the following example, which modifies the value held in a box that is passed through a parameter value.

```
public class BoxTest {
   static public void main (String [ ] args) {

      Box x = new Box( );
```

```
        x.setValue (7);

        sneaky (x);

        System.out.println("contents of x " + x.getValue( ));
    }

    static void sneaky (Box y) {
        y.setValue (11); // change value of parameter
        }
}
```

A programmer who passes a box to this method, as shown in the main method, could subsequently see the resulting change in a local variable. In this example, the local variable x, has its value initially set to 7. The class sneaky(x) changes the value to 11, which is then printed out.

A Java programmer should always keep in mind that when a value is passed to a method, a certain degree of control over the variable is lost. In particular, the method is free to invoke any method applicable to the parameter type, which could result in the state of the variable being changed, as in this example.

11.4   EQUALITY TEST

For basic data types the concept of equality is relatively simple. The value 7 should clearly be equivalent to $3 + 4$, for example, because we think of integers as being unique entities—there is one and only one 7 value. This is true even when there are two syntactic representations for the same quantity, for example the ASCII value of the letter a is 141, and thus '\141' is the same as 'a'.

The situation becomes slightly more complicated when the two values being defined are not the same type. For example, should the value 2 (an integer constant) be considered equal to 2.0 (a floating-point constant)? The Java language says that the two values are equivalent in this case, since the integer value can be *converted* into a floating-point value, and the two floating values compared. Thus, all the following expressions will yield a true result.

```
7 == (3 + 4)
'a' == '\141'
2 == 2.0
```

When the concept of equality testing is expanded to include objects, the most natural interpretation becomes less obvious. In Section 11.3 it was argued that because objects are internally represented by pointers, the natural interpretation of assignment uses reference semantics. One interpretation of equality testing follows the same reasoning. That is, two objects can be considered equal if they are identically the same. This form of equality testing is often termed "testing object *identity*," and is the interpretation provided by the operator == and its inverse, the operator ! =. This can cause certain anomalies. For example, although 7 is equal to 3 + 4, the following code fragment will nevertheless show that an Integer value 7 is a distinct object from a different Integer object, even if it has the same value:

```
Integer x = new Integer(7);
Integer y = new Integer(3 + 4);
if (x == y)
    System.out.println("equivalent");
else
    System.out.println("not equivalent");
```

The Java compiler does apply type checking rules to the two arguments, which will help detect many programming errors. For example, although a numeric value can be compared to another numeric, a numeric cannot be compared to a different type of object (for example, a String). Two object values can be compared if they are the same type, or if the class of one can be converted into the class of the second. For example, a variable that was declared to be an instance of class Shape could be compared with a variable of type Circle, since a Circle would be converted into a Shape. A particular instance of the conversion rule is one of the more frequent uses of the == operator; namely, any object can be compared to the constant null, since the value null can be assigned to any object type.

Often object identity is not the relation one would like to test, and instead one is interested in object *equality*, based on value, not reference, comparison. This is provided by the method equals, which is defined by the base class Object and redefined by a number of classes. The following, for example, would return true using the equals method but would not be true using the == operator:

```
String a = new String("abc");
String b = new String("abc");
Integer c = new Integer(7);
Integer d = new Integer(3 + 4);
if (a.equals(b)) // uses equals redefined for String
    System.out.println("strings are equal");
if (c.equals(d))
    System.out.println("integers are equal");
```

Because the equals method is defined in class Object, it can be used with any object type. However, for the same reason, the argument is declared only as type Object. This means that any two objects can be compared for equality, even if there is no possible way for either to be assigned to the other:

```
if (a.equals(c)) // can never be true
    System.out.println("string equal to integer");
```

The developer of a class is free to override the equals operator and thereby allow comparison between objects of the same class. Since the argument is an Object it must first be tested to ensure it is the correct type. By convention, the value false is returned in cases where the type is not correct. The following, for example, would be how one could define a method to compare two instances of class Circle (Figure 11.1).

```
class Circle extends Shape {
    .
    .
    .
    public boolean equals (Object arg) {
        if (arg instanceof Circle) {
            // convert argument to circle
            Circle argc = (Circle) arg;
            if (radius == argc.radius)
                return true;   // just test radius
        }
        return false; // return false otherwise
    }
}
```

Because the type of the argument is not necessarily the same as the type of the receiver, unusual situations can occur if the programmer is not careful. For example, suppose we defined equals in class Shape from Figure 11.1 to test equality of the x and y values, but forgot to also override the method in class Square. It could happen in this situation that if we tried to compare a square and a circle, the comparison would be true one way and false the other.

```
Square s = new Square(10, 10, 5);
Circle c = new Circle(10, 10, 5);
if (s.equals(c)) // true, since method in shape is used
    System.out.println("square equal to circle");
if (c.equals(s)) // false, since method in circle is used
    System.out.println("circle equal to square");
```

When overriding the equals method the programmer should be careful to avoid this problem and should ensure that the resulting methods are both symmetric (if x is equal to y, then y is equal to x) and transitive (if x is equal to y and y is equal to z, then x is equal to z).

A good rule of thumb is to use == when testing numeric quantities, and when testing an object against the constant null. In all other situations the method equals should be used.

11.5 GARBAGE COLLECTION

In Section 11.2 it was argued that support for polymorphic variables naturally implies that values are allocated to the heap, rather than to the stack. Memory of any type is always a finite resource, which must be managed if a program is to avoid running out of storage. In order to prevent this problem, both stack-based and heap-based memory is recycled, with new memory requests being assigned the same locations as previous memory values that are no longer being used.

Unlike stack-based memory allocation, heap-based memory management is not tied to method activation, and is thus not automatically recovered when a method returns. This means an alternative mechanism must be introduced.

Two different approaches to the recovery of heap-based memory values are found in programming languages. In languages such as Object Pascal or C++, it is up to the programmer to explicitly indicate when a memory value is no longer being used and can therefore be reused to satisfy new memory requests. In Object Pascal, for example, this is accomplished by means of the statement dispose:

```
var
   aShape : Shape;
begin
   new (aShape); (* allocate a new shape *)
   .
   .
   .
   dispose (aShape); (* free memory used by variable *)
end.
```

In such languages, if an object is to be freed, it must be "owned" by some variable (the variable that will be the target for the free request). But Java values are simply references, and are shared equally by all variables that refer to the same value. If a programmer assigns a value to another variable, or passes the value as an argument, the programmer may no longer be aware of how many references a value might have.

Leaving to the programmer the responsibility for freeing memory in this situation exposes a program to a number of common errors, such as freeing the same memory location twice. Even more commonly, programmers avoid committing this error by simply never freeing memory, causing long-running programs to slowly degrade as they consume more and more memory resources.

For these reasons, the designers of Java elected a different approach. Rather than having the programmer indicate when a value is no longer needed, a run-time system is provided that periodically searches the memory being used by a program to discover which heap values are being accessed and, more importantly, which heap values are no longer being referenced by any variable and can therefore be recovered and recycled. This mechanism is known as the *garbage collection* system.

The use of a garbage collection system in Java is a compromise. The task of garbage collection does exact a toll in execution time. However, in return a garbage collection system greatly simplifies the programming process and eliminates several categories of common programming errors. For most programs, the improvements in reliability are well worth the execution time overhead.

11.6   CHAPTER SUMMARY

The idea of a polymorphic variable is an extremely powerful concept, one we will explore in detail in later chapters. However, the decision to support the concept of a polymorphic variable raises a number of subtle and difficult issues in other aspects of the language. In this chapter we have investigated some of these, showing how inheritance alters the way the language must handle storage management, the concept of assignment, and the testing of two values for equality.

STUDY QUESTIONS

1. What is a polymorphic variable?

2. Given the class definitions shown in Figure 11.1, which of the following statements are legitmate in Java and why?

   ```
   Shape s = new Square(6, 8, 3);
   Circle c = new Square(10, 12, 4);
   ```

3. From the language implementation point of view, what are the two major categories of memory values?

4. How does the idea of a polymorphic variable conflict with the ability to determine memory requirements at compile time?

5. What does it mean to say that Java uses reference semantics for assignment of object values?

6. What does it mean to say that Java uses copy semantics for assignment of primitive data values?

7. What must a programmer do to create a class that supports the Cloneable interface?

8. What is the difference between a deep and shallow copy?

9. In what way is passing a parameter similar to assignment?

10. What is the difference between the == operator and the equals( ) method?

11. What task is being performed by the garbage collection system in the Java run-time library?

12. What are some advantages of a language that uses garbage collection? What are some disadvantages?

EXERCISES

1. Rewrite the Shape classes shown in Figure 11.1 so that they support the Cloneable interface.

2. Rewrite the class Box so that it also has a data field that refers to a Shape object. It should be cloneable in such a way that a deep-copy is created.

3. Rewrite the class Box so that it supports the equals method.

4. Rewrite the Shape classes so that they support the equals method.

5. The concepts of shallow and deep copy have a correspondance with the equals( ) method. Explain the ideas of shallow equals and deep equals, and give an implementation of each.

IV

Understanding Polymorphism

12 Polymorphism

The term *polymorphic* has Greek roots and means roughly "many forms." (*poly* = many, *morphos* = form. Morphos is related to the Greek god Morphus, who could appear to sleeping individuals in any form he wished and hence was truly polymorphic.) In biology, a polymorphic species is one, such as *Homo sapiens*, that is characterized by the occurrence of different forms or color types in individual organisms or among organisms. In chemistry, a polymorphic compound is one that can crystallize in at least two distinct forms, such as carbon, which can crystallize both as graphite and as diamond.

12.1 VARIETIES OF POLYMORPHISM

In object-oriented languages, polymorphism is a natural result of the *is-a* relationship and of the mechanisms of message passing, inheritance, and the concept of substitutability. One of the great strengths of the OOP approach is that these devices can be combined in a variety of ways, yielding a number of techniques for code sharing and reuse.

Pure polymorphism occurs when a single function can be applied to arguments of a variety of types. In pure polymorphism, there is one function (the code body) and a number of interpretations (different meanings). The other extreme occurs when we have a number of different functions (code bodies) all denoted by the same name—a situation known as *overloading* or sometimes *ad hoc polymorphism*. Between these two extremes are *overriding* and *deferred methods*.[1]

---

[1] Note that there is little agreement regarding terminology in the programming language community. In [Horowitz 1984], [Marcotty and Ledgard 1987], [MacLennan 1987], and [Pinson and Wiener 1988] for example, *polymorphism* is defined in a manner roughly equivalent to what we are here calling *overloading*. In [Sethi 1989] and [Meyer 1988] and in the functional programming languages community (such as [Wikström 1987] and [Milner, Tofte, and Harper 1990]), the term is reserved for what we are calling *pure polymorphism*. Other authors use the term for one, two, or all of the mechanisms described in this chapter. Two complete, but technically daunting, analyses are [Cardelli and Wegner 1985] and [Danforth and Tomlinson 1988].

12.2   POLYMORPHIC VARIABLES

With the exception of overloading, polymorphism in object-oriented languages is made possible only by the existence of *polymorphic variables* and the idea of substitutability. A polymorphic variable is one with many faces; that is, it can hold values of different types. Polymorphic variables embody the principle of substitutability. In other words, although there is an expected type for any variable, the actual type can be from any value that is a subtype of the expected type.

In dynamically bound languages (such as Smalltalk), all variables are potentially polymorphic—any variable can hold values of any type. In these languages the desired type is defined by a set of expected behaviors. For example, an algorithm may make use of an array value, expecting the subscripting operations to be defined for a certain variable; any type that defines the appropriate behavior is suitable. Thus, the user could define his or her own type of array (for example, a sparse array) and, if the array operations were implemented using the same names, use this new type with an existing algorithm.

In statically typed languages, such as Java, the situation is slightly more complex. Polymorphism occurs in Java through the difference between the declared (static) class of a variable and the actual (dynamic) class of the value the variable contains.

A good example of a polymorphic variable is the array allPiles in the Solitaire game presented in Chapter 9. The array was declared as maintaining a value of type CardPile, but in fact it maintains values from each of the different subclasses of the parent class. A message presented to a value from this array, such as display in the example code shown below, executes the method associated with the dynamic type of the variable and not that of the static class.

```
public class Solitaire {
    .
    .
    .
   static CardPile allPiles [ ];
    .
    .
    .
   public void paint(Graphics g) {
      for (int i = 0; i < 13; i++)
         allPiles[i].display(g);
   }
    .
    .
    .
}
```

12.3 OVERLOADING

We say a method name is *overloaded* if two or more function bodies are associated with it. Note that overloading is a necessary part of overriding, described in the next section, but the two terms are not identical and overloading can occur without overriding.

In overloading, it is the method *name* that is polymorphic—it has many forms. Another way to think of overloading and polymorphism is that there is a single abstract function that takes various types of arguments; the actual code executed depends on the arguments given. The fact that the compiler can often determine the correct method at compile time (in a strongly typed language) and the fact that it can therefore generate only a single code sequence are simply optimizations.

12.3.1 Overloading Messages in Real Life

In Chapter 1 we saw an example in which overloading occurred without overriding, when I wanted to surprise my friend with flowers for her birthday. One possible solution was to send the message sendFlowersTo to my local florist; another was to give the *same* message to my wife. Both my florist and my wife (an instance of class Spouse) would have understood the message, and both would have acted on it to produce a similar result. In a certain sense, I could have thought of sendFlowersTo as being one method understood by both my wife and my florist, but each would have used a different algorithm to respond to my request.

Note, in particular, that there was no inheritance involved in this example. The first common superclass for my wife and my florist was the category Human. But certainly the behavior sendFlowersTo was not associated with all humans. My dentist, for example, who is also a human, would have been very puzzled by the message.

12.3.2 Overloading and Coercion

As an example more closely tied to programming languages, suppose a programmer is developing a library of classes representing common data structures. A number of data structures can be used to maintain a collection of elements (sets, bags, dictionaries, arrays, and priority queues, for example), and these might all define a method, add, to insert a new element into the collection.

This situation—in which two totally separate functions are used to provide semantically similar actions for different data types—occurs frequently in all programming languages, not simply in object-oriented languages. Perhaps the most common example is the overloading of the addition operator, +. The code generated by a compiler for an integer addition is often radically different from the code generated for a floating-point addition, yet programmers tend to think of the operations as a single entity, the "addition" function.

In this example it is important to point out that overloading may not be the only activity taking place. A semantically separate operation, *coercion*, is also usually associated with arithmetic operations. It occurs when a value of one type is converted into one of a different type. If mixed-type arithmetic is permitted, the addition of two values may be interpreted in a number of different ways:

- There may be four different functions, corresponding to integer + integer, integer + real, real + integer, and real + real. In this case, there is overloading but no coercion.

- There may be two different functions for integer + integer and real + real. In integer + real and real + integer, the integer value is coerced by being changed into a real value. In this situation there is a combination of overloading and coercion.

- There may be only one function, for real + real addition. All arguments are coerced into being real. In this case there is coercion only, with no overloading.

12.3.3   *Overloading from Separate Classes*

Two different forms of overloading can be distinguished. One form occurs when the same method name is found in two or more classes that are not linked by inheritance. The second form occurs when two or more methods with the same name are found within one class definition. The latter form will be described in the next section.

A good example of overloading of the first type is the method isEmpty. This method is used to determine if an object is empty; however, the exact meaning of empty will differ depending upon circumstances. The message is understood by the classes Vector, Hashtable, and Rectangle. The first two are collection classes, and the message returns true when there are no elements in the collection. In the class Rectangle the message returns true if either the height or width of a rectangle is zero, and thus the rectangle has no area.

```
Rectangle r1 = new Rectangle ();
if (r1.isEmpty()) ...
```

Overloading Does Not Imply Similarity

There is nothing intrinsic to overloading that requires the methods associated with an overloaded name to have any semantic similarity. Consider a program that plays a card game, such as the Solitaire game we examined in Chapter 9. The method draw was used to draw the image of a card on the screen. In another application we might also have included a draw method for the pack of cards, that is, to draw a single card from the top of the deck. This draw method is not even remotely similar in semantics to the draw method for the single card, and yet they share the same name.

Note that this overloading of a single name with independent and unrelated meanings should *not* necessarily be considered bad style, and generally it will not contribute to confusion. In fact, the selection of short, clear, and meaningful names such as add, draw, and so on, contributes to ease of understanding and correct use of object-oriented components. It is far simpler to remember that you can add an element to a set than to recall that to do so requires invoking the addNewElement method, or, worse, that it requires calling the routine Set_Module_Addition_Method.

All object-oriented languages permit the occurrence of methods with similar names in unrelated classes. In this case the resolution of overloaded names is determined by observation of the class of the receiver for the message. Nevertheless, this does not mean that functions or methods can be written that take arbitrary arguments. The statically typed nature of Java still requires specific declarations of all names.

12.3.4 *Parametric Overloading*

Another style of overloading, in which procedures (or functions or methods) in the same context are allowed to share a name and are disambiguated by the number and type of arguments supplied, is called *parametric overloading*; it occurs in Java as well as in some imperative languages (such as Ada) and many functional languages. Parametric overloading is most often found in constructor methods. A new Rectangle, for example, can be created either with no arguments (generating a rectangle with size zero and northwest corner 0,0), with two integer arguments (a width and height), with four integer arguments (width, height, northwest corner), with a Point (the northwest corner, size is zero), with a Dimension (height and width, corner 0,0), or with both a Point and a Dimension.

```
Rectangle r1 = new Rectangle ();
Rectangle r2 = new Rectangle (6, 7);
Rectangle r3 = new Rectangle (10, 10, 6, 7);
Point p1 = new Point (10, 10);
Dimension d1 = new Dimension (6, 7);
Rectangle r4 = new Rectangle (p1);
Rectangle r5 = new Rectangle (d1);
Rectangle r6 = new Rectangle (p1, d1);
```

There are six different constructor methods in this class, all with the same name. The compiler decides which method to execute based on the number and type of arguments used with the method call.

Overloading is a necessary prerequisite to the other forms of polymorphism we will consider: overriding, deferred methods, and pure polymorphism. It is also often useful in reducing the "conceptual space," that is, in reducing the amount of information that the programmer must remember. Often, this reduction in programmer-memory space is just as significant as the reduction in computer-memory space permitted by code sharing.

12.4   OVERRIDING

In Chapter 8 we described the mechanics of overriding, so it is not necessary to repeat that discussion here. Recall, however, the following essential elements of the technique. In one class (typically an abstract superclass), a general method is defined for a particular message that is inherited and used by subclasses. In at least one subclass, however, a method with the same name is defined that hides access to the general method for instances of this class (or, in the case of refinement, subsumes access to the general method). We say the second method *overrides* the first.

Overriding is often transparent to the user of a class, and, as with overloading, frequently the two methods are thought of semantically as a single entity.

12.4.1   *Replacement and Refinement*

In Chapter 9 it was briefly noted that overriding can occur in two different forms. A method can *replace* the method in the parent class, in which case the code in the parent is not executed at all. Alternatively, the code from the child can be used to form a *refinement*, which combines the code from the parent and the child classes.

Normally, overridden methods use replacement semantics. If a refinement is desired, it can be constructed by explicitly invoking the parent method as a function. This is accomplished by using the pseudovariable super as the receiver in a message-passing expression. An example from the Solitaire program described in Chapter 9 showed this:

```
class DiscardPile extends CardPile {

    public void addCard (Card aCard) {
        if (! aCard.faceUp( ))
            aCard.flip( );
        super.addCard(aCard);
        }

}
```

Constructors, on the other hand, *always* use refinement semantics. A constructor for a child class will always invoke the constructor for the parent class. This invocation will take place *before* the code for the constructor is executed. If the constructor for the parent class requires arguments, the pseudovariable super is used as if it were a method:

```
class DeckPile extends CardPile {

    DeckPile (int x, int y) {
            // first initialize parent
        super(x, y);
            // then create the new deck
            // first put them into a local pile
        for (int i = 0; i < 4; i++)
            for (int j = 0; j <= 12; j++)
                addCard(new Card(i, j));

            // then shuffle the cards
        Random generator = new Random( );
        for (int i = 0; i < 52; i++) {
            int j = Math.abs(generator.nextInt( )) % 52;
                // swap the two card values
            Object temp = thePile.elementAt(i);
            thePile.setElementAt(thePile.elementAt(j), i);
            thePile.setElementAt(temp, j);
        }
    }
}
```

When used in this fashion, the call on the parent constructor must be the first statement executed. If no call on super is made explicitly, an implicit call will be made to the constructor in the parent class that takes no arguments (if there is one). If the parent class only defines a constructor(s) with arguments, a compiler error will be generated. If the parent class defines no constructors at all, then a default constructor will be created automatically, and it will be this default constructor that is called implicitly.

12.5 ABSTRACT METHODS

A method that is declared as *abstract* can be thought of as defining a method that is *deferred*; it is specified in the parent class but must be implemented in a descendent class. Interfaces can also be viewed as a method for defining deferred classes. Both can be considered to be a generalization of overriding. In both cases, the behavior described in a parent class is modified by the child class. In an abstract method, however, the behavior in the parent class is essentially null, a place holder, and *all* useful activity is defined as part of the code provided by the child class.

One advantage of abstract methods is conceptual, in that their use allows the programmer to think of an activity as associated with an abstraction at a higher level than may actually be the case. For example, in a collection of classes representing geometric shapes, we can define a method to draw the shape in each of the subclasses Circle, Square, and Triangle. We could have defined a similar method in the parent class Shape, but such a method cannot, in actuality, produce any useful behavior since the class Shape does not have sufficient information to draw the shape in question. Nevertheless, the mere presence of this method permits the user to associate the concept *draw* with the single class Shape, and not with the three separate concepts Square, Triangle, and Circle.

There is a second, more practical reason for using abstract methods. In statically typed object-oriented languages, such as Java, a programmer is permitted to send a message to an object only if the compiler can determine that there is in fact a corresponding method that matches the message selector. Suppose the programmer wishes to define a polymorphic variable of class Shape that will, at various times, contain instances of each of the different shapes. Such an assignment is possible, according to our rule of substitutability; nevertheless, the compiler will permit the message draw to be used with this variable only if it can ensure that the message will be understood by any value that may be associated with the variable. Assigning a method to the class Shape effectively provides this assurance, even when the method in class Shape is never actually executed.

12.6   PURE POLYMORPHISM

Many authors reserve the term *polymorphism* (or *pure polymorphism*) for situations where one method can be used with a variety of arguments, and the term *overloading* for situations where multiple methods are all denoted by a single name.[2] Such facilities are not restricted to object-oriented languages. In Lisp or ML, for example, it is easy to write functions that manipulate lists of arbitrary elements; such functions are polymorphic, because the type of the argument is not known at the time the function is defined. The ability to form polymorphic functions is one of the most powerful techniques in object-oriented programming. It permits code to be written once, at a high level of abstraction, and to be tailored as necessary to fit a variety of situations. Usually, the programmer accomplishes this tailoring by sending further messages to the receiver for the method. These subsequent messages often are not associated with the class at the level of the polymorphic method, but rather are deferred methods defined in the lower classes.

---

[2] The extreme cases may be easy to recognize, but discovering the line that separates overloading from polymorphism can be difficult. In both Java and ML a programmer can define a number of functions, each having the same name, but which take different arguments. Is it overloading in Java because the various functions sharing the same name are not defined in one location, whereas in ML-style polymorphism they must all be bundled together under a single heading?

An example of pure polymorphism is the method valueOf, found in the class String. This method is used to generate a textual description of an object, and has roughly the following definition:

```
public class String {

    public static String valueOf (Object obj)
    {
        if (obj == null)
            return "null";
        return obj.toString();
    }
}
```

The method toString is defined in class Object and redefined in a large number of different subclasses. Each of these definitions of toString will have a slightly different effect; a Double will produce a textual representation of its numeric value, a Color will generate a string that describes the red, green, and blue values in the color, a Button will create a string representing the class name followed by a hexadecimal number that represents the location of the object in memory, and so on.

Because these various versions of toString produce a variety of different effects, the method valueOf will similarly produce a number of different results. This variety of effects is achieved despite the fact that there is only one definition of method valueOf.

The important defining characteristic of pure polymorphism, as opposed to overloading and overriding, is that there is one function with the given name, used with a variety of different arguments. Almost always, as in this case, the body of such an algorithm will make use of other forms of polymorphism, such as a polymorphic variable used as an argument, which in turn invokes an overridden method.

12.7 EFFICIENCY AND POLYMORPHISM

An essential point to note is that programming always involves compromises. In particular, programming with polymorphism involves compromises among ease of development and use, readability, and efficiency. In large part, efficiency has been already considered and dismissed; however, it would be remiss not to admit that it is an issue, however slight.

A method, such as the valueOf method described in the last section, that does not know the type of its arguments can seldom be as efficient as a method that has more complete information. Nevertheless, the advantages of rapid development and consistent application behavior and the possibilities of code reuse usually more than make up for any small losses in efficiency.

12.8 CHAPTER SUMMARY

Polymorphism is an umbrella term used to describe a variety of different mechanisms found in programming languages. In object-oriented languages the most important forms of polymorphism are tied to the polymorphic variable—a variable that can hold many different types of values. For example, overloading occurs when two or more functions share the same name. If these methods happen to be found in classes that have a parent class/child class relationship, then it is called overriding. If an overridden method is used with a polymorphic variable, then the particular method executed will be determined by the run-time value of the variable, not the compile-time declaration for the variable.

Other forms of polymorphism include overloading from independent classes, parametric overloading (overloading that is disambiguated by the types of arguments used in a function call), and abstract methods.

Note that the use of polymorphism tends to optimize program development time and reliability, at the cost of run-time efficiency. For most programs, the benefits far exceed the costs.

FURTHER READING

In the interests of completeness, it should be mentioned that there is at least one important style of polymorphism, found in other computer languages, that is not found in Java. A *generic* (sometimes called a template) is a technique that allows a class description to be parameterized with a type. In C++, for example, one could declare a class as follows:

```
template <class T> class box {
public:
    box (T init) { value = init; }
    T getValue( ) { return value; }
private
    T value;
};
```

The result is a "box of T", and not simply a box. To create such a value, one must also specify a type for the parameter value T:

```
box<int> aBox(5); // create a box with an integer
box<Shape> aBox(aCircle); // create a box with a circle
```

One important place where this mechanism is useful is in the creation of collection classes (see Chapter 19). A language with generics, for example, would allow one to declare a vector *of Cards*, rather than (as in Java) simply a vector of objects. The compiler can then verify that the collection contains only the indicated type of values. More importantly, the compiler can avoid the cast necessary in Java when an object is removed from a container.

A discussion of generics in relation to other forms of polymorphism can be found in [Budd 1997].

STUDY QUESTIONS

1. What does the term *polymorphic* mean in common usage?

2. What is a polymorphic variable?

3. How is the characterization of polymorphic variables different in dynamically typed languages than in statically typed languages?

4. What does it mean to say that a method name is overloaded?

5. What does it mean to say that a value has been coerced to a different type?

6. What is parametric overloading?

7. What is overriding, and how is it different from overloading?

8. What is the difference between overriding using replacement and overriding using refinement?

9. What is the default semantics for overriding for methods? For constructors?

10. What is an abstract method?

11. How is an abstract method denoted?

12. What characterizes pure polymorphism?

13. Why should a programmer not be overly concerned with the loss of efficiency due to the use of polymorphic programming techniques?

EXERCISES

1. Describe the various types of polymorphism found in the PinBall Game application presented in Chapter 7.

2. Describe the various types of polymorphism found in the Solitaire application presented in Chapter 9.

13 The AWT and Swing

Java's Abstract Windowing Toolkit, or AWT, is the portion of the Java run-time library that is involved with creating, displaying, and facilitating user interaction with window objects. The AWT is an example of a software *framework*. A framework is a way of structuring generic solutions to a common problem, using polymorphism as a means of creating specialized solutions for each new application. Thus, examining the AWT will illustrate how polymorphism is used in a powerful and dynamic fashion in the language Java.

Beginning with Java 1.2, the AWT has been augmented with a newer library, called Swing. A problem with the earlier AWT components was that they depended upon the underlying operating system. For instance, an AWT button will look like a Windows button on a Windows based PC and like a Macintosh button on a Macintosh. The Swing library overcomes this limitation, and a swing component will look the same on any platform. This means you do not have to worry about inconsistences in the GUI between platforms. The downside is that Swing components are much more computationally intensive, since they operate with only minimal operating system support. This means a Swing-based interface may take longer to draw than would an interface based on the earlier AWT components. Nevertheless, the newer Swing library is slowly becoming the preferred technique for creating user interfaces.

13.1 THE AWT/SWING CLASS HIERARCHY

From the very first, we have said that class JFrame represents the Java notion of an application window, a two-dimensional graphical surface that is shown on the display device and through which the user interacts with a computer program. All our applications have been formed by inheriting from JFrame, overriding various methods, such as the paint method for repainting the window. In actuality, much

211

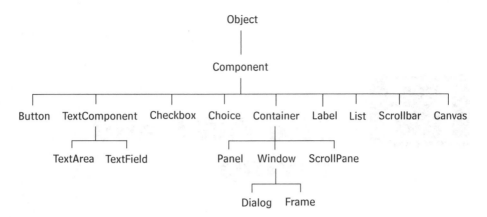

Figure 13.1   The AWT class hierarchy.

of the behavior provided by class JFrame is inherited from parent classes (see Figure 13.1). Examining each of these abstractions in turn will help illustrate the functioning of the Java windowing system, as well as illustrate the power of inheritance as a mechanism for code reuse and sharing.

The class Object is the parent class of all classes in Java. It provides the ability to compare two objects for equality, compute a hash value for an object, and determine the class of an object. Methods defined in class Object include the following:

equals (anObject)	Return true if object is equal to argument
getClass ( )	Return the class of an object
hashCode ( )	Return a hash value for an object
toString ( )	Return a string representation of an object

A Component is something that can be displayed on a two-dimensional screen and with which the user can interact. Attributes of a component include a size, a location, foreground and background colors, whether or not it is visible, and a set of listeners for events. Methods defined in class Component include the following:

setEnabled(boolean)	Enable/disable a component
setLocation(int,int), getLocation( )	Set and get component location
setSize(int,int), getSize( )	Set and get size of component
setVisible(boolean)	Show or hide the component
setForeground(Color), getForegound( )	Set and get foreground colors
setBackground(Color), getBackground( )	Set and get background colors

setFont(Font), getFont( )	Set and get font
repaint(Graphics)	Schedule component for repainting
paint(Graphics)	Repaint component appearance
addMouseListener(MouseListener)	Add a mouse listener for component
addKeyListener(KeyListener)	Add a keypress listener for component

In the AWT library graphical elements such as buttons, checkboxes, scroll bars, and the like are declared as types of components. We will see shortly that the Swing library has moved the Swing versions of these components (JButton and the like) further down the class hierarchy.

A Container is a type of component that can nest other components within it. A container is the way that complex graphical interfaces are constructed. A container maintains a list of the components it manipulates, as well as a layout manager to determine how the components should be displayed. Methods defined in class Container include the following:

| setLayout (LayoutManager) | Set layout manager for display |
| add (Component), remove (Component) | Add or remove component from display |

A Window is a type of Container. A window is a two-dimensional drawing surface that can be displayed on an output device. A window can be stacked on top of other windows and can be moved either to the front or back of the visible windows. Methods defined in class Window include the following:

show( )	Make the window visible
toFront( )	Move window to front
toBack( )	Move window to back

A Frame is a type of window with a title bar, a menu bar, a border, a cursor, and other properties. Methods defined in class Frame include:

setTitle(String), getTitle( )	Set or get title
setCursor(int)	Set cursor
setResizable( )	Make the window resizable
setMenuBar(MenuBar)	Set menu bar for window

Finally, the Swing class JFrame is a subclass of the earlier AWT class Frame. A JFrame will maintain a Container, called the *contentPane*, that will hold all the graphical elements of the window. In addition, the method overrides several of the methods inherited from parent classes.

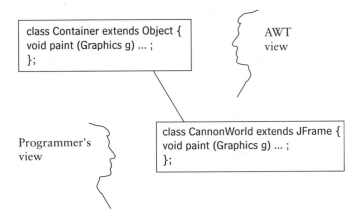

Figure 13.2   Two views of a component.

getContentPane()   Return container for window

If we consider a typical application, such as the CannonWorld application of Chapter 6, we see that it uses methods from a number of different levels of the class hierarchy:

getContentPanel( )   Inherited from class JFrame

setTitle(String)   Inherited from class Frame

setSize(int, int)   Inherited from class Component

show( )   Inherited from class Window

repaint( )   Inherited from class Component

paint( )   Inherited from Component, overridden in application class

The power of the AWT, indeed the power of any framework, comes through the use of a polymorphic variable, that is, a variable declared as a parent type with a value from a child class. When the method show in class Window is invoked, it calls the method setVisible in class Component. This method calls repaint, which in turn calls paint. The code for the algorithm used by setVisible and repaint resides in class Component. When it is being executed, the framework "thinks" that it is dealing only with an instance of Component. However, in actuality the method paint that is being executed is the version that has been overridden in the application class. Thus, there are two views of the method being executed, as described in Figure 13.2.

The code in the parent classes (Component, Container, Window, Frame and JFrame) can all be written without reference to any particular application. Thus, this code can be easily carried from one application to the next. To specialize the design

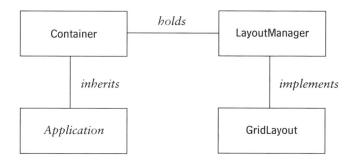

Figure 13.3 Relationships between Layout Manager Components

framework to a new application it is only necessary to override the appropriate methods (such as paint or event listeners) to define application-specific behavior. Thus, the combination of inheritance, overriding, and polymorphism permits design and software reuse on a grand scale.

13.2 THE LAYOUT MANAGER

The idea of a layout manager, which is the technique used by the AWT to assign the locations of components within a container, is an excellent illustration of the combination of polymorphic techniques of composition and inheritance. The layout manager is charged with assigning positions on the surface of a container to the components held in that container. There are a variety of standard layout managers, each of which will place components in slightly different ways. The programmer developing a graphical user interface creates an instance of a layout manager and hands it to a container. Generally, the task of creation is the only direct interaction the programmer will have with the layout manager, as thereafter all commands will be handled by the container itself.

The connections between the application class, the container, and the layout manager illustrate yet again the many ways that inheritance, composition, and interfaces can be combined (Figure 13.3). The application class may inherit from the container (as is usually the case when an application is formed using inheritance from class Frame in the AWT) or it may hold the container as a component (as is usually the case when an application is formed from JFrame using the Swing). In either case the container itself, however, holds the layout manager as a data field, as part of the internal state of the container. But in actual fact, the variable that holds the layout manager is polymorphic. While the Container thinks that it is maintaining a value of type LayoutManager, in fact it will be holding a value from some other type, such as GridLayout, that is implementing the LayoutManager interface.

Figure 13.4   Locations recognized by Border Layout Manager.

There are three different mechanisms at work here: inheritance, composition, and implementation of an interface. Each is serving a slightly different purpose. Inheritance is the *is-a* relation that links the application class to the parent window class. This allows the code written in the AWT class Window to perform application-specific actions, by invoking methods in the application class that override methods in the parent class (paint( ), for example). The fact that composition is used to link the container with the layout manager makes the link between these two items very dynamic—the programmer can easily change the type of layout manager being employed by a container. This dynamic behavior is very difficult to achieve using inheritance alone, since the inheritance relationship between a parent and child is established at compile time. Finally, the fact that LayoutManager is simply an interface; and as well as the fact that various different classes of objects implement this interface, means that the programmer is free to develop alternative layout managers using a wide variety of techniques. (This freedom would be much more constrained if, for example, LayoutManager was a class that alternative layout managers needed to extend.)

13.2.1   *Layout Manager Types*

There are five standard types of layout managers: BorderLayout, GridLayout, Card-Layout, FlowLayout, and GridBagLayout. The BorderLayout manager can manage no more than five different components. This is the default layout manager for applications constructed by subclassing from JFrame. The five locations are shown in Figure 13.4. They correspond to the left and right, top and bottom, and center of the display. Not all five locations need be filled. If a location is not used, the space is allocated to the remaining components.

When a border layout manager is employed, the first argument in the add method is used to specify which position a component is filling in a collection. (With JFrame we must first use the method getContentPane in order to access the container holding the window contents.)

```
getContentPane().add("North", new JButton("quit"));
getContentPane().add("Center", colorField);
```

The next most common type of layout is the GridLayout. The manager for this layout creates a rectangular array of components, each occupying the same size portion of the screen. Using arguments with the constructor, the programmer specifies the number of rows and the number of columns in the grid. Two additional integer arguments can be used to specify a horizontal and vertical space between the components. An example of a panel formatted using a GridLayout is shown in Figure 13.13. The section of code for that application that creates the layout manager is as follows:

```
JPanel p = new JPanel( );
   // make a 4 by 4 grid,
   // with 3 pixels between each element
p.setLayout (new GridLayout(4, 4, 3, 3));

p.add (new ColorButton(Color.black, "black"));
p.add (new ColorButton(Color.blue, "blue"));
```

A FlowLayout manager places components in rows left to right, top to bottom. Unlike the layout created by a GridLayout manager, the components managed by a flow layout manager need not all have the same size. When a component cannot be completely placed on a row without truncation, a new row is created. The flow manager is the default layout manager for the class JPanel (as opposed to JFrame, where the default manager is a BorderLayout).

A CardLayout manager stacks components vertically. Only one component is visible at any one time. The components managed by a card layout manager can be named (using the string argument to the add method). Subsequently, a named component can be made the visible component. This is one of the few instances where the programmer would have direct interaction with the layout manager.

```
CardLayout lm = new CardLayout( );
JPanel p = new JPanel (lm);
p.add ("One", new JLabel ("Number One"));
p.add ("Two", new JLabel ("Number Two"));
p.add ("Three", new JLabel ("Number Three"));
   .
   .
   .
lm.show (p, "Two"); // show component "Two"
```

The most general type of layout manager is the GridBagLayout manager. This manager allows the programmer to create a nonuniform grid of squares, and place components in various positions within each square. However, the details of the use of this manager are complex and will not be described here.

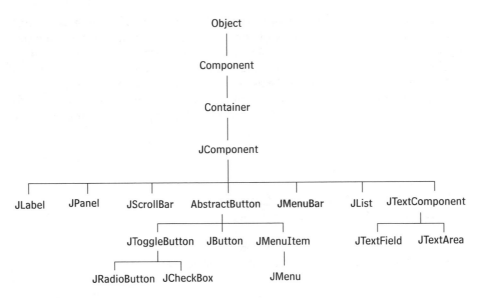

Figure 13.5   The Swing class hierarchy.

13.3   USER INTERFACE COMPONENTS

The variety of user interface components in the Java and Swing frameworks are again a good illustration of the power of polymorphism provided both through inheritance and interfaces. In the Swing extensions of the AWT, all the user interface components are subclasses of the parent class JComponent (Figure 13.5). Containers assume only that the elements they will hold are instances of subclasses of class Component. In fact, the values they maintain are polymorphic and represent more specialized values, such as buttons or scroll bars. Thus, the design of the user interface construction system depends upon the mechanisms of inheritance, polymorphism, and substitutability.

13.3.1   *Labels*

The simplest type of user interface component is a JLabel. A label has only the text it will display. It will display as much of the text as it can in the area it is given.

```
JLabel lab = new JLabel("score: 0 to 0");
getContentPane().add ("South", lab); // put label on bottom of window
```

Unlike other components, a label does not respond to any type of event, such as a mouse click or a key press. However, the text of the label can be changed using the method setText(String), and the current text of a label can be retrieved using getText( ).

13.3.2 *Button*

A JButton is a labeled component, represented by a rounded box, that can respond to user interaction. As we have seen in earlier programs, interaction with a button is achieved by attaching an ActionListener object to the button. The ActionListener object is then notified when the button is pressed.

```
JButton b = new JButton ("do it!");
b.addActionListener (new DoIt( ));
   .
   .
   .
private class DoIt implements ActionListener {
   public void actionPerformed (ActionEvent e) {
      // whatever DoIt does
        .
        .
        .
   }
}
```

A useful technique is to combine the button object and the button listener in one new class. This new class both subclasses from the original JButton class and implements the ActionListener interface. For example, in the case study presented in Section 13.5, we create a set of buttons for different colors. Each button holds a color value, and when pressed it invokes a method using the color as argument. This class is written as follows:

```
private class ColorButton
      extends JButton implements ActionListener {
   private Color ourColor;

   public ColorButton (Color c, String name) {
      super (name); // create the button
      ourColor = c; // save the color value
      addActionListener (this); // add ourselves as listener
   }

   public void actionPerformed (ActionEvent e) {
         // set color for middle panel
      setFromColor (ourColor);
   }
}
```

Notice how the object registers itself as a listener for button actions. The pseudovariable this is used when an object needs to denote itself. When pressed, the button will invoke the method actionPerformed, which will then invoke the method setFromColor that is found in the surrounding class.

We can even take this technique one step further, and define a generic Button-Adapter class that is both a button and a listener. The actions of the listener will be encapsulated by an abstract method, which must be implemented by a subclass:

```
abstract class ButtonAdapter
     extends JButton implements ActionListener {
  public ButtonAdapter (String name) {
     super (name);
     addActionListener (this);
  }

  public void actionPerformed (ActionEvent e) { pressed( ); }

  public abstract void pressed ( );
}
```

To create a button using this abstraction, the programmer must create a subclass and override the method pressed. This, however, can be done easily using a class definition expression (see Section 10.5.3). The following, for example, creates a button that when pressed will halt the application.

```
JPanel p = new JPanel( );

p.add (new ButtonAdapter("Quit"){
   public void pressed ( ) { System.exit(0); }});
```

13.3.3 *Scroll Bars*

A JScrollBar is a slider, used to specify integer values over a wide range. Scroll bars can be displayed in either a horizontal or a vertical direction. The maximum and minimum values can be specified, as well as the line increment (the amount the scroll bar will move when it is touched in the ends), and the page increment (the amount it will move when it is touched in the background area between the slider and the end). Like a button, interaction is provided for a scroll bar by defining a listener that will be notified when the scroll bar is modified.

The case study at the end of this chapter uses a technique similar to the one described earlier in the section on buttons. Figure 13.13 offers a a snapshot of this application, which includes three vertical scroll bars. The class ColorBar represents a scroll bar for maintaining colors. The constructor for the class creates a vertical scroll bar with an initial value of 40 and a range between 0 and 255. The background color for the scroll bar is set using a given argument. Finally, the object itself is made a listener for scroll bar events. When the scroll bar is changed, the method adjustmentValueChanged will be executed. Typically, within this method the current value of the scroll bar would be accessed using getValue( ).

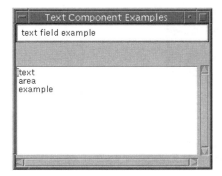

Figure 13.6   A window with two text components.

In this particular application, a bank of three scroll bars will be created, and the value of all three will be recovered in a shared method named setFromBar.

```
private class ColorBar
      extends JScrollBar implements AdjustmentListener {
   public ColorBar (Color c) {
      super (JScrollBar.VERTICAL, 40, 0, 0, 255);
      setBackground (c);
      addAdjustmentListener (this);
   }

   public void adjustmentValueChanged (AdjustmentEvent e) {
      // method setFromBar will get scroll bar
      // value using getValue();
      setFromBar ( );
   }
}
```

13.3.4   *Text Components*

A text component is used to display editable text. There are two varieties of text components, JTextField and JTextArea. The first is a fixed-size block, while the second uses scroll bars to display a larger block of text, not all of which might be viewable at any one time. Figure 13.5 illustrates these two types of items. ←13.6

The text in a text component can be set or accessed by the program using the methods setText(String) and getText(). Additional text can be added to the text area using the method append(String). Various other methods can be used to indicate whether or not the text is editable and to select a subportion of the text. A TextListener can be attached to a text component. The listener must implement the TextListener interface:

Figure 13.7   A window with a checkbox.

```
interface TextListener extends EventListener {
    public void textValueChanged (TextEvent e);
    }
```

13.3.5   *Checkbox*

A JCheckBox is a component that maintains and displays a labeled binary state.
The state described by a checkbox can be either on or off. The current state of the
checkbox can be set or tested by the programmer. A checkbox is typically used
in an application to indicate a binary (on/off, yes/no) choice (see Figure (13.6)).

Both the label and the state of the checkbox can be set by the programmer,
using the methods getText, setText, isSelected, and setSelected. Changing the state of
a checkbox creates an ItemEvent, that is registered with any ItemListener objects.
The following simple application illustrates the use of these methods:

```
import javax.swing.*;
import java.awt.event.*;

class CheckTest extends JFrame {
    private JCheckBox cb = new JCheckBox ("the checkbox is off");

    public static void main (String [ ] args)
        { CheckTest world = new CheckTest(); world.show(); }

    public CheckTest () {
        setTitle("Check box example"); setSize(300, 70);
        cb.addItemListener (new CheckListener());
        getContentPane().add ("Center", cb);
        }

    private class CheckListener implements ItemListener {

        public void itemStateChanged (ItemEvent e) {
            if (cb.isSelected())
                cb.setText ("The checkbox is on");
            else cb.setText ("The checkbox is off");
        }
```

13.7 →

```
      }
   }
```

13.3.6 *Radio Button Groups, Choices, and Lists*

Three types of interface components are typically employed to allow the user to select one item from a large number of possibilities. The first is a group of connected buttons, called a ButtonGroup, that has the property that only one can be set at any one time. Such a collection is sometimes called a *radio button* group, since their behavior is similar to the way buttons in car radios work. The second form is termed a JComboBox. A JComboBox object displays only one selection, but when the user clicks the mouse in the selection area, a pop-up menu appears that allows the choice to be changed to a different selection. A third possibility is termed a JList. A JList is similar to a JComboBox, however several possibilities out of the range can be displayed at one time.

Figure 13.7 illustrates all three possibilities. The code to produce this example ← 13.8 is shown in Figure 13.9.

A ButtonGroup group should be used when the number of alternatives is small. A JComboBox or a JList should be used if the number of alternatives is five or more. A combo box takes up less space in the display, but makes it more difficult to view all the alternatives.

To create a JComboBox or a JList object, the programmer specifies the alternatives as an array of objects passed to the constructor. An ItemListener can be attached to the object. When a selection is made, the listener will be informed

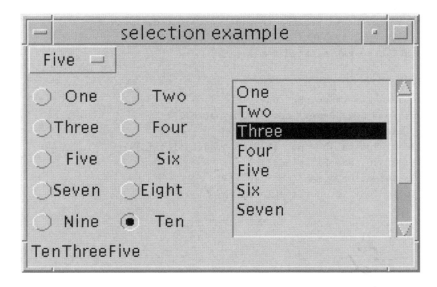

Figure 13.8   Three selection possibilities: radio button Checkbox group, Choice object, and a List.

```
public class ChoiceTest extends JFrame {
    public static void main (String [ ] args)
        { ChoiceTest world = new ChoiceTest( ); world.show( ); }

    private String [ ] choices = {"One", "Two", "Three", "Four",
        "Five", "Six", "Seven", "Eight", "Nine", "Ten"};
    private JLabel display = new JLabel();
    private JComboBox theChoice = new JComboBox(choices);
    private JList theList = new JList(choices);
    private ButtonGroup theGroup = new ButtonGroup();
    private ItemListener theListener = new ItemListener() {
            public void itemStateChanged (ItemEvent e) { setDisplay(); }};

    public ChoiceTest ( ) {
        setTitle ("selection example"); setSize (300, 300);
        theChoice.addItemListener(theListener);
        theList.addListSelectionListener (new ListSelectionListener() {
            public void valueChanged (ListSelectionEvent e)
                { setDisplay( ); }});
        getContentPane().add("West", makeRadioButtons());
        getContentPane().add("North", theChoice);
        getContentPane().add("East", theList);
        getContentPane().add("South", display);
    }

    private void setDisplay ( ) {
        display.setText( (String) theList.getSelectedValue() +
            theGroup.getSelection().getActionCommand() +
            theChoice.getSelectedItem());
    }

    private JPanel makeRadioButtons( ) {
        JPanel p = new JPanel (new GridLayout(5,2));
        for (int i = 0; i < 10; i++) {
            JRadioButton jb = new JRadioButton(choices[i]);
            theGroup.add(jb); p.add(jb);
            jb.setActionCommand(choices[i]);
            jb.addItemListener(theListener);
        }
        return p;
    }
}
```

Figure 13.9 Alternative ways to display choices.

using the method itemStateChanged. The text of the selected item can be recovered using the method getSelectedItem.

To structure a group of radio buttons as a group, the programmer first creates a ButtonGroup. Each button is registered with the button group. As a checkbox group is constructed out of several components, it is almost always laid out on a JPanel. The JPanel is then placed as a single element in the original layout. This is shown in Figure 13.9. Here a 5 by 2 grid is used as layout for the 10 checkboxes.

13.4   PANELS

A JPanel is a Container that acts like a Component. A panel represents a rectangular region of the display. Each panel holds its own layout manager, which can differ from the layout manager for the application display. Items can be inserted into the panel. The panel, as a single unit, is then inserted into the application display.

The use of a panel is illustrated by the application described in Figure 13.9. *← 13.10* Here the method makeRadioButtons creates a panel to hold the 10 radio buttons that make up the group. This panel is structured, using a GridLayout as a 5 by 2 element matrix. This group of 10 components can then be treated as a single element, and is placed on the left side of the application layout.

More examples of the use of panels will be provided by the application that will be described in the next section. A snapshot of the window for this application is shown in Figure 13.13. The three scroll bars on the left are placed on a panel. This panel is laid out using a BorderLayout manager. The method to create and return this panel is described as follows:

```
private JPanel makeScrollBars ( ) {
   JPanel p = new JPanel( );
   p.setLayout (new BorderLayout( ));
   p.add("West", redBar);
   p.add("Center", greenBar);
   p.add("East", blueBar);
   return p;
}
```

The panel returned as the result of this method is then placed on the left side of the application window.

13.4.1   ScrollPane

A JScrollPane is in many ways similar to a JPanel. Like a panel, it can hold another component. (See Figure 13.9.) However, a JScrollPane can only hold one *← 13.10* component, and it does not have a layout manager. If the size of the component being held is larger than the size of the ScrollPane itself, scroll bars will be automatically generated to allow the user to move the underlying component.

We illustrate the use of a ScrollPane with a simple test program, shown in Figure 13.11. The application window in this program will be set to 300 by 300 pixels, but a scroll pane is created that holds a canvas that has been sized to 1000 by 1000 pixels. Scroll bars will therefore be added automatically that allow the user to see portions of the underlying canvas. As mouse events are detected by the canvas, points will be added to a Polygon. The listener is here doing double duty, trapping both mouse presses (subclassing from frame MouseAdapter and overriding the message mousePressed) and scroll bar movements (implementing the AdjustmentListener interface and implementing the method adjustmentValueChanged). To paint the application window, the canvas simply draws the polygon values.

13.5   CASE STUDY: A COLOR DISPLAY

A simple test program will illustrate how panels and layout managers are used in developing user interfaces. The application will also illustrate the use of scroll bars and the use of methods provided by the class Color. Finally, we can also use this program to illustrate how nested classes can be employed to combine the actions of creating a new graphical component (such as a button or a slider) and listening for actions relating to the component.

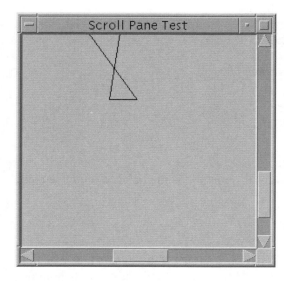

Figure 13.10   A ScrollPane test.

```java
import javax.swing.*;
import java.awt.*;
import java.awt.event.*;

public class BigCanvas extends JFrame {
   public static void main ( String [ ] args) {
      BigCanvas world = new BigCanvas( );
      world.show( );
   }

   private Polygon poly = new Polygon( );
   private JPanel jp = new JPanel( );
   private MouseKeeper mouseListener = new MouseKeeper();

   public BigCanvas( ) {
      setSize (300, 300); setTitle ("Scroll Pane Test");
         // make canvas larger than window
      jp.setPreferredSize(new Dimension(1000, 1000));
      jp.addMouseListener(mouseListener);
         // add scroll pane to manage canvas
      JScrollPane jsp = new JScrollPane(jp);
      jsp.getHorizontalScrollBar().addAdjustmentListener(mouseListener);
      jsp.getVerticalScrollBar().addAdjustmentListener(mouseListener);
      getContentPane().add("Center", jsp);
   }

   public void paint (Graphics g) {
      super.paint(g);
      Graphics gr = jp.getGraphics( );
      gr.drawPolygon (poly);
   }

   private class MouseKeeper
            extends MouseAdapter implements AdjustmentListener {
      public void mousePressed (MouseEvent e) {
         poly.addPoint (e.getX( ), e.getY( ));
         repaint( );
      }

      public void adjustmentValueChanged (AdjustmentEvent e)
         { repaint( ); }
   }
}
```

Figure 13.11   Test program for scrollpanes.

```
class ColorTest extends JFrame {
   static public void main (String [ ] args)
      { ColorTest world = new ColorTest( ); world.show( ); }

   private JTextField colorDescription = new JTextField( );
   private JPanel colorField = new JPanel( );
   private Color current = Color.black;
   private JScrollBar redBar = new ColorBar(Color.red);
   private JScrollBar greenBar = new ColorBar(Color.green);
   private JScrollBar blueBar = new ColorBar(Color.blue);

   public ColorTest( ) {
      setTitle ("color test"); setSize (400, 600);
      getContentPane().add("North", colorDescription);
      getContentPane().add("East", makeColorButtons( ));
      getContentPane().add("Center", colorField);
      getContentPane().add("West", makeScrollBars( ));
      setFromColor (current);
   }

   private void setFromColor (Color c) {
      current = c; colorField.setBackground (current);
      redBar.setValue(c.getRed( )); greenBar.setValue(c.getGreen( ));
      blueBar.setValue(c.getBlue( ));
      colorDescription.setText(c.toString( ));
   }

   private void setFromBar ( ) {
      int r = redBar.getValue( ); int g = greenBar.getValue( );
      int b = blueBar.getValue( ); setFromColor (new Color(r, g, b));
   }

   private JPanel makeColorButtons ( ) { ... }
   private JPanel makeScrollBars ( ) { ... }
private class BrightenButton extends JButton implements ActionListener ...
private class ColorButton extends JButton implements ActionListener ...
private class ColorBar extends JScrollBar implements AdjustmentListener ...
}
```

Figure 13.12   The class ColorTest.

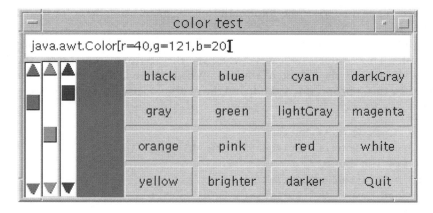

Figure 13.13   Snapshot of ColorTest application.

The class ColorTest (Fig. 13.12) creates a window to display color values. The window (Fig. 13.13) is divided into four regions. The regions are managed by the default layout manager for class Frame, which is a value of type BorderLayout.

At the top (the "north" side) is a text region, a component of type JTextField, that describes the current color. To the left (the "west" region) is a trio of sliders that can be used to set the red, green, and blue values. To the right (the "east" region) is a 4 by 4 bank of 16 buttons. These are constructed on a JPanel that is organized by a GridLayout manager. Thirteen of the buttons represent the predefined color values. Two more represent the actions of making a color brighter and darker. The final button will halt the application. Finally, in the middle will be a square panel that represents the specified color.

The class ColorTest holds six data fields. The first represents the text field at the top of the page. The second represents the color panel in the center. the third represents the current color of this center panel. The remaining three represent the three scrollbars that will be placed in the panel on the left.

The three sliders make use of the class ColorBar described earlier in Section 13.3.3. The argument used with the constructor for each class is the color to be used in painting the buttons and background for the scroll bar. You will recall that when adjusted, the scroll bar will invoke its listener, which will execute the method adjustmentValueChanged. This method will then execute the method setFromBar.

A method makeScrollBars, used to create the panel that holds the three scroll bars, was described earlier in Section 13.4.

The idea of combining inheritance and implementation of an interface is used in creating the buttons that represent the 13 predefined colors. Each instance of ColorButton, shown earlier in Section 13.3.2, both extends the class JButton and implements the ActionListener interface. When the button is pressed, the method setFromColor will be used to set the color of the middle panel using the color stored in the button.

The class BrightenButton is slightly more complex. An index value is stored with the button. This value indicates whether the button represents the "brighten" button or the "darken" button. When pressed, the current color is modified by the appropriate method, and the new value used to set the current color.

```java
private class BrightenButton
      extends JButton implements ActionListener {
   private int index;
   public BrightenButton (int i) {
      super ( i == 0 ? "brighter" : "darker");
      index = i;
      addActionListener(this);
   }

   public void actionPerformed (ActionEvent e) {
      if (index == 0)
         setFromColor (current.brighter( ));
      else
         setFromColor (current.darker( ));
   }
}
```

A panel is used to hold the 16 button values. In this case the layout is described by a 4 by 4 grid pattern. Thirteen represent the predefined buttons. Two represent the brighter and darker buttons. And the final creates a button that when pressed exits the application.

```java
private JPanel makeColorButtons ( ) {
   JPanel p = new JPanel( );
   p.setLayout (new GridLayout(4,4,3,3));
   p.add (new ColorButton(Color.black, "black"));
   p.add (new ColorButton(Color.blue, "blue"));
   p.add (new ColorButton(Color.cyan, "cyan"));
   p.add (new ColorButton(Color.darkGray, "darkGray"));
   p.add (new ColorButton(Color.gray, "gray"));
   p.add (new ColorButton(Color.green, "green"));
   p.add (new ColorButton(Color.lightGray, "lightGray"));
   p.add (new ColorButton(Color.magenta, "magenta"));
   p.add (new ColorButton(Color.orange, "orange"));
   p.add (new ColorButton(Color.pink, "pink"));
   p.add (new ColorButton(Color.red, "red"));
   p.add (new ColorButton(Color.white, "white"));
```

```
    p.add (new ColorButton(Color.yellow, "yellow"));
    p.add (new BrightenButton(0));
    p.add (new BrightenButton(1));
    p.add (new ButtonAdapter("Quit"){
       public void pressed( ) { System.exit(0); }});
    return p;
}
```

13.6 DIALOGS

A JDialog is a special purpose window that is displayed for a short period of time during the course of execution, disappearing thereafter. Dialogs are often used to notify the user of certain events, or to ask simple questions. A dialog must always be attached to an instance of JFrame, and disappears automatically when the frame is hidden (such as when the application halts).

Dialog windows can be modal or nonmodal. A modal dialog demands a response from the user, and it prevents the user from performing any further action until the dialog is dismissed. A nonmodal dialog, sometimes called a modeless dialog, can be ignored by the user. The processing of actions for a nonmodal dialog is often placed in a separate Thread (see Chapter 20), so that the actions produced by the dialog will not disrupt the continuing processing of the rest of the application. Whether or not a dialog is modal is determined when the dialog is created. The two arguments used in the constructor for the dialog are the application Frame and a Boolean value that is true if the dialog is modal.

```
    // create a new nonmodal dialog in current application
    JDialog dig = new JDialog (this, false);
```

Because a JDialog is a type of Window, graphical components can be placed in the dialog area, just as in a JFrame or JPanel. The default layout manager for a dialog is BorderLayout, the same as with JFrame.

The most common methods used with a dialog are not actually defined in the class JDialog but are inherited from parent classes. These include the following:

setSize(int, int)	Set window size
show( )	Display window
setVisible(false)	Remove window from display
setTitle(String), getTitle( )	Set or get title of window

For modal dialogs, the show method does not return until the dialog is dismissed. Such dialogs must therefore invoke the setVisible(false) method sometime during their processing.

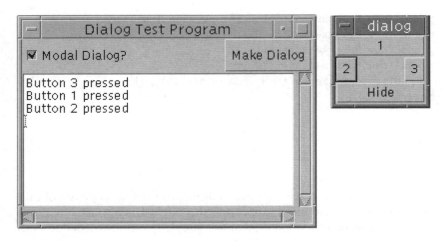

Figure 13.14   Dialog example window.

233 →

13.6.1   *Example Program for Dialogs*

An example program will illustrate the creation and manipulation of dialogs. The application shown in Figure 13.15, on page ⟨226⟩ creates a window with a checkbox, a button, and a text area. The application window, as well as an example dialog box window, is shown in Figure 13.14. The checkbox allows the user to specify either a modal or modeless dialog box should be created. The button creates the dialog, while the text area records button presses performed by the dialog.

The method makeDialog creates the dialog box. The size of the box is set at 100 by 100 pixels, and four buttons are placed on the box. Three buttons simply type text into the display when pressed, while the last button will hide the dialog. For a modal dialog hiding the dialog is the same as dismissing the dialog box, and it returns control to the method that created the dialog.

13.7   THE MENU BAR

A Swing menu bar is a graphical component, it is declared as a sub-class of JComponent. Both menu bars and menus act like containers. A menu bar contains a series of menus, and each menu contains a series of menu items.

An instance of *JMenuBar* can be attached to a Frame using the method setJ-MenuBar:

```
          .
          .
          .
JMenuBar bar = new JMenuBar( );
setJMenuBar (bar);
```

```
class DialogTest extends JFrame {
   static public void main (String [ ] args)
      { DialogTest world = new DialogTest( ); world.show( ); }

   private JTextArea display = new JTextArea( );
   private JCheckBox cb = new JCheckBox("Modal Dialog?");

   public DialogTest( ) {
      setTitle ("Dialog Test Program");
      setSize (300, 220);

      getContentPane().add ("West", cb);
      getContentPane().add ("East", new Makebutton( ));
      getCOntentPane().add ("South", display);
   }

   private class Makebutton extends ButtonAdapter {
      public Makebutton ( ) { super ("Make Dialog"); }
      public void pressed ( ) { makeDialog (cb.isSelected( )); }
   }

   private void makeDialog (boolean modalFlag) {
      final JDialog dlg = new JDialog (this, modalFlag);
      dlg.setSize (100, 100);
      dlg.add ("North", new CountButton(1));
      dlg.add ("West", new CountButton(2));
      dlg.add ("East", new CountButton(3));
      dlg.add ("South", new ButtonAdapter("Hide") {
         public void pressed ( ) { dlg.setVisible(false); }});
      dlg.show( );
   }

   private class CountButton extends ButtonAdapter {
      public CountButton (int val) { super ("" + val); }
      public void pressed ( ) {
         display.append("Button " + getLabel( ) + " pressed\n");}
   }
}
```

Figure 13.15 Example program for creating dialogs.

.
.
.

Individual menus are named, and are placed on the menu bar using the method add:

.
.
.

```
JMenu helpMenu = new JMenu ("Help");
bar.add (helpMenu);
```

.
.
.

Menu items are created using the class JMenuItem. Each menu item maintains a list of ActionListener objects, the same class used to handle JButton events. The listeners will be notified when the menu item is selected.

.
.
.

```
JMenuItem quitItem = new JMenuItem ("Quit");
quitItem.addActionListener (new QuitListener());
helpMenu.add (quitItem);
```

.
.
.

A number of techniques can be used to create special purpose menus, such as tear-off menus, cascading menus, and so on. However, these will not be described here.

13.7.1 *A Quit Menu Facility*

On many platforms it is sometimes difficult to stop a running Java application. For this reason, it is useful to define a general purpose "Quit" menu bar facility. The class QuitItem (Figure 13.16, on page 228) creates a listener that will halt the running application when the associated menu item is selected. By overloading the constructor, we make it trivial to add this functionality to any application.

The constructor for QuitItem can be given a JMenuItem as argument. In this case it merely attaches itself as a listener to the menu item. Alternatively, it can be given a JMenu, in which case it creates a menu item labeled "Quit." Or it can be given a JMenuBar, in which case it creates a new menu labeled "Quit" that contains only the quit menu item. Finally, the constructor can be given an application as argument, in which case it creates a new menu bar containing only the one menu that contains only the single quit item. Using the application constructor, a quit menu selection can be added to an application by placing only a single line in the constructor for the application:

```
class QuitItem implements ActionListener {

  public QuitItem (JFrame application) {
      JMenuBar mBar = new JMenuBar( );
      application.setJMenuBar (mBar);
      JMenu menu = new JMenu("Quit");
      mBar.add (menu);
      JMenuItem mItem = new JMenuItem("Quit");
      mItem.addActionListener (this);
      menu.add (mItem);
  }

   public QuitItem (JMenuBar mBar) {
      JMenu menu = new JMenu("Quit");
      mBar.add (menu);
      JMenuItem mItem = new JMenuItem("Quit");
      mItem.addActionListener (this);
      menu.add (mItem);
  }

   public QuitItem (JMenu menu) {
      JMenuItem mItem = new JMenuItem("Quit");
      mItem.addActionListener (this);
      menu.add (mItem);
  }

  public QuitItem (JMenuItem mItem)
     { mItem.addActionListener (this); }

  public void actionPerformed (ActionEvent e)
       { System.exit(0); }
}
```

Figure 13.16   A general purpose QuitItem class.

```
class ColorTest extends Frame {
    .
    .
    public ColorTest ( ) {
       .
       .
          // add quit menu item to application
       new QuitItem (this);
```

```
            .
            .
            .
        }
    }
```

13.8 CHAPTER SUMMARY

The Abstract Windowing Toolkit, or AWT, is the portion of the Java library used for the creation of graphical user interfaces. The design of the AWT is an excellent illustration of the power of object-oriented techniques. The Swing library is an extension to the AWT that allows graphical user interfaces to have the same look and feel across different platforms. In this chapter we have described the various AWT and Swing components, and the way in which they are used to develop user interfaces.

STUDY QUESTIONS

1. What do the letters *AWT* stand for?

2. What is a Component object in the Java AWT?

3. What are the parent classes of class JFrame?

4. In what class is the method setBackground defined?

5. How is a container different from other types of components?

6. What is the difference between a frame, a window, and a container?

7. Explain why in a framework there are two views of an overridden method, such as paint.

8. What is the task performed by the layout manager?

9. Explain how the three mechanisms of inheritance, composition, and implementation of an interface are all involved in the task of attaching a layout manager to a container.

10. What are the five different layout manager types? Which mangers use the one argument add method, and which use the method in which the first argument is a String value and the second a component?

11. What two roles are being combined in a ButtonAdapter?

12. Show how the class ColorButton could have been written using a ButtonAdapter.

13. What is the difference between a TextArea and a TextField?

14. What are the three different types of components that allow the user to select one item out of many possibilities?

15. What is a JPanel?

16. What are the 13 predefined values provided by class Color?

17. What do the three numerical values that define a color represent?

18. In what ways is a MenuBar similar to a Component? In what ways is it different?

Exercises

1. Add a menu bar to the Solitaire program described in Chapter 9. Then, add two menu items, one to quit the application, and one to reset the application for a new game.

2. Write code to create a panel having a 2 by 2 grid layout with 3 pixels horizontal space and 5 pixels vertical space between components. Place buttons labelled "one" to "four" in the panels of the grid. Place this panel in the center of your frame.

3. After placing the panel from the last question into the center portion of a window, add a small text box at the top. As each button is pressed, display the button number in the text box.

4. Using a text box and a grid of buttons, create a simple calculator application. Buttons correspond to digits and the four arithmetic functions +, −, ∗ and /, as well as the equals sign.

14

Input and Output Streams

At first glance, the input/output facilities in Java seem to present a confusing profusion of alternatives. At the highest level, there is the distinction between the *stream* classes, used to manipulate binary 8-bit quantities, and the *reader/writer* classes, used to manipulate string and 16-bit Unicode character values. Underneath each of these major categories are a plethora of subclasses. In all, over 40 classes are used to provide input and output. However, standing behind this multitude is an elegant logical structure that makes efficient and effective use of inheritance, composition, and polymorphism. Understanding how to manipulate the network and file facilities provided by Java will be much easier once you appreciate the structure and purpose of the I/O classes.

14.1 STREAMS VERSUS READERS AND WRITERS

The term *stream* conjures up an image of a narrow conduit through which values must pass. And indeed, at the lowest level, a stream is a device for transmitting or retrieving 8-bit (or *byte*) values. Note the emphasis on the action of reading or writing, as opposed to the data itself. A *file* is a collection of items stored on an external device, such as a floppy disk or CD-ROM. The Java object through which the file is accessed—for instance, a FileStream—provides the means to access the data values in the file but does not actually hold the file contents. And although we emphasize that at the lowest levels streams are always pipelines for transmitting 8-bit values, we also note that much of the functionality provided by the various different stream abstractions is intended to permit the programmer to think in terms of higher level units—for example, transmitting strings or integers or object values, instead of their 8-bit internal representation. For example, a method such as readInt() (found in class DataInputStream) will process four 8-bit values in the process of reading a single 32-bit integer.

239

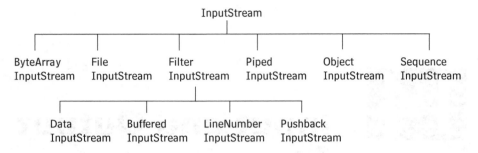

Figure 14.1   Subclasses of InputStream.

Next note that there are two independent and largely parallel systems involved in I/O. The hierarchy rooted in the two classes InputStream and OutputStream are used to read and write 8-bit quantities. Most networking software and file systems are still based around the 8-bit unit, and for the time being these classes will therefore be the ones most commonly used. The alternative hierarchy is rooted in two different classes, Reader and Writer. These abstractions are used to read and write 16-bit Unicode character values.

Figure 14.1 gives the hierarchy of classes that descend from InputStream. (Figure 14.3 will later show a similar hierarchy for the class Reader.) The majority of this chapter will discuss the stream abstractions, as they will likely be the more commonly used for the near future (until 16-bit characters become more of the norm). However, we will briefly discuss the reader/writer classes in Section 14.7, and will use them in the networking examples presented in Chapter 22.

14.2   INPUT STREAMS

The class InputStream is an abstract class, parent to 10 subclasses in the Java library. Each class implements roughly the same behavior. This input stream protocol can be described as follows:

```
abstract class InputStream {

    // read a single byte from the input
    int read( ) throws IOException;

    // read an array of values from the input
    int read (byte [ ] buffer) throws IOException;

    // skip the indicated number of values from input
    long skip (long n) throws IOException;

    // determine number of bytes readable without blocking
```

```
int available( ) throws IOException;

    // close this input stream
void close( ) throws IOException;
}
```

An IOException will be generated if a file cannot be opened, or if an interrupt is encountered while reading from a pipe, or in other exceptional conditions.

The differences among the variety of input stream classes can best be understood by dividing them into two major categories. The first are classes tied to a *physical* input source. These read values from a byte array, a file, or a pipe. The second are those input streams that are *virtual*, depending upon another input stream for the actual reading operations but extending the functionality of the input stream in some fashion. For example, a PushbackInputStream reads values from another input stream but also allows the program to "unread" characters, "pushing them back" into the input stream. In reality the pushed back characters are stored in a local buffer within the PushbackInputStream. When a subsequent read operation is performed, the characters will be read first from the local buffer, before once again reading from the underlying input stream once the buffer is emptied.

14.2.1 *Physical Input Streams*

There are three input stream classes that read from actual data areas. These are distinguished by their names and the arguments used in their constructors. A ByteArrayInputStream, for example, must be given an array of byte values as an argument. A FileInputStream requires either a file or a file name, and so on.

```
    // constructors for various input streams
ByteArrayInputStream (byte [ ] buffer);
ByteArrayInputStream (byte [ ] buffer, int offset, int count);
FileInputStream (File f);
FileInputStream (String fileName);
PipedInputStream (PipedOutputStream p);
```

Note that for simple reading and writing, a FileInputStream or FileOutputStream can be manipulated without first creating a File object. Generally, a File object is necessary only if one is doing operations to the file itself, such as renaming or removing the file. Another reason for creating a File object would be to test whether a file is readable or writable before beginning a sequence of input/output operations.

14.2.2 *Virtual Input Streams*

four

The classes SequenceInputStream, ObjectInputStream, and the three subclasses of FilterInputStream can be thought of as *virtual* input classes. None of these actually read characters from any input area, but instead they rely on one or more underlying input streams for their data source. Each adds useful functionality as values are passed through the class.

For example, a SequenceInputStream takes a sequence of two or more input streams, and logically places them end to end. When one input stream is exhausted, the next stream in sequence is started without interruption or any action on the user's part. The underlying streams can be specified either as two arguments to the constructor (if there are only two input streams to be catenated) or as an enumeration to an underlying collection of input streams (if there are more than two input streams).

```
InputStream f1 = new FileInputStream ("file1.text");
InputStream f2 = new FileInputStream ("file2.text");
InputStream f3 = new SequenceInputStream (f1, f2);
    // f3 now represents the catenation of file1 and file2
Vector fv = new Vector ( );
fv.addElement (f1); fv.addElement (f2);
InputStream f4 = new SequenceInputStream (fv.elements( ));
    // f4 also now represents the same catenation
```

The structure of the class SequenceInputStream is an example of the *composite* design pattern (see Section 15.2).

The class ObjectInputStream is used to provide *serialization*, the ability to convert an object value into a representation that can be transmitted as a sequence of 8-bit values. These values are themselves written to or read from an underlying stream, typically a file stream although any type of stream abstraction will work. We will discuss this class in more detail in Section 14.5.

As noted in Chapter 10, the subclasses of FilterInputStream represent an interesting combination of the object-oriented mechanisms of inheritance and composition, characteristic of the *wrapper* design pattern (see Section 15.9). Because each class inherits from InputStream, they can be used in all situations where an input stream is expected. But each also holds as a component an underlying input stream, used to read the actual character values. One way to envision these classes is as an adapter, or filter, that sits between the client (the code making the request for values) and the physical input stream producing the values.

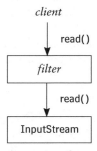

Because they support the interface common to all input streams, such filters can be easily added or removed as needed.

The PushbackInputStream allows a single character to be unread. A value pushed back into the input stream will subsequently be returned as the result of the next read operation. This facility is useful when scanning textual input. Imagine, for example, reading the textual representation of a numeric value, such as 456. It is only *after* the first nondigit character is read that one knows that all of the digits of the number have been seen. But the last character, the nondigit, should not be considered part of the number. Thus, this value is "pushed back" into the input, to be read again later.

The PushbackInputStream allows only a single character to be reprocessed. The BufferedInputStream is a more general facility, allowing the input operations to be backed up over a larger range. A BufferedInputStream reads values from the underlying input stream in large blocks, which for external devices such as a file is much more efficient than reading values byte-by-byte. The BufferedInputStream then responds to the read operation by returning characters from its internal buffer, refilling the buffer with new values if necessary. The method mark() tells the stream to mark a location in this internal buffer. A subsequent reset() then resets the input back to the marked location. All characters between the mark and the reset will then be read again. Although declared only as an instance of InputStream, on most systems the standard input stream System.in is *implemented* by an instance of a buffered input stream. Thus, on most platforms, characters cannot be read from this input stream until an entire line of text has been entered.

The input filter that adds the most additional functionality is the class DataInputStream. In this class, methods are provided to read bytes from the source and return them as a primitive data type. To read an int, for example, will require reading four characters from the underlying input stream. In response to a call on readInt, the four-byte values are read in and combined together to form the new integer value, which is then returned as the result of the call on readInt. Similar methods are provided for each of the primitive data types.

```
class DataInputStream extends FilterInputStream
    implements DataInput {
    .
    .
    public boolean readBoolean () throws IOException

    public byte readByte () throws IOException

    public char readChar () throws IOException

    public double readDouble () throws IOException

    public int readInt () throws IOException
```

```
    public int readLong () throws IOException

    public short readShort () throws IOException

    public int readUnsignedByte () throws IOException

    public int readUnsignedShort () throws IOException
}
```

Note that these methods read a binary representation, not a textual representation of the values. Most generally, the input stream being processed will have been produced using a DataOutputStream. The DataInput interface is also used by the class RandomAccessFile.

14.3 STREAM TOKENIZER

Although not specifically an InputStream, the class StreamTokenizer provides a useful mechanism for breaking a textual file into a sequence of tokens. The stream tokenizer recognizes words (sequences of letters separated by nonletter characters) and numbers (sequences of digit characters), and it can even be set up to recognize comments or convert all tokens to lowercase. Each token returned is characterized by a token type, which is either one of several symbol constants defined in the class or the integer value of the last character read. The following program illustrates several of the methods provided by this class:

```
class TokenTest {
    public static void main (String [ ] args) {
        StreamTokenizer tok = new StreamTokenizer (System.in);
        try {
        while (tok.nextToken() != tok.TT_EOF) {
            switch (tok.ttype) { // ttype is token type
                case StreamTokenizer.TT_NUMBER: // nval is numeric value
                    System.out.println("number " + tok.nval);
                    break;
                case StreamTokenizer.TT_EOL:
                    System.out.println("end of line");
                    break;
                case StreamTokenizer.TT_WORD: // sval is text value
                    System.out.println("word " + tok.sval);
                    break;
```

```
            default:
                System.out.println("token " + (char) tok.ttype);
                break;
            }
        }
    } catch (IOException e) { }
    }
}
```

Giving this program the input "23-skidoo, kid!" yields the output:

```
number 23.0
token -
word skidoo
token ,
word kid
token !
```

The class StringTokenizer (Section 17.8.3) provides a similar facility for breaking apart a string value.

14.4   OUTPUT STREAMS

Although not as extensive as the input stream classes, the subclasses of OutputStream (Figure 14.2) also exhibit the same interesting use of polymorphism, composition, and inheritance. Like InputStream, the abstract parent class OutputStream defines minimal functionality:

```
abstract class OutputStream {
    // write a single byte value
    public abstract void write (int b) throws IOException
```

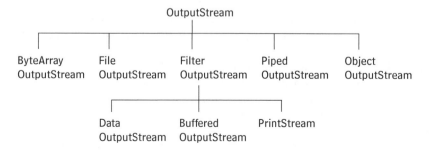

Figure 14.2   Subclasses of OutputStream.

```
        // write an array of byte values
    public void write (byte [ ] buffer) throws IOException

        // flush all output from buffers
    public void flush () throws IOException

        // close stream
    public void close () throws IOException
}
```

The OutputStream abstraction views writing as a task performed one character at a time. However, for many devices (files or networks, for example), such character-by-character processing can be very inefficient. For this reason many subclasses of OutputStream will *buffer* their values, collecting characters in an internal data area until a sufficiently large number of values have been generated, and then writing them out in one step. For the most part this buffering is transparent to the programmer and is of little concern. Occasionally, however, the buffering process is undesirable. We will see an example in Chapter 22, where input and output streams are used to conduct a dialog between two computers. One computer will send a question along an output stream and then wait for the response to arrive in an input stream. Here it is necessary that an output operation be performed, even if the internal buffers have not yet been filled, since the response will not be generated until the computer at the other end of the network receives the question. It is for this reason that the OutputStream abstraction provides the method flush. Issuing a flush will force the completion of all pending output operations, even if internally maintained buffers have not been completely filled. Closing a stream will automatically flush all pending operations.

As we did with input streams, we can divide the description of output streams into two major categories: (1) those classes that characterize the physical location of the output and (2) those classes that add more behavior to an output stream.

In the first group are the three classes: (1) ByteArrayOutputStream, (2) FileOutputStream, and (3) PipedOutputStream. The first writes values into an in-memory byte array, the second on to an external file, and the third on to a pipe (see Section 14.6).

The second category is represented by the class ObjectOutputStream and by the class FilterOutputStream and its subclasses. Just as FilterInputStream provided an orthogonal way of adding additional functionality to an input stream regardless of the physical source of the data, a filtered output stream adds new functionality to an output operation. Whereas a filtered input stream generally performs new operations after reading from the underlying stream, a filtered output stream generally performs some task *before* sending the values (which are perhaps transformed) to the underlying output stream. There are three subclasses of FilterOutputStream: (1) BufferedOutputStream, (2) DataOutputStream, and (3) PrintStream.

A BufferedOutputStream maintains an internal buffer of values that have been output. Rather than writing bytes one by one, values are written to the underlying output stream only when the buffer becomes full or when the output is flushed. This is useful if writing an individual byte to the output stream involves a high overhead that can be amortized if many characters are written at once.

A DataOutputStream is the output equivalent of DataInputStream. This class adds methods to write the binary values for each of the primitive data types. The output will be read subsequently by a DataInputStream. A program in Section 14.6 will illustrate the use of a DataOutputStream.

A PrintStream is similar but generates a textual representation rather than a binary representation. The methods print() and println() are overloaded with functions specific to each of the primitive data types. Typically, a print stream is used to generate output that will be read by human users, as opposed to processing by another program. Both the streams System.out and System.err are instances of PrintStream.

```
class PrintStream extends FilterOutputStream  {
   .
   .
   .
   // print textual representation of primitive value
   public void print (boolean bool)
   public void print (int inum)
   public void print (float fnum)
   public void print (double dnum)
   public void print (String str)
   public void print (Object obj) { print (obj.toString()); }
   .
   .
   .
}
```

The implementation of the method print() when used with an object as argument is an example of pure polymorphism combined with an abstract, or deferred method. Because all objects are subclasses of Object, any value can be used as argument with this method. When executed, the method uses the function toString() to convert the object into a string representation. The implementation of this method in class Object simply returns the name of the class of the receiver. However, this method is overridden in many classes to provide more meaningful output. The function executed will be determined by the dynamic, run-time type of the argument, not by the static type Object. In this fashion, whatever text the programmer has provided using the toString() method will be the output produced.

The stream accessed through System.out will likely continue to be an instance of PrintStream, since so much existing Java code depends upon this feature. However,

the creation of new data streams using PrintStream is being discouraged, in favor
of the more general PrintWriter facility that provides similar functionality and also
supports 16-bit Unicode character values. We will discuss the writer classes in
Section 14.7.

The class ObjectOutputStream is used to provide object serialization, a topic we
will discuss in the next section.

14.5   OBJECT SERIALIZATION

The class ObjectOutputStream is designed for writing object values to a stream in a
form that allows them to be easily read back in using an ObjectInputStream. This
process of converting an object into a representation that can be accommodated
in 8-bit units is termed *object serialization*. The concept of object serialization
is essential to almost all network programming, as it is the process that allows
arguments to be passed along a network to an application running on another
machine. It is also the key to providing object *persistence*, the ability to save an
object's state across program invocations.

A serialized object can be stored in an 8-bit form—for example, on a file—
and yet be read back and restored to its exact representation. This process is
not as easy as it seems. For example, objects almost always have internal state
that must also be restored. Worse yet, the same object may be referenced two
or more times within an object. When restored, these common references must
also be restored to a single value. Fortunately, the classes ObjectOutputStream and
ObjectInputStream and the Serializable interface hide most of these details from the
programmer.

A few simple classes will illustrate the difficulties of object serialization, and
the use of the serialization abstractions. Imagine a class Pair that holds two object
values, and a class Holder that maintains a single value:

```
import java.io.Serializable;

class Pair implements Serializable {
    public Object first;
    public Object second;
}

class Holder implements Serializable {
    public Object value;
}
```

Using these, we construct an instance of class Pair in which each field is a
Holder, and in which the two holder objects point to the same value, say the
current date:

```
import java.util.Date;

Date today = new Date();
Holder a = new Holder();
a.value = today;
Holder b = new Holder();
b.value = today;
Pair c = new Pair();
c.first = a;
c.second = b;
```

We can visualize the value of c as a diamond; each of its two child fields eventually pointing to the same value:

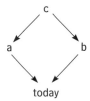

To save the current value we create an ObjectOutputStream. Note that an object output stream must be built on top of another stream that is used for the actual values. In this case we use a file stream:

```
try {
        // Open output stream
    FileOutputStream f = new FileOutputStream("saveState");
    ObjectOutputStream s = new ObjectOutputStream(f);
        // Write string, followed by representation of object
    s.writeObject("The Value of c is");
    s.writeObject(c);
    s.flush();
} catch (IOException e) {
    System.out.println("received error " + e);
}
```

The end result is that the state of the variable c, along with an identifying string, will have been been saved in the file. This value can be read, generally in another program, as follows:

```
try {
        // Open input stream
    FileInputStream f = new FileInputStream("saveState");
```

```
ObjectInputStream s = new ObjectInputStream(f);
    // Read string, then representation of object
String tag = (String) s.readObject();
Pair c = (Pair) s.readObject();
} catch (IOException e) {
    System.out.println("received IO exception " + e);
} catch (ClassNotFoundException e) {
    System.out.println("received class exception " + e);
}
```

Note that it is necessary to cast the value returned by the readObject method to the correct type, and that the readObject method declares the ClassNotFoundException which must be handled. The following test will ensure that, as we hope, only one copy of the Date object will be found in the restored state:

```
Holder a = (Holder) c.first;
Holder b = (Holder) c.second;
if (a.value == b.value)
    System.out.println("its the same object");
```

Note that to make an object serializable requires almost no effort whatsoever. All we have done is to indicate that the new classes will satisfy the Serializable interface. Because the interface is empty and it defines no additional behavior, this is very easy to do. This is all that is needed for the vast majority of situations. More complex actions may be necessary if, for instance, only a portion of an object's state is to be saved on the output stream.

14.6   PIPED INPUT AND OUTPUT

In some types of applications a common situation is for one portion of a program to be producing values that are being consumed by a different portion of the same program. Such an arrangement is called a *producer/consumer* relationship. Java provides an elegant way of organizing this type of program, through the use of multiple threads of execution and pipes. The producer and consumer each run in their own thread of execution, communicating through a pipe.

A *pipe* is a buffered data area that is used for both reading and writing. A pipe can hold only a limited number of values. Either reading from or writing to a pipe can cause a thread to be temporarily suspended. A write will be suspended if the current pipe buffer is full, whereas a read operation will be suspended if the buffer is empty. In both cases, execution will continue when the condition is resolved—for example, when a subsequent read frees up space in the buffer, or a subsequent write adds a new element.

Each pipe is manifested by a matched pair of stream pointers, a PipedOutput-Stream and a PipedInputStream. The second value created (either input or output pipe) is passed the first value as an argument, and the connection is thereby made between the two:

```
PipedInputStream in = new PipedInputStream( );
PipedOutputStream out = new PipedOutputStream (in);
```

Values can subsequently be written to the piped output stream as if it were any other type of output stream, and these values can then be read, in the same order they were inserted, from the corresponding input stream.

We can illustrate the use of pipes by means of a program designed to find all the integers smaller than 100,000 that are both prime numbers and Fibonacci numbers. A prime number, you will recall, is a value with no divisors other than 1 and itself. A Fibonacci number is defined by the recurrence relation $f_0 = 0$, $f_1 = 1$, $f_n = f_{n-2} + f_{n-1}$. [1]

A separate thread of control (see Chapter 20) is created to generate both sequences of numbers. The thread, in fact, need not even know that it is dealing with a pipe. The Fibonacci thread simply creates a sequence of values and writes them to an output stream. Using a DataOutputStream makes it easier to write integer values. Although it looks as if the thread produces all the values at once, a print( ) statement placed inside the loop will demonstrate that this is not so, and that production of values will be delayed until they are required.

```
class FibMaker extends Thread {
   private DataOutputStream out;

   public FibMaker (DataOutputStream o) { out = o; }

   public void run ( ) {
      int n = 0;
      int m = 1;
      try {
         out.writeInt (m);
```

---

[1] Tradition has it that Fibonacci numbers describe the population growth of rabbits. Rabbits take two years to mature. Once mature, they give birth each year to a single offspring. Thus, each new year the number of rabbits is the number of rabbits in the previous year plus the number of mature rabbits in the previous year, each of which has given birth. Hardly realistic, but the sequence of numbers produced by this relation has some fascinating properties.

```
        while (m < 100000) {
            int newValue = n + m;
            n = m;
            m = newValue;
            System.out.println("writing new Fibonacci " + newValue);
            out.writeInt (newValue);
            }
        out.close();
        } catch (IOException e) { return; }
    }
}
```

A similar thread creates prime numbers:

```
class PrimeMaker extends Thread {
    private DataOutputStream out;

    public PrimeMaker (DataOutputStream o) { out = o; }

    public void run () {
        int newValue = 1;
        try {
            while (newValue < 100000) {
                newValue = newValue + 1;
                boolean isPrime = true;
                for (int i = 2; i * i <= newValue; i++)
                    if (newValue % i == 0) {
                        isPrime = false; break; // no use checking further
                        }
                if (isPrime) {
                    System.out.println("writing new prime " + newValue);
                    out.writeInt (newValue);
                    }
                }
            out.close();
            } catch (IOException e) { return; }
    }
}
```

The main program shows how these are connected. The thread for each generator and for the pipes as well is created in the methods makeFibs() and makePrimes(). Note how all the pipe mechanism is encapsulated in these two routines, and the remainder of the program simply views input as coming from a DataInputStream. The main program simply reads values as long as they are available, comparing them and outputting those that match.

```
class PipeTest {
   static public void main (String [ ] args)
      { PipeTest world = new PipeTest(System.out); }

   private PipeTest (PrintStream out) {
      DataInputStream fibs = makeFibs();
      DataInputStream primes = makePrimes();
      try {
         int x = fibs.readInt();
         int y = primes.readInt();
         while (x < 100000) {
            if (x == y) {
               out.println ("integer " + x + " is both fib
                  and prime");
               x = fibs.readInt();
               y = primes.readInt();
               }
            else if (x < y)
               x = fibs.readInt();
            else
               y = primes.readInt();
            }
         } catch (IOException e) { System.exit(0); }
      }

   private DataInputStream makeFibs () {
      try {   // create the Fibonacci number generator
         PipedInputStream in = new PipedInputStream();
         PipedOutputStream out = new PipedOutputStream (in);
         Thread fibThread = new FibMaker
            (new DataOutputStream(out));
         fibThread.start();
         return new DataInputStream (in);
         } catch (IOException e) { return null; }
      }

   private DataInputStream makePrimes () {
      try {   // create the prime number generator
         PipedInputStream in = new PipedInputStream();
         PipedOutputStream out = new PipedOutputStream (in);
```

```
        Thread primeThread = new PrimeMaker
           (new DataOutputStream(out));
        primeThread.start( );
        return new DataInputStream (in);
        } catch (IOException e) { return null; }
    }
}
```

An examination of the output will show that values are being generated on demand, rather than being all computed at once.

```
writing new Fibonacci 1
writing new Fibonacci 2
writing new prime 2
writing new prime 3
writing new prime 5
writing new prime 7
writing new Fibonacci 3
writing new Fibonacci 5
writing new prime 11
writing new prime 13
writing new prime 17
writing new Fibonacci 8
writing new Fibonacci 13
writing new Fibonacci 21
integer 2 is both fib and prime
integer 3 is both fib and prime
integer 5 is both fib and prime
integer 13 is both fib and prime
writing new Fibonacci 34
  .
  .
  .
writing new prime 19
writing new prime 23
  .
  .
  .
writing new prime 31
writing new Fibonacci 233
  .
  .
  .
integer 89 is both fib and prime
  .
  .
  .
integer 233 is both fib and prime
```

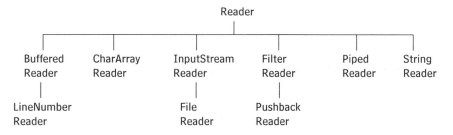

Figure 14.3 Subclasses of Reader.

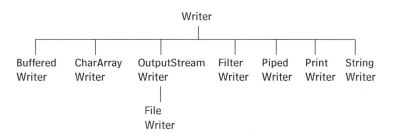

Figure 14.4 Subclasses of Writer.

14.7 READERS AND WRITERS

The class hierarchies rooted at Reader and Writer largely mirror the functionality provided by the classes InputStream and OutputStream and their dependents. However, readers and writers manipulate 16-bit Unicode character values, rather than 8-bit bytes. The class hierarchy for readers is shown in Figure 14.3, and for writers in Figure 14.4.

As with input streams, we can divide the various types of readers into those that directly manipulate a data area (CharArrayReader, StringReader, FileReader) and those that add functionality to data being generated by another reader (BufferedReader, LineNumberReader, FilterReader).

Readers and writers are useful whenever the input or output values are purely textual, as opposed to binary data such as colors or images. For example, the class BufferedReader provides a method readLine, which yields a line of text stored in a value of type String. We use this facility in a case study discussed in Chapter 19 (see Figure 19.2). The application in this example generates a concordance, a table of words and the lines on which they appear. The heart of the algorithm that generates the concordance is a loop that reads the input line by line:

```
public void readLines (BufferedReader input) throws IOException
```

```
{
    .
    .
    for (int line = 1; true; line++) {
        String text = input.readLine();
        if (text == null)
            return; // a null value signals end of input
        .
        .
    }
}
```

The class BufferedReader is a filter, which must be built on top of another reader. To use the above code with text drawn from a file, for example, one would first create a FileReader, and then use the file reader to construct the BufferedReader:

```
try {
    FileReader f = new FileReader("filename");
    BufferedReader input = new BufferedReader(f);
    .
    .
} catch (FileNotFoundException e) { ... }
```

A reader can also be built on top of an InputStream using an instance of InputStreamReader, a class that acts as a filter for input streams. Similarly, writers can be directed to any type of output stream by means of an OutputStreamWriter. An *encoding algorithm* is used to translate between the 16-bit Unicode character representation and the 8-bit byte representation used by streams and low-level devices (such as files). There are a large number of encoding algorithms provided by the standard library to support the various foreign alphabets that can be represented by the Unicode character set. The programmer can specify one of these encodings when creating a reader. The following, for example, could be used to read lines from a file that contained cyrillic characters:

```
    // first get access to the file
FileInputStream f = new FileInputStream("fileName");
    // then convert bytes to characters
InputStreamReader r = new InputStreamReader(f, "MacCyrillic");
    // then buffer the input
BufferedReader input = new BufferedReader(r);

    // now read text line by line
String text = input.readLine();
```

```
while (text != null) {
    .
    .
    .
    text = input.readLine();
}
```

Many of the output stream writers will buffer their values internally. In situations where this is undesirable the flush method can be used to force the processing of all pending characters.

14.8 CHAPTER SUMMARY

Although the number of different classes can initially make the input/output facilities of Java seem confusing, the structure of these classes is very simple and a good illustration of the use of inheritance and polymorphism.

Input and output can be divided into the *stream* abstractions, which read and write 8-bit values, and the *reader/writer* classes, which manipulate 16-bit Unicode character values.

Input streams can be divided into those based on a physical input source (reading input from a file, for example), and those based on adding new functionality to a logical input stream. An example of the latter is the class PushbackInput-Stream, which adds the ability to unread already processed characters, returning them once more in response to a subsequent read operation. The design of the subclasses of FilterInputStream combines both the techniques of inheritance and composition.

Although not specifically an input stream, the class StreamTokenizer provides a way to break a stream into individual tokens. A similar facility for strings will be described in Chapter 17.

Object serialization is the process of encoding an object's state into a form that can be represented as a series of 8-bit values. This serialized form can then be transferred across a network, or stored on a permanent storage device to provide object *persistence*.

Like input streams, the various subclasses of output streams differ in the physical location to which the output is directed. Although the output stream abstraction describes writing only a single character value, many subclasses will maintain values in an internal buffer and only perform a physical output operation when the buffer is full, or when the user explicitly requests, using the method flush, that the output be processed. Closing a stream will automatically flush all pending operations.

Pipes provide a mechanism for structuring programs that include both the production and consumption of a given resource. The producer writes values to the pipe, while the consumer reads values. The pipe facility will automatically suspend either the producer or the consumer tasks if values are not available or the pipe buffer becomes full.

The reader/writer abstractions provide the ability to work with character and string data types that may contain extended Unicode character values. The translation betweeen 16-bit Unicode characters and an 8-bit physical representation is handled automatically behind the scenes. Readers and writers should be used whenever input or output values are entirely textual.

STUDY QUESTIONS

1. What is the difference between the *stream* class hierarchies and the *Reader/ Writer* hierarchies?

2. Describe the methods that are common to all subclasses of InputStream.

3. What are the different types of physical locations from which an input stream can read?

4. Describe how a FilterInputStream combines both inheritance and composition.

5. What is the difference between the InputStream class and the DataInputStream class?

6. What does it mean to say that a PushBackInputStream permits a character to be unread?

7. What task is performed by a StreamTokenizer?

8. What is the purpose of the method flush in both output stream and writer abstractions?

9. Describe the different targets to which an output stream can write.

10. What is object serialization? How is the concept linked to network computing? How is the concept linked to persistence?

11. In what ways is a pipe different from a file? In what ways are they the same?

12. How are readers and writers linked to streams?

13. What task is performed by a byte encoding algorithm?

EXERCISES

1. Create a new subclass of FilterInputStream that reads values from an input stream and converts all uppercase characters to lowercase. How would you test your program?

2. Using BufferedReader.readLine() and a StringTokenizer, write an application that will count and display the number of lines, words, and characters in

a file. The name of the file should be taken from the argument list for the application.

3. Write the class description for a new class SequenceOutputStream, which is the output analog to SequenceInputStream. The constructor for this class will take two output streams as arguments. Each write to the SequenceOutputStream will thereafter be translated into a write on each of the argument streams.

4. Extend the class you developed in the preceding exercise so that the constructor can take an enumeration of output streams as an argument.

5. Write a subclass of FilterInputStream that looks for positive integer digit characters, such as "4231", and replaces them with the textual equivalent, in this example the words "four thousand two hundred and thirty one". Do this in several steps:

   (a) Convert the input stream into a PushbackInputStream.

   (b) As long as the source input stream is not a digit character, return it.

   (c) When a digit character is encountered, read the number until the end of digit is found.

   (d) Push the terminating nondigit character back into the input.

   (e) Translate the number into its textual equivalent, stored in a String. Create an InputStream to read characters from this string.

   (f) For subsequent requests, read from the string buffer input stream until no further characters remain, then revert to reading from the original push back input stream.

15 Design Patterns

Like most complex structures, good computer programs are often formed by imitating the structure of older, similar programs that have already proven successful. A *design pattern* is an attempt to capture and formalize this process of imitation. The basic idea is to characterize the features of a proven solution to a small problem, summarizing the essential elements and omitting the unnecessary detail. A catalog of design patterns is a fascinating illustration of the myriad ways that software can be structured so as to address different problems. Later, patterns can give insight into how to approach new problems that are similar to those situations described by the pattern.

This chapter will introduce the idea of design patterns by describing several found in the Java library. The terminology used in describing the patterns is adapted from the book *Design Patterns: Elements of Reusable Object-Oriented Software*, by Erich Gamma, Richard Helm, Ralph Johnson, and John Vlissides [1995]. This was one of the first books to describe the concept of design patterns and provide a systematic cataloging of patterns. Many more patterns than are described in the present chapter can be found in this book, as well as in the recent literature on design patterns.

The format used in describing each pattern is to first characterize the problem the pattern is addressing, then to summarize the essential features of the solution. In some cases this is followed by a discussion of some of the context for the problem or of alternative design possibilities. This is followed by a more detailed description of the pattern as it is manifested in the Java Library. Finally, a sentence or two summarizes the situations where the pattern is applicable.

15.1 ADAPTER

Problem: How do you use an object that provides appropriate behavior but uses a different interface than is required in some situation?

Figure 15.1   The adapter pattern.

Solution: Define an *adapter* class that acts as an intermediary (Figure 15.1). The adapter does little work itself but merely translates commands from one form into the other.

Discussion: International travelers frequently overcome the problem of differing electrical plug and voltage standards by using adapters for their appliances. These adapters are connectors that allow an electrical appliance with a plug for one type of outlet to be plugged into a different type of electrical outlet. Like an electrical adapter, a software adapter uses the functionality of an existing class, and maps it to a new interface.

Example: In Section 10.2 we discussed two different techniques for creating a Stack abstraction using the facilities provided by the class Vector. One approach used inheritance, having the class Stack inherit from Vector. The second approach used composition, having Stack maintain a data field of type Vector. Both these techniques are forms of adaptors. In both cases the majority of the effort is being provided by the Vector, and the Stack is solely used to change the Vector interface.

   Another example is provided by the classes InputStreamReader and OutputStreamWriter discussed in Chapter 14. Here again it is the underlying stream abstractions that are doing the actual work, and the InputStreamReader and OutputStreamWriter classes merely provide the mechanism for changing the *input/output* stream interfaces into the required *reader/writer* interfaces.

   An adapter can be used whenever there is the need for a change in interface, but no, or very little, additional behavior beyond that provided by the worker.

15.2   COMPOSITE

Problem: How do you permit the creation of complex objects using only simple parts?

Solution: Provide a small collection of simple components, but also allow these components to be nested arbitrarily. The resulting composite objects allow individual objects and compositions of objects to be treated uniformly. Frequently, an interesting feature of the *composition* pattern is the merging of the *is-a* relation with the *has-a* relation.

Example: A good example of composition in the Java library is the creation of design layouts through the interaction of Components and Containers. Only five simple types of layouts are provided by the standard library, and of these five only two, border layouts and grid layouts, are commonly used. Each item in a layout

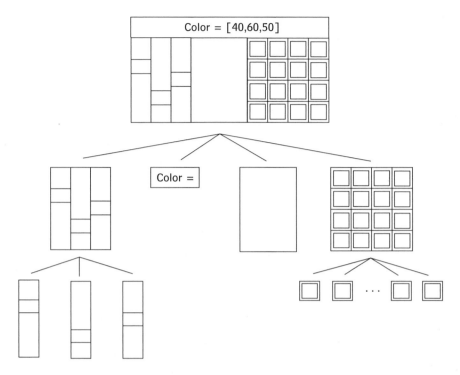

Figure 15.2   An example of a Composite.

is a Component. Composition occurs because Containers are also Components. A container holds its own layout, which is again one of only a few simple varieties. Yet the container is treated as a unit in the original layout.

The structure of a composite object is often described in a treelike format. Consider, for example, Figure 15.2, the layout of the window shown in Figure 13.13 of Chapter 13. At the application level there are four elements to the layout. These are a text area, a simple blank panel, and two panels that hold composite objects. One of these composite panels holds three scroll bars, while the second is holding a grid of 16 buttons.

By nesting panels one within another, arbitrarily complex layouts can be created. Another example of composition is the class SequenceInputStream, which is used to catenate two or more input streams so that they appear to be a single input source (see Section 14.2.2). A SequenceInputStream *is-a* InputStream (meaning it extends the class InputStream). But a SequenceInputStream also *has-a* InputStream as part of its internal state. By combining inheritance and composition, the class permits multiple sequences of input sources to be treated as a single unit.

This pattern is useful whenever it is necessary to build complex structures out of a few simple elements. Note that the merging of the *is-a* and *has-a* relations is characteristic of the *wrapper* pattern (Section 15.9), although wrappers can be constructed that are not composites.

15.3 STRATEGY

Problem: How do you allow the algorithm that is used to solve a particular problem to be easily and dynamically changed by the client?

Solution: Define a family of algorithms with a similar interface. Each algorithm provides a different strategy for solving the problem at hand. Encapsulate each algorithm, and let the client select the strategy to be used in any situation.

Discussion: If a complex algorithm is embedded in a larger application, it may be difficult to extract the algorithm and replace it with another, alternative version. If several alternative algorithms are included in the same object, both the complexity and the code of the resulting object may be increased unnecessarily. Separating problem and solution makes it easier for the client to select the solution (strategy algorithm) appropriate for any particular situation.

Example: An example of the use of the strategy pattern is the creation of layout managers in the AWT. Rather than coding in the component library the details of how items are laid out on the screen, these decisions are left to the layout manager. An interface for LayoutManager is defined, and five standard layout managers are provided. The ambitious programmer is even allowed, should he or she choose, to define a new object that satisfies the LayoutManager interface. (See Figure 15.3.)

The activities of the design component (such as a Panel or a Window) are independent of the particular layout manager that is being used. This both simplifies the container component and permits a much greater degree of flexibility in the

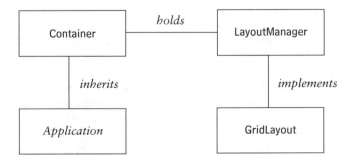

Figure 15.3 An example of the strategy pattern.

structure of the resulting layout than would be possible if layout decisions were an intrinsic part of the container.

The strategy pattern is useful whenever it is necessary to provide a set of alternative solutions to a problem and the algorithms used to address the problem can be encapsulated with a simple interface.

15.4 OBSERVER

Problem: How do you allow two or more independent and loosely coupled objects to change in synchrony with each other?

Solution: Maintain a list of objects that are tied, or dependent, on another object. When the target object changes, the dependents, or observers, are notified that they should update themselves.

Discussion: It is easy to maintain tightly coupled objects in synchrony. For example, if a new class is defined as a subclass of an existing parent class, modifications of the parent that are made via method invocations can be monitored by simply overriding the methods. It is much more difficult to keep objects in step with one another when links are formed and broken dynamically at run time, or when no obvious class relationship exists between the separate elements.

Example: There are two good examples of the use of the observer pattern in the Java library. The first we have seen in many earlier case studies, such as the Cannon World examined in Chapter 6. Each of the user interface components that permits interaction, such as buttons, scroll bars, and checkboxes, maintains a collection of *listener* objects. This list is dynamic; listeners for any component can be easily added or removed at run time. Furthermore, the structure of the listeners is not specified, they are only required to satisfy the necessary interface. When the component changes state (the button is pressed, the slider moved, the checkbox changed), each of the listeners is notified that a change has occurred. It is up to the listener to decide what action should be taken as a result of the change.

The idea behind listeners is also found in a more general facility that can be used by programmers for situations that do not involve user interaction. The library class Observable represents objects that can be "observed," the equivalent of the components in the AWT mechanism. Programmers can either subclass a new class from Observable, or simply create an Observable field within a class. Other objects can implement the Observer interface. These correspond to "listener" objects. An instance of Observer registers itself with the object being observed.

At any time, the Observable object can indicate that it has changed, by invoking the message notifyObservers( ). An optional argument can be passed along with this message. Each observer is passed the message update(Observable, Object), where the first argument is the Observable that has changed, and the second is the optional argument provided by the notification. The observer takes whatever action is necessary to bring the state into synchrony with the observed object.

The *observer* pattern is applicable whenever two or more objects must be loosely coupled but must still maintain synchronization in some aspect of their behavior or state.

15.5 FLYWEIGHT

Problem: How can one reduce the storage costs associated with a large number of objects that have a similar state?

Solution: Share state in common with similar objects, thereby reducing the storage required by any single object.

Example: With the exception of primitive values, all objects in Java are an instance of some class. With each class it is necessary to associate certain information. Examples of information are the name of the class (a String), and the description of the interface for the class. If this information were duplicated in each object, the memory costs would be prohibitive. Instead, this information is defined once by an object of type Class, and each instance of the class points to this object.

The objects that share the information are known as *flyweights*, since their memory requirements are reduced (often dramatically) by moving part of their state to the shared value. The flyweight pattern can be used whenever there are a large number of objects that share a significant common internal state.

15.6 ABSTRACT FACTORY

Problem: How to provide a mechanism for creating instances of families of related objects without specifying their concrete representations.

Solution: Provide a method that returns a new value that is characterized only by an interface or parent class, not by the actual type produced.

Discussion: There are several instances where the value returned by a method in the standard library is characterized by either an abstract class or an interface. Clearly the actual value being returned is a different type, but normally the client using the method is not concerned with the actual type, but only the behavior described by the characterizing attributes.

Example: Two examples out of the many found in the Java library will be described. Each of the collection classes Vector, Hashtable, and Dictionary define a method named elements( ) that is described as returning a value of type Enumeration. As Enumeration is only an interface, not a class, the value returned is clearly formed as an instance of some other class. Almost always, the client has no interest in the actual type being yielded by elements( ) and is only interested in the behavior common to all values that satisfy the Enumeration interface.

A similar situation occurs with the classes Font and FontMetrics. The class FontMetrics is used to describe the characteristics of a Font, such as the height and width of characters, the distance characters extend above or below the baseline, and so on. A FontMetrics is an abstract class, one that cannot be instanciated directly by the programmer using the new command. Instead, a value of type FontMetric is returned by a Graphics object in response to the message getFontMetrics. Clearly, the graphics object is returning a value derived from a subclass of FontMetric, but the particular value returned is normally of no concern to the client.

A similar facility is used by class Applet, which can return an AppletContext that describes the current execution environment.

The abstract factory pattern should be used whenever the type of the actual value to be created cannot be predicted in advance and therefore must be determined dynamically.

15.7 FACTORY METHOD

Problem: You have a method that returns a newly created object, but you want subclasses to have the ability to return different types of objects.

Solution: Allow the subclass to override the creation method and return a different type of object.

Discussion: This pattern is very similar to the abstract factory but is specialized for the situation where new abstractions are formed using inheritance.

Example: The method clone( ) is a good example of a factory method. This method returns a copy of an object, provided the object supports the Cloneable interface. The default method in class Object raises an exception, indicating that the cloneable interface is not supported. Subclasses that wish to permit clones must override this method and return a different type of value.

Note that the value returned by a factory method must be the same for all classes. For the Cloneable interface this type is Object. Any class that permits cloning will still return a value of type Object in response to the message clone( ). This value must then be cast to the appropriate type.

The factory method pattern is useful when there is a hierarchy of abstractions formed using inheritance, and part of the behavior of these abstractions is the creation of new objects.

15.8 ITERATOR

Problem: How to provide a way to access elements of an aggregate object sequentially without exposing the underlying representation.

Solution: Provide a mediator object for the sole purpose of sequential access. This mediator can be aware of the representation of the aggregate although the client using the object need not be aware of these details.

Example: The Enumeration interface for container access actually addresses two related problems. It provides a uniform means of accessing elements from many different types of containers and it hides the details of the underlying container representation. It is the second aspect that makes the Enumeration a good example of the iterator pattern.

Consider, for example, an enumeration that is generating elements from a Hashtable. Internally, a hash table is implemented as an array, each element of the array being a list. Values that hash into the same locations are found on the same list. (See Figure 15.4.)

The programmer who uses a hash table and wishes to iterate over the values should not be concerned with the representation, such as moving from one list to the next when the elements in one hash location have been exhausted. The hash table enumeration hides these difficulties behind a simple interface. The programmer sees only the two methods hasMoreElements() and nextElement(). With these, a loop can be written that does not even hint at the complex actions needed to access the underlying elements.

```
HashTable htab = new HashTable( );
.
.
for (Enumeration e = htab.elements( ); e.hasMoreElements( ); ) {
   Object val = e.nextElement( );
   .
   .
   .
   }
```

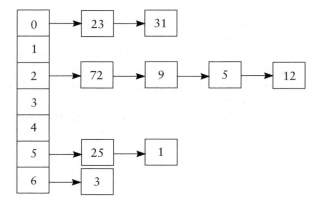

Figure 15.4   Internal representation of a hash table.

The fact that the method elements returns a value that is not directly an Enumeration, but is rather a value from another class that implements the Enumeration interface, is an example of the *abstract factory* pattern (Section 15.6).

The iterator pattern is useful whenever an aggregate object is created that can hold an arbitrary number of values, and it is necessary to provide access to values without exposing the underlying representation.

15.9 DECORATOR (FILTER OR WRAPPER)

Problem: How can you attach additional responsibilities to an object dynamically?

Solution: By combining the *is-a* and *has-a* relations, create an object that wraps around an existing value, adding new behavior without changing the interface.

Discussion: Inheritance is one technique for providing new functionality to an existing abstraction. But inheritance is rather heavyhanded, and is often not flexible enough to accommodate situations that must dynamically change during the course of execution. A decorator wraps around an existing object and satisfies the same requirements (for example, is subclassed from the same parent class or implements the same interface). The wrapper delegates much of the responsibility to the original but occasionally adds new functionality. (See Figure 15.5.)

Example: The class InputStream provides a way to read bytes from an input device, such as a file. The class BufferedInputStream is a subclass of InputStream, adding the ability to buffer the input so that it can be reset to an earlier point and values can be reread two or more times. Furthermore, a BufferedInputStream can take an InputStream as an argument in its constructor.

Because a BufferedInputStream both *is* an InputStream and *has* an input stream as part of its data, it can be easily wrapped around an existing input stream. Due to inheritance and substitutability, the BufferedInputStream can be used where the original InputStream was expected. Because it holds the original input stream, any

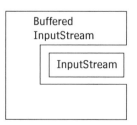

Figure 15.5 Buffered InputStream as an example of the wrapper or filter pattern.

actions unrelated to the buffering activities are simply passed on to the original stream.

A decorator, or wrapper class, is often a flexible alternative to the use of subclassing. Functionality can be added or removed simply by adding or deleting wrappers around an object.

15.10 PROXY

Problem: How do you hide details such as transmission protocols to remote objects?

Solution: Provide a proxy that acts as a surrogate or placeholder for another object.

Discussion: A proxy is an object that stands in place of another. The first object receives requests for the second, and generally forwards the requests to the second, after processing them in some fashion. (See Figure 15.6.)

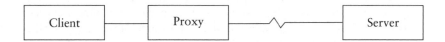

Figure 15.6 The proxy pattern.

Example: An example proxy in the Java Library is the Remote Method Invocation (RMI) system. RMI is a mechanism that can be used to coordinate Java programs running on two or more machines. RMI creates a proxy object that runs on the same machine as the client. When the client invokes a method on the proxy, the proxy transmits the method across the network to the server on another machine. The server handles the request, then transmits the result back to the proxy. The proxy hands the result back to the client. In this fashion, the details of transmission over the network are handled by the proxy and the server, and are hidden from the client.

15.11 BRIDGE

Problem: How to decouple an abstraction from its implementation so that the latter can vary independently.

Solution: Remove implementation details from the abstraction, placing them instead in an object that is held as a component in the abstraction.

Example: Most of the component classes in the AWT make use of the *bridge* pattern. Fundamentally, this is because the actions necessary to implement a graphical component vary in great detail from one platform to another. For example, the actions needed to display a window are different depending upon whether the underlying display is X-Windows/Motif, Windows-95, or the Macintosh. Rather than placing platform specific details in the class Window, instead each window maintains a component of type WindowPeer. The interface WindowPeer has different implementations, depending upon the platform on which the application is being executed. This separation allows a Java program that depends only on the class Window to be executed in any environment for which there is a corresponding peer.

The bridge pattern is in many ways similar to the strategy pattern described earlier. Differences are that bridges are almost always hidden from the client (for example, the average Java programmer is generally unaware of the existence of the peer classes), and are generally dictated by environmental issues rather than reflecting design decisions.

15.12   Chapter Summary

An emerging new area of study in object-oriented languages is the concept of design patterns. A design pattern captures the salient characteristics of a solution to a commonly observed problem, hiding details that are particular to any one situation. By examining design patterns, programmers learn about techniques that have proven to be useful in previous problems, and are therefore likely to be useful in new situations.

Further Reading

The most important reference for design patterns is the 1995 book of the same name by Gamma, Helm, Johnson, and Vlissides (commonly known as the Gang of Four, or GOF). Another recent book on patterns is by Richard Gabriel [1996].

Study Questions

1. In what ways is an adapter similar to a proxy? In what ways are they different?

2. What does the link between an Adapter and a Worker represent? Composition or Inheritance?

3. In what way is the composition design pattern similar to the idea of composition examined in Chapter 10?

4. Explain how the Composite pattern works in the AWT, and explain how this relies on both inheritance and composition.

5. In what ways is a strategy design pattern similar to a bridge pattern? In what ways are they different?

6. In what ways is an iterator similar to an adapter?

EXERCISE

1. What design pattern is exhibited by the class PrintStream (see Section 14.4)? Explain your answer.

V

Understanding
the Java World

16 Exception Handling

From the start, Java was designed with the understanding that errors occur, that unexpected events happen, and that programmers should always be prepared for the worst. Part of this outlook is the inclusion in the language of a simple yet powerful mechanism for handling *exceptions*.

An exception is an event that occurs during the execution of a program that disrupts the flow of instructions and prevents the program from continuing along its normal course. An example that is easy to understand is the exception that occurs when a file cannot be opened. The programmer developing a file-processing application starts out with a structure that perhaps looks something like the following:

```
ask the user for the name of a file
open the file
read the contents
do something with the contents
close the file
```

The programmer probably develops the application using some simple test cases and might not even think about the possibility that the file cannot be opened. What happens if the user enters incorrect values, a name that is not a valid file name? In most languages, the likely answer is that the program will fail in totally unexpected and inexplicable ways.

In Java, the programmer cannot simply forget to think about this possibility, because the language will not allow the programmer to write a statement that opens a file without providing the code that will be executed should a failure occur. The file-opening method is declared as a function that can potentially "throw an exception", and the compiler will refuse to recognize any use of the method that does not handle the exception.

As we saw earlier in the case study described in Chapter 7, a method that can potentially raise an exception must be invoked within the framework of a *try/catch* block. This is written as a nested statement following the keyword try, and an associated set of statements following the keyword catch:

```
try {
    File fd = new File(filename);
} catch (FileOpenFailed e) {
    System.err.println("Cannot open file " + filename);
}
```

The exception mechanism is in fact dealing with an actual object, which is an instance of class Throwable. When an error occurs, the value of this object is assigned to the variable e in the statements shown above.

Multiple statements can be nested within the try block. In fact, often almost the entire application will be held within a surrounding block.

```
try {
    File fd = new File(filename);
    processFile (fd);
    fd.close( );
} catch (FileOpenFailed e) {
    System.err.println("Cannot open file " + filename);
}
```

Multiple exceptions can also be tested, by writing a series of catch clauses

```
try {
    File fd = new File(filename);
    processFile (fd);
    fd.close( );
} catch (FileNotFoundException e) {
    System.err.println("Cannot find file " + filename);
} catch (FileOpenFailed e) {
    System.err.println("Cannot open file " + filename);
}
```

Exceptions are a useful programming construct because the location where an error is detected is usually not the place where the appropriate solution is known. For example, suppose you are the programmer developing the file-processing library routines. That is, you are the person developing the code for the class File. Certainly you are aware of the fact that the string passed to the constructor for your class might not represent a valid file name. But what should you do in this situation? Without knowledge of the surrounding application, there is no good answer.

One common solution is to return a special value, such as the value null, when a command cannot be processed. But constructors are not permitted to return a null value, furthermore there might be multiple reasons for a failure. Does a null value returned by a file open operation mean the file does not exist, or that it exists but cannot be read? Finally, what if a null value is perfectly legal? How would one indicate an error in that case?

The exception mechanism not only gives the programmer who detects the message the ability to return precise information, it also places responsibility for dealing with the error on the shoulders of the programmer, who knows the appropriate action to take.

16.1 INFORMATION TRANSMITTED TO THE CATCH BLOCK

You will note that a catch block looks something like a method declaration. Like a method heading, the catch block defines a *variable* that is given a value when the exception is handled. Each of the various exceptional conditions is in fact a class name, a subclass of Throwable. The variable that is thrown often contains useful information pertaining to the exception, such as the name of the file that cannot be opened, or the value of an illegal array index. If the exception is converted to a String value, as in many of the examples shown in this chapter, then this information will be printed.

The class Throwable also defines several methods. One of the most useful is a method that will print a stack trace, which describes the sequence of method calls up to the point where the exception occurred. The following shows how this could be used:

```
try {
    File fileOne = new File (fileName);
    processfile (fileOne);
    fileOne.close( );
} catch (FileNotFoundException e) {
    System.error.println("Cannot find file " + e);
    e.printStackTrace( );
}
```

16.2 CATCHING MULTIPLE ERRORS

There need not be a one-to-one correspondence between methods that can throw an exception and the try block that handles the error. The Java language only requires that the statement that can throw the exception must be handled somewhere. For example, if two or more files are being opened, they can be surrounded by a single try/catch statement. An error opening either file will be handled in the same way.

```
try {
    File fileOne = new File (filenameOne);
    File fileTwo = new File (filenameTwo);
    processFile (fileOne, fileTwo);
    fileOne.close( );
    fileTwo.close( );
} catch (FileNotFoundException e) {
    System.err.println("Cannot find file " + e);
} catch (FileOpenFailed e) {
    System.err.println("Cannot open file " + e);
}
```

16.3 THE FINALLY CLAUSE

The try/catch statement permits an optional last clause, labeled finally. Statements contained in the finally block will be executed, regardless of whether or not an exception is raised. Consider, for example, the following:

```
try {
    System.out.println("start");
    File fileOne = new File (filenameOne);
    System.out.println("open worked");
} catch (FileNotFoundException e) {
    System.out.println("not found error");
} catch (FileOpenFailed e) {
    System.out.println("open error");
} finally {
    System.out.println("all done");
}
```

One possible sequence of output is *start-open worked-all done*. Another sequence, should it happen that the file name is not valid, is *start-not found error-all done*. Yet another might be *start-open error-all done*. The key feature to note in all of these is that it is not possible to execute the try/catch statement without executing the finally block. This is true even if a return statement is executed inside the body of the try/catch statement!

16.4 TERMINATION OR RESUMPTIVE MODELS

When an exception is thrown, control transfers directly to the catch block that handles the error. Unless the programmer explicitly reinvokes the same method, control will not return to the point at which the error occurred. This is sometimes referred to as the *termination model* of exception handling. There exist other programming languages that permit control to be returned to the point of error. Such languages are said to use the *resumptive model* of exception handling.

16.5 EXCEPTIONS THROWN IN THE STANDARD LIBRARY

Exceptions come in several varieties, which are all subclasses of the class Throwable. The two major subclasses of Throwable are Error and Exception. Some of the more common exceptions are described in Figure 16.1.

The subclasses of Error represent "hard" failures, such as the virtual machine detecting an error in the bytecode representation. Processing will immediately halt once such an error is detected. Fortunately, it is unlikely that a typical Java program will ever see or throw such an error.

```
Throwable
   Error
      LinkageError
         IncompatibleClassChangeError
            InstantiationError
      VirtualMachineError
         InternalError
         OutOfMemoryError
         StackOverflowError
   Exception
      IllegalAccessException
      IOException
         EOFException
         FileNotFoundException
         InterruptedIOException
         MalformedURLException
      RuntimeException
         ArithmeticException
         ClassCastException
         EmptyStackException
         IndexOutOfBoundsException
            ArrayIndexOutOfBoundsException
            StringIndexOutOfBoundsException
         NegativeArraySizeException
         NullPointerException
         SecurityException
```

Figure 16.1 Some of the exceptions issued in the standard library.

Most programmers will write code to throw and catch objects that derive from the class Exception. Once again, these can be divided into categories, the two most important being RuntimeException and IOException.

The subclasses of RuntimeException represent conditions that arise within the Java virtual machine itself during the processing of the bytecodes that represent a program. Examples include the use of a variable that has not been initialized (NullPointerException), an improper cast conversion, or an arithmetic operation that overflows. Because the source for such an error could potentially be almost any Java statement, the compiler does not insist that the programmer test for or catch these errors. (Think about what a program would look like if every variable reference needed to be surrounded by a try statement to detect null value possibilities.)

The subclasses of IOException represent errors that can occur during the processing of input and output statements. Examples include not being able to open files, attempting to read past the end of a file, or attempting to access information across the network using a badly formed URL.

16.6 THROWING EXCEPTIONS

A method that will in some situations throw an exception must declare so in the method heading. For example, suppose one is developing a stack abstraction (see Chapter 19) making use of an array. Popping from an empty stack might be a condition that would trigger an exception. To throw an exception, a new value is created (using the new operator). This value must be a subclass of Throwable.

```
class Stack {
   private int index;
   private Vector values;
   .
   .
   .

   Object pop( ) throws Exception {
      if (index < 0)
         throw new Exception("pop on empty stack");
      Object result = values.elementAt(index);
      index--;
      return result;
   }
}
```

It is possible to convey more precise information by first creating a subclass of Exception, then throwing an instance of this class. The class Exception has two constructor forms, and subclasses generally follow the same pattern.

```
class StackUnderflowException extends Exception {
   StackUnderflowException ( ) { super( ); }
```

```
      StackUnderflowException (String gripe) { super(gripe); }
   }

   class Stack {
      private int index;
      private Vector values;
      .
      .
      .

      Object pop( ) throws StackUnderflowException {
         if (index < 0)
            throw new StackUnderflowException( );
         Object result = values.elementAt(index);
         index--;
         return result;
      }
   }
```

A child class that overrides a method inherited from a parent class is not permitted to introduce new exceptions that were not already declared in the parent.

16.7 PASSING ON EXCEPTIONS

Occasionally it is useful for a method not to handle an exceptional condition and simply to pass the exception back to the caller. This can be accomplished by simply adding the exception type to the method header. An example occurs in the concordance program examined in Chapter 19.

```
class Concordance {

   public void readLines (DataInputStream input) throws IOException {
      String delims = " \t\n.,!?;:";
      for (int line = 1; true; line++ ) {
         String text = input.readLine( );
         if (text == null) return;
         text = text.toLowerCase( );
         Enumeration e = new StringTokenizer(text, delims);
         while (e.hasMoreElements( ))
            enterWord ((String) e.nextElement( ), new Integer(line));
      }
   }
   .
   .
   .
}
```

Here the IOException could be thrown by the method readLine. However, the method readLines really had no better way of dealing with this particular error than did the readLine method itself. Thus, the error is simply passed back to the caller of readLines, who could take the appropriate action. We will see further examples of this usage in the client-server programs in Chapter 22.

16.8 CHAPTER SUMMARY

The exception-handling mechanism in Java is a powerful technique for increasing the reliability and robustness of Java programs. Exceptions handle unexpected conditions that can disrupt the normal flow of control in the execution of a program. By properly declaring and catching exceptions, programmers are provided with a way to recover gracefully from potentially error-producing situations.

STUDY QUESTIONS

1. What is an exception?

2. Before exceptions were part of programming languages, a common technique used to indicate errors was to have a function return a special value, such as a null pointer. How is the exception mechanism an improvement over this technique?

3. In what ways is a catch clause similar to a method heading? In what ways is it different?

4. What is the difference between the termination and resumptive models of exception handling?

5. What is the difference between exceptions formed as subclasses of Error, and those that are subclasses of Exception?

EXERCISES

1. Modify the Stack data abstractions given in Chapter 10 so that they will throw an EmptyStackException if an attempt is made to read or remove a value from an empty stack.

17 Utility Classes

The Java library provides a number of small utility classes that are useful in a wide variety of situations. In this chapter we will consider several of these, including Point, Dimension, Date, Math, Random, Toolkit, and the data field named System. In addition, we will consider strings and their related classes.

17.1 POINT

A Point represents a location in two-dimensional space. The point is described by a pair of integer values, called the x and y values. Points are used in conjunction with a number of the AWT painting operations and with layout managers. An important feature to remember is that in the AWT coordinate system, the y coordinates increase as locations move downward, rather than decreasing as is true in classical geometry.

The following summarizes the characteristics of the class Point:

```
class Point {
    // constructor
    public Point (int x, int y)

    // public accessible data fields
    public int x
    public int y

    // operations
    public void move (int x, int y) // move to given location
    public void translate (int x, int y) // change by offset
    public boolean equals (Object p) // compare two points
    public String toString ( ) // convert to string
}
```

17.2   DIMENSION

A dimension is used to represent a rectangular size. Dimensions are characterized by a width and a height. Dimensions are used in many AWT methods and returned as the result of methods that need to characterize a size. The following summarizes the features of the class Dimension:

```
class Dimension {
      // constructors
   public Dimension ()
   public Dimension (int w, int h)
   public Dimension (Dimension d) // make copy

      // public accessible data fields
   public int width
   public int height

      // operations
   public String toString()
}
```

17.3   DATE

The class Date is used to represent both data and time values. Two dates can be compared to determine if one comes after the other. Once set, any of the fields in a date can be changed. The following summarizes the methods provided by the class Date:

```
class Date {
      // constructors
   public Date () // return current date and time
   public Date (int year, int month, int day)
   public Date (int year, int month, int day, int hours,
      int minutes)
   public Date (int year, int month, int day,
      int hours, int minutes, int seconds)

      // field access methods
   public int getDate () // returns day of month, 1-31
   public int getDay () // returns day of week, 0-6
   public int getHours () // returns hour, 0-23
   public int getMinutes () // returns minute of hour, 0-59
   public int getMonth () // returns month of year, 0-11
   public int getSeconds () // returns second of minute 0-59
```

```
public int getYear ( ) // returns year number - 1900
public int getTimezoneOffset ( ) // returns offset from GMT

    // epoch methods
public long getTime ( ) // returns milliseconds since epoch
public void setTime (long lval) // set time from epoch

    // field setting methods
public void setDate (int date)
public void setHours (int hour)
public void setMinutes (int minutes)
public void setMonth (int month)
public void setSeconds (int seconds)
public void setYear ( )

    // comparison methods
public boolean after (Date day)
public boolean before (Date day)
public boolean equals (Object day)

    // output
public String toString ( )
}
```

When provided with no constructors, the class Date returns the current time and day. Otherwise, the date is set from the argument values given. The year value is given as the year minus 1900, that is, 97 represents 1997, and 112 represents 2012.

Notice that the method equals overrides the similarly named method inherited from class Object. Thus, the argument to this method must be simply Object. However, the methods after and before, which are defined here for the first time, can be restricted to working only with Date objects.

The recently released 1.2 revision of the Java language introduced a number of changes in the class Date. In order to reduce the connection between dates and the western style Gregorian calendar, a new class Calendar was added. Some functions formerly provided by class Date are now performed using a combination of Date and Calendar values. For example, the method getDate, which returns a day of the month, is now discouraged in favor of the following command:

```
Calendar.get(Calendar.DAY_OF_MONTH)
```

17.3.1 *After the Epoch*

Recent dates and times can be compactly represented by a single long value that represents the number of milliseconds since January 1, 1970, which is termed the start of the *epoch*. This quantity is returned by the method getTime. Most often these values are used in pairs, to obtain the amount of time used to perform a certain operation:

```
Date start = new Date( ); // starting time

int j = 0;
for (int i = 0; i < 100000; i++)
    j = j + 1;

Date end = new Date( ); // ending time
System.out.println("That took " + (end.getTime( )
    - start.getTime( )) + " milliseconds");
```

Epoch values for dates prior to January 1, 1970 are returned as negative numbers.

17.4 MATH

The class Math provides a number of constants, as well as useful mathematical functions. All values and methods are declared as static. Thus, these elements are accessible without creating an instance of the class. The class can be summarized as follows:

```
final class Math {
    // constants
    public static final double E   // 2.71828 ...
    public static final double PI  // 3.1415926 ...

    // trigonometric operations, angles in radians
    public static double sin (double num)
    public static double cos (double num)
    public static double tan (double num)
    public static double asin (double num)
    public static double acos (double num)
    public static double atan (double num)
    public static double atan2 (double s, double c)

    // rounding operations
    public static double ceil (double num)
    public static double floor (double num)
    public static double rint (double num)
    public static int round (float num)
    public static long round (double num)
```

```
    // exponential and powers
public static double exp (double y) // e raised to x
public static double pow (double x, double y) // x raised to y
public static double log (double x) // log base e
public static double sqrt (double x) // x raised to 1/2

    // other operations
public static int abs (int num)
public static long abs (long num)
public static float abs (float num)
public static double abs (double num)
public static int max (int x, int y)
public static float max (float x, float y)
public static double max (double x, double y)
public static int min (int x, int y)
public static float min (float x, float y)
public static double min (double x, double y)
public static double random ( ) // value between 0 and 1
}
```

The method random( ) returns a value that is larger than or equal to 0.0, and strictly smaller than 1.0, uniformly distributed over the range. The following, for example, could be used to return a random number between 1 and 10 (inclusive of both endpoints):

```
int val = (int) Math.floor(Math.random( ) * 10 + 1);
```

More extensive random number operations are provided by class Random.

17.5 RANDOM

The method Math.random( ) can be used to generate random floating-point values larger than or equal to 0.0 and smaller than 1.0 with a uniform distribution. The class Random provides more general facilities, allowing not only the generation of random integers, but also the ability to reset the random number generator with a *seed* value. This latter feature provides a way to recreate the same random sequence of values many times, a property that is often useful in testing programs, as well as other situations. The facilities provided by Random can be summarized as follows:

```
class Random {
    // constructors
    public Random ( )
    public Random (long seed)
```

```
    // operations
    public void setSeed (long seed)
    public double nextDouble ()
    public float nextFloat ()

    // integer value, can be either positive or negative
    public int nextInt ()
    public long nextLong ()

    // alternative distribution
    public double nextGaussian ()
}
```

All methods use a uniform distribution, with the exception of nextGaussian, which uses a Gaussian distribution. Other distributions can often be constructed from these. The following method, for example, takes as argument an integer array of weights and computes a random number with weighted distribution. It sums the array of weights, computes a random integer between 0 and the sum, then locates the integer in the array of weights:

```
static public int weightedDistribution (int [ ] weights) {
    int sum = 0; // compute sum of weights
    for (int i = 0; i < weights.length; i++)
       sum += weights[i];
       // compute random value less than sum
    int val = (int) Math.floor(Math.random() * sum + 1);
       // find point in distribution
    for (int i = 0; i < weights.length; i++) {
       val -= weights[i];
       if (val < 0)
          return i;
    }
    return 0; // should never happen
}
```

Given an array of weights $(1, 3, 2)$, for example, the value 0 would be returned 1/6 of the time, the value 1 returned 1/2 of the time, and the value 2 returned 1/3 of the time.

17.6 TOOLKIT

The class Toolkit is mostly used to create the peer objects used in providing the device independent aspects of the AWT (see Section 15.11). However, in addition to creating the windows, buttons, menus, and other features of a graphical interface, the class also provides a few utilities useful to the programmer.

Toolkit is an abstract class, specialized for each type of platform on which a Java program can be executed. The implementation of Toolkit appropriate to the current environment is found by executing the method Toolkit.getDefaultToolkit().

The method getFontList() returns an array of string values, containing the names of the fonts available on the current system.

The method getImage() takes as argument either a string or a URL (see Section 21.4.1). If a string argument is used it should contain the name of a file. The image is loaded from the file or the URL address, and returned as a value of type Image.

The methods getScreenSize() and getScreenResolution() together return the size of the screen. The first returns the number of pixels in the screen, both height and width in a value of type Dimension. The second returns the number of dots per inch. Dividing one by the other will yield the physical size of the screen.

17.7 SYSTEM

The class System, and the instance data field of the same name provided by class Frame, give access to several systemwide resources. The most commonly used values are the input and output streams for the standard input, standard output, and error output. These are found at System.in, System.out, and System.err, respectively.

The method System.exit(int) immediately halts the currently running program, yielding to the operating system the integer status value given in the argument.

The method currentTimeMillis() returns the current time in milliseconds. The value is returned as a signed long value, representing the number of milliseconds since January 1, 1970 (see Section 17.3.1). Since the value is returned as a long, overflow will occur sometime in the year 292280995.

17.8 STRINGS AND RELATED CLASSES

The handling of strings in Java is similar enough to the handling of strings in other languages to seem natural to the programmer learning the language, yet sufficiently different in subtle points to be a potential source of trouble. In this chapter we will describe strings, string buffers, string tokenizers, and related classes.

The most important fact to remember is that in Java a String is an immutable value; it cannot be changed. One should think of a string as a constant, like a double-precision value. Just as a variable declared as holding a double can be assigned a new value, a variable assigned as holding a String can be assigned a new string, but this is not the same as changing the string value. A second class, StringBuffer, is closer, for example, to the C concept of a string as simply an array of character values. A string buffer can be subscripted, and individual elements modified. The following shows, for example, how to change *hope* into *cope* in both C and in Java.

C version	*Java version*
`char * str = "hope";`	`String str = "hope";`
`str[0] = 'c';`	`StringBuffer strbuf(str);`
	`strbuf.setCharAt(0, 'c');`

17.8.1   *Operations on Strings*

The most common way to create a string is with a literal:

```
String name = "John Smith";
```

The various constructors for String also allow a string to be created from another string, from an array of characters or bytes, or from a string buffer:

```
char data[ ] = {'q','e','d'};
String quod = new String(data);
    // quod erat demonstrandum
```

The addition operator, +, is overloaded with a new meaning when either the left or the right argument is a string. In this case, the nonstring argument (if any) is converted into a string and a string catenation is performed. This is most often used to produce formatted output:

```
System.out.println(" The answer is: " + answer);
```

Note that the addition operator groups left to right, so that the meaning of the addition in the following two expressions is very different:

```
System.out.println("Catch-" + 2 + 2); // catch-22
System.out.println(2 + 2 + "warned"); // be forewarned
```

The String class defines a number of methods for returning portions of a string, converting values to a string, and comparing strings. These can be summarized as follows:

```
final class String { // declared final so it cannot be subclassed

    // constructors
    public String (String src)
    public String (char [ ] charArray)
    public String (byte [ ] byteArray)
    public String (StringBuffer buffer);
```

```
    // methods for creating new strings
    // catenate string with argument string
public String concat (String str)
    // replace old characters with new
public String replace (char oldChar, char newChar)
    // return subportion of string
public String substring (int offset)
public String substring (int offset, int endIndex)
    // convert case of all letters
public String toLowerCase ()
public String toUpperCase ()
    // return reference of current string
public String toString ()
    // trim leading and trailing whitespace
public String trim ()
    // create string from primitive data type
public static String valueOf (boolean bool)
public static String valueOf (char ch)
public static String valueOf (char [ ]  charArray)
public static String valueOf (int i)
public static String valueOf (long l)
public static String valueOf (float f)
public static String valueOf (double d)
public static String valueOf (Object obj)


    // comparison methods
    // compare ordering, return negative, zero or positive
public int compareTo (String str)
    // compare for equality
public boolean equals (Object obj)
public boolean equalsIgnoreCase (String str)
    // test front or end of string
public boolean endsWith (String str)
public boolean startsWith (String str)
    // find first occurrence of char or string
public int indexOf (char c)
public int indexOf (char c, int startingOffset)
public int indexOf (String str, int startingOffset)
public int lastIndexOf (char c)
public int lastIndexOf (char c, int startingOffset)
public int lastIndexOf (String str, int startingOffset)
}
```

There are a few subtle points that can trap the unwary programmer. Note that the identity operator, ==, tests whether two variables refer to exactly the same value. This is not the same as testing whether two string values have exactly the same character representation. In general, one should always use equals( ) to test the equality of objects, including strings, and not use the == operator. Because equals overrides the method inherited from Object, the argument must be an Object and not a String. A string value will always return false when compared to a nonstring. The method equalsIgnoreCase tests whether two values are the same, ignoring uppercase and lowercase distinctions.

The method compareTo( ) returns an integer result. This value is negative if the current string is lexicographically smaller than the argument, zero if they are equal, and positive if the string is larger than the argument. The exact integer value returned is implementation-dependent and should not be counted upon in any program.

The static method String.valueOf (Object obj) is a good example of a polymorphic method. The argument can be any type of object, including a null object. If it is not null, the method toString is used to convert the object into a string value:

```
final class String {
   .
   .
   .

   public static String valueOf (Object obj) {
      if (obj == null)
         return "null";
      else
         return obj.toString( );
   }
   .
   .
   .

}
```

The method toString is defined in class Object (where it returns the class name of the receiver as a string), and redefined in many classes. The value yielded by toString( ), and hence by valueOf( ), will be whatever method is appropriate for the dynamic, run-time type of the argument.

Because String.valueOf returns a legal result regardless whether or not the argument is null, it is a safer alternative to the use of toString directly:

```
Shape aShape = null;
   .
   .

String a = String.valueOf(aShape); // will return "null" as string
String b = aShape.toString( ); // will generate null value exception
```

This property of the == operator can be used to demonstrate one subtle difference between creating a new string using the String constructor, and creating a string using the valueOf operator. One case generates a copy of the original string, while the other simply returns a reference to the original.

```
String one = "One";
String two = new String(one);
String three = String.valueOf(one);
System.out.println(" is one == two " + (one == two));
    // returns false
System.out.println(" is one == three " + (one == three));
    // returns true
```

17.8.2 *String Buffers*

A StringBuffer is similar to the C language concept of a string as an array of character values. A string buffer, like a vector, has a buffer of positions that may be larger than the number of character values it currently holds. This makes the representation useful when a sequence of insertion operations must be performed on the same string value. The methods provided by class StringBuffer can be described as follows:

```
final class StringBuffer {
    // constructors
    public StringBuffer (int capacity) // initially null string
    public StringBuffer (String str)

    // methods that change contents, return reference to ourselves
    public StringBuffer append (boolean bool)
        ... // and all other primitive data types
    public StringBuffer insert (int offset, boolean bool)
        ... // and all other primitive data types
    public StringBuffer reverse ()
    public void setCharAt (int index, char c)

    // methods to access values
    public char charAt (int index);

    // misc methods
    public int length ()
    public void setLength (int length)
    public void ensureCapacity ()
    public String toString ()
}
```

Note that the methods append, insert, and reverse both change the current string buffer and return a reference to the updated string buffer. This is different from the transformation methods in class String, which leave the receiver string unchanged but return a new string in which the transformations have been applied.

The append operator is used internally by the Java compiler to implement the + operator. A statement such as:

```
System.out.println("answer: " + answer);
```

is compiled as if it were written:

```
System.out.println(new StringBuffer("answer: ").append(answer)
    .toString());
```

17.8.3 *String Tokenizers*

The class StringTokenizer is useful for breaking a string into a sequence of *tokens*. Tokens are defined by a set of delimiter characters. Common delimiters include spaces, tabs, and punctuation such as periods or commas. The class StringTokenizer implements the Enumeration protocol (see Section 19.2), and can therefore be manipulated in an enumeration-style loop.

The methods provided by StringTokenizer can be described as follows:

```
class StringTokenizer implements Enumeration {
    // constructors
    public StringTokenizer (String str)
    public StringTokenizer (String str, String delims)
    public StringTokenizer (String str, String delims,
        boolean returnDelims)

    // enumeration protocol
    public boolean hasMoreElements ()
    public Object nextElement ()
    public String nextToken ()

    // return number of remaining tokens
    public int countTokens ()
}
```

The enumeration protocol requires that the method nextElement() return a value of type Object. In order to avoid the consequent casting of this value to a String, the equivalent method nextToken() can be used instead. The concordance program to be described in Section 19.7.1 will illustrate the use of a string tokenizer in breaking a line into a sequence of words:

```
class Concordance {
    public void readLines (DataInputStream input) throws IOException
    {
```

```
        String delims = " \t\n.,!?;:";
        for (int line = 1; true; line++ ) {
            String text = input.readLine( );
            if (text == null) return;
            text = text.toLowerCase( );
            Enumeration e = new StringTokenizer(text, delims);
            while (e.hasMoreElements( ))
                enterWord ((String) e.nextElement( ), new Integer(line));
        }
    }
}
```

The class StreamTokenizer (Section 14.3) provides a similar facility to breaking an input stream into tokens.

17.8.4 *Parsing String Values*

A StringTokenizer provides one method for breaking a string into component parts, resulting in a sequence of string tokens. If the string tokens represent primitive data values, the programmer requires a method to change the string representation into the primitive value. This functionality is provided by the wrapper classes, Boolean, Integer, Double, Float, and Long. One form of the constructor in each of these classes takes a String as argument and parses the string to ascertain the underlying value. The original value can then be obtained from the wrapper class, as shown in the following example:

```
String dstr = "23.7";
Double dwrap = new Double(dstr); // parse the string
double dval = dwrap.doubleValue( );
```

The wrapper classes also provide the reverse; that is, a way to change a primitive value into a string. Often there are a variety of different formats available. These facilities are summarized in Table 17.1.

Most of the conversion methods will throw a NumberFormatException if the characters do not represent a value in the correct format.

17.9 CHAPTER SUMMARY

The Java run-time system provides a number of useful utility classes. In this chapter we have explored several of these. A Point represents a location in a two-dimensional space, described by a pair of integer coordinates. A Dimension has the same representation—a pair of integer values—but is used to represent a two-dimensional size (height and width). A Date represents a calendar date and time value. The class Math provides access to a number of mathematical constants and useful functions. The Toolkit provides the means for accessing fonts, and retrieving

Table 17.1   Wrapper class conversions to and from strings

Class	Conversion from string	Conversion to string
Boolean	new Boolean(str)	toString( )
	Boolean.valueOf(Boolean bval)	
Double	new Double(str)	toString( )
	Double.valueOf(double dval)	
Float	new Float(str)	toString( )
	Float.valueOf(Float fval)	
Integer	new Integer(str)	toString( )
	Integer.parseInt(String str, int radix)	toBinaryString( )
	Integer.valueOf(int ival)	toOctalString( )
		toHexString( )

images over a network. The class System provides access to standard input and output areas.

A String in the Java language is an immutable (constant) value. The String data type provides a number of high-level operations. A related class, StringBuffer, permits changes to the individual fields in a string. The class StringTokenizer can be used to break a string into individual parts.

STUDY QUESTIONS

1. What type of values does a Point represent?

2. What type of values does a Dimension represent?

3. Both points and dimensions have the same internal representation; a pair of integer data values. What makes them different?

4. What type of values does a Date represent?

5. Write a Java expression that prints the current day of the month and hour.

6. What is the start of the epoch?

7. Why are data fields and constants in class Math declared as static?

8. How is a String different from a StringBuffer?

18 Understanding Graphics

The Java language provides one of the richest collections of graphical commands of any general purpose programming language. In this chapter we will explain some of the basic aspects of the classes associated with graphical operations in Java. Topics discussed include colors, fonts, images, and animation.

18.1 COLOR

The class Color is used to represent a color value. We know from optics that all colors can be formed by combinations of red, green, and blue. Color televisions use this principle, displaying colors as combinations of red, green, and blue dots. In order to represent colors in a computer more easily, each of the three amounts of red, green, and blue is represented by an integer value between 0 and 255. (There is nothing magic about the value 255; it was simply chosen so that each quantity could be stored in an eight-bit byte.) For each quantity, the larger the value, the brighter the component. A value of (0,0,0) is therefore black, while a value of (255, 255, 255) is white.[1] While in theory this encoding can represent 2^{24} different colors ($2^8 \times 2^8 \times 2^8$), in practice most display devices can handle only a limited range. When the exact color is unavailable, the actual color produced by a display device will usually be the closest matching color.

The Java library class Color allows colors to be specified using three integer values. The class also defines predefined constants for a number of commonly used colors. These are described in Table 18.1. The constructor for color takes as

---

[1] There is an alternative system that represents each color by a triple of floating-point values that represent the Hue, Saturation, and Brightness of the color. The HSB system is not used as much as the RGB system and will not be described here. The class Color provides methods for converting between the two systems.

Table 18.1   Methods for Class Color.

Predefined Colors

Color.black	Color.magenta
Color.blue	Color.orange
Color.cyan	Color.pink
Color.darkGray	Color.red
Color.gray	Color.white
Color.green	Color.yellow
Color.lightGray	

Description of Methods in Class Color

new Color (int, int, int)	constructor
brighter()	create brighter version of color
darker()	create darker version of color
getBlue()	return blue component of color
getGreen()	return green component of color
getRed()	return red component of color
toString()	return string representation of color

argument the three integer values representing the red, green, and blue components. These values can subsequently be retrieved from a color using the methods getRed, getGreen, and getBlue. The methods brighter and darker return brighter and darker versions of the current color. Finally, the method toString returns a string representation of the current color. A program that illustrates the use of many of the features of class Color is described in Section 13.5.

18.2   RECTANGLES

There are two classes in the Java library used for manipulating polygon shapes. The class Rectangle represents a rectangular area on a two-dimensional plane. The class Polygon represents more general polygon shapes.

We have used the class Rectangle already in the Cannon World program described in Chapter 6. In that program, every graphical object, each ball as well as each target, was placed on top of a rectangle that represented the location of the item. The application used the fact that a rectangle not only records a position on the two-dimensional surface but also can be easily moved to a new position and can tell whether or not it intersects with another rectangle.

A new rectangle can be created in a variety of ways. If no arguments are provided with the constructor, then an empty rectangle whose northwest corner is the origin is created. If two integers are specified, they are taken to be a width and height for a rectangle with the northwest corner at the origin. If four integer arguments are specified, the first two are the locations of the northwest corner, and the remaining arguments are the width and height.

```
Rectangle r = new Rectangle ();
Rectangle rTwo = new Rectangle (3, 4); \\ width 3, height 4
Rectangle rThree = new Rectangle (7, 6, 3, 4); \\ corner 7,6
```

Operations that test the state of a rectangle can be summarized as follows:

r.equals (rTwo)	Tell whether two rectangles are equal
r.inside (int, int)	Tell whether a point is inside the rectangle
r.intersects (rTwo)	Tell whether two rectangles intersect
r.isEmpty( )	Tell whether rectangle has nonempty extent

The size of a rectangle can be changed in a variety of ways. The add operation takes two integers that represent a point, and increases the size of the rectangle until it includes the point. The union operation does the same with another Rectangle argument, returning the smallest rectangle that encloses both. The grow operation takes two integer arguments and moves each of the horizontal sizes by the first argument amount and each of the vertical sides by the second, which can be either positive or negative. The method intersection calculates the intersection of two rectangles. The setLocation method moves a rectangle to a given location, while the translate method moves a rectangle by a given amount. The setSize method sets a rectangle size. Both the size and location of a rectangle can be changed by the method reshape, which takes four integer arguments in the same form as the constructor.

18.2.1 *Rectangle Sample Program*

A sample program, shown in Figure 18.1, illustrates the use of many Rectangle methods. Two rectangles are initially placed on the window. In each step all rectangles are either resized or moved, and a test is performed to see if any two rectangles intersect. If so, a new rectangle is generated with the same size as their intersection.

The method to move rectangles generates two random numbers. Using these, the rectangle is either changed in size or moved. Tests are performed to ensure the rectangle does not become negative in size or move off the board.

```
private void moveAllRectangles() {
    for (Enumeration e = rects.elements(); e.hasMoreElements(); ) {
        Rectangle r = (Rectangle) e.nextElement();
        int i = rand(5);
        int j = rand(5);
```

```
class RectTest extends JFrame {
   public static void main (String [ ] args)
      { Frame window = new RectTest(); window.show(); }

   private Vector rects = new Vector();
   private Random rnd = new Random();
   private static int FrameWidth = 400;
   private static int FrameHeight = 400;

   public RectTest () {
      setSize (400, 400);
      setTitle ("Rectangle test");
      rects.addElement (new Rectangle(4, 5));
      rects.addElement (new Rectangle(100, 100, 6, 7));
      }

   public void paint (Graphics g) {
      g.setColor(Color.green);
      for (Enumeration e = rects.elements(); e.hasMoreElements(); ) {
         Rectangle r = (Rectangle) e.nextElement();
         g.fillRect (r.x, r.y, r.width, r.height);
         }
      moveAllRectangles();
      spawnNewRectangles();
      repaint();
      }

   private int rand (int max) { return rnd.nextInt() % max; }

   private void moveAllRectangles() { ... }

   private void spawnNewRectangles() { ... }
}
```

Figure 18.1   The rectangle example program.

```
      if ((i + j) % 5 == 0) {
         r.grow (i, j);
         if (r.height < 0)
            r.setSize (r.width, - r.height);
         if (r.width < 0)
            r.setSize (- r.width, r.height);
      }
      else {
```

```
            r.translate (i, j);
            if (r.x < 0)
                r.setLocation (r.x + FrameWidth, r.y);
            if (r.y < 0)
                r.setLocation (r.x, r.y + FrameWidth);
            if (r.x > FrameWidth)
                r.setLocation (r.x - FrameWidth, r.y);
            if (r.y > FrameWidth)
                r.setLocation (r.x, r.y - FrameWidth);
        }
    }
}
```

The routine to test for intersections uses doubly-nested enumeration loops. If it locates two intersecting rectangles, a new rectangle is created and placed in the upper corner. Only one new rectangle is created in each move, in order to slow the process of filling the window.

```
private void spawnNewRectangles( ) {
    for (Enumeration e = rects.elements( ); e.hasMoreElements( ); ) {
        Rectangle r1 = (Rectangle) e.nextElement( );
        for (Enumeration f = rects.elements( ); f.hasMoreElements( ); )
        {
            Rectangle r2 = (Rectangle) f.nextElement( );
            if (r1.intersects(r2) && ! r1.equals(r2)) {
                Rectangle nr = r1.intersection(r2);
                nr.setLocation (0, 0);
                rects.addElement(nr);
                return;
            }
        }
    }
}
```

<h2>18.3 FONTS</h2>

A Font object describes the characteristics used to display printed text. Features of a font that the programmer can modify are the style, size, and font family (or logical name).

The logical font name describes the family of font styles being used. There are six recognized logical font names, Dialog, Helvetica, TimesRoman, Courier, DialogInput, and Symbol. The last is used to represent nonalphabetic symbols and is seldom used. Courier is a font with fixed-width characters, much like a typewriter. Helvetica and Times Roman are variable-width fonts, which are the type

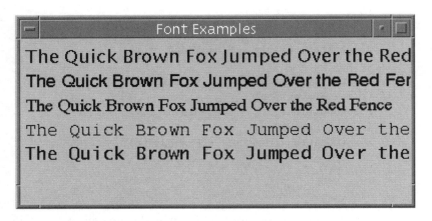

Figure 18.2   Example text printed in different fonts.

normally used for printed text. An example of text printed in each of the first five fonts is shown in Figure 18.2.

A font style describes the thickness and slant of the characters. In the Java library there are two characteristics that describe a style. These are the Bold attribute and the Italic attribute. Each is represented by an integer value, which can be combined. Thus, there are four different representations for each font family: plain (neither bold nor italic), bold, italic, and both bold and italic.

A font point size represents the size of the individual characters. Points are units used in typesetting. One point is approximately 1/72 of an inch.

The following chart describes the most commonly used methods recognized by instances of class Font.

Font(String name, int style, int size)	Construct new font
Font.PLAIN	Constant used to describe plain fonts
Font.BOLD	Constant used to describe bold fonts
Font.ITALIC	Constant used to describe italic fonts
getName( )	Return logical name
getSize( )	Return point size
getStyle( )	Return style characteristics
isBold( )	Determine if font is bold
isItalic( )	Determine if font is italic
isPlain( )	Determine if font is plain
toString( )	Return string representation of font

An instance of class Font can be created by providing the logical font name, a style, and a size. The name *must* be one of the six recognized family names (Dialog, Helvetica, TimesRoman, Courier, DialogInput, and Symbol). The style is formed using the class constants. A font that is both bold and italic can be created by adding the two values Font.BOLD and Font.ITALIC. The size can be any integer value, although not all sizes can be represented by all font families on any particular output device. In general, the size used in a display will be the closest available size to the one specified.

18.3.1 *Font Metrics*

A separate class, FontMetrics, is occasionally needed to get more detailed information about a font or about a string printed in a given font. For example, a font metric can be used to determine the width (in pixels) of a text that is to be printed in a particular font. Font metrics is an abstract class, and therefore you cannot directly construct instances of the class. The most common way to access a font metric object is by means of the method getFontMetrics provided by an object of type Graphics, as in the following example:

```
public void paint (Graphics g) {
   .
   .
   g.setFont (aFont);
   FontMetric fm = g.getFontMetrics();
   .
   .
   .
}
```

To determine the width of an individual character or a string, the methods fm.charWidth(char) or fm.stringWidth(String) can be used. The result is described in pixel units. Various other characteristics of a font are accessible using a font metric, for example fm.getHeight() will return the height (maximum character size) of the font. There are other methods. However these are rarely used.

18.3.2 *Font Example Program*

A small test program will illustrate both the use of methods in class Font and the way to program using checkboxes. The application will have a bank of six checkboxes on the bottom of the window, corresponding to the six logical font family names. Two buttons on the right (the east) will set either bold, or italic, or both, while a text edit field will allow the size to be set. An example text that illustrates the selected characteristics is then displayed in the middle of the application window. The main program is shown in Figure 18.3. The two banks of checkboxes are created by the two routines makeStyles and makeNames.

```
class FontTest extends JFrame {
   static public void main (String [ ] args)
      { Frame window = new FontTest( ); window.show( ); }

   private int style = 0;
   private int size = 15;
   private String fontName = "Helvetica";

   public FontTest ( ) {
      setTitle("Font Test"); setSize(600, 150);
      add("East", makeStyles( ));
      add("South", makeNames( ));
   }

   private void display ( ) { repaint( ); }

   public void paint (Graphics g) {
      Font f = new Font(fontName, style, size);
      g.setFont(f);
      FontMetrics fm = g.getFontMetrics( );
      g.drawString(f.toString( ), 5, 10 + 2 * fm.getHeight( ));
   }

   private Panel makeStyles( ) { ... }

   private class StyleBox extends Checkbox implements ItemLextener ...

   private class SizeBox extends TextField implements ActionListener ...

   private class NameBox extends Checkbox implements ItemLextener ...

   private Panel makeNames( ) { ... }
}
```

Figure 18.3   The FontTest program.

The method makeStyles creates a grid layout of four horizontal panels. The first two are filled by instances of a class StyleBox that will allow a style to be set. The third is a SizeBox that will set the size of the example text. The final element is a quit button using the class ButtonAdapter defined earlier in Chapter 13.

```
private Panel makeStyles( ) {
   Panel p = new Panel( );
   p.setLayout(new GridLayout(4,1));
```

```
      p.add (new StyleBox(Font.ITALIC, "italic"));
      p.add (new StyleBox(Font.BOLD, "bold"));
      p.add (new SizeBox( ));
      p.add (new ButtonAdapter("Quit"){
         public void pressed( ){System.exit(0);}});
      return p;
   }
```

A StyleBox uses a technique we have seen earlier in Chapter 13. The class both extends the library class Checkbox and implements the class ItemListener. Thus, the class can encapsulate within itself both the creation of a Checkbox item and the task of listening when the Checkbox has been selected. When each box is selected it either turns on or off the given modifier bits, depending upon the state of the box. Notice that when checkboxes are created in this fashion, they are independent of each other, and can be set or unset individually. (For example, both the bold and italic checkbox can be set, in order to display bold italic output.)

```
private class StyleBox extends Checkbox implements ItemListener {
   private int modifiers;

   public StyleBox (int m, String name)
      { super (name);
      addItemListener (this); modifiers = m; }

   public void itemStateChanged (ItemEvent e) {
      if (getState( ))
         style |= modifiers; // turn on modifiers
      else
         style &= ~ modifiers; // turn off modifiers
      display( );
   }
}
```

A SizeBox is a type of TextField, that when edited changes the size value in the application class.

```
private class SizeBox extends TextField implements ActionListener {
   public SizeBox ( ) { super ("" + size); addActionListener(this); }

   public void actionPerformed (ActionEvent e) {
      String sz = getText( );
      size = (new Integer(sz)).intValue( );
      display( );
   }
}
```

The method makeNames( ) illustrates the creation of a different type of checkbox. In this form, only one of the collection can be set at any one time. Setting one item will automatically unset all others. Such a group is sometimes referred to as *radio buttons*, as they operate in a fashion similar to the buttons on a car radio. To create a radio button collection, a CheckBoxGroup is created. This checkbox group is then passed with the constructor to each checkbox that will be part of the group.

```
private class NameBox extends Checkbox implements ItemListener {
    public NameBox (String name, CheckboxGroup cg)
       { super(name, cg, false); addItemListener(this); }

    public void itemStateChanged (ItemEvent e)
       { fontName = getLabel( ); display( ); }
}

private Panel makeNames( ) {
    Panel p = new Panel( );
    p.setLayout(new GridLayout(1,6));
    CheckboxGroup cg = new CheckboxGroup( );
    p.add (new NameBox("Courier", cg));
    p.add (new NameBox("Dialog", cg));
    p.add (new NameBox("DialogInput", cg));
    p.add (new NameBox("Helvetica", cg));
    p.add (new NameBox("TimesRoman", cg));
    p.add (new NameBox("Symbol", cg));
    return p;
}
```

When any button is pressed, the fontName field will be changed, and the display method activated.

18.4   IMAGES

An image is really nothing more than a two-dimensional collection of pixel values. Most commonly images are created by some video device, such as a digital camera, and stored in a file in a standard format, such as JPEG or GIF. A picture stored in such a format can be read into a Java program by first creating a URL (see Section 21.4.1), then using the toolbox routine getImage. The following program illustrates this technique. The first command-line argument is assumed to be a URL for a file stored in one of the standard formats. This image is read from the file and displayed as the value of the application window.

```
import java.awt.*;
import java.net.*;

class ImageTest extends JFrame {
   public static void main (String [ ] args) {
      Frame world = new ImageTest (args[0]);
      world.show( );
   }

   private Image image = null;

   public ImageTest (String fileName) {
      setSize (300, 300);
      setTitle ("Image Test");
      try { // read image from URL given in argument
         URL imageAddress = new URL (fileName);
         image = getToolkit( ).getImage(imageAddress);
      } catch (Exception e) { image = null; }
   }

   public void paint (Graphics g) {
      if (image != null)
         g.drawImage (image, 0, 0, this);
   }
}
```

18.4.1 *Animation*

Animation is simply the process of displaying a sequence of still pictures one after another. Just as with a movie, the eye is fooled into linking the pictures together, giving the appearance of smooth motion. The simplest animation program is shown below. Here a series of GIF files is read into an array of images. The paint routine selects one of these for display, then updates an index value so that the next image in sequence will be selected by the following display. Calling repaint ensures that the next image will then be displayed.

```
class AnimationTest extends JFrame {

   public static void main (String [ ] args) {
      Frame world = new AnimationTest ( );
      world.show( );
   }

   private Image [ ] imageArray;
```

```
    private int index = 0;

    public AnimationTest ( ) {
        setSize(300, 300);
        setTitle("Simple Animation");
        imageArray = new Image [ 17 ];
        for (int i = 0; i < 17; i++) {
            String name = "T" + (i+1) + ".gif";
            try {
                URL address = new URL (name);
                imageArray[i] = getToolkit( ).getImage(address);
            } catch (Exception e) { imageArray[i] = null; }
        }
    }

    public void paint (Graphics g) {
        if (imageArray[index] != null)
            g.drawImage(imageArray[index++], 0, 0, this);
        if (index >= imageArray.length)
            index = 0;
        try {
            Thread.sleep(200);
        } catch (Exception e) { }
        repaint( );
    }
}
```

In order to slow down the animation, the paint routine will sleep for 200 milliseconds after drawing the image. On some platforms the animation will show an annoying flicker. This is because the method update, called by repaint, will redraw the screen in the background color before calling paint. This can sometimes be eliminated by simply overriding the method update to avoid redrawing the background:

```
    // override update to simply paint window
    public void update (Graphics g) {
        paint(g);
    }
```

18.5 GRAPHICS CONTEXTS

As we have seen in almost all of our example programs, the majority of graphics in Java are generated using an object of class Graphics. Such an object is termed the *graphics context*. As we noted in Chapter 6, graphics contexts maintain a

Table 18.2 Operations Provided by Graphics Context.

clearRect	Clear a rectangular region
copyArea	Copy a rectangular region to another location
draw3DRect	Paint a three-dimensional rectangle
drawArc	Draw elliptical arc
drawBytes	Display bytes as text
drawChars	Display characters as text
drawImage	Display pixel image
drawLine	Draw a line from one point to another
drawOval	Draw oval outline
drawPolygon	Draw polygon outline
drawRect	Draw rectangle
drawRoundRect	Draw rounded rectangle
drawString	Draw string at given location
fillArc	Paint a filled elliptical arc
fillOval	Paint a filled oval shape
fillRect	Paint a filled rectangular area
fillRoundRect	Paint a filled rounded rectangular area
getColor	Retrieve the current foreground color
getFont	Retrieve the font used to print text
getFontMetrics	Retrieve font metrics object for current font
setColor	Set the current foreground color
setFont	Set the font for future printing operations
setPaintMode	Set drawing to paint mode
setXORMode	Set drawing to XOR mode

coordinate system in which the 0,0 location is the upper left corner, and values increase as they move down and to the right. Graphics contexts also maintain both a foreground and a background color, in a fashion we have already seen used with windows. Table 18.2 summarizes the most commonly used method provided by class Graphics. We have used many of these in our earlier case studies.

Drawing operations in graphics contexts can be performed in one of two different *modes*. The common mode is *paint* mode, established by calling the method setPaintMode. An alternative is XOR mode. The unique property of XOR mode is that if the same object is drawn twice, the second drawing command *erases* the object, restoring the image to the state it had prior to the first command.

This property is similar to the logical exclusive-or (XOR) command, hence the name. The common use for this property is to draw cursors, or other graphics images that track the position of the mouse as it moves across a window. We will see an example of this in the program described in the next section.

18.6   A SIMPLE PAINTING PROGRAM

An example program will illustrate the use of many of the graphics context commands. The program will also show how one can create a static image that can be generated as a sequence of graphical commands, rather than all at one time.

The window for the application (Figure 18.4) has a row of buttons across the top. Pressing one of these buttons selects the type of figure to be drawn. Pressing the mouse in the canvas window then begins a drawing operation. As the mouse moves while still being pressed, a "ghost" image of the figure tracks the mouse location. When the mouse is released, the selected figure is drawn.

The source code for the painting application is shown in Figure 18.5. A Panel is used to hold the three buttons. The buttons themselves are defined as subclasses of an inner class Shape, which will do double duty as both a button listener class, and a recording of the currently selected shape. When pressed, the button will simply save its value in the variable currentShape. In addition to representing a button, each shape will know how to draw itself in a rectangular region (Figure 18.6).

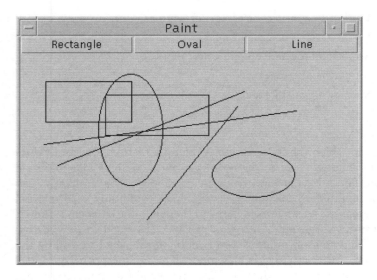

Figure 18.4   Window for painting application.

```
class Paint extends JFrame {
   public static void main (String [ ] args)
      { Frame world = new Paint( ); world.show( ); }

   private Image image = null;
   private Shape currentShape = null;

   public Paint ( ) {
      setTitle("Paint");
      setSize(400, 300);
         // change layout manager
      getContentPane( ).setLayout(new BorderLayout( ));

         // create panel of buttons
      Panel p = new Panel( );
      p.setLayout(new GridLayout(1,3));
      p.add(new Rectangle( ));
      p.add(new Oval( ));
      p.add(new Line( ));
      getContentPane( ).add("North", p);
         // add mouse event listener
      MouseKeeper k = new MouseKeeper( );
      addMouseListener(k);
      addMouseMotionListener(k);
   }

   public void paint (Graphics g) {
      if (image == null) // will happen only once
         image = createImage(400, 300);
      if (image != null)
         g.drawImage(image, 0, 0, this);
   }

   private abstract class Shape
      extends Button implements ActionListener { ... }
   private class Rectangle extends Shape { ... }
   private class Oval extends Shape { ... }
   private class Line extends Shape { ... }

   private class MouseKeeper
      extends MouseAdapter implements MouseMotionListener { ... }
}
```

Figure 18.5   Source for painting application.

The class Shape, as well as the drawing method, have been declared abstract. This means that it is not possible to create an instance of the class without first subclassing. Furthermore, each subclass *must* implement the method draw.

The first time the application is asked to draw its window, it copies the Image associated with the application component into a variable named image. Thereafter, to render the application window it is only necessary to draw the contents of this image.

Most applications that interact with the mouse need to recognize the mouse moving down. Of these, a few (such as the current application) need to differentiate between the mouse going down and the mouse going up. Fewer still need also to track the position of the mouse as it is moving. Because the latter action is relatively infrequent, the Java event library separates this task into a different listener. A MouseListener tracks only mouse presses and releases. A MouseMotionListener also tracks mouse movements, either while pressed or not. The mouse class we created for this class implements both interfaces, by extending the MouseAdapter, and implementing the MouseMotionListener interface (Figure 18.7, on page 314).

When the mouse is first pressed, the location of the mouse press is saved in a pair of local integer variables. A second pair of integer variables records the new location and is initially the same as the source location. As the mouse moves, the method mouseDragged is repeatedly executed. This method sets the graphical display mode to XOR, then repaints the current shape using the old coordinate locations. The effect will be the *erase* of the previous image. The end point locations are then set to the current mouse position and the shape redrawn. The effect is that the shape is continually erased and redrawn as the mouse is moved. When the mouse is finally released, the method mouseReleased is executed. This erases the old image one last time, changes the mode to paint, and draws the shape in its final location.

18.7 CHAPTER SUMMARY

A Java run-time library provides a rich collection of classes that can be used to manipulate graphical images. In this chapter we have investigated several of these. A Color represents a color value. Colors are specified by a trio of integer values, representing the amount of red, green and blue in the color. A Rectangle represents a rectangular region of the plane. A Font describes the characteristics of a printed letter. An Image is a picture composed of pixel values. A succession of images can be displayed one after the other in an animation. A Graphics object provides the tools necessary to perform simple graphical operations, such as drawing a line or oval.

STUDY QUESTIONS

1. What do the three integer values in a color represent?

```
private abstract class Shape
      extends JButton implements ActionListener {

   public Shape (String name) {
      super(name);
      addActionListener (this);
   }

   public abstract void draw (Graphics g, int a, int b, int c, int d);

   public void actionPerformed (ActionEvent e)
      { currentShape = this; }
}

private class Rectangle extends Shape {

   public Rectangle () { super("Rectangle"); }

   public void draw (Graphics g, int a, int b, int c, int d) {
      int w = c - a; // width
      int h = d - b; // height
      g.drawRect(a, b, w, h);
   }
}

private class Oval extends Shape {
   public Oval () { super("Oval"); }

   public void draw (Graphics g, int a, int b, int c, int d) {
      int w = c - a; int h = d - b;
      g.drawOval(a, b, w, h);
   }
}

private class Line extends Shape {
   public Line () { super("Line"); }

   public void draw (Graphics g, int a, int b, int c, int d)
      { g.drawLine(a, b, c, d); }
}
```

Figure 18.6 Shape subclasses.

```
private class MouseKeeper
     extends MouseAdapter implements MouseMotionListener {
  private int startx, starty; // upper right corner
  private int lastx, lasty; // current position

  public void mousePressed (MouseEvent e) {
     lastx = startx = e.getX( );
     lasty = starty = e.getY( );
  }

  private void drawShape (Graphics g) {
     if (currentShape != null)
        currentShape.draw(g, startx, starty, lastx, lasty);
  }

  public void mouseDragged (MouseEvent e) {
     Graphics g = image.getGraphics( );
     g.setXORMode(Color.white);
        // erase old image
     drawShape(g);
        // draw new rectangle
     lastx = e.getX( ); lasty = e.getY( );
     drawShape(g); repaint( );
  }

  public void mouseReleased (MouseEvent e) {
     Graphics g = image.getGraphics( );
        // erase old image
     g.setXORMode(Color.white);
     drawShape(g);
        // now paint new image
     g.setPaintMode( );
     lastx = e.getX( ); lasty = e.getY( );
     drawShape(g); repaint( );
  }

  public void mouseMoved (MouseEvent e) { }
}
```

Figure 18.7   The mouse listener for the painting application.

2. What are the predefined colors available to the Java run-time system?

3. How does one tell whether or not a point is found inside a rectangle?

4. What are the style modifiers used with a value of type Font?

5. What is an animation? How can an animation be produced in Java?

6. How is a MouseMotionListener different from a MouseActionListener?

EXERCISES

1. Add buttons to the painting program described in Section 18.6 to create filled rectangles and ovals, as well as the outline rectangles and ovals it currently produces.

2. Add a panel with three sliders for selecting colors, similar to the panel described in Chapter 13. Use the colors selected by these sliders for the fill color in the figures you added in the previous question.

3. By adding a KeyListener object, add the ability to enter text and have it displayed at the current mouse location.

4. Add menu items to change the font and style of text values.

19

Collection Classes

Collections are classes designed for holding groups of objects. Almost all non-trivial programs need to maintain one or more collections of objects. Although the Java library provides only a few different forms of collection, the features provided by these classes are very general, making them applicable to a wide variety of problems. In this chapter we will first describe some of the basic concepts common to the collection classes, then summarize the basic collections provided by Java, and finally describe a few container types that are not provided by the standard library, but which can be easily constructed by the programmer.

19.1 ELEMENT TYPES AND PRIMITIVE VALUE WRAPPERS

With the exception of the array data type, all the collections provided by the Java library maintain their values in variables of type Object. There are two important consequences of this feature:

- Since primitive types, such as integers, Booleans, characters, and floating-point values, are not subclasses of Object, they cannot be directly stored in these collections.

- When values are removed from the collection, they must be cast back to their original type.

One way to circumvent the first restriction is through the use of *wrapper classes*. A wrapper class maintains a primitive data value but is itself an object and can thus be stored in a container. Methods are typically provided both to construct an instance of the wrapper class from a primitive value, and to recover the original value from the wrapper. The following, for example, stores two integers into instances of class Integer, then recovers the original values so that an arithmetic operation can be performed:

```
Integer a = new Integer(12);
Integer b = new Integer(3);
   // must recover the int values to do arithmetic
int c = a.intValue() * b.intValue();
```

In addition, many wrapper classes provide other useful functionality, such as the ability to parse string values. A common way to convert a string containing an integer value literal into an int, for example, is to use an Integer as a middle step:

```
String text = "123"; // example string value
Integer val = new Integer(text); // first convert to Integer
int ival = val.intValue(); // then convert Integer to int
```

Table 19.1 summarizes the most common wrapper classes and a few of their more useful behaviors.

Table 19.1 Wrapper Classes and Selected Behaviors.

Integer Wrapper	
new Integer(int value)	Build Integer from int
Integer(String value)	Parse integer in String
intValue( )	Value of Integer as int
toString( )	Return decimal string representation of Integer
toBinaryString( )	Return binary representation
toOctalString( )	Return octal representation
toHexString( )	Return hex representation
Character Wrapper	
new Character(char value)	Convert char to Character
charValue( )	Return char value of Character
isLetter( )	Determine if character is letter
isDigit( )	True if character is digit
Boolean Wrapper	
new Boolean (boolean value)	Convert boolean to Boolean
booleanValue ( )	Retrieve boolean value from Boolean
toString( )	Generate string representation of boolean
Double Wrapper	
new Double(double)	Convert double to Double
new Double(String)	Construct Double from string
doubleValue( )	Return double value of Double

19.2 ENUMERATORS

All collections can be envisioned as a linear sequence of elements. However, the particular means used to access each element differs from one collection type to another. For example, a vector is indexed using an integer position key, whereas a hash table can use any type of object as a key. It is frequently desirable to abstract away these differences and access the elements of the collection in sequence without regard to the technique used to obtain the underlying values. This facility is provided by the Enumeration interface and its various implementations. The Enumeration interface specifies two methods:

hasMoreElements( )	A Boolean value that indicates whether or not there are any more elements to be enumerated
nextElement( )	Retrieves the next element in the enumeration

These two operations are used together to form a loop. The following code, for example, shows how all the elements of a hash table could be printed:

```
for (Enumeration e = htab.elements( ); e.hasMoreElements( ); ) {
    System.out.println (e.nextElement( ));
    }
```

The methods hasMoreElements and nextElement should always be invoked in tandem. That is, nextElement should never be invoked unless hasMoreElements has first determined that there is another element, and nextElement should never be invoked twice without an intervening call on hasMoreElements. If it is necessary to refer more than once to the value returned by nextElement, the result of the nextElement call should be assigned to a local variable:

```
for (Enumeration e = htab.elements( ); e.hasMoreElements( ); ) {
    Object value = e.nextElement( );
    if (value.equals(Test))
        System.out.println ("found object " + value);
    }
```

With the exception of the array, all the collections provided by the Java library provide a method that generates an enumeration. In addition, several other classes that are not necessarily collections also support the enumeration protocol. For example, a StringTokenizer is used to extract words from a string value. The individual words are then accessed using enumeration methods. Section 19.6.1 describes how the programmer can create a new type of enumeration.

19.3 THE ARRAY

The most basic collection form in Java is the array. As noted in earlier chapters, the creation and manipulation of an array value is different in Java than in many other programming languages. The Java language makes a separation between (a) declaring a variable of array type, (b) defining the size of the array and allocating space, and (c) assigning values to the array. In many other languages the first and second tasks are merged. Combining these concepts makes it difficult to, for example, write functions that will operate on arrays of any size. These problems are largely eliminated in Java's approach to arrays.

An array variable is declared by indicating the type of elements the array will contain, and a pair of square brackets that indicate an array is being formed. The following, for example, is from the Solitaire game case study examined in Chapter 9.

```
static public CardPile allPiles [ ];
```

The brackets can be written either after the variable name or after the type. The following, for example, is an equivalent declaration:

```
static public CardPile [ ] allPiles;
```

Note that the array is the only collection in the Java library that requires the programmer to specify the type of elements that will be held by the container. An important consequence of this is that the array is the *only* collection that can maintain nonobject types, such as integers, Booleans, or characters. Other containers hold their values as instances of class Object, and can therefore only hold primitive values if they are surrounded by wrapper classes (Integer, Double, and so on).

An array *value* is created, as are all values, using the new operator. It is only when the array value is created that the size of the array is specified.

```
allPiles = new CardPile [ 13 ]; // create array of 13 card piles
```

Arrays can also be created as an initialization expression in the original declaration. The initialization expression provides the values for the array, as well as indicating the number of elements.

```
int primes [ ] = {2, 3, 5, 7, 11, 13, 17, 19};
```

Elements of an array are accessed using the subscript operator. This is used both to retrieve the current value held at a given position and to assign a position a new value:

```
primes[3] = primes[2] + 2;
```

Legal index values range from zero to one less than the number of elements held by the array. An attempt to access a value with an out-of-range index value results in an IndexOutOfBoundsException being thrown.

The integer field length describes the number of elements held by an array. The following loop shows this value being used to form a loop to print the elements in an array:

```
for (int i = 0; i < primes.length; i++)
    System.out.println("prime " + i + " is " + primes[i]);
```

Arrays are also *cloneable* (see Section 11.3.1). An array can be copied and assigned to another array value. The clone operation creates a shallow copy.

```
int numbers [ ];
numbers = primes.clone( ); // creates a new array of numbers
```

19.4   THE Vector COLLECTION

The Vector data abstraction is similar to an array of objects. However, it provides a number of high-level operations not supported by the array abstraction. Most importantly, a vector is *expandable*, meaning it grows as necessary as new elements are added to the collection. Thus, the programmer need not know the eventual collection size at the time the vector is created. To use this collection the Vector class must be imported from java.util.Vector. A new vector is created using the new operator.

```
import java.util.Vector;
.
.
.
Vector numbers = new Vector ( );
```

Because objects held by a Vector must be subclasses of Object, a vector can not be used to hold primitive values, such as integers or floats. However, wrapper classes can be used to convert such values into objects.

Table 19.2 summarizes the most useful operations provided by the Vector data abstraction. The class has been carefully designed so that it can be used in a variety of different ways. The following sections describe some of the more common uses.

19.4.1   *Using a Vector as an Array*

Unlike an array, a vector is not created with a fixed size. A vector can be given a specific size either by adding the appropriate number of elements (using the

Table 19.2   Operations Provided by the Vector Data Type.

Size Determination	
size( )	Returns number of elements in collection as an int
isEmpty( )	Returns true if collection is empty
capacity( )	Return current capacity of vector as an int
setSize(int newSize)	Set size of vector, truncating or expanding as necessary
Element Access	
contains(Object elem)	Determines whether a value is in this vector
firstElement( )	Returns first element of collection
lastElement( )	Returns last element of collection
elementAt(int index)	Returns element stored at given position
Insertion and Modification	
addElement(Object value)	Add new value to end of collection
setElementAt(Object value, int index)	Change value at position
insertElementAt(Object value, int index)	Insert value at given index
Removal	
removeElementAt(int index)	Remove element at index, reducing size of vector
removeElement(Object value)	Remove all instances of value
removeAllElements( )	Delete all values from vector
Search	
indexOf(Object value)	Return index of first occurrence
lastIndexOf(Object value)	Return index of last occurrence
Miscellaneous	
clone( )	Return shallow copy of vector
toString( )	Return string representation of vector

addElement operation) or by using setSize. In the latter case, a null value will be stored in any index locations that have not previously been assigned a value.

```
Vector aVec = new Vector ( ); // create a new vector
aVec.setSize (20); // allocate 20 locations, initially undefined
```

Once sized, the value stored at any position can be accessed using the method elementAt, while positions can be modified using setElementAt. Note that in the latter, the index of the position being modified is the second parameter, while the value to be assigned to the location is the first parameter. The following illustrates how these methods could be used to swap the first and final elements of a vector:

```
Object first = aVec.elementAt(0); // store first position
aVec.setElementAt(aVec.lastElement( ), 0); // store last in location 0
aVec.setElementAt(first, aVec.size( )-1); // store first at end
```

19.4.2   *Using a* Vector *as a Stack*

A *stack* is a data structure that allows elements to be inserted and removed at one end, and it always removes the last element inserted. A stack of papers on a desk is a good intuitive picture of the stack abstraction.

Although the Java standard library includes a Stack data abstraction (see Section 19.5), it is easy to see how a Vector can be used as a stack. The characteristic operations of a stack are to insert or remove an item from the top of the stack, peek at (but do not remove) the topmost element, or/and test the stack for emptiness. The following shows how each of these can be performed using operations provided by the vector class:

aVec.addElement (value)	Push a value on the stack
aVec.lastElement( )	Peek at the topmost element of the stack
aVec.removeElementAt(aVec.size( ) - 1)	Remove the topmost element of the stack

As will be noted in Section 19.5, the Stack abstraction is slightly more robust, since it will throw more meaningful error indications if an attempt is made to remove an element from an empty stack.

19.4.3   *Using a* Vector *as a Queue*

A *queue* is a data structure that allows elements to be inserted at one end, and removed from the other. In this fashion, the element removed will be the *first* element that was inserted. Thinking about a line of people waiting to enter a theater provides a good intuition.

In a manner analogous to the way that the vector can be used as a stack, the vector operations can also be used to simulate a queue:

aVec.addElement (value)	Push a value on the queue
aVec.firstElement( )	Peek at the first element in the queue
aVec.removeElementAt(0)	Remove the first element of the queue

There is one important difference between this abstraction and the earlier simulation of the stack. In the stack abstraction, all the operations could be performed in constant time, independent of the number of elements being held by the stack.[1] Removing the first element from the queue, on the other hand, *always* results in all elements being moved and therefore always requires time proportional to the number of elements in the collection.

19.4.4   *Using a* Vector *as a Set*

A *set* is usually envisioned as an unordered collection of values. Characteristic operations on a set include testing to see if a value is being held in the set, and adding or removing values from the set. The following shows how these can be implemented using the operations provided by the Vector class:

aVec.contains(value)	See if value is held in set
aVec.addElement(value)	Add new element to set
aVec.removeElement(value)	Remove element from set

The equals method is used to perform comparisons. Comparisons are necessary to determine whether or not a value is held in the collection and whether a value is the element the user wishes to delete. For user-defined data values the equals method can be overridden to provide whatever meaning is appropriate (see Section 11.4).

Operations such as union and intersection of sets can be easily implemented using a loop. The following code, for example, places in setThree the union of the values from setOne and setTwo.

```
Vector setThree = new Vector( );
setThree = setOne.clone( ); // first copy all of set one
    // then add elements from set two not already in set one
for (Enumeration e = setTwo.elements( ); e.hasMoreElements( ); ) {
    Object value = e.nextElement( );
    if (! setThree.contains(value))
        setThree.addElement(value);
}
```

For sets consisting of positive integer values, the BitSet class (Section 19.6) is often a more efficient alternative.

---

[1] The assertion concerning constant time operation of stack operations is true with one small caveat. An insertion can, in rare occasions, result in a reallocation of the underlying vector buffer and thus require time proportional to the number of elements in the vector. This is usually, however, a rare occurrence.

19.4.5 *Using a* Vector *as a List*

Characteristic operations of a *list* data abstraction give the abilities to insert or remove elements at any location and the ability to find the location of any value.[2]

aVec.firstElement( )	First element
aVec.lastElement( )	Last element
aVec.insertElementAt(value, 0)	Insert to front of list
aVec.addElement(value)	Insert to end of list
aVec.contains(value)	See if value is in collection
aVec.removeElementAt(0)	Remove first element
aVec.removeElementAt(aVec.size( ) - 1)	Remove last element
aVec.indexOf(value)	Find location of element
aVec.removeElementAt(index)	Remove value from middle

Again, this use of the Vector abstraction to simulate a list differs from the classical description of the *list* abstraction in the algorithmic execution time of certain operations. In particular, the insertion or removal from the front of the collection may result in the entire set of values being moved, thereby requiring time proportional to the size of the collection. This is a critical concern only when the size of the collections is large or when this is a frequent operation. A more direct implementation of a list is described in Section 19.9.

19.5 THE STACK COLLECTION

Section 19.4.2 described how a stack could be simulated using a Vector. However, the Java standard library also provides the Stack as a data value. The names of the methods used to operate on this data type are slightly different from the Vector operations described in Section 19.4.2, and the structure is slightly more robust. Stack operations can be described as follows:

Stack aStack = new Stack( )	Create a new stack
aStack.push (value)	Push a value onto the stack
aStack.peek( )	Peek at the topmost element of the stack
aStack.pop( )	Remove the topmost element of the stack
aStack.size( )	Number of elements in the collection

---

[2] The list referred to here is the traditional data abstraction known by that name. The Java library unfortunately uses the class name List to refer to a graphical component that allows the user to select a value from a series of string items.

| aStack.empty( ) | Test for empty stack |
| aStack.search(value) | Position of element in stack |

The pop operation both removes and returns the topmost element of the stack. Both the pop and the peek operations will throw an EmptyStackException if they are applied to an empty stack.

The search method returns the index of the given element starting from the top of the stack; that is, if the element is found at the top of the stack, search will return 0, if found one element down in the stack, search will return 1, and so on. Because the Stack data structure is built using inheritance from the Vector class it is also possible to access the values of the stack using their index. However, the positions returned by the search operation do not correspond to the index position. To discover the index position of a value the Vector operation indexOf can be used.

In Chapter 10 we described some of the advantages and disadvantages of creating the stack using inheritance from class Vector.

19.6   THE BitSet COLLECTION

A BitSet is abstractly a set of positive integer values. The BitSet class differs from the other collection classes in that it can only be used to hold integer values. Like an array or a Vector, each element is given an index position. However, the only operations that can be performed on each element are to set, test, or clear the value. A BitSet is a compact way to encode either a collection of positive integer values or a collection of Boolean values (for example, on/off settings).

To create a BitSet, the user can specify the number of positions the set will represent. However, like the Vector, the bit set is extensible and will be enlarged automatically if a position outside the range is accessed.

```
// create a BitSet that initially contains 75 elements
BitSet bset = new BitSet(75);
```

The following list summarizes the operations used to set or test an individual position in the bit set:

bset.set (index)	Set a bit position
bset.get (index)	Test a bit position
bset.clear (index)	Clear a bit position

The get method returns a boolean value, which is true if the given bit is set, and false otherwise. Each of these operations will throw an IndexOutOfBoundsException if the index value is smaller than zero.

A BitSet can be combined with another BitSet in a variety of ways:

bset.or(setTwo)	Form bitwise union with argument set
bset.and(setTwo)	Form bitwise intersection with argument set
bset.xor(setTwo)	Form bitwise symmetric difference with argument set

The method toString returns the string representation of the collection. This consists of a comma-separated list of the indices of the bits in the collection that have been set.

19.6.1 *Example Program: Prime Sieve*

A program that will generate a list of prime numbers using the sieve of Eratosthenes can be used to illustrate the manipulation of a bit set. The constructor for the class Sieve (Figure 19.1) takes an integer argument n, and creates a bit set of n positions. These are initially all set to 1, using the member function set. The sieve algorithm then walks through the list, using get to find the next set value. A loop then walks through the remainder of the collection, throwing out (via the clear( ) member function) values that are multiples of the earlier value. When we are finished, any value not crossed out must be prime.

The remaining two functions illustrate how a new enumeration can be created. The value index will maintain the current "position" in the list, which will change as values are enumerated. The method hasMoreElements loops until a prime value is found, or until the size of the bit set is exceeded. The first results in a true value, the latter a false one. The method nextElement simply makes an object out of the integer value. A small test method is also included in the class, to illustrate how this class could be used.

19.7 THE Dictionary INTERFACE AND THE Hashtable COLLECTION

A *dictionary* is an indexed collection, similar to an array or a Vector. However, unlike array values, the index values need not be integer. Instead, any object type can be used as an index (called a *key*), and any object value can be stored as the element selected by the key. To place a new value into the collection, the user provides both the key and value. To access an element in the collection, the user provides a key, and the associated value is returned.

In the Java library, the class Dictionary is an abstract class that defines the behavior of the *dictionary* abstraction but does not provide an implementation. This interface can be described as follows:

dict.get(key)	Retrieve value associated with given key
dict.put(key, value)	Place value into collection with given key
dict.remove(key)	Remove value from collection

```java
import java.util.*;

class Sieve implements Enumeration {
    private BitSet primes;
    private int index = 2;

    public Sieve (int n) {
        primes = new BitSet(n);
        // first set all the bits
        for (int i = 1; i < n; i++)
            primes.set(i);
        // then erase all the nonprimes
        for (int i = 2; i * i < n; i++)
            if (primes.get(i))
                for (int j = i + i; j <= n; j += i)
                    primes.clear(j);
    }

    public boolean hasMoreElements () {
        index++;
        int n = primes.size();
        while (! primes.get(index))
            if (++index > n)
                return false;
        return true;
    }

    public Object nextElement() { return new Integer(index); }

    // test program for prime sieve algorithm
    public static void main (String [ ] args) {
        Sieve p = new Sieve(100);
        while (p.hasMoreElements())
            System.out.println(p.nextElement());
    }
}
```

Figure 19.1   Prime Sieve program.

dict.isEmpty( )	See if collection is empty
dict.size( )	Return number of elements in collection
dict.elements( )	Return enumeration for collection values
dict.keys( )	Return enumeration of collection keys

The get method will return null if the given value is not found in the collection. Otherwise, the value is returned as an Object, which must then be cast into the appropriate type. The remove method returns the value of the association being deleted, again returning null if the key is not a legal index element. There are two enumeration generating methods, one to return an enumeration of keys and one to return an enumeration of values.

The class Hashtable provides an implementation of the Dictionary operations. A hash table can be envisioned as an array of collections called *buckets*. To add an element to the collection, an integer value, called the *hash value*, is first computed for the given key. The method hashCode is used for this purpose. This method is defined in class Object and is therefore common to all object values. It is overridden in various classes to provide alternative algorithms. Using this integer, one of the buckets is selected and the key/value pair inserted into the corresponding collection.

In addition to the methods matching the Dictionary specification, the hash table provides the method clear( ), which removes all values from the container, contains(value), which determines whether an element is contained in the collection, and containsKey(key), which tests to see if a given key is in the collection.

The default implementation of the hashCode method, in class Object, should be applicable in almost all situations, just as the default implementation of equals is usually adequate. If a data type that is going to be used as a hash table key overrides the equals method, it is a good idea to override hashCode as well, so that two objects that test equal to each other will also have the same hash value.

19.7.1   *Example Program: A Concordance*

A concordance is a listing of words from a printed text, each word being followed by the lines on which the word appears. A class that will create a concordance will illustrate how the Dictionary data type is used, as well as how different collection classes can be combined with each other.

In the program shown in Figure 19.2, the primary data structure is a dictionary, implemented using the Hashtable class. The keys for this dictionary will be the individual words in the input text. The value associated with each key will be a set of integer values, representing the line numbers on which the word appears. A Vector will be used to represent the set, using the techniques described in Section 19.4.4.

```
import java.util.*;
import java.io.*;

class Concordance {
    private Dictionary dict = new Hashtable( );

    public void readLines (DataInputStream input) throws IOException {
        String delims = " \t\n.,!?;:";
        for (int line = 1; true; line++ ) {
            String text = input.readLine( );
            if (text == null) return;
            text = text.toLowerCase( );
            Enumeration e = new StringTokenizer(text, delims);
            while (e.hasMoreElements( ))
                enterWord ((String) e.nextElement( ), new Integer(line));
        }
    }

    public void generateOutput (PrintStream output) {
        Enumeration e = dict.keys( );
        while (e.hasMoreElements( ) ) {
            String word = (String) e.nextElement( );
            Vector set = (Vector) dict.get(word);
            output.print (word + ": ");
            Enumeration f = set.elements( );
            while (f.hasMoreElements( ))
                output.print (f.nextElement( ) + " ");
            output.println (" ");
        }
    }

    private void enterWord (String word, Integer line) {
        Vector set = (Vector) dict.get(word);
        if (set == null) { // word not in collection
            set = new Vector( ); // make new set
            dict.put (word, set);
        }
        if (! set.contains(line)) set.addElement(line);
    }
}
```

Figure 19.2   The class Concordance.

The method readLines reads the input line by line, maintaining a counter to indicate the line number. The method readLine, provided by the class DataInputStream, returns a null value when end of input is encountered, at which time the method returns. (This method is also the potential source for the IOException, which can be thrown if an error occurs during the read operation. In our program we simply pass this exception back to the caller.) Otherwise, the text is converted to lowercase, using the method toLowerCase provided by the String class; then a StringTokenizer is created to split the text into individual words. A StringTokenizer is a form of Enumeration, and so an enumeration loop is used to enter each word into the concordance.

The private method enterWord is used to place each new word in the concordance. First, the value associated with the key (the word) is determined. Here the program handles the first of two exceptional conditions that might arise. If this is the first time the word has been seen, there will be no entry in the dictionary, and so the result of calling get will be a null value. In this case a new and empty Vector is created and is inserted into the dictionary using the word as key. Using the Vector in the fashion of a set, the method contains is invoked to determine if the line has already been placed in the collection. (This is the second exceptional condition, which will occur if the same word appears two or more times on one line.) If not, the line is then added to the list.

Finally, once all the input has been processed, the method generateOutput is used to create the printed report. This method uses a doubly nested enumeration loop. The first loop enumerates the keys of the Dictionary, generated by the keys method. The value associated with each key is a set, represented by a Vector. A second loop, using the enumerator produced by the elements method, then prints the values held by the vector.

An easy way to test the program is to use the system resources System.in and System.out as the input and output containers, as in the following:

```
static public void main (String [ ] args) {
   Concordance c = new Concordance( );
   try {
      c.readLines(new DataInputStream(System.in));
   } catch (IOException e) { return; }
   c.generateOutput (System.out);
}
```

19.7.2 *Properties*

The Java run-time system maintains a special type of hash table, termed the *properties list*. The class Properties, a subclass of Hashtable, holds a collection of string key/value pairs. These represent values that describe the current executing environment, such as the user name, operating system name, home directory, and so on. The following program can be used to see the range of properties available to a running Java program:

```java
public static void main (String [ ] args) {
   Dictionary props = System.getProperties( );
   Enumeration e = props.keys( );
   while (e.hasMoreElements( )) {
      Object key = e.nextElement( );
      Object value = props.get(key);
      System.out.println("property " + key + " value " + value);
   }
}
```

19.8 WHY ARE THERE NO ORDERED COLLECTIONS?

If one considers the "classic" data abstractions found in most data structures textbooks, a notable omission from the Java library are data structures that maintain values in sequence. Examples of such abstractions are ordered lists, ordered vectors, or binary trees. Indeed, there is not even any mechanism provided in the Java library to sort a vector of values. Rather than being caused by oversight, this omission reflects some fundamental properties of the Java language.

All of the Java collections maintain their values in variables of type Object. The class Object does not define any ordering relation. Indeed, the only elements that can be compared using the < operator are the primitive numeric types (integer, long, double, and so on). One could imagine defining in class Object a method lessThan(Object), similar to the method equals(Object). However, while there is a clear default interpretation for the equality operator (namely, object identity), it is difficult to imagine a similar meaning for the relational operator that would be applicable to all objects. Certainly it could not provide a total ordering on all objects. What, for example, would be the result of comparing the String "abc" and the integer 37? In short, ordered collections are not found in the Java library because there is no obvious general mechanism to define what it means to order two values.

One could imagine that an alternative to placing the method lessThan in class Object would be to create an Ordered interface, such as the following:

```java
interface Ordered {
   public boolean compare (Ordered arg);
}
```

One could then create a collection in which all values need to implement the Ordered interface, rather than simply being Object. However, there are two major objections to this technique. The first is that since the argument is only known to be an object that implements the Ordered interface, one must still decide how to compare objects of different types (a Triangle and an Orange, for example). The second problem is that restricting the type of objects the collection can maintain to only those values that implement the Ordered relation severely limits the utility of the classes.

Another possibility is to imagine an interface for an object that is used to create comparisons. That is, the object takes both values as arguments, and returns their ordering. Such an interface could be written as follows:

```
interface ComparisonObject {
    public boolean Compare (Object one, Object two);
}
```

To manipulate an ordered collection, one would then create an implementation of this interface for the desired elements. The following, for example, would be a comparison class for Integer objects:

```
class IntegerComparison implements ComparisonObject {
    public boolean Compare (Object one, Object two) {
        if ((one instanceof Integer) && (two instanceof Integer)) {
            Integer ione = (Integer) one;
            Integer itwo = (Integer) two;
            return ione.intValue( ) < itwo.intValue( );
        }
        return false;
    }
}
```

The following program illustrates how such an object could be used. The static method sort is an implementation of the insertion sort algorithm. The main method creates a vector of integer values, then creates a comparison object to be passed as argument to the sort algorithm. The sorting algorithm orders the elements in place, using the comparison object to determine the relative placement of values.

```
class VectorSort {
    public static void sort (Vector v, ComparisonObject test) {
        // order a vector using insertion sort
        int n = v.size( );
        for (int top = 1; top < n; top++) {
            for (int j = top-1; j >= 0 &&
                test.Compare(v.elementAt(j+1), v.elementAt(j)); j--) {
                // swap the elements
                Object temp = v.elementAt(j+1);
                v.setElementAt(v.elementAt(j), j+1);
                v.setElementAt(temp, j);
```

```
        }
      }

    }

    public static void main (String [ ] args) {
       Vector v = new Vector( );
       Random r = new Random( );
       for (int i = 0; i < 10; i++)
          v.addElement(new Integer(r.nextInt( )));

          // sort the vector
       sort (v, new IntegerComparison( ));

       for (Enumeration e = v.elements( ); e.hasMoreElements( ); )
          System.out.println(e.nextElement( ));
    }
  }
```

19.9 BUILDING YOUR OWN CONTAINERS

Even though the containers in the Java library are flexible, they cannot handle all situations in which a collection class is needed. It is therefore sometimes necessary to create new collection classes. To see how this can be done we will create a class that implements the idea of a linked list. The major advantage of the linked list over a vector is that insertions or removals to the beginning or the middle of a linked list can be performed very rapidly (technically, in constant time). In the vector these operations require the movement of all the elements in the collection and can therefore be much more costly if the collection is large.

The LinkedList class abstraction is shown in Figure 19.3.[3] The actual values are stored in instances of class Link, which is a nested inner class. In addition to a value, links maintain references to the previous and next element in the list. A private internal value firstLink will reference the first link. A link with an empty value is used to mark the end of the list. The private internal value lastLink points to this value.

Values can be inserted either to the front or the back of the list. An enumeration value can also be used to insert new elements into the middle of a list. The value is inserted immediately before the element referred to by the enumeration. All three methods make use of a common insertion routine provided by the inner class Link.

---

[3] It would have been preferable to call this class List. However, as we noted in an earlier footnote, the Java library already has a List class, which implements a graphical component used for selecting one string item out of many alternatives.

```
class LinkedList {
   private Link firstLink;
   private Link lastLink;
   private int  count = 0;

   public LinkedList ()
      { firstLink = lastLink = new Link(null, null, null); }

   private class Link { ... }

   private class ListEnumeration implements Enumeration { ... }

   public boolean isEmpty () { return firstLink == lastLink; }

   public int size () { return count; }

   public Object firstElement () { return firstLink.value; }

   public Object lastElement () { return lastLink.prev.value; }

   public void addFront (Object newValue) { firstLink.insert(newValue); }

   public void addBack (Object newValue) { lastLink.insert(newValue); }

   public void addElement (Enumeration e, Object newValue) {
      ListEnumeration le = (ListEnumeration) e;
      le.link.insert (newValue);
   }

   public Object removeFront () { return firstLink.remove(); }

   public Object removeBack () { return lastLink.prev.remove(); }

   public Object removeElement (Enumeration e) {
      ListEnumeration le = (ListEnumeration) e;
      return le.link.remove ();
   }

   public Enumeration elements () { return new ListEnumeration(); }
}
```

Figure 19.3   The LinkedList class.

```java
class LinkedList {
  private class Link {
      public Object value;
      public Link next;
      public Link prev;

      public Link (Object v, Link n, Link p)
         { value = v; next = n; prev = p; }

      public void insert (Object newValue) {
         Link newNode = new Link (newValue, this, prev);
         count++;
         if (prev == null) firstLink = newNode;
         else prev.next = newNode;
         prev = newNode;
      }

      public Object remove () {
         if (next == null)
            return null; // cannot remove last element
         count--;
         next.prev = prev;
         if (prev == null) firstLink = next;
         else prev.next = next;
         return value;
      }
  }

  private class ListEnumeration implements Enumeration {
      public Link link = null;

      public boolean hasMoreElements () {
         if (link == null) link = firstLink;
         else link = link.next;
         return link.next != null;
      }

      public Object nextElement () { return link.value; }
  }
  .
  .
  .
}
```

Figure 19.4   The inner classes in LinkedList.

This method is also used to maintain the count of the number of elements in the list. The classes Link and ListEnumeration are shown in Figure 19.4.

The class ListEnumeration implements the Enumeration protocol and is used for iterating over list elements. Note that the Enumeration protocol assumes that the methods hasMoreElements and nextElement will work in tandem and does not specify which of the two will actually advance the internal reference to the next element. Implementations of the Enumeration protocol use a variety of different schemes. This is why, for example, one should never invoke nextElement twice without an intervening call on hasMoreElements. In the LinkedList class, however, we assume that having examined the current value (the value yielded by nextElement), the programmer may wish to either insert a new value or remove the current value. Thus, in this case the task of advancing to the next value is given to the method hasMoreElements.

19.10 CHAPTER SUMMARY

In this chapter we have described the classes in the Java library that are used to hold collections of values. The simplest collection is the array. An array is a linear, indexed homogenous collection. A difficulty with the array is that the size of an array is fixed at the time the array is created. The Vector class overcomes this restriction, growing as necessary as new values are added to the collection. Vectors can be used to represent sets, queues, and lists of values. The Stack datatype is a specialization of the vector used when values are added and removed from the collection in a strict first-in, first-out fashion. A BitSet is a set of positive integer values. A Dictionary is an interface that describes a collection of key and value pairs. The HashTable is one possible implementation of the Dictionary interface.

The lack of any ordered collections is a reflection of the problem that there is, in general, no way to construct an ordering among all Java values.

The chapter concludes by showing how new collection classes can be created, using as an example a linked list container.

STUDY QUESTIONS

1. What are collection classes used for?

2. Because the standard library collection classes maintain their values as an Object, what must be done to a value when it is removed from a collection?

3. What is a wrapper class?

4. What is an enumerator?

5. What is the protocol for the class Enumerator? How are these methods combined to form a loop?

6. How is the Java array different from arrays in other languages?

7. What does it mean to say that the Vector data type is expandable?

8. How does the use of the Stack data type differ from the use of a Vector as a stack?

9. What concept does the class BitSet represent?

10. What is the relationship between the classes Dictionary and Hashtable?

11. Why are there no ordered collections in the Java library?

EXERCISES

1. Assume two sets are implemented using vectors, as described in Section 19.4.4. Write a loop that will place the intersection of the two sets into a third set.

2. Assume two sets are implemented using vectors, as described in Section 19.4.4. Write a loop that will place the symmetric difference of the two sets into a third set. (The symmetric difference is the set of elements that are in one or the other set, but not both.)

3. Add the following methods to the LinkedList class described in Section 19.9:

setElement(Enumeration e, Object v)	Change value at given location
includes(Object v)	Test whether value is in collection
find(Object v)	Return enumeration if value is in collection, or null

4. Modify the LinkedList class of Section 19.9 so that linked lists support the cloneable interface. (The cloneable interface is described in Section 11.3.1.)

5. Write an OrderedList class. This class will be like a linked list, but will maintain a comparison object, as described in Section 19.8. Using this object, elements will be placed in sequence as they are inserted into the container.

20 Multiple Threads of Execution

Most users of a computer are familiar with the idea of *multitasking*—for example, editing a spreadsheet at the same time that the computer is printing a report or receiving a fax. The computer appears to be doing more than one activity at the same time. Whether this is actually true depends upon the hardware involved. Unless you are using a machine with multiple processors, what is in fact occurring is that the operating system is rapidly cycling between the different activities, allowing each to execute for a small amount of time.

Multithreading is the same concept applied to an individual program. Each program has the ability to execute a number of tasks at the same time. Each of these computational tasks is called a *thread*. Unlike separate computer applications, multiple threads exist in the same executing environment (technically speaking, we say they have the same *context*). This means they share the same data variables, access the same methods, and so on. As with multitasking, this parallel behavior is usually just a charade; in fact the operating system is still executing only one thread at any one time and is cycling among all the different threads to give each an equal share.

20.1 CREATING THREADS

Recall the BallWorld application from Chapter 5 (Figure 5.2). This program created a bouncing ball, then moved the ball around on the window 2000 times before halting. You may recall that this is *all* the program did. It did not allow any sort of user interaction, and if you tried to stop the program before 2000 steps you could not.

In practice it is desirable to have programs that are more user friendly. Part of this is being able to interact with an application while it is running. One way to do this is to place the execution of the program in a separate thread, leaving the main program thread free to listen for user activity.

In Java, threads are created using the class Thread. There are two common ways that this class is used. One way is to subclass from Thread, and override the method run, which is the method that is executed to perform the task assigned to a thread. We could, for example, modify the BallWorld application (Figure 5.2) and create a bouncing ball thread as follows:

```java
public class ThreadedBallWorld extends JFrame {
    .
    .
    .
    private class BallThread extends Thread {
        public void run () {
            while (true) {
                aBall.move();
                if ((aBall.x() < 0) || (aBall.x() > FrameWidth))
                    aBall.setMotion (-aBall.xMotion(), aBall.yMotion());
                if ((aBall.y() < 0) || (aBall.y() > FrameHeight))
                    aBall.setMotion (aBall.xMotion(), -aBall.yMotion());
                repaint();
                try {
                    sleep(50);
                } catch (InterruptedException e) { }
            }
        }
    }
    .
    .
    .
}
```

When started, the thread continually moves the ball, changing the direction of motion when the sides of the window are hit. Each time the ball moves the window is repainted, and the thread "sleeps" for 50 milliseconds.

The revised ball world application is shown in Figure 20.1. In the constructor for the application ThreadedBallWorld a Ball is created, and then a BallThread is produced to control the movement of the ball. Execution of the new thread is initiated by the call to start for the thread object. To illustrate that the user can now interact with the application as the ball moves, we have added a mouse listener object. When the mouse is clicked in the application window, the ball is moved to the mouse location. Notice how the paint method in Figure 20.1 needs only to call the paint method in Ball, since all the ball-moving code it carried in Figure 5.2 has been moved into the run method of BallThread.

Ignore

Platforms differ on how they assign time to threads. On some systems threads are run until they sleep or until they yield to another thread. On other systems threads are given a fixed amount of time to execute, then halted automatically if they have not yet given up control when their time unit is finished. In order

```
public class ThreadedBallWorld extends JFrame {

    public static void main (String [ ] args) {
        ThreadedBallWorld world = new ThreadedBallWorld (Color.red);
        world.show ();
    }

    private static final int FrameWidth = 600;
    private static final int FrameHeight = 400;
    private Ball aBall;
    private int counter = 0;

    private ThreadedBallWorld (Color ballColor) {
        // constructor for new ball world
            // resize our frame
        setSize (FrameWidth, FrameHeight);
        setTitle ("Ball World");
        addMouseListener (new BallListener());

            // initialize object data field
        aBall = new Ball (10, 15, 5);
        aBall.setColor (ballColor);
        aBall.setMotion (3.0, 6.0);
        Thread ballThread = new BallThread();
        ballThread.start();
    }

    private class BallThread extends Thread { ... }

    private class BallListener extends MouseAdapter {
        public void mousePressed (MouseEvent e)
            { aBall.moveTo(e.getX(), e.getY()); }
    }

    public void paint (Graphics g) { super.paint(g); aBall.paint (g); }
}
```

Figure 20.1   BallWorld application using threads.

to provide maximum portability, threads should either sleep occasionally (as is done here) or periodically invoke the method yield that is inherited from class Thread. Either of these actions will halt the current thread, allowing other threads a chance to perform their actions.

It is sometimes not convenient to create a thread class by subclassing from Thread. For example, it can happen that the thread class is already inheriting from some other class. Since in Java a class cannot extend from two classes, the designers of the language have provided an alternative technique. Instead of inheriting from Thread, the action portion of a thread can be declared as implementing the interface Runnable. The ball thread could be rewritten in this form as follows:

```java
public class ThreadedBallWorld extends JFrame {
   .
   .
   .
   private class BallThread implements Runnable {
      public void run () {
         while (true) {
            aBall.move( );
            if ((aBall.x( ) < 0) || (aBall.x( ) > FrameWidth))
               aBall.setMotion (-aBall.xMotion( ), aBall.yMotion( ));
            if ((aBall.y( ) < 0) || (aBall.y( ) > FrameHeight))
               aBall.setMotion (aBall.xMotion( ), -aBall.yMotion( ));
            repaint( );
            try {
               Thread.sleep(50);
            } catch (InterruptedException e) { }
         }
      }
   }
   .
   .
   .
}
```

Note the format used for the call on sleep. Because the new class is not tied to Thread, the method sleep is not automatically inherited. Instead, the class name Thread must be explicitly provided in this case.

When a new thread class is defined by extending Thread, it inherits a start method from Thread and overrides the run method defined in the parent class. A thread belonging to such a class is started by applying start to it, which in turn will call run. However, when a new thread class, like BallThread, is defined by implementing Runnable, it has a run method but no start method. Consequently a different mechanism is required to start and run such a thread. This involves creating two objects. The first is the instance of Runnable (in this case a BallThread object). The second is an object of type Thread created using a constructor that takes the runnable object as argument:

```java
Thread ballThread = new Thread(new BallThread( ));
ballThread.start( );
```

The Thread object provides the start method that is necessary to schedule for execution the actions of the runnable object.

20.1.1 *Synchronizing Threads*

Two or more threads frequently need to share the same data fields. If two threads attempt to modify the same data area, it is possible for erroneous values to be produced. Assume we have two threads that share an integer data field, and assume that they each try to increment the value by 10. Internally an addition statement is divided into several separate steps. For example, the statement

```
a = a + 10
```

is executed as something similar to the following:

```
push the value of a on a stack
push the value 10 on the stack
add the two values on the stack
pop the top of stack, assign value to a
```

Assume that this same sequence of instructions is performed by two threads, and the original value of a is 50. Assume further that the thread that is running the first process is stopped immediately after the first push instruction above. The first thread will push the value 50 on its stack, then stop temporarily. The second thread will push the value 50 on its stack, increment by 10, then store the resulting value of 60 on its stack. Suppose now the first thread is restarted. It will continue with its actions, pushing 10 on the stack, adding the two values, and assigning the sum, 60, back to a. The end result will be that the value a will ultimately hold 60, not the value 70 that it should have held.

Although it might seem that a problem such as this might be rare, the speed with which computers execute means that a situation such as that described here, if possible at all, is not at all uncommon. Such errors are also exceedingly difficult to uncover, since they occur in such a rare situation. Fortunately, the designers of Java have foreseen this and provided a simple and elegant solution. A method that is declared as synchronized cannot be executed by more than one process at any time. In fact, if an object has more than one method declared as synchronized, then an attempt to execute any synchronized method will be delayed until the first synchronized method has been completed. If one thread is executing a synchronized method and a second thread tries to execute any other synchronized method with the same object, the second thread will be halted until the first thread completes. The solution to the problem just described is therefore to place the increment operation inside a method that is declared as synchronized:

```
public synchronized void increment ( ) {
      // only one thread can execute this
      // at any time
   a = a + 10;
   }
```

We will illustrate the use of a synchronized method in the case study presented in Section 20.2. There are many more advanced features of threads; however, they are generally not needed in most programs and will not be described here.

20.2 CASE STUDY: A TETRIS GAME

A video game is a good illustration of the need for multiple threads of control. In a typical game, the user is constantly entering information, and the game itself is constantly moving. In a conventional single-thread programming language, one or the other of these tasks must be selected as the primary structure. Either the main program is a large loop that listens for the user's commands and every now and then moves the game forward, or it is a large loop that moves the elements of the game and every now and then listens for the user's instructions. Either form will end up being clumsy and difficult to debug.

A much more elegant solution is possible in the language Java. Each of these two tasks can be assigned its own process. Each thread is executed in parallel with other threads. One thread is simply listening for the user's commands, while the other thread is charged with moving the pieces (see Figure 20.2).

Of course, there must be some sort of communication between the two threads, and this is where most of the complexity in multithreaded programming occurs. In the Tetris game presented here, the communication consists only of one integer value, which maintains the next command to be performed.

In addition to demonstrating multiple threads of control, the Tetris game presented in this section will illustrate how to read keyboard events, and an important technique for preventing flickering in graphical displays.

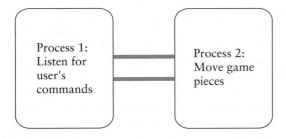

Figure 20.2   A double-thread program.

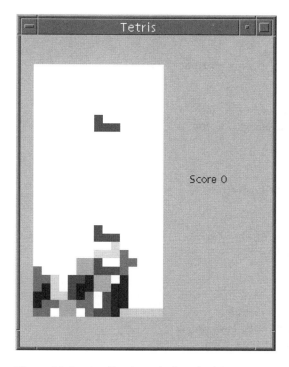

Figure 20.3 Application window for Tetris game.

20.2.1 *The Tetris Game Class*

Tetris is a popular video game. Playing pieces of several different forms fall from the sky and can merge together when they reach the ground. The player can move a piece left or right or rotate a piece as it falls to the ground. The player scores by arranging pieces as they fall so as to form a completely filled row in the ground. Figure 20.3 shows an example of a game in execution.

The primary class for the Tetris game is shown in Figure 20.4. As with all applications, execution begins with a static method named main. The main method creates an instance of the class Tetris, which is a type of JFrame, and places this window on the display using the method show.

The constructor for the Tetris class sizes the application window, gives it a name, adds a listener for key presses, then creates and starts the second process. The game playing process will be an instance of a second class, named PieceMover. We will examine the structure of this class shortly. Once created, the thread of execution that will play the game is initiated by the issuing of the command start.

```
public class Tetris extends JFrame {

    public static void main(String [ ] args)
        { Tetris world = new Tetris( ); world.show( ); }

        // data fields
    public static final int FrameWidth = 300;
    public static final int FrameHeight = 400;
    private PieceMover player;

    public Tetris ( ) {
        setSize (FrameWidth, FrameHeight);
        setTitle("Tetris");

        addKeyListener (new keyDown( ));
        player = new PieceMover(this);
        player.start( );
    }

        // interface point between two threads
        // data shared by event handler and piece mover
    private int currentCommand = Piece.Down;

        // synchronized method for accessing shared data
    public synchronized int getCommand (int nextCommand) {
        int oldCommand = currentCommand;
        currentCommand = nextCommand;
        return oldCommand;
    }

    private class keyDown extends KeyAdapter { ... }

    public void update (Graphics g)
        { player.paint(sg); }
}
```

Figure 20.4   The Controller class for the Tetris game.

Communication Between Threads

Communication between the two threads of control is accomplished via a single integer variable (currentCommand). This value represents the next command to be executed. This variable is both set and accessed by means of the method getcommand. Note that this method is declared as synchronized. This means that only one of the two threads can be executing the method at any one time. If the other process attempts to execute the method, it will be held up until the first process completes. (In truth, the synchronization here is largely unnecessary, since the only penalty for simultaneous access will be that one process may receive an out-of-date value. Nevertheless, the use of the synchronized designation also helps to document the connection between the two threads.)

Handling Keyboard Events

Keyboard events are handled in a fashion similar to the mouse click events we have examined previously. A component maintains a collection of key listeners, which must each implement the KeyListener interface:

```
interface KeyListener extends EventListener {
    public void keyTyped (KeyEvent e);
    public void keyPressed (KeyEvent e);
    public void keyReleased (KeyEvent e);
}
```

As with mouse presses, the programmer can elect to either treat a key press and the key release as independent events, or simply examine one event for both actions. Implementing the KeyListener interface requires defining a body for all three methods. As normally one is interested in only one of these, an adapter class, named KeyAdapter, is provided that implements a null method for each of the three methods. To create a listener, one can inherit from this adapter and redefine the meaning of one of the methods. This is how key presses are handled in our application:

```
public class Tetris extends JFrame {
      .
      .
      .
    private class keyDown extends KeyAdapter {
        public void keyPressed (KeyEvent e) {
            char key = e.getKeyChar( );
            switch (key) {
                case 'g': player.newGame( ); break;
                case 'j': getCommand(Piece.Left); break;
                case 'k': getCommand(Piece.Rotate); break;
                case 'l': getCommand(Piece.Right); break;
                case 'q': System.exit(0);
            }
        }
    }
      .
      .
      .
}
```

Avoiding Flicker

As the game is being played, the screen is constantly being updated. This update process consists largely of drawing each individual square of the display. If this is done as separate graphical commands, the result can be an annoying flicker. There are several common ways to avoid this. Perhaps one of the easiest is the technique shown here. The method update() inherited from class Component normally first redraws the entire screen in the background color, then invokes paint to refresh the screen. If one overrides update rather than overriding paint, then the redrawing in the background color is avoided.

One often confusing feature to note is that although the update method invokes the paint method in the class of the player object (namely, the class PieceMover), the resulting actions are not performed by the piece mover thread. Updating the image is performed by the first thread, and it is independent of the piece mover thread, which continues to run on its own.

20.2.2   *The* PieceMover *Thread*

The class PieceMover is shown in Figure 20.5. The fact that the class extends class Thread and the presence of the method named run indicate that this class can potentially be executed as an independent thread.

The constructor for the class will be executed when the instance of PieceMover is created, as in Figure 20.4. The constructor sets the values of local variables, including creating an array of colors for the playing area. The playing area will be 15 elements wide by 30 elements deep. Because we think of the playing area as a graphical object, it will be easier to describe this by placing the horizontal movement first and the vertical movement second.

The thread starting point is a method named run. This method will be executed when the thread is started. Note that the method the programmer writes is called run, while the method used to initiate the thread is called start (the call on start in this case appears in Figure 20.4). The start method performs some other actions, such as setting up a schedule for thread execution, before invoking run. In our simple example, the run method will simply repeatedly create and drop playing pieces.

As the playing pieces move, they will indicate the change by altering the colors stored in the color table. Thus, the paint method simply cycles through the table, displaying each color in a small rectangle.

```
public void paint (Graphics g) {
    for (int i = 0; i < 30; i++)
        for (int j = 0; j < 15; j++) {
            g.setColor(table[j][i]);
            g.fillRect(20+10*j, 350-10*i, 10, 10);
        }
```

```
class PieceMover extends Thread {

   private Tetris controller;
   private Color table[ ][ ];
   private Piece currentPiece;
   private int score = 0;

   public PieceMover (Tetris t) {
      controller = t;
      table = new Color[15][30];
      currentPiece = null;
      newGame();
   }

      // thread starting point
   public void run ()
      { while (dropPiece()) { } }

      // other methods
   public void newGame () {
      for (int i = 0; i < 30; i++)
         for (int j = 0; j < 15; j++)
            table[j][i] = Color.white;
   }

   public void paint (Graphics g) { ... }

   public boolean dropPiece () { ... }

   private void moveDown (int start) { ... }

   private void checkScore() { ... }
}
```

Figure 20.5 The PieceMover class.

```
      g.setColor (Color.blue);
      g.drawString("Score " + score, 200, 200);
   }
```

The heart of the piece movement thread is the method dropPiece. This method creates a new piece, selecting the type of piece randomly from among the seven possibilities. If the piece cannot be moved downward once initially created at the top of the scene, the game is over, and the method returns false. Otherwise, a loop then reads the commands placed in the buffer shared with the controller, and acts on them, passing the command value to the individual piece for action. After every move the controller is asked to repaint, and control of the processor is yielded, allowing the other process time to execute. When control is returned, the piece movement process still sleeps for 100 milliseconds before reading the next command and moving once more.

```java
private boolean dropPiece () {
   int piecetype = 1 + (int) (7 * Math.random ());
   currentPiece = new Piece (piecetype);
   if (! currentPiece.move (Piece.Down, table))
      return false;
   int command = controller.getCommand (Piece.Down);
   while (currentPiece.move (command, table)) {
      controller.repaint ();
      yield ();
      try {
         sleep (100);
      } catch (InterruptedException e) { }
      command = controller.getCommand (Piece.Down);
   }
   // piece cannot move, check score
   checkScore();
   return true;
}
```

The while loop terminates when the piece can no longer move. At this point the method checkScore is called to determine if any points have been scored. Points are scored by completely filling a row. If such a row is found, the controller is notified that a score has been made, and the entire image is moved downward.

```java
private void checkScore()
{
   for (int i = 0; i < 30; i++) {
      boolean scored = true;
      for (int j = 0; j < 15; j++)
         if (table[j][i] == Color.white)
            scored = false;
      if (scored) {
         score += 10;
         moveDown(i);
         i = i - 1; // check row again
      }
   }
}
```

```
private void moveDown (int start) {
   for (int i = start; i < 30; i++)
      for (int j = 0; j < 15; j++)
         if (i < 29)
            table[j][i] = table[j][i+1];
         else
            table[j][i] = Color.white;
}
```

The method moveDown copies the colors from the row above into the current row, copying white values into the topmost row.

20.2.3 *The Game Piece Class*

An individual game piece is composed of a number of blocks. Each block is identified only by an x and y coordinate, maintained in a pair of parallel arrays. A piece also has its own color. The constructor for the class Piece (Figure 20.6) takes an integer that represents the piece type and initializes the locations appropriately. Only the initialization of the "S" shaped piece is shown; the others are all similar.

Other than the constructor, the only publicly accessible method for the game piece is the method named move. This method tries to move the piece according to the command given. The method returns false if the command is a move down and the piece cannot move, which indicates that no further actions are possible.

```
class Piece {
   .
   .
   .
   public boolean move (int command, Color [ ][ ] table)
   {
      erase(table);
      boolean canDoIt = false;
      switch (command) {
         case Down: canDoIt = testDown(table); break;
         case Right: canDoIt = testMoveRight(table); break;
         case Left: canDoIt = testMoveLeft(table); break;
         case Rotate: canDoIt = testRotate(table); break;
      }
      if (canDoIt)
         switch (command) {
            case Down: moveDown( ); break;
            case Right: moveRight( ); break;
            case Left: moveLeft( ); break;
            case Rotate: moveRotate( ); break;
         }
```

```
class Piece {
      // data fields
   private int x[ ];
   private int y[ ];
   private Color color;
      // moves
   public static final int Down = 1;
   public static final int Left = 2;
   public static final int Rotate = 3;
   public static final int Right = 4;

      // constructor
   public Piece (int type)
   {
      switch(type) {
         case 1: // s shaped piece
            x = new int[4];
            y = new int[4];
            x[0] = 7; y[0] = 29;
            x[1] = 7; y[1] = 28;
            x[2] = 8; y[2] = 28;
            x[3] = 8; y[3] = 27;
            color = Color.green;
            break;
            .
            .
            .
      }
   }
   .
   .
   .
}
```

Figure 20.6   The class Piece.

```
      draw(table);
      if (command == Down)
         return canDoIt;
      return true;
   }
}
```

Erasing and redrawing the piece are performed by transferring colors to the color table:

```
class Piece {
    .
    .
    .
    private void erase (Color [ ][ ] table) {
        for (int i = 0; i < x.length; i++)
            table[x[i]][y[i]] = Color.white;
    }

    private void draw (Color [ ][ ] table) {
        for (int i = 0; i < x.length; i++)
            table[x[i]][y[i]] = color;
    }
}
```

Before any command is performed, a test is conducted to see if the spaces the blocks will occupy subsequent to the command are open. The following demonstrates one of these routines; the others are similar. If the target locations are open, the corresponding move routine performs the actual transformation.

```
class Piece {
    .
    .
    .
    private boolean testPosition (int x, int y, Color[ ][ ] table)
    {
        if ((x < 0) || (x > 14))
            return false;
        if ((y < 0) || (y > 29))
            return false;
        if (table[x][y] != Color.white)
            return false;
        return true;
    }

    private boolean testDown (Color [ ][ ] table) {
        for (int i = 0; i < x.length; i++)
            if (! testPosition(x[i], y[i]-1, table))
                return false;
        return true;
    }

    private void moveDown () {
        for (int i = 0; i < x.length; i++)
            y[i] = y[i] - 1;
    }
}
```

The only tricky method is the rotation. One square, the square at position 1, is designated the square around which rotation will be performed. The differences in coordinates from this square are computed, and the updated coordinates determined.

```
class Piece {
    .
    .
    .
    private boolean testRotate (Color [ ][ ] table) {
        for (int i = 0; i < x.length; i++) {
            int dx = x[i] - x[1];
            int dy = y[i] - y[1];
            int nx = x[1] + dy;
            int ny = y[1] - dx;
            if (! testPosition(nx, ny, table))
                return false;
        }
        return true;
    }
}
```

20.3 CHAPTER SUMMARY

Java programs can have several independent sequences of execution, or threads. Each is represented by a different instance of class Thread. Threads share a common execution environment and can communicate with each other through the use of shared data values. Problems involving simultaneous access to these data values can be avoided by declaring methods to be synchronized. Only one thread is permitted to be executing a synchronized method at any one time.

In this chapter we have illustrated the use of threads by describing the implementation of a video game, similar to the game of Tetris.

CROSS REFERENCES

The BallWorld case study appears originally in Chapter 5. Placing balls in their own thread of control is also shown in the pinball game application described in Chapter 7.

STUDY QUESTIONS

1. What is the difference between multitasking and multithreading?

2. Describe the two ways to create a new thread.

3. What are the two ways described in this chapter to temporarily halt the execution of a thread?

4. When used in a method heading, what does the keyword synchronized mean?

EXERCISES

1. Add a keyboard listener to the BallWorld application shown in Figure 20.1. When the user types the keys u or d, change the ball direction to move upward or downward, respectively. When the user types q quit the application.

2. Change the mouse down method so that when the user presses the mouse a new ball is created and set in motion. To do this you will need to create a collection of ball objects (see Chapter 5). Each new object should execute in its own separate thread.

3. The Tetris game can be made to "speed up" by reducing the amount of time the piece mover sleeps between commands. Change the code so that this time is reduced by 5 milliseconds for every 100 points the user scores.

4. Change the program so that instead of scoring 10 points for each filled row, the player gets additional points for multiple rows scored with the same piece. For example, a second row will get 20 points, a third row 30 points, and a fourth row 40 points.

5. Change the program to score 50 extra points if an entirely filled row is all one color.

21 Applets and Web Programming

As noted in Chapter 2, although Java is a general purpose programming language that can be used to create almost any type of computer program, much of the excitement surrounding Java has been generated by its employment as a language for creating programs intended for execution across the World Wide Web. Programs written for this purpose must follow certain conventions, and they differ slightly from programs designed to be executed directly on a computer, such as the ones we have developed up to now. In this chapter we will examine these differences and see how to create programs for the Web.

21.1 APPLETS AND HTML

Applications written for the World Wide Web are commonly referred to as *applets*. Applets are attached to documents distributed over the World Wide Web. These documents are written using the HyperText Markup Language (HTML) protocol. A Web browser that includes a Java processor will then automatically retrieve and execute the Java program. Two HTML tags are used to describe the applet as part of an HTML document. These are the <applet> tag and the <param> tag. A typical sequence of instructions would be the following:

```
<applet codebase="http://www.sun.com" code=Main width=300
      height=200>
<param name=name1 value="value1">
You do not have a Java enabled browser
</applet>
```

The <applet> tag indicates the address of the Java program. The codebase parameter gives the URL Web address where the Java program will be found,

357

while the code parameter provides the name of the class. The height and width attributes tell the browser how much space to allocate to the applet.

Just as users can pass information into an application using command-line arguments, applets can have information passed into them using the <param> tags. Within an applet, the values associated with parameters can be accessed using the method getParameter( ).

Any code other than a <param> tag between the beginning and end of the <applet> tag is displayed only if the program cannot be loaded. Such text can be used to provide the user with alternate information.

21.2 SECURITY ISSUES

Applets are designed to be loaded from a remote computer (the server) and then executed locally. Because most users will execute the applet without examining the code, the potential exists for malicious programmers to develop applets that would do significant damage, for example erasing a hard drive. For this reason, applets are much more restricted than applications in the type of operations they can perform.

1. Applets are not permitted to run any local executable program.

2. Applets cannot read or write to the local computer's file system.

3. Applets can only communicate with the server from which they originate. They are not allowed to communicate with any other host machine.

4. Applets can learn only a very restricted set of facts about the local computer. For example, applets can determine the name and version of the operating system, but not the user's name or e-mail address.

In addition, dialog windows that an applet creates are normally labeled with a special text, so the user knows they were created by a Java applet and are not part of the browser application.

The Java security model has been extended in Java 1.2. It is now possible to attach a digital signature to applets, so that they can be run in a less restricted environment. Discussion of this is beyond the scope of this book.

21.3 APPLETS AND APPLICATIONS

All the applications created prior to this chapter that made use of graphical resources have been formed as subclasses of class JFrame. This class provided the necessary underpinnings for creating and managing windows, graphical operations, events, and the other aspects of a standalone application.

A program that is intended to run on the Web has a slightly different structure. Rather than subclassing from JFrame, such a program is subclassed from Applet.

Just as JFrame provides the structure necessary to run a program as an application, the class Applet provides the necessary structure and resources needed to run a program on the Web. The Swing class JApplet is a sublass of its AWT equivalent, Applet. Applet, in turn, is a subclass of Panel (see section 13.4) and thus JApplet inherits the applet functionality of Applet and the graphical component attributes of Panel.

Rather than starting execution with a static method named main, as applications do, applets start execution at a method named init, which is defined in class Applet but can be overridden by users. The method init is one of four routines defined in Applet that is available for overriding by users. These four can be described as follows:

init( ) Invoked when an applet is first loaded; for example, when a Web page containing the applet is first encountered. This method should be used for one-time initialization. This is similar to the code that would normally be found in the constructor for an application.

start( ) Called to begin execution of the applet. Called again each time the Web page containing the applet is exposed. This can be used for further initialization or for restarting the applet when the page on which it appears is made visible after being covered.

stop( ) Called when a Web page containing an applet is hidden. Applets that do extensive calculations should halt themselves when the page on which they are located becomes covered, so as to not occupy system resources.

destroy( ) Called when the applet is about to be terminated. Should halt the application and free any resources being used.

For example, suppose a Web page containing an applet as well as several other links is loaded. The applet will first invoke init( ), then start( ). If the user clicks on one of the links, the Web page holding the applet is overwritten, but it is still available for the user to return to. The method stop( ) will be invoked to temporarily halt the applet. When the user returns to the Web page, the method start( ), but not init( ), will once again be executed. This can happen many times before the user finally exits altogether the page containing the applet, at which time the method destroy( ) will be called.

Figure 21.1 shows portions of the painting application described in Section 18.6, now written as an applet rather than as an application. In place of the main method, the applet contains an init method. The init takes the place both of main and of the constructor for the application class. Other aspects of the applet are the same. Because an applet is a subclass of Panel, events are handled in exactly the same fashion as other graphical components. Similarly, an applet repaints the window in exactly the same fashion as an application. Because an applet is a panel, it is possible to embed components and construct a complex

```
import java.applet.*;
import java.awt.*;
import java.awt.event.*;
import javax.swing.*;

public class PaintApplet extends JApplet {

    private Image image = null;
    private Shape currentShape = null;

    public void init () {
        // change our layout manager
        getContentPane().setLayout(new BorderLayout());
        // create panel for buttons
        Panel p = new Panel();
        p.setLayout(new GridLayout(1,3));
        p.add(new Rectangle());
        p.add(new Oval());
        p.add(new Line());
        getContentPane().add("North", p);
        MouseKeeper k = new MouseKeeper();
        addMouseListener(k);
        addMouseMotionListener(k);
    }
        .
        .
        .
}
```

Figure 21.1   Painting program written as an applet.

graphical interface (see Chapter 13). Note, however, that the default layout manager for an Applet is a flow layout rather than the border layout that is default to applications.

21.4   OBTAINING RESOURCES USING AN APPLET

The class Applet provides a number of methods that can be used to load resources from the server machine. The method getImage(URL), for example, takes a URL and retrieves the image stored in the given location. The URL must specify a file in jpeg or gif format. The method getAudioClip(URL) similarly returns an audio object from the given location. The audioClip can subsequently be asked to play itself. A shorthand method play(URL) combines these two features.

The method getCodeBase( ) returns the URL for the codebase specified for the applet (see the earlier discussion on HTML tags). Since Java programs are often stored in the same location as associated documents, such as gif files, this can be useful in forming URL addresses for related resources.

The method getParameter( ) takes as argument a String, and returns the associated value (again, as a string) if the user provided a parameter of the given name using a <param> tag. A null value is returned if no such parameter was provided.

21.4.1 *Universal Resource Locators*

Resources, such as Java programs, gif files, or data files are specified using a universal resource locator, or URL. A URL consists of several parts, including a protocol, a host computer name, and a file name. The following example shows these parts:

> ftp://ftp.cs.orst.edu/pub/budd/java/errata.html

This is the URL that points to the errata list for this book. The first part, ftp:, describes the protocol to be used in accessing the file. The letters stand for *File Transfer Protocol*, and is one common protocol. Another common protocol is http, which stands for *Hypertext Transfer Protocol*. The next part, ftp.cs.orst.edu, is the name of the machine on which the file resides. The remainder of the URL specifies a location for a specific file on this machine. File names are hierarchical. On this particular machine the directory pub is the area open to the public, the subdirectory budd is my own part of this public area, java holds files related to the Java book, and finally errata.html is the name of the file containing the errata information.

URLs can be created using the class URL.[1] The address is formed using a string, or using a previous URL and a string. The latter form, for example, can be used to retrieve several files that reside in the same directory. The directory is first specified as a URL, then each file is specified as a URL with the file name added to the previous URL address. The constructor for the class URL will throw an exception called MalformedURLException if the associated object cannot be accessed across the Internet.

The class URL provides a method openStream, which returns an inputStream value (see Chapter 14). Once you have created a URL object, you can use this method to read from the URL using the normal InputStream methods, or convert it into a Reader in order to more easily handle character values. In this way, reading from a URL is as easy as reading from a file or any other type of input stream. The following program reads and displays the contents of a Web page. The URL for the Web page is taken from the command-line argument.

---

[1] It is important to distinguish the idea of a URL as a concept from the Java class of the same name. We will write URL in the normal font when we want to refer to a universal resource locator, and URL when we specifically wish to refer to the Java class.

```
import java.net.*;
import java.io.*;

class ReadURL {
   public static void main (String [ ] args) {
      try {
         URL address = new URL(args[0]);
         InputStreamReader iread = new InputStreamReader(
            address.openStream( ));
         BufferedReader in = new BufferedReader(iread);

         String line = in.readLine( );
         while (line != null) {
            System.out.println(line);
            line = in.readLine( );
         }
         in.close( );
      } catch (MalformedURLException e) {
         System.out.println("URL exception " + e);
      } catch (IOException e) {
         System.out.println("I/O exception " + e);
      }
   }
}
```

If you run the program, you should see the HTML commands and textual content displayed for the Web page given as argument. Since not all files are text files, the class URL also provides methods for reading various other formats, such as graphical images or audio files.

21.4.2   *Loading a New Web Page*

Applets used with Web browsers can instruct the browser to load a new page. This feature is frequently used to simulate links or buttons on a Web page, or to implement image maps. The method appletContext.showDocument(URL) takes a URL as argument, then instructs the Web browser to display the indicated page.

21.5   COMBINING APPLICATIONS AND APPLETS

The class Applet pays no attention to any static methods that may be contained within the class definition. We can use this fact to create a class that can be executed both as an applet and as an application. The key idea is that an JApplet contains a content pane in the same way as a JFrame. We can nest within the applet class an inner class that creates the JFrame necessary for an application.

The only component of the window created for this frame will be the content pane of the applet. The main program, which is ignored by the applet, will when executed as an application create an instance of the applet. The applet can then create an instance of JFrame for the application, placing itself in the center of the window. The constructor for the JFrame executes the methods init( ) and start( ) required to initialize the applet. The following shows this technique applied to the painting applet described earlier:

```
import java.applet.*;
import java.awt.*;
import java.awt.event.*;
import javax.swing.*;

public class PaintApplet extends JApplet {

      // executed for applications
      // ignored by applet class
   public static void main (String [ ] args) {
      JFrame world = new PaintApplet( ).application( );
      world.show( );
   }

   private JFrame application( )
      { return new JAppletFrame (this); }

   private class JAppletFrame extends JFrame {
      public JAppletFrame (JApplet p) {
         setTitle("Paint Application");
         setSize (400, 300);
         p.init( ); p.start( );
         getContentPane().add("Center", p);
      }
   }

   ... // remainder as before
}
```

Trace carefully the sequence of operations being performed here and the order in which objects are created. Since the Frame is nested within the Applet, it is only possible to create the frame (in the method application) after the applet has already been created.

21.6 CHAPTER SUMMARY

An *applet* is a Java application designed to be executed as part of a Web browser. Although much of the code for an applet is similar to that of an application, the two differ in some significant respects. Applets are created by subclassing from the class Applet, rather than from the class Frame. Applets begin execution with the method init, rather than main. Finally, applets can be halted and restarted, as the Web browser moves to a new page and returns.

Security over the Web is a major concern, and for this reason applets are restricted in the actions they can perform. For example, applets are not permitted to read or write files from the client system.

The chapter concludes by showing how it is possible to create a program that can be executed both as an application and as an applet.

STUDY QUESTIONS

1. What is an applet?

2. What is html?

3. How can a web page be made to point to an applet?

4. What is the purpose of the param tag? How is information described by this tag accessed within an applet?

5. What happens if a web browser cannot load and execute an applet described by an applet tag?

6. Why are applets restricted in the variety of activities they can perform?

7. What is the difference between the init and start methods in an applet? When will each be executed?

8. What is the function of a URL? What are the different parts of a URL?

9. How can one read the contents of a file addressed by a URL?

EXERCISES

1. Convert the pinball game described in Chapter 7 to run as an applet, rather than as an application.

2. Convert the Tetris game described in Chapter 20 to run as an applet rather than as an application.

3. Section 18.6 presented a simple painting program. Convert this program to run as an applet, rather than as an application.

22 Network Programming

In Chapter 2 we noted that much of the excitement being generated around Java is due to the potential use of the language in network programming–a process that deals with the task of connecting two or more computers together so that they, and the users working on them, can communicate and share resources.

Network programming is often described using the concepts of client and server (see again Figure 2.1). A *server* is an application that runs on one computer, called the *host computer*, and provides both a means of connection and useful information once a connection is established. Often we blur the lines between the computer and the application, and use the term server to mean both the application and the host computer on which it runs. A *client* is an application that runs on a different computer, and seeks to establish a connection to the server. Oftentimes there will be many clients for a single server (Figure 22.1).

Applets, such as those we examined in Chapter 21, are one form of client/server network computing. An applet, you will recall, is a program that is stored on a server computer, but when requested is transmitted across the network and executes on the client computer. However, applets are only a very simple example of a much more powerful concept. In general, we would like to perform computation on both the client and server sides of the network. In this chapter we will explore how this idea is realized in Java.

22.1 Addresses, Ports, and Sockets

In order to communicate with each other, computers must first be connected. This connection can take various forms. Computers in a small area, such as a single office, might be connected over a *local area network*, or LAN. Computers connected over much longer distances, such as across a city or around the world, are typically connected by a *wide area network*, or WAN. The best-known WAN

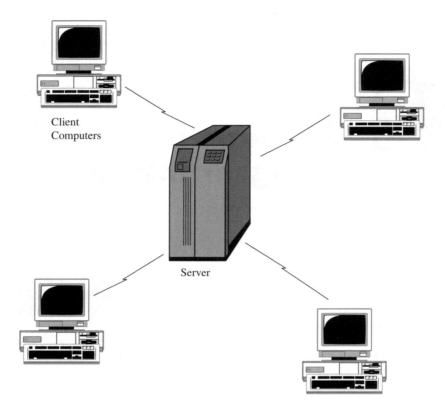

Figure 22.1   Many clients connected to a single server.

is the Internet, which is simply a loose connection of computers (really, a network of networks) that have agreed to communicate with each other following certain rules, or *protocols*.

For a computer to be able to select one application running on one computer out of the multitude of computers (tens of millions, in the case of the Internet) connected to a network, there must be an addressing scheme. On the Internet this address is known as an IP address, and is usually written in the form of four numbers, each between 0 and 255, separated by dots. An example might be 100.12.11.13. Humans are not very good at remembering or dealing with numbers of this form. Thus, computer names can also be written in an alternative, and more human-friendly representation.

A *domain name* address is another way to designate a specific computer. Like IP addresses, domain names are also written as a series of items separated by periods, although the connection between the two forms is not as direct as one might expect. Domain names denote a specific machine by means of a number of levels, the levels reading from more general on the right to more specific on the left. The computer this book is being written on, for example, is addressed as oops.cs.orst.edu. This address can be read as follows. oops (the name of my machine) on the network for cs (the computer science department at my university) at the institution orst (Oregon State University), which is in the highest level group edu (educational institutions in the United States). The series of names can be imagined as being analogous to the way that a physical address is often described as a building address, street address, city name, and country name.

In order to exchange data, clients and servers need more than just an address. Many servers, for example, can be running simultaneously on the same computer, and hence have the same IP address. Within a computer, the mechanism used to establish a rendezvous is termed a *port*. A port is a location where information can be exchanged between a client and a server. One can think of the term as analogous to a shipping port, where goods come in from abroad and are picked up for delivery to the interior, and vice versa. Ports are designated by integer numbers. Typically the values smaller than 1024 are reserved for predefined services (e-mail, file transfer, Web access), and user defined ports have larger numbers.

The combination of IP address and port number is used to create an abstraction termed a *socket*. Again, one can think of this as an analogy to a connection, such as an electrical socket. A client can "plug into" the server, creating a connection along which information can flow, and can subsequently "disconnect" leaving the socket free for another use. As we will see in the programming examples, a socket provides the facilities for creating input and output streams, which allow data to be exchanged between the client and server.

Finally, files that reside on a specific computer are described using the now ubiquitous URL, or *universal resource locator*. A URL consists of a number of parts. As we described in Section 21.4.1, three of these are the protocol that indicates the communication method used to obtain the item (for example, ftp for file transfer, or http for Web pages), a domain name address, and a file name within the computer. A fourth part, not mentioned in Section 21.4.1, is an optional port number. The port number is necessary only when the default port for the particular protocol is, for some reason, not being used.

22.2 A SIMPLE CLIENT/SERVER PROGRAM

In Section 21.4.1 we described how to open a stream and read the information stored at the location described by a URL. However, in general we would like to do more than simply read a file across the network. We would like to perform computation on both ends of a network connection. We earlier noted that this

```
import java.util.Date;
import java.net.*;
import java.io.*;

public class DateServer {
   static public void main (String [ ] args) {
      try {
         DateServer world = new DateServer();
      } catch (IOException e) {
         System.out.println("IO exception " + e);
      }
   }

   static final public int portNumber = 4291;

   public DateServer () throws IOException {
      ServerSocket server = new ServerSocket(portNumber);
      while (true) {
         System.out.println("Waiting for a client");
             // wait for a client
         Socket sock = server.accept();
         System.out.println("Got a client, send a message");
             // create an output stream
         OutputStreamWriter out =
             new OutputStreamWriter(sock.getOutputStream());
         String message =
             "Current date and time is " + new Date() + "\n";
             // write the message, then close the stream
         out.write(message);
         out.close();
      }
   }
}
```

Figure 22.2   The DateServer Application.

style of computing is generally known as client/server programming. We will illustrate the basic ideas of client/server programming using a pair of simple programs. The server is shown in Figure 22.2. In addition to the classes found in java.io and java.net, we use the class Date found in java.util. The application is named DateServer.

The port number is arbitrarily chosen as 4291. In fact any integer value larger than 1024 and not already in use on the server computer could have been selected.

The class ServerSocket is used to register the server with the port number on the underlying computer. Having registered itself, the server then sits and waits for a client.[1] The method accept will return when a client requests a connection. (An alternative form of accept allows the programmer to specify a time period for the wait, so the program can time out if no client ever comes by.)

The constructor for the ServerSocket, the accept method, and the write method for the output writer can all generate an IOException. We can simplify the program by declaring this exception as part of the constructor interface, and catching any such errors in the main method. By naming the exception in the method header for the constructor, any exceptions thrown by the library routines will pass through the constructor up to the calling procedure, where we catch them (in a try block) and simply print a message and halt.

The result returned by the accept message is a Socket, the connector that will allow a communication path to be established to the client. In particular, we can use the socket to create an OutputStream, which we here convert into a OutputStreamWriter (recall we discussed the various different forms of output streams in Chapter 14). Having made a connection, the server then sends whatever information has been requested back to the client. In this case, we simply write the current date and time as yielded by the Date class.

We explicitly close the output stream, since the program will thereafter go back to waiting for another client. Closing the stream will flush any pending output, and will free up certain system resources that are then available for use by this program or others. Oftentimes an explicit close will be omitted, since all such bookkeeping tasks will be performed automatically when a program terminates. However, if a program is finished with a resource and not yet ready to exit, as in this case, then it is considered good practice to explicitly release the resource.

On the other side, we need a client. The DateClient code is shown in Figure 22.3. The client requests a socket to be created to the given port on a specific computer. In this simple example, we are assuming the client and server run on the same computer. The IP address of the computer on which an application is run can be accessed using the method InetAddress.getLocalHost(). A more general facility is provided by InetAddress.getByName(domainName), which takes a string representation of a domain name and converts the name into an IP address.

Having created a socket, the socket can then be used to create an input stream, which we first convert into a Reader, and then to a BufferedReader (see Chapter 14). The buffered reader provides a method to read an entire line of input, which we simply print out.

---

[1] Here the server is waiting in an infinite loop. On platforms where it is difficult to terminate programs running in the background, the reader may wish to replace the while loop with a finite loop, such as a for loop that will make three connections and then halt.

```
import java.io.*;
import java.net.*;

public class DateClient {
   public static void main (String [ ] args) {
      try {
         DateClient world = new DateClient();
      } catch (IOException e) {
         System.out.println("Received an IO exception " + e);
      }
   }

   static final public int portNumber = 4291;

   public DateClient () throws IOException {
         // open socket as a reader
      Socket sock = new Socket(InetAddress.getLocalHost(), portNumber);
      Reader isread = new InputStreamReader(sock.getInputStream());
      BufferedReader input = new BufferedReader(isread);

         // now read one line
      System.out.println("message is " + input.readLine());
   }
}
```

Figure 22.3   The DateClient Application.

If we run both programs on the same computer we will observe the expected outcome–namely, that the client will print the date and time given by the server.

22.3   MULTIPLE CLIENTS

There are many limitations to our first simple client/server system, but the two most important are that it only provided communication one way, from the server to the client, and it only permitted one client for one server. In our second example program we will address both of these points.

The Therapist program, Figure 22.4, is a rewriting of a classic and well-known computer game, originally called *Eliza* [Weizenbaum 1976]. The application simulates a Gestalt psychotherapist, and conducts a sort of question-and-answer session with the user. An example session might be the following:

```
Hello.  Welcome to therapy. What is your name?
Tim
```

```
import java.net.*;
import java.io.*;

public class Therapist {
    static public void main (String [ ] args) {
        try {
            Therapist world = new Therapist();
        } catch (IOException e) {
            System.out.println("Received an IO Exception" + e);
        }
    }

    static final public int portNumber = 5321;

    public Therapist () throws IOException {
        ServerSocket server = new ServerSocket(portNumber);
        while (true) {
            Socket sock = server.accept();
            // start new thread to handle session
            Thread session = new TherapySession
                (sock.getInputStream(), sock.getOutputStream());
            session.start();
        }
    }
}
```

Figure 22.4   The Therapist Application.

```
Well Tim what can we do for you today?
I am writing a book on Java.
Tell me more
Do you know Java?
Why do you want to know?
Even my mother is learning how to program in Java.
Tell me more about your mother
    .
    .
    .
```

The therapist application is very similar to the date server described earlier. One important difference is that when a socket is requested by a client, a new *thread* is created to service this request. As we discussed in Chapter 20, this new thread then begins execution in parallel with the original task, which meanwhile completes the while loop and goes back to waiting for another client. In this

```java
import java.io.*;
import java.util.Vector;
import java.util.StringTokenizer;

public class TherapySession extends Thread {
    public TherapySession (InputStream ins, OutputStream outs) {
        Reader isread = new InputStreamReader(ins);
        in = new BufferedReader(isread);
        out = new OutputStreamWriter(outs);
    }

    private String name = "";
    private BufferedReader in;
    private Writer out;

    private String response (String text) {
        .
        .
        .
    }

    public void run () {
        try {
                // get name
            out.write("Hello.  Welcome to therapy. What is your name?\n");
            out.flush();
            name = in.readLine();
            out.write("Well " + name + " what can we do for you today?\n");
            out.flush();

                // now read and respond
            while (true) {
                String text = in.readLine();
                out.write(response(text) + "\n");
                out.flush();
            }
        } catch (IOException e) { stop(); }
    }
}
```

Figure 22.5 The TherapySession class.

fashion, many clients can be serviced simultaneously because each will be given their own thread of execution.

The servicing of the client is handled by an instance of TherapySession, shown in Figure 22.5. Note that the therapist passes both an input and output stream to the constructor for this class, permitting two-way communication between the client and the server. The class TherapySession is declared to be a subclass of Thread, which means that most of its processing will be performed by the run method, invoked when the therapist starts the thread.

For the moment, we have omitted some of the code used in the execution of this thread, so that the overall structure can be more easily seen. In order to simplify input and output processing, the constructor for the class converts the input and output streams into buffered readers and writers.

The run method begins by writing a generic greeting. The flush method is needed to transfer the output across the network, since otherwise the buffering of the writer will wait until more output has been generated. The next line is assumed to be a one-word name. Another generic response is then given, and the program moves into the loop which is the heart of the application.

The infinite while loop simply reads a line of text from the user, then determines and writes a response. We will return to the issue of how the response is generated after discussing the client side code.

The client program is named TherapyClient (Figure 22.6) and is again very similar to the Date client. The program creates readers and writers to handle the socket input and output, and it then simply reads lines of text from the standard input and passes them across the network to the server, printing the response on the standard output.

Although the therapy session application clearly has no innate intelligence, people are frequently fooled into thinking otherwise. This effect is achieved by a clever selection of simple rules for responding to what the user writes. Figure 22.7 shows the code that embodies these rules. If the user asks a question (a condition discovered by checking the final character), then the program will answer with a question. Otherwise the line of text is converted into lowercase, and broken into individual words. A StringTokenizer, which we discussed briefly in Chapter 14, is used in this process.

Once the line is broken into words, there are several simple rules that can be applied. If the user started a sentence with "I feel," then we can ask why they feel that way. Otherwise, we check every word to see if they mentioned a family member. If so, then we ask for more information on that relative. Finally, if nothing else has been applicable, we ask a general open-ended question. These are only a small sample of the rules that can be written—all to simulate intelligence when there is none.

```java
import java.io.*;
import java.net.*;

public class TherapyClient {
    public static void main (String [ ] args) {
        try {
            TherapyClient world = new TherapyClient();
        } catch (IOException e) {
            System.out.println("Received an IO exception " + e);
        }
    }

    static final public int portNumber = 5321;
    private BufferedReader input, term;
    private Writer output;

    public TherapyClient () throws IOException {
        // open standard input as buffered reader
        term = new BufferedReader(new InputStreamReader(System.in));

        // open socket as a reader and a writer
        Socket sock = new Socket(InetAddress.getLocalHost(), portNumber);
        Reader isread = new InputStreamReader(sock.getInputStream());
        input = new BufferedReader(isread);
        output = new OutputStreamWriter(sock.getOutputStream());

        // now read and print
        while (true) {
            // read and print something from therapist
            String line = input.readLine();
            System.out.println(line);
            // get our response
            line = term.readLine();
            if (line.equals("Quit"))
                break;
            output.write(line + "\n");
            output.flush();
        }
    }
}
```

Figure 22.6 The TherapyClient class.

```
private String response (String text) {
    // answer a question with a question
    if (text.endsWith("?"))
        return "Why do you want to know?";
        // break up line
    Vector words = new Vector();
    StringTokenizer breaker =
        new StringTokenizer(text.toLowerCase(), " .,?!");
    while (breaker.hasMoreElements())
        words.addElement(breaker.nextElement());

        // look for "I feel"
    if ((words.size() > 1) &&
        words.elementAt(0).equals("i") &&
        words.elementAt(1).equals("feel"))
        return "Why do you feel that way?";

        // look for relatives
    for (int i = 0; i < words.size(); i++) {
        String relative = (String) words.elementAt(i);
        if (isRelative(relative))
            return "Tell me more about your " + relative;
    }

        // nothing else, generic response
    return "Tell me more";
}

private boolean isRelative (String name) {
    return name.equals("mother") || name.equals("father")
        || name.equals("brother") || name.equals("sister")
        || name.equals("uncle");
}
```

Figure 22.7 The response generator.

22.4 TRANSMITTING OBJECTS OVER A NETWORK

Objects can be transmitted over a network using the technique of *object serialization* described in Section 14.5. We illustrate this mechanism by presenting a portion of another client/server application. This application is an on-line pocket-change exchange calculator. The application will take a description of a collection

```
import java.io.Serializable;

abstract public class PocketChange implements Serializable {
    public int penny = 0;
}

class BritishCoins extends PocketChange {
    public int twoPence = 0; // worth 2 pennies
    public int fivePence = 0; // worth 5 pennies
    public int tenPence = 0; // worth 10 pennies
    public int twentyPence = 0; // worth 20 pennies
    public int fiftyPence = 0; // worth 50 pennies
    public int pound = 0; // worth 100 pennies
    public int twoPound = 0; // worth 200 pennies
}

class AmericanCoins extends PocketChange {
    public int nickel = 0; // worth 5 pennies
    public int dime = 0; // worth 10 pennies
    public int quarter = 0; // worth 25 pennies
}
```

Figure 22.8   The Coin class hierarchy.

of coins, either in British or American coinage, and calculate the equivalent in the other system.

To start, we need a class hierarchy to describe a collection of coins. This is provided by the three classes shown in Figure 22.8. The class PocketChange is an abstract class, parent to the two classes BritishCoins and AmericanCoins. Since both currencies share the concept of a penny, that is the only data field found in the parent class. Each subclass gives names for the various different types of coins in use in the country. (Fifty-cent pieces and dollar coins have actually been minted in the United States, but have never been widely popular.) This class description must be available on both the client and server sides of the network connection.

The class PocketChange has been declared as implementing the Serializable interface. This is all that is necessary to permit instances of the class to be written to and read from an object stream (see Section 14.5). It is not necessary to repeat the implements clause in the child classes BritishCoins and AmericanCoins, since they will inherit the Serializable characteristic from their parent class PocketChange.

We give only a portion of the server program (Figure 22.9), leaving the completion of the server program and the development of a client application as an exercise for the reader. The ChangeMaker application waits for a client to request a connection. When a connection is made, the program reads a value from

```
public class ChangeMaker {
    static final public int portNumber = 3347;
    static final public double exchangeBPenniestoAPennies = 1.615;

    public ChangeMaker () throws IOException {
        ServerSocket server = new ServerSocket(portNumber);
        while (true) {
            Socket sock = server.accept();
                // got a client, make the connections
            ObjectInputStream in =
                new ObjectInputStream(sock.getInputStream());
            ObjectOutputStream out =
                new ObjectOutputStream(sock.getOutputStream());

                // read the value
            PocketChange coins;
            try { coins = (PocketChange) in.readObject();
            } catch (ClassNotFoundException e) { continue; }

                // now convert the value
            if (coins instanceof BritishCoins) {
                    // convert British to American
                BritishCoins bc = (BritishCoins) coins;
                int bPennies = bc.penny + 2 * bc.twoPence +
                    5 * bc.fivePence + 10 * bc.tenPence +
                    20 * bc.twentyPence + 50 * bc.fiftyPence +
                    100 * bc.pound + 200 * bc.twoPound;
                int amPennies = (int) (bPennies
                    * exchangeBPenniestoAPennies);
                AmericanCoins ac = new AmericanCoins();
                ac.quarter = amPennies / 25; amPennies %= 25;
                ac.dime = amPennies / 10; amPennies %= 10;
                ac.nickel = amPennies / 5; amPennies %= 5;
                ac.penny = amPennies;
                    // write out american object
                out.writeObject(ac);
            } else {
                .
                :  convert American to British
                .
            }
            sock.close();
        }
    }
}
```

Figure 22.9 The ChangeMaker Server Application.

the input stream. Notice that the actual value read will be either an instance of AmericanCoins or an instance of BritishCoins, but the server has no idea which one. Instead, the server reads the value as an instance of the parent class PocketChange. Nevertheless, the *actual* value transferred will be an instance of one of the child classes.

The server determines which class has been transferred using the Java instanceof operator. The result of this test is used to determine which conversion should be performed, either from British to American coins, or the reverse. We show only the British to American conversion.

To calculate the correct amount, the value of the coins is first reduced to penny units, and then multiplied by the current exchange rate. (A more sophisticated program could, at this point, make another network connection to a server that would yield the current exchange rate.) Having determined the American penny equivalent to the British coins, a series of assignments are then used to convert this quantity into quarters, dimes, nickels, and pennies. The idiom

```
ap %= 25;
```

by the way, is a shorthand way of expressing the statement

```
ap = ap % 25;
```

that finds the remainder after dividing by 25. Any of the binary arithmetic operators can be written using the assignment-operator form.

Once the equivalent number of coins has been determined, the object representing the collection of coins is written to the output stream using the method writeObject. On the client side this quantity will be read using a corresponding readObject method. The server then closes the socket and goes back to waiting for the next connection.

22.5   PROVIDING MORE COMPLEXITY

We have only scratched the surface of the techniques that can be used in network programming. We will here describe some of the ways that further functionality can be added to our examples.

The *Remote Method Invocation* package (java.rmi) provides a framework for creating distributed applications (applications that run on two or more computers) in which the actual physical location of an object is transparent to the user. An object will support the same interface whether it is local to the machine, or on a remote machine connected by a socket.

A common type of network application involves a server providing access to a data base. The Java Database Connectivity (JDBC) library provides a simple and uniform interface that can be used to access a wide variety of different commercial database systems.

Servlets are an alternative to applets. While applets originate on the server computer but run on the client computer, servlets both originate and run on the server computer, and only transmit their results to the client. This technique is useful since programs running on the server are often permitted to perform tasks that are not allowed to be performed by applets. Just as the class Applet provides much of the mechanism for creating applets in a systematic and relatively easy fashion, the servlet library provides facilities for creating server software.

22.6 CHAPTER SUMMARY

Network programming involves applications running on two or more computers working in a cooperative fashion to solve a particular problem.

To work in tandem, applications must communicate. Computers establish connections by means of a series of different mechanisms. An *address* is used to designate a specific computer out of the many computers that may be connected to a network. A *port* is used to identify an individual application on a computer that is waiting to make a connection. Once the application is found, a *socket* is used to create the actual communication medium that links the two communicating applications.

The *streams* created by a socket can be used to transmit 8-bit byte values between the two communicating parties. By using the *stream* and *reader/writer* abstractions provided by the Java library, higher level objects can also be trasmitted easily across the network connection.

By processing requests in a separate thread of execution, a single server can be made to service many different clients simultaneously.

STUDY QUESTIONS

1. Explain what is meant by the terms *client* and *server*.

2. Explain how applets represent one form of client/server computing.

3. How are different machines in a network addressed?

4. What is a port? What is the difference between a port and a socket?

5. In what way is a URL object similar to a Socket object?

6. What is the difference between a Socket object and an object of type Server-Socket?

7. What information is needed in order to form a socket?

8. How does a client create a connection with a server? How does a server create a connection with a client?

9. Having established a socket connection, how is communication between client and server effected?

10. What is the benefit of having the Therapist server create separate threads to handle communiction with the client?

11. In the communication between the Therapist server and the client, why is it important for the writers to be flushed after a line of text has been output?

12. What Java facilities are required for transmitting objects over a network?

EXERCISES

1. Create an array of "fortune cookies," one-line comments offering advice or information. Then write a server program that will, when requested, return a randomly selected value from this list.

2. Many more rules can be added to the response generator for the therapist program. Examples include responding to "I want" or "I think" with a question that asks why the client wants or thinks that way (perhaps even including the text of the material that follows the first two words), a randomly generated generic response if nothing else is appropriate, searching for key words such as "computer" and making a response such as "Computers can be so annoying, can't they?" Think of some more question and answer patterns and implement them in your own version of the therapist.

3. Complete the ChangeMaker server, and write a client program that will interface with this server. Allow the user the ability to specify input as either American or British currency, using forms for the various numeric fields.

4. Unlike the Therapist program, the ChangeMaker does not service each client in a separate thread. Thus, each client must be completely serviced before the next client can be handled. Modify the ChangeMaker program to correct this, so that servicing a client is performed in a separate thread and can be performed in parallel with the main program waiting for a new connection to be established.

23 What's New in 1.2

Java is a language that continues to evolve and change, sometimes at an annoyingly rapid pace. This means that any book that tries to describe Java–and this one is no exception—can represent only an overview that captures a point in time. It is a certainty that some of the information described in this book will eventually become outdated and will have to be revised, replaced, modified or discarded. As a reader you can try to keep abreast of this process by by perusing articles in trade journals, by reading books that describe the latest versions of languages, by attending conferences or trade shows, by taking continuing education classes, and in general, by being aware of what is happening in the computing world.

In large part the evolution of Java involves not changes to the basic syntax of the language (although there have been some of those) but modifications to the library of packages that are included as part of most Java programs. This evolution involves both the basic libraries provided by Sun (the developers of the language), and third-party packages created and marketed by others.

To date (meaning, middle 1999) there have been three major stages in the life of Java as a language. The first version of the language to become widely popular was known as Java 1.0.2, after the version number assigned by Sun. This was replaced by Java 1.1, which was the reference version used in the writing of the first edition of this book. The major change between the earlier language and Java 1.1 was the introduction of the new and simpler event-handling model, based around listeners, that we have here been using since Chapter 6. Subsequent to the publication of the first edition of this book, Sun released Java 1.2. In this chapter we will discuss some of the more important changes and innovations that were included in that release.

23.1 COLLECTION CLASSES

The collection classes are a revision of the 1.1 (and earlier) container library described in Chapter 19. The collection API now includes linked lists and sets, in addition to the classes for vectors and hashtables found in the earlier library. Also many new operations have been added to the existing abstractions.

There has been some objection to the new classes because they include the concept of an *optional method*. An interface can claim to provide an operation, and a class can claim to implement the interface, and yet the class is permitted to throw an UnsupportedOperationException when the operation is invoked. This means that users need to be aware of this possibility, and check carefully which classes support which operations.

In Section 19.8 we explained why there were no ordered collections in the Java library, and discussed a technique that could be used to provide such data abstractions. The new 1.2 collection library now includes a number of ordered collections (SortedSet is the most useful example), and uses a technique almost identical to the one described in Chapter 19 to form the ordering between elements. Wrapper classes such as Integer and Double have been modified to make them integrate well with the ordered container abstractions.

23.2 SWING USER INTERFACE COMPONENTS

The *Swing* library is a significant extension to the AWT windowing toolkit described in Chapter 13. Many new graphical components have been added (such as split panes, and progress bars), and new abilities have been incorporated into existing components (such as the ability to put images on a button label). End users now have greater control over the appearance of graphical components and can change this appearance dynamically. Greater support is now provided for assistive technologies–for example, alternative input devices such as sound or braille output devices.

23.3 IMPROVEMENTS TO THE GRAPHICS LIBRARY

The Graphics class introduced in Chapter 5 has been greatly expanded to provide new operations for rendering two-dimensional graphics. The new class is called Graphics2D and provides tools for mixing overlapping images, transforming and clipping images, and alternative rendering techniques.

A new Graphics3D library has been added to assist in the transformation of three-dimensional images into a two-dimensional display.

23.4 INTERNATIONALIZATION

Building on the idea of *properties* described in Section 19.7.2, users can now create *Resource Bundles* that describe features that can be dynamically loaded. For example, rather than having a program print the text strings "Hello" and "Good-bye", a programmer can create resource bundles that describe the standard greetings in various different languages. After determining the correct language for a given user, a program can then dynamically load the appropriate resource bundle for the language and use the properties defined by the resource to print a greeting in the user's language.

Other support is provided for various currencies, descriptions of dates, times, measurements, and postal addresses. For example, the Date class may print a date in the United States as 14-Apr-98, and print the same date in France as 14 Avr 98. A time printed in the United States as 3:58:42 PM might be printed in Germany as 15:58:42.

23.5 JAVA BEANS

In the distributed computing world a *component* is a self-contained independent reusable software unit that can be dynamically loaded into memory. Collections of components are composed to create new applications. Components are higher-level abstractions than classes and may be written in many different languages.

Using the idea of *reflection* (the ability for a program to discover information about itself), the Java Beans API provides the tools to create and distribute reusable components in Java. Components examine themselves to discover what methods they support, and can automatically share this information with other components. Components then interact with each other by passing *events*, which are a more general form of messages.

23.6 SOUND

Java 1.2 now provides the ability to manipulate and play sounds recorded in a wide variety of formats and sampling rates.

23.7 DATABASES

The JDBC API provides a platform-independent way to connect with and perform operations on databases from a wide variety of different vendors.

23.8 REMOTE METHOD INVOCATION

The RMI API defines a simple way to hide much of the detail involved in client/server applications. Using RMI, a programmer can deal with a remote object, an object on another computer that is accessed across the network, in exactly the same way as if it were present on the local computer.

23.9 SERVLETS

As we described in Chapter 21, *applets* are programs that are downloaded across a network from a server computer to a client computer but run on the client machine. A *servlet* is similar, but it runs on the server side, not the client side. Thus servlets are typically permitted to perform operations that applets may not be allowed (and vice versa as well).

23.10 CHAPTER SUMMARY

Java 1.2 is the latest version of the Java programming language and associated libraries. The transition from Java 1.1 to Java 1.2 introduced many new libraries that provided significant functionality in a form that is easy for the programmer to use.

It is almost guaranteed that this will not be the last revision of the Java language or its libraries. The conscientious programmer should be aware of these changes and strive to understand the importance of developments as they occur in the programming field.

FURTHER READING

The most authoratative information is obtained directly from SUN, at their Web site http://java.sun.com/docs. Of the many Java 1.2 tutorials available, the one I like best is the addition to *The Java Tutorial*, called *The Java Tutorial Continued: The Rest of the JDK* [Campione 1999].

 **Java Syntax**

This appendix gives an overview of the Java language as it is used in this book. The method of description is informal, and it is not intended to replace a reference manual for the language. For example, statements that are legal in Java but are not used in the book are not described.

We will divide the presentation of the language into three major sections:

1. *Program structure*, where the overall organization of a Java program is defined; this includes packages, interfaces, classes, and methods.

2. *Statements*, where dicussion focuses on declaration statements, assignment statements, and statements that control the flow of execution within a method.

3. *Expressions*, where individual values are computed.

A.1 PROGRAM STRUCTURE

A Java program is written as a collection of files. Each file can contain an optional package name, an optional sequence of import declarations, and finally a sequence of class or interface declarations.

A.1.1 Import Declaration

An import declaration names an item from another package that will be used in the subsequent class or interface declarations. An asterisk can be used to include all the items in a package.

```
// Example from program found in Chapter 22
import java.util.Date;
import java.net.*;
import java.io.*;
```

A.1.2   *Class Declaration*

A class declaration consists of an optional sequence of modifiers, the keyword
class, the class name, an optional parent class name, an optional sequence of
interfaces, and the class body. The class body is a sequence of class member or
constructor declarations, surrounded by a pair of curly brackets.

```java
// Class definition from Chapter 4
public class FirstProgram {

   public static void main (String [ ] args ) {
      System.out.println ( "My first Java program!" );
   }
}
```

The modifiers discussed in this book have been public, abstract and final. A public
class can be used outside of the package in which it is declared. An abstract class
is one that cannot be instantiated, one that must be subclassed before instances
can be created. A final class is one that cannot be subclassed.

```java
// Class definition from Section 8.4.2
public abstract class Number {
   .
   .
   .
}
```

The optional parent class name is used to denote that this class is being constructed using inheritance from an existing class. The keyword extends indicates
that inheritance is being performed.

```java
// Class definition from Chapter 7
public class PinBall extends Ball {
   .
   .
   .
}
```

The optional sequence of interfaces is used to indicate that the class being
defined implements all the methods described in an interface declaration. Note
that a class can satisfy many different interfaces but can have only one parent
class.

```java
// Class definition from Chapter 7
class Hole extends Ball implements PinBallTarget {
   .
   .
   .
}
```

A.1.3   *Interface Declaration*

An interface declaration substitutes the keyword interface for the keyword class. The body of an interface contains methods but no data fields. In addition, the methods specify only the function and argument names, but do not have a function body. In place of the method body, a semicolon is used to mark the end of a method declaration.

```
    // Interface definition from Chapter 7
interface PinBallTarget {
    public boolean intersects (Ball aBall);
    public void moveTo (int x, int y);
    public void paint (Graphics g);
    public void hitBy (Ball aBall);
}
```

A.1.4   *Method Declaration*

A method declaration consists of an optional series of modifiers, a return type, a method name, an optional throws part, a list of arguments, and (in class declarations) a method body. A method body is a sequence of statements, surrounded by a pair of curly brackets.

```
    // Class found in Chapter 8
class Stack extends Vector {

    public synchronized Object pop( ) {
        Object obj = peek( );
        removeElementAt(size( ) - 1);
        return obj;
    }
}
```

The following modifiers have been used in the book:

public   The method can be invoked by messages sent to instances of this class. (Many examples occur, starting in Chapter 4.)

protected   The method can be invoked only within other methods associated with the class of the object, within other classes in the same package, or in methods defined as part of subclasses.

private   The method can be invoked only within other methods associated with this class.

final   The method cannot be overridden in subclasses. An example occurs in Chapter 9.

abstract   The method must be overriden in subclasses. (A semicolon replaces the method body when this modifier is used.) An example occurs in Chapter 8.

static   The method can be invoked without first creating an instance of the class. The main method must always be declared static.

synchronized   At any point in time only one thread can be executing this method. An example was presented in Chapter 8.

The return type for a method can be a primitive type, a class type, or void. The type void is used to indicate that the method does not return a value as a result.

A throws part indicates the exceptions this method might potentially throw. It is indicated by the keyword throws, followed by a list of exception names, separated by commas.

```
// Example from Chapter 14
class DataInputStream extends FilterInputStream {

    public byte readByte () throws IOException {
        .
        .
        .
    }
}
```

The optional sequence of formal arguments is a list of zero or more formal argument declarations, separated by commas. Each formal argument is a type (either a primitive type or a class name) followed by a variable name:

```
// From the concordance program in Chapter 19
private void enterWord (String word, Integer line) {
    .
    .
    .
}
```

A.1.5   *Constructors*

A syntax of a *constructor* is similar to a method but eliminates the return type, and the method name must match the class name. A constructor is invoked automatically when an instance of the class is created.

```
// Ball class from Chapter 5
public class Ball {

    public Ball (Point lc, int r) {
        loc = lc;
        rad = r;
        color = Color.blue;
```

```
        }
        ·
        ·
        ·
    }
```

A.1.6 *Data Field Declaration*

A data field declaration has an optional modifier part, a type, a variable name, and an optional initialization.

```
    // Ball class from Chapter 5
public class Ball { // a generic round colored object that moves
    protected Rectangle location; // position on graphic surface
    protected double dx, dy; // x and y components of motion vector
    protected Color color;  // color of ball
    ·
    ·
}
```

An initialization, if present, consists of an equals sign followed by a value:

```
    // From an example in Chapter 7
public class PinBallGame extends Frame {
    public static final int FrameWidth = 400;
    public static final int FrameHeight = 400;
    ·
    ·
}
```

A.2 STATEMENTS

The following describes only those statements that we have used in the book. The Java language also permits other statement forms that we will not describe.

A.2.1 *Declaration Statement*

A declaration statement consists of a type (either a primitive or a class type) and a variable name. It can have an optional initialization part, which provides an initial value for the variable.

```
    int size;
    double pi = 3.14159;
    Ball aBall;
```

A.2.2   *Assignment Statement*

An assignment statement is used to modify the value of a variable. The target variable (the value to the left of the equal sign) can be a simple variable, an array expresssion, or a field name. The right side can be any legal expression.

```
size = 3 + 4;
```

Binary operators can also be combined with an assignment statement. The effect is as if the target variable were used as the left argument with the binary operator, and the result assigned to the target:

```
i += 3; // same as i = i + 3
```

A.2.3   *Procedure Calls*

A method can be invoked as a statement. A method that is declared as void can be executed only in this fashion. If the method returns a non-void result, the value will be ignored.

```
aBall.move(12, 13);
```

The expression to the left of the period is known as the *receiver*. The class of the receiver will determine which method will be executed. If no receiver is specified, a method in the current class will be executed.

A.2.4   *If Statement*

If statements and switch statements are sometimes together termed *conditional statements*. They allow the programmer to select one alternative out of many. The if statement makes a decision based on a boolean-valued expression; if the expression is true, a statement is selected. The else portion of the statement is optional; if present and if the expression is false, the else statement will be executed.

```
    // From cannon ball game in Chapter 6
if ((cannonBall.x() > targetX) &&
    (cannonBall.x() < (targetX+50)))
    message = "You Hit It!";
else
    message = "Missed!";
```

Curly brackets can be used to group a series of statements together to form a *compound statement*. These statements will then be executed as a unit, either all together or (if the condition is not satisfied) not at all.

```
    // From Figure 7.6
if (state == 1) { // draw compressed spring
    g.fillRect(x, y, pad.width, pad.height);
    g.drawLine(x, y+3, x+30, y+5);
    g.drawLine(x+30, y+5, x, y+7);
    g.drawLine(x, y+7, x+30, y+9);
    g.drawLine(x+30, y+9, x, y+11);
    }
else {  // draw extended spring
    g.fillRect(x, y-8, pad.width, pad.height);
    g.drawLine(x, y+5, x+30, y-1);
    g.drawLine(x+30, y-1, x, y+3);
    g.drawLine(x, y+3, x+30, y+7);
    g.drawLine(x+30, y+7, x, y+11);
    state = 1;
}
```

A.2.5 Switch Statement

A switch statement selects one alternative out of many. The selection is determined by the value of an expression. The result of the expression is compared against a list of constants, and when a match is found the associated statement is executed. One statement can be labelled as default, and will be executed if no other match is successful.

```
    // From pinball game described in Chapter 7
switch (y / 40) {
    case 2: element = new Hole(0, 0); break;
    case 3: element = new Peg(0, 0, 100); break;
    case 4: element = new Peg(0, 0, 200); break;
    case 5: element = new ScorePad(0, 0, 100); break;
    case 6: element = new ScorePad(0, 0, 200); break;
    case 7: element = new Spring(0, 0); break;
    case 8: element = new Wall(0, 0, 2, 15); break;
}
```

The break statement is necessary in order to break out of the switch. If the break is omitted, then after execution of the case statements, control will drop into the next case statement. There are rare situations where this is useful; however, the normal situation is to break after each case statement.

A.2.6 While Statement

The while and for statements are often termed *looping statements*, since they have the effect of executing a statement repeatedly until a condition is satisfied. The statement can be executed zero times if the condition is false the first time the statement is encountered.

```
// From pinball game described in Chapter 7
while (theBall.y( ) < FrameHeight) {
    theBall.move ( );
        .
        .
        .
}
```

A.2.7 *For Statement*

A for statement consists of an initialization part, a test for completion, an update statement, and the body of the loop. The for statement is actually just a convenient shorthand for a while loop. That is, a statement such as the following:

```
for (int i = 0; i < 10; i++) {
    a[i] = 3 * i;
}
```

can be rewritten, and has the same effect, as the following:

```
int i = 0;
while (i < 10) {
    a[i] = 3 * i;
    i++;
}
```

A.2.8 *Return Statement*

A return statement is used to indicate the end of execution for a method. If an expression is provided, it will be the value returned as the result of the method execution. Otherwise, if no value is given in the result statement, the method must be declared as void.

```
return 3 + 4;
```

A.2.9 *Throw Statement*

A throw statement is used to raise an exception. Control will immediately halt in the current procedure, and the most recent matching catch block from a calling procedure will be invoked.

```
throw new StackUnderflowException( );
```

A.2.10 *Try Statement*

Any code that can generate an exception should be invoked in a try block. The try statement is followed by an optional sequence of catch clauses. Each catch block specifies the type of exception it can handle. If the associated exception is thrown during the course of executing the statements in the try block, then the code in the matching catch statement will be executed. An optional finally block is executed at the end of the statement, whether or not an exception has occurred.

```
try {
   URL address = new URL(args[0]);
   .
   .
   .
} catch (MalformedURLException e) {
   System.out.println("URL exception " + e);
} catch (IOException e) {
   System.out.println("I/O exception " + e);
}
```

A.3   EXPRESSIONS

An expression is a programming construct that, when executed, will cause a value to be computed. Expressions are found in various types of statements, such as assignment statements, the conditional test in a while loop, or the selecting expression in a switch statement.

An expression can be placed in parentheses to form a new expression. This is often used to indicate grouping, or when the precedence of operators does not provide the desired value. For example, $2 + 3 * 4$ will be evaluated and produce the result 14, but $(2 + 3) * 4$ will yield the value 20.

A.3.1 *Literal*

The simplest type of expression is a literal. A literal (sometimes called a *constant*) has a self-evident type and value.

```
7 // integer literal
3.14159 // floating-point literal
true // boolean literal
'a' // character literal
"name" // string literal
null // object literal
```

The value null is a literal value that is used with variables of class type. This value is the initial value of all variables before they are assigned. Thus, the value null can be thought of as asserting that the variable does not refer to any object.

The following escape characters can be used in a character or string literal:

\b   backspace

\n   newline

\r   carriage return

\t   tab stop

For example, the following statement:

```
System.out.println("Hello\n\n\tWorld");
```

will produce the following output:

```
Hello

    World
```

A.3.2 *Variable*

A variable is a storage location that has been declared in a declaration statement. When used as an expression, the value currently stored in the variable is the value returned.

The name this is sometimes called a *pseudo-variable*. It is a variable that does not have to be declared. When used as an expression inside a method, it denotes the object executing the method (the object that was targeted as the *receiver* in the message expression that caused the method to be executed).

Data fields and methods declared within the class in which an expression occurs, and protected or public data fields or methods declared in parent classes, can be accessed simply by naming them as a variable. The meaning is the same as a data field access using this as the base expression, however the more complete form is seldom written:

```
public class Ball {
    protected Rectangle location;
    protected double dx, dy;
    protected Color color;

    public Ball (int x, int y, int r) {
        location = new Rectangle(x-r, y-r, 2*r, 2*r);
        dx = 0;
        dy = 0; // same as this.dy = 0;
        color = Color.blue;
    }
}
```

The name super is another pseudo-variable, one that can be used only as a receiver for a message, or in a constructor. The first form is used when a method defined in a parent class is overridden, and the programmer wishes to execute the parent method from inside the method appearing in the child class. In a constructor it is used to indicate the parameters to be passed to the parent class. Both forms are found in the following methods from Chapter 7.

```
public class PinBall extends Ball {

    public PinBall (int sx, int sy)
    {
        super(sx, sy, 10);
            // start out moving (roughly) vertically
        setMotion (-2 + Math.random()/4, -15);
    }

    public void move ()
    {
        dy = dy + gravityEffect;
        super.move();    // execute move method in class Ball
    }
}
```

A.3.3 Data Field and Method Access

Public fields within an object can be accessed by naming the object, followed by a period, followed by the field name:

```
aBall.location
```

Static fields can be accessed using a class name to the left of the period. As we noted earlier, data fields declared within the same class can be accessed without any base expression.

A method invocation uses the same notation as a data field access, but is followed by a parenthesis, an optional list of comma-separated parameter values, and a closing parenthesis.

```
aBall.setColor (ballColor);
```

A.3.4 Operators

A unary operator takes one expression as an argument. An example is the increment operator, ++, which is used to increment a variable. A binary operator takes two expressions as arguments. An example is the addition operator, +, which adds two numeric values. (The addition operator can also be used with

String values, in which case it means string catenation.) The list below gives the set of binary operators recognized by Java. They are shown in precedence order, with higher precedence operators appearing before lower precedence operators. Higher precedence operators will be performed before lower precedence operators; thus, $2 + 3 * 4 + 3$ will yield 17, not 23.

postfix operator	*expr++ expr--*
unary operator	*++expr --expr +expr -expr*
creation or cast	`new` (*type*) *expr*
multiplicative	`* / %`
additive	`+ -`
shift	`<< >> <<<`
relational	`< > <= >= instanceof`
equality	`== !=`
bitwise and	`&`
bitwise or	`|`
logical and	`&&`
logical or	`||`
assignment	`= += -= etc.`

A.3.5 *Object Creation*

An object is created using the `new` operator. As part of the creation process, a constructor may be executed to initialize the object. If any arguments are supplied with the call, they are passed to the constructor for the class, to be used in initializing the object.

```
aBall = new Ball (10, 15, 5);
```

A.3.6 *Arrays*

An array is a homogeneous (same-typed) collection of values that is declared using a pair of square brackets, without indicating the size.

```
Ball [] balls;
```

The number of elements in the array is determined when the array value is allocated, using a `new` statement:

```
balls = new Ball[20]; // create an array of 20 balls
```

An element in the array is accessed by an index position, which must be an integer value between larger than or equal to zero and smaller than the number of values in the array.

```
balls[8].moveTo(23, 17);
```

B Packages in the Java API

The table below lists the principle packages in the Java API. From time to time new libraries are added to the Java run-time system.

Package Name	Contents
java.applet	Applet classes
java.awt	User interface classes
java.awt.event	Event-processing and listener classes
java.beans	JavaBeans component model classes
java.io	Input and output classes
java.lang	Core classes
java.lang.reflect	Reflection classes
java.math	Arbitrary precision arithmetic classes
java.net	Network classes
java.rmi	Remote method invocation classes
java.security	Security classes
java.sql	Java database connectivity classes
javax.swing	Swing user interface classes
javax.swing.event	Event-processing for Swing classes
java.text	Text manipulation classes for internationalization
java.util	Various utility classes

 **Conversion between AWT and Swing**

As we noted in Chapter 13, the Java user interface library underwent a major revision between Java version 1.1 and version 1.2. The newer Swing library promised greater platform independence and a consistency of apperance between components. On the negative side the newer library tends to run more slowly than the older AWT library.

Depending upon what platform is being used readers may encounter either the earlier and the later libraries. If applets are being developed (see Chapter 21) then the programmer should be aware that many web broswers do not yet support the Java 1.2 libaries. In this appendix we will describe the most important differences between the two systems.

C.1 IMPORT LIBRARIES

To use the older AWT library it was only necessary to import java.awt.* and java.awt.event.*. To include the newer Swing libraries it is necessary to import javax.swing.* and javax.swing.event.*. Since Swing is built on top of AWT, it is usually necessary to import both sets of libraries.

C.2 DIFFERENT COMPONENTS

The AWT components had names like Button, Scrollbar and the like. The Swing components have, for the most part, simply prepended the letter J to the name, as in JButton. (Although there are exceptions to this rule, for example Scrollbar became JScrollBar, with a capital B).

There are minor differences in the methods supported by the two sets of
components, and the Swing library has introduced many new components not
found in AWT. But generally backwards compatibility has been preserved, so that
methods that formerly worked with the AWT should still work with the Swing
library.

C.3 DIFFERENT PAINT PROTOCOL

In the Swing library it is almost always necessary to invoke the parent class paint
method from inside an overridden paint method. This is accomplished by calling
super.paint:

```
public class BallWorld extends JFrame {
   .
   .
   .
   public void paint (Graphics g) {
       super.paint(g); // first call parent, then do
       aBall.paint(g); // class-specific painting
   }
   .
   .
   .
}
```

C.4 ADDING COMPONENTS TO A WINDOW

In the AWT library the user generally attached a component to a window by
issuing an add method in the constructor for an application class. In the Swing
library it is necessary to first invoke the method getContentPane, then add the
component to the value returned by this method:

```
public class CannonWorld extends JFrame {

   public CannonWorld () {
      .
      .
      getContentPane().add("East", scrollbar);
   }
}
```

Glossary

abstract A keyword applied to either a **class** or a **method**. When applied to a class, the keyword indicates that no **instances** of the class can be created, and the class is used only as a **parent class** for subclassing. When applied to a method within an **abstract class**, it indicates that the method must be **overridden** in subclasses before any instance of the subclass can be created.

abstract class Syn. *deferred class, abstract superclass*. A class that has been declared using the abstract keyword. Classes can be declared to be abstract even if they do not contain any **abstract methods**.

abstract method A method that has been declared using the abstract keyword. Abstract methods can only appear in classes that have themselves been declared abstract.

abstract windowing toolkit A Java package which provides the graphical user interface facilities for a Java program. The AWT is an example of a **framework**.

abstraction A technique in problem solving in which details are grouped into a single common concept. This concept can then be viewed as a single entity and nonessential information ignored.

access specifier A keyword (private, protected, or public) that controls access to **data members** and **methods** within user-defined classes.

accessor function A function that is used to access the values of an **instance variable**. By restricting access through a function, the programmer can ensure that instance variables will be read but not modified. *See also* **mutator**.

ad hoc polymorphism Syn. *overloading*. A procedure or method identifier (or name) that denotes more than one procedure.

agent Syn. *object, instance*. A nontechnical term sometimes used to describe an object in order to emphasize its independence from other objects and the fact that it is providing a service to other objects.

anonymous class *See* unnamed class.

Application Programmers Interface (API) The Java class library is generally referred to as the Java API. It is arranged in **packages** of related classes which can be accessed by a program using an import statement.

argument signature An internal encoding of a list of argument types; the argument signature is used to disambiguate **overloaded** function invocations, selecting the **method body** that matches most closely the signature of the method call. *See also* **parametric overloading**.

ASCII ordering A standard mapping between textual character values and an integer **internal representation**. The character value 'a', for example, is mapped on to the integer value 97, which can be stored in a single **byte** value. **Unicode** character values use 16 bits, or two bytes, and can thus represent a wider variety of symbols.

automatic storage management A policy in which the underlying run-time system is responsible for the detection and reclamation of memory values no longer accessible, and hence of no further use to the computation. *See also* **garbage collection**.

AWT See *Abstract Windowing Toolkit*.

base class Syn. *ancestor type, superclass, parent class*. A class from which another class is derived.

binary representation The encoded form of a value used at the machine level. For example, int values in Java are represented by a 4-**byte** machine word, short values by a 2-byte sequence, ASCII characters by a single byte, and **Unicode characters** by a two-byte sequence. Note that two different values may have the same internal binary representation, for example the short value 97 and the **Unicode** character 'a' are both represented by 00000000 01100001. *See also* **textual representation**.

binding The process by which a name or an **expression** is associated with an attribute such as a variable and the type of value the variable can hold.

binding time The time at which a binding takes place. *Early* or *static binding* generally refers to binding performed at compile time, whereas *late* or *dynamic binding* refers to binding performed at run time.

byte The smallest grouping of binary bits used by the computer to represent data. A byte consists of 8 bits. Although a byte may have only one value, a byte can be *interpreted* in a number of different ways. The value 01100001, for example, can be interpreted as the number 97, or as the **character** value 'a'.

bytecode The assembly language for an imaginary Java **virtual machine**. So-called because most instructions can be encoded in a form that is one or two **bytes** in length.

cast A unary **expression** that converts a value from one type to another.

character A value used to represent a single printed symbol. Historically characters were encoded as one-**byte** integer values, using the **ASCII** convention. However, this only permitted the representation of 256 different symbolic values. Java represents characters using a two-bit **Unicode** convention. The sixteen bits in a unicode character allow for the representation of most of the world's letters.

child class Syn. *subclass*, *derived class*. A class defined as an extension of another class, which is called the *parent class*.

class Syn. *object type*. An abstract description of the data and behavior of a collection of similar objects. The representatives of the collection are called **instances** of the class.

Class The class that maintains behavior related to class instance and subclass creation.

class description protocol The set of messages that an object understands.

class hierarchy A hierarchy formed by listing classes according to their class-subclass relationship. *See also* **hierarchy**.

class member *See* **member**.

client An application running on one computer that wishes to obtain information from another application, the **server**, running on a different computer. The two computers must be connected over a **network**.

client-side computing In a network environment, a program that is executed on the client side rather than on the server side of the network. The Java programming language is intended to perform client-side computing and so is more efficient than programs that must wait for execution on the (generally more overloaded) server machine.

cohesion The degree to which components of a single software system (such as members of a single class) are tied together. Contrast with **coupling**.

collaborator Two classes which depend upon each other for the execution of their behaviors are said to be collaborators.

collection classes Classes used as data structures that can contain a number of elements. Examples include Vector, Stack, Hashtable and arrays.

command line argument Arguments supplied to a program as part of the command that causes it to execute. The way these are written will depend upon your platform. These are transmitted to the Java program in an array of String values passed to the main program.

composition The technique of including user-defined object types as part of a newly defined object, as opposed to using **inheritance**.

constant A data field that is declared static and final, which is then guaranteed to exist in only one place and cannot change value. The identifier of such a data field is sometimes called a *symbolic name* and hence the constant is sometimes referred to as a *symbolic constant*.

constructor A **method** used to create a new object. The constructor handles the dual tasks of allocating memory for the new object and ensuring that this memory is properly initialized. The programmer defines how this initialization is performed. In Java, a constructor has the same name as the class in which it appears.

contravariance A form of overriding in which an argument associated with a method in the child class is restricted to a less general category than the corresponding argument in the parent class. Contrast with *covariance*. Neither covariant nor contravariant overriding is common in object-oriented languages.

coupling The degree to which separate software components are tied together. Contrast with *cohesion*.

covariance A form of overriding in which an argument associated with a method in the child class is enlarged to a more general category than the corresponding argument in the parent class. Contrast with *contravariance*. Neither covariant nor contravariant overriding is common in object-oriented languages.

CRC card An index card that documents the name, responsibilities, and collaborators for a class, used during the process of system analysis and design.

data field A class member in the form of a variable or constant that holds an instance of a primitive data type or a reference to an object.

data hiding An encapsulation technique that seeks to abstract away the implementation details concerning what data values are maintained in order that an object may provide a particular service.

data member *See* **instance variable**.

deferred class *See* **abstract class**.

derived class Syn. *descendant type, subclass, child class*. A class that is defined as an extension or a **subclass** of another class, which is called the **base class**.

descendant type Syn. *subclass, child class*. *See also* **derived class**.

design pattern A simple, elegant software design that captures, in generic terms, a solution that has been developed over time.

early binding *See* **binding time.**

encapsulation The technique of hiding information within a structure, such as the hiding of instance data within a class.

escape character A multi-character sequence used to represent an otherwise unprintable character value. For example, the sequence \n represents a newline character. When printed, this character terminates a line of output and moves the current position back to the left margin.

event An action, such as the user clicking on a button, pressing a key, selecting a menu item, or inserting a disk into a drive. The system will respond to such an event by carrying out certain actions, provided the program defines an appropriate **listener** for that event. *See also* **event listener** and **event handler.**

event-driven execution A style of programming where the program largely responds to user-generated events, such as a mouse click or a keypress.

event handler The part of the Java run-time system that enables events to be recognized and responded to.

event listener A class that defines what will happen when a particular kind of event occurs. For example, a button object must be associated with a **listener** object that knows what to do when the button is "pressed". *See also* **event** and **event handler.**

exception An unusual condition that prevents the normal sequence of instructions from going forward. An example would be attempting to use an uninitialized value (a null value) as the target of a message-passing expression.

exception handling The portion of a Java program devoted to responding to the occurrence of an exception.

expression A programming construct that returns a value. For example $1 + 2$ is an expression since it returns the value 3. A function is an expression because it returns a value that is an instance of its return type. *See also* **statement.**

extends A keyword used in forming a new class as a subclass of an existing class, or a new interface as an extension of an existing interface.

final A keyword used in forming either a final class or a final method within a class.

final class A class declared using the keyword final. This keyword indicates that the class cannot be used as a base class for inheritance.

final method A method declared using the keyword final. This keyword indicates that the method cannot be overridden in subclasses.

finalizer   A method with the name finalize, no arguments, and no return type. This method will be invoked automatically by the run-time system prior to the object in which it is declared being recycled by garbage collection.

Frame   A class in the Java library that defines behavior common to all application windows.

framework   A collection of classes that together provide the behavior common to a large variety of applications. The programmer creates a new application by specializing and extending the behavior of the classes contained in the framework, thereby providing the solution to a specific problem.

function   A method that has a return type other than void. A function is a form of **expression**. *See also* **procedure**.

function member   *See* **method**.

garbage collection   A memory-management technique whereby the run-time system determines which memory values are no longer necessary to the running program and automatically recovers and recycles the memory for different use.

Graphical User Interface   The graphical display for a program, through which the user interacts with a running application.

GUI   See *Graphical User Interface*.

has-a **relation**   The relation that asserts that instances of a class possess fields of a given type. *See* *is-a* **relation**.

hierarchy   An organizational structure with components ranked into levels of subordination according to some set of rules. In object-oriented programming the most common hierarchy is that formed by the **class-subclass** relationship.

immediate superclass   The closest parent class from which a class inherits. The superclass relationship is a transitive closure of the immediate superclass relationship.

immutable value   A value that is not permitted to change once it has been set. Variables that hold such values are sometimes called **single-assignment variables,** or **symbolic constants**. In Java, immutable values can be identified via the keywords final and static.

implements   A keyword used to indicate that a class provides the behavior described by an **interface**.

information hiding   The principle that users of a software component (such as a class) need to know only the essential details of how to initialize and access the component, and do not need to know the details of the implementation. By reducing the degree of interconnectedness between separate elements of a software system, the principle of information hiding helps in the development of reliable software.

inheritance   The property of objects by which instances of a **class** can have access to **data fields** and **methods** contained in a previously defined class, without those definitions being restated. *See* **ancestor class**.

inheritance graph   An abstract structure that illustrates the inheritance relationships with a collection of classes.

inner class   A **class** definition that appears inside another class. Inner classes are allowed access to both the **data members** and **methods** of the surrounding class. Inner classes are used frequently in building **listener** objects for handling events.

instance   Syn. **object**.

instance variable   An internal variable maintained by an instance. Instance variables represent the state of an object.

interaction diagram   A diagram that documents the sequence of messages that flow between objects participating in a scenario.

interface   A description of behavior. Classes that claim to implement the interface must provide the services described by the interface.

Internet   A world-wide collection of machines that have agreed to communicate with each other using a common protocol.

***is-a* relation**   The relation that asserts that instances of a subclass must be more specialized forms of the superclass. Thus, instances of a subclass can be used where quantities of the superclass type are required. *See has-a* **relation**.

interpreter   A computer program that simulates the actions of the imaginary Java **virtual machine**. The interpreter examines and executes the **bytecode** representation of a Java program.

iterator   A class that is used mainly to provide access to the values being held in another class, usually a container class. The iterator provides a uniform framework for accessing values, without compromising the encapsulation of the container.

Java API   *See* **Application Programmers Interface**

Java library   *See* **Application Programmers Interface**

JIT   *See* **just-in-time compiler**.

just-in-time (JIT) compiler   A technique whereby immediately before a program is to execute, the device-independent **bytecode** representation of a Java program is converted into machine code for a specific platform. The machine code representation will often execute much faster than will an **interpreter** running the bytecode representation.

late binding   *See* **binding time.**

layout manager   A component in the **AWT** that controls the layout of graphical components in a panel or window. Part of the graphical user interface system.

listener   An object that waits for an **event** to occur, then executes certain actions to respond to the event.

member   A **data field** or **method.** Sometimes referred to as a **class member.**

message   Syn. *message selector, method designator, method selector, selector.* The textual string that identifies a requested action is a **message-passing** expression. During message passing, this string is used to find a matching **method** as part of the method-lookup process.

message passing   The process of locating and executing a method in response to a message. *See also* **method lookup.**

message selector   Syn. *method designator, method selector, selector.* The textual string that identifies a **message** in a **message-passing** expression. During message passing, this string is used to find a matching **method** as part of the method-lookup process.

method   A class member which is an operation. A method has a **method header** and a **method body.** A method is invoked in a message passing style.

method body   The section of a **method** that specifies what operations will be invoked when the method is executed. The method body is written as a series of statements surrounded by a pair of curly brackets.

method invocation   *See* **message passing.**

method header   The portion of a **method** that describes the return type, the name, and the argument names and types. If the return type of a method is void it can only be used as a **procedure.** If it is not void it can be used as a **function** in an expression.

method declaration   The part of a **class** declaration specific to an individual **method.**

method designator   Syn. *message selector.* A method name identifier used as a **procedure** or **function** name in a **message-passing** expression. The method designator is used to search for the appropriate **method** during message sending. In general, you cannot determine from the program text which method a method designator will activate during execution.

method lookup   The process of locating a **method** matching a particular **message**, generally performed as part of the **message-passing** operation. Usually, the run-time system finds the method by examining the **class hierarchy** for the **receiver** of the message, searching from bottom to top until a method is found with the same name as the message.

method selector   *See* **message selector.**

mouse listener   A **listener** that sits and waits for mouse events (mouse press or mouse release) and then performs the appropriate action.

mutator   A **method** that is used to modify the value of an **instance variable.** By requiring such modifications to be mediated through a function, a class can have greater control over how its internal state is being modified.

native method   A **method** that is implemented in another language, such as C or assembly language. *See also* **primitive.**

network   The physical connections between two or more computers, plus the **protocol,** or message format and interpretation, that they use to communicate with each other. The Internet, for example, refers to both the physical connections and the fact that machines on the Internet agree to communicate using a standard called TCP/IP.

object   A value that can both maintain data fields and perform actions. The behavior of an object is characterized by the object **class.** *See also* **instance.**

object initialization   The process of ensuring that an object is in a proper state after it has been created. Usually this is the task of a **constructor.**

object-oriented programming   A style of design that is centered around the delegation of responsibilities to independent interacting **agents,** and a style of programming characterized by the use of **message passing** and **classes** organized into one or more **inheritance hierarchies.**

overload   Used to describe an identifier that denotes more than one object. Procedures, functions, methods, and operators can all be overloaded. A method that is overridden can also be said to be overloaded. *See* **parametric overloading.**

override   The action that occurs when a method in a **subclass** with the same name as a method in a **superclass** takes precedence over the method in the superclass. Normally, during the process of binding a method to a message (see **message passing**), the overriding method will be the method selected.

paradigm   An illustrative model or example, which by extension provides a way of organizing information. The object-oriented paradigm emphasizes organization based on behaviors and responsibilities.

parametric overloading Overloading of method names in which two or more method bodies are known by the same name in a given context, and are disambiguated by the type and number of parameters supplied with the method invocation. (Overloading of functions, methods, and operators can also occur.)

parent class Syn. *superclass*, *ancestor class*. An immediate superclass of a class.

Parnas's principles Principles that describe the proper use of modules, originally developed by the computer scientist David Parnas.

pattern *See* **design pattern**.

persistent object An object that continues to exist outside of the execution time of programs that manipulate the object.

polymorphic Literally, 'many shapes.' A feature of a variable that can take on values of several different types. The term is also used for a method name that denotes serveral different methods. *See* **pure polymorphism**.

polymorphic function (or **method**) A function (or method) that has at least one argument that is a **polymorphic variable**.

polymorphic variable A variable that can hold many different types of values. Object-oriented languages often restrict the types of values to being **subclasses** of the declared type of the variable.

primitive An operation that cannot be performed in the programming language and must be accomplished with the aid of the underlying run-time system.

private method A method that is not intended to be invoked from outside an object. More specifically, the receiver for the message that invokes a private method should always be the receiver for the method in which the invocation is taking place (see self). Contrast with *public method*.

procedure A term sometimes used to describe a method that does not return a value (indicated by declaring the return type void). A procedure can only be used as a complete statement, it cannot be invoked as part of an expression.

procedure call The transfer of control from the current point in execution to the code associated with a procedure. Procedure calling differs from **message passing** in that the selection of code to be transferred to is decided at compile time (or link time) rather than run time.

process See *thread*.

protocol A particular form that messages must adhere to when requesting a service or services from a server. For example, the HTTP internet protocol for accessing web pages. In an OO context, the term is also used in the description of a **class description protocol**.

pseudo-variable A variable that is never declared but can nevertheless be used within a method, although it cannot be directly modified (a pseudo-variable is therefore by definition read-only). The most common pseudo-variable is used to represent the receiver of a method. *See also* this *and* super.

public class A **class** that is global and can be accessed from other packages. One public class may be declared in each compilation unit.

public method A **method** that can be invoked at any time from outside an object.

pure polymorphism A feature of a single function that can be executed by arguments of a variety of types. *See also* **ad hoc polymorphism.**

rapid prototyping A style of software development in which less emphasis is placed on creation of a complete formal specification than on rapid construction of a prototype pilot system, with the understanding that users will experiment with the initial system and suggest modifications or changes, probably leading to a complete redevelopment of a subsequent system.

receiver The **object** to which a **message** is sent. The receiver is the object to the left of the field qualifier (period). Within a **method**, the current receiver is indicated by the variable this.

redefinition The process of changing an inherited operation to provide different or extended behavior.

refinement A style of overriding in which the inherited code is merged with the code defined in the child class.

replacement A style of overriding in which the inherited code is completely replaced by the code defined in the child class.

responsibility-driven design A design technique that emphasizes the identification and division of responsibilities within a collection of independent agents.

scope When applied to a variable identifier, the (textual) portion of a program in which references to the identifier denote the particular variable.

selector *See* **message selector.**

server An application running on one computer that will make information available to applications running on other computers. The computer making the request for information is known as a **client**. The two computers must be connected over a **network**.

shadowed name A name that matches another name in a surrounding **scope**; the new name effectively makes the surrounding name inaccessible. An example is a local variable with the same name as that of a global or instance variable. Within the procedure, the local variable will be attached to all references of the name, making references to the surrounding name difficult. In Java, access to such values can be provided by a fully qualified name.

single-assignment variable   A variable the value of which is assigned once and cannot be redefined. In Java, single-assignment variables can be created using the keyword final.

socket   A network connection between two applications running on different computers. The socket permits information to be transmitted from one application to the other.

statement   A programming construct which carries out an action. A **method body** consists of a sequence of statements.

static   A declaration modifier that, when applied to instances variables and functions, means that the variables and functions are shared by all instances of a class and exist even when no instances have yet been created.

static method   A **method** that is declared static. Since such functions exist even when no instances have been created, they can be invoked using the class name as receiver.

stream   A programming abstraction that views a file, an array, or a network connection as a sequence of **byte** values. Operations are provided to read and write values to a stream. Higher level operations are then built on top of these stream abstractions to read and write more complex values.

strongly typed language   A language in which the type of any expression can be determined at compile time.

subclass   Syn. *descendant type, derived class, child class.*

subclass coupling   The connection formed between a parent and child class. Subclass coupling is a very weak form of coupling, since instances of the subclass can be treated as though they were simply instances of the parent class. *See also* **coupling** *and* **cohesion.**

substitutability, principle of   The principle that asserts one should be able to substitute an instance of a child class in a situation where an instance of the parent class is expected. The principle is valid if the two classes are subtypes of each other, but not necessarily in general.

subtype   A type A is said to be a subtype of a type B if an instance of type A can be substituted for an instance of type B with no observable effect. Subtypes can be formed through **inheritance**, although not all **subclasses** need be subtypes. Subtypes can also be formed using **interfaces.**

super   A keyword which is used in two ways: as a message inside a constructor to indicate that the constructor for the parent class should be invoked using the arguments which follow (if any); and as a pseudo-variable inside a method to show that the method after super is the method in the parent class and not the one from the child class which has been overridden.

superclass Syn. *ancestor class*, *base class*. A class from which another class inherits attributes.

symbolic constant *See* **constant**.

textual representation A value that has been converted into characters in order to be more easily read by humans. Compare to **internal representation**. The internal value 00000000 0011001 would have a textual representation of 97 if it is a short integer, and a textual representation of 'a' if it is a character.

this When used inside a method, a reference to the receiver for the message that caused the method to be invoked.

thread A separate task or process that can proceed in parallel with other threads.

Unicode character A 16-bit character value. Unicode characters can be used to represent a variety of non-roman alphabets.

unnamed class Also known as an **anonymous class**. This is a Java device for defining a class (without a name) as a single expression, the value of which is a new object of that class. It is used in cases where only one object of the class is constructed.

URL A *Universal Resource Locator*. A textual address that encodes the information necessary to obtain a resource across a **network**. This information includes a machine name, a file on the machine, the type of **server** that will provide the information, and the **port** through which connections to the server will be made.

virtual machine An imaginary Java machine. Java programs are translated into assembly language instructions for this imaginary machine. To execute a Java program, an actual computer must simulate the working of the virtual machine.

void A type name used to indicate a method returning no value—that is, a **procedure**.

World Wide Web A collection of machines on the Internet that have agreed to distribute information according to a common protocol. This information is usually accessed with a *browser*.

yo-yo problem Repeated movements up and down the class hierarchy that may be required when the execution of a particular method invocation is traced.

Bibliography

Actor Language Manual. 1987. Evanston, IL: The Whitewater Group, Inc.

Beck, Kent and Ward Cunningham. 1989. "A Laboratory for Teaching Object-Oriented Thinking." *Proceedings of the 1989 OOPSLA—Conference on Object-Oriented Programming Systems, Languages and Applications.* Reprinted in *Sigplan Notices* 24(10): 1–6.

Bellin, David and Susan Suchman Simone. 1997. *The CRC Card Book.* Reading, MA: Addison-Wesley.

Budd, Timothy A. 1997. *An Introduction to Object-Oriented Programming,* 2nd ed. Reading, MA: Addison-Wesley.

Campione, Mary, Kathy Walrath and Alison Huml. 1999. *The Java Tutorial Continued: The Rest of the JDK.* Reading, MA: Addison-Wesley.

Cardelli, Luca and Peter Wegner. 1985. "On Understanding Types, Data Abstraction, and Polymorphism." *Computing Surveys* 17(4): 471–523.

Chan, Patrick and Rosanna Lee. 1996. *The Java Class Libraries: An Annotated Reference.* Reading, MA: Addison-Wesley.

Cox, Brad J. 1986. *Object Oriented Programming: An Evolutionary Approach.* Reading, MA: Addison-Wesley.

Cox, Brad J. 1990. "Planning the Software Industrial Revolution." *IEEE Software* 7(6): 25–35, November.

Dahl, Ole-Johan and Kristen Nygaard. 1966. "Simula, An Algol-Based Simulation Language." *Communications of the ACM* 9(9): 671-678, September.

Danforth, Scott and Chris Tomlinson. 1988. "Type Theories and Object-Oriented Programming." *ACM Computing Surveys* 20(1): 29–72.

Gabriel, Richard P. 1996. *Patterns of Software.* New York: Oxford University Press.

Gamma, Erich, Richard Helm, Ralph Johnson, and John Vlissides. 1995. *Design Patterns: Elements of Reusable Object-Oriented Software.* Reading, MA: Addison-Wesley.

Gosling, James, Bill Joy, and Guy Steele. 1996. *The Java Language Specification.* Reading, MA: Addison-Wesley.

Horowitz, Ellis. 1984. *Fundamentals of Programming Languages.* Rockville, MD: Computer Science Press.

Ingalls, Daniel H. H. 1981. "Design Principles Behind Smalltalk." *Byte* 6(8): 286–298.

Kay, Alan. 1977. "Microelectronics and the Personal Computer." *Scientific American.* 237(3): 230–244.

Kay, Alan C. 1993. "The Early History of Smalltalk." The Second ACM SIGPLAN History of Programming Languages Conference (HOPL-II), *ACM SIGPLAN Notices* 28(3): 69–75, March.

Keller, Daniel. 1990. "A Guide to Natural Naming." *Sigplan Notices* 25(5): 95–102, May.

Kim, Won, and Frederick H. Lochovsky (Eds.). 1989. *Object-Oriented Concepts, Databases, and Applications.* Reading, MA: Addison-Wesley.

Lindholm, Tim, and Frank Yellin. 1997. *The Java Virtual Machine Specification.* Reading, MA: Addison-Wesley.

MacLennan, Bruce J. 1987. *Principles of Programming Languages.* New York: Holt, Rinehart & Winston.

Marcotty, Michael, and Henry Ledgard. 1987. *The World of Programming Languages.* New York: Springer-Verlag.

Meyer, Bertrand. 1988. *Object-Oriented Software Construction.* London: Prentice-Hall International.

Micallef, Josephine. 1988. "Encapsulation, Resuability and Extensibility in Object-Oriented Programming Languages." *Journal of Object-Oriented Programming Languages* 1(1): 12–35.

Milner, Robin, Mads Tofte, and Robert Harper. 1990. *The Definition of Standard ML.* Cambridge, MA: MIT Press.

Morehead, Albert H., and Geoffrey Mott-Smith. 1949. *The Complete Book of Solitaire and Patience Games.* New York: Grosset & Dunlap.

Nygaard, Kristen, and Ole-Johan Dahl. 1981. "The Development of the Simula Languages." In Richard L. Wexelblat (Ed.). *History of Programming Langauges.* New York: Academic Press.

Pinson, Lewis J., and Richard S. Wiener. 1988. *An Introduction to Object-Oriented Programming and Smalltalk.* Reading, MA: Addison-Wesley.

Sethi, Ravi. 1989. *Programming Languages: Concepts and Constructs.* Reading, MA: Addison-Wesley.

Stroustrup, Bjarne. 1982. "Classes: An Abstract Data Type Facility for the C Language." *ACM Sigplan Notices* 17(1):42–51, January.

Stroustrup, Bjarne. 1988. "What is 'Object-Oriented Programming?'" *IEEE Software* 5(3): 10–20, May.

Stroustrup, Bjarne. 1994. *The Design and Evolution of C++.* Reading, MA: Addison-Wesley.

Taenzer, David, Murthy Ganti, and Sunil Podar. 1989. "Object-Oriented Software Reuse: The Yoyo Problem." *Journal of Object-Oriented Programming* 2(3): 30–35.

Wegner, Peter. 1986. "Classification in Object-Oriented Systems." *Sigplan Notices* 21(10): 173–182, October.

Weizenbaum, Joseph. 1976. *Computer Power and Human Reason.* San Francisco: W. H. Freeman and Company.

Wikström, Åke. 1987. *Functional Programming Using Standard ML.* London: Prentice-Hall International.

Wirfs-Brock, Rebecca, and Brian Wilkerson. 1989. "Object-Oriented Design: A Responsibility-Driven Approach." *Proceedings of the 1989 OOPSLA—Conference on Object-Oriented Programming Systems, Languages and Applications.* Reprinted in *Sigplan Notices* 24(10): 71–76, October.

Wirfs-Brock, Rebecca, Brian Wilkerson, and Lauren Wiener. 1990. *Designing Object-Oriented Software.* Englewood Cliffs, NJ: Prentice-Hall.

Wulf, William A. 1972/1979. "A Case Against the GOTO." *Proceedings of the Twenty-Fifth National ACM Conference.* 1972; Reprinted in Edward Yourdon (Ed.). *Classics in Software Engineering.* Englewood Cliffs, NJ: Prentice-Hall.

Index